A Duty of Remembrance

A Duty of Remembrance

The Story of My German Family

GUDRUN MOORE

WORKBOOK PRESS LLC
187 E Warm Springs Rd,
Suite B285 Las Vegas NV 89119 USA

Website: https://workbookpress.com/
Hotline: 1-888-818-4856
Email: admin@workbookpress.com

Ordering Information:

Quantity sales. Special discounts are available on quantity purchases by corporations, associations, and others. For details, contact the publisher at the address above.

Library of Congress Control Number:

ISBN-13:   978-1-965732-74-8   Paperback Version
                 978-1-965732-75-5   Digital Version

REV. DATE: 28/01/2026

Contents

ACKNOWLEDGEMENT

This is the story of my German family. My father Gustel, (pronounced Goostel), my Aunt Erika and Uncle Manfred tell their own story in their own words. I had asked them to speak on tapes and they most willingly complied and also answered questions I put to themtat that time. Irmgard, my mother, sent me her story in letter form just a few years before her death. The story of my maternal grandfather Herbert is pulled from his Diary, a copy of which was graciously given to me by his youngest daughter Sigrid. What I tell about the lives of the Haefner family is based on my paternal grandfather's diary from WWI and on the notes, stories and tapes of my father and, of course, my own memories, in what I think is my duty of remembrance.

I also wish to acknowledge my husband Jim and my good friend Maureen Johnston who spent countless hours listening, suggesting, editing and proof reading my manuscript. My deepest thanks to both.

Gudrun Moore

FOREWORD

Everyone on my mother's side of the family was an ardent National Socialist. They supported the ideas of the Third Reich with enthusiasm and idealism and contributed to its growth each in his or her fashion. After the fall of the Third Reich grandfather Herbert Ernst, a deputy Kreisleiter, lost not only all his possessions but also his position as a school superintendent in Silesia when he and his family fled west from the advancing Russians. Erika, his daughter, my mother's sister, had been married by proxy to a steel helmet in Germany while her new husband was in Russia at the front. A few months later he was allowed a short holiday and they loved for a few weeks. He committed suicide in a field hospital in Russia rather than fall into the hands of Russian soldiers. In January of 1945 Erika became one of a group of women and children fleeing west to escape from the advancing Russians. She was one of the very few to survive the trek. Manfred, my mother's brother, was in Wehrmacht uniform at the age of eighteen and was just twenty one years old when he was captured by the Russians and sent to Siberian Gulags. After several unsuccessful attempts to escape he ended up in the Lubyanka Prison in Moscow. He was lucky enough to make it to the west in the very last train filled with prisoners of war that the Russians allowed out of the country; he was repatriated in 1950. My mother, driven out of her home by French soldiers in May of 1945, left, pushing a pram that held her two small girls and little else. In the Alps she found work milking cows for a few months before she walked north to find refuge at her parents-in-law.

My paternal grandfather August Haefner spent the four years of WWI in France and Flanders, carting the wounded from the battle field to the field hospital with horse and wagon. Once home again he hid his medals and the tattered diary that he brought home and never spoke of war again. Liese, his daughter and my father's only sister, married young. Her husband, a prisoner of war in Russia, starved to death in 1945 leaving her a widow at the age of twenty three. Gustel, my father and the only Nazi in his family, joined the volunteer SS at a young age. Very much a military man and very ambitious, he left the Waffen SS after a dispute and rather than becoming a member of the Gestapo he joined the border guards. When the Sicherheitsdienst, the German equivalent of Homeland Security, was created, the border guards were incorporated into the border police who eventually came under the jurisdiction of the Gestapo. Gustel first became an instructor at a police academy not far from Berlin from where he was later sent to university for further training. He then worked for the Gestapo until the end of the war. After the collapse of the German Reich he spent three years as a prisoner of war, during which time he was called to Nuremberg as a witness in the trial of Otto Ohlendorf, the commander of the Einsatzgruppe D. My father was arrested in 1965 and stood trial in Darmstadt for his involvement in the murder of Jewish children in Belaya Cerkov and having been part of the Sonderkommando that murdered 33,771 Jews of Kiev in Babi Yar.

I have used diaries, memories and memoirs, letters and many spoken tapes to tell the story of my German family: housewives and secretaries, coopers and teachers, farmers and innkeepers, soldiers in WWI under Kaiser Wilhelm, soldiers in WWII under Hitler, members of the Reichswehr, the Wehrmacht, the SS, the Gestapo, and the new Bundeswehr after 1945. The chronicle tells of army widows, refugees, prisoners of war under the Russians and the Americans. Most of my family stayed in Germany after the war; four women immigrated to the United States, one to Canada. Their lives span the time from the late eighteen hundreds to this day. None was born to wealth or title; they were ordinary people who had to work to make a decent life for themselves and their families. They are my German family; their lives touched my life. It is also my story.

INTRODUCTION

I became a Canadian citizen on April 20, 1970. An RCMP officer in red serge represented law and order and a black robed judge spoke serious words about freedom and democracy to somber people who were trying hard to hide their happy smiles. I was instructed to lay my hand on the Bible and to swear loyalty to the Queen. These symbolic actions expunged my German citizenship. I felt good. But I knew that back in Germany my mother and my father did not feel the same way. They were sad, if not hurt, that I had decided to no longer be a German. I am very sure that my mother also acknowledged the date: April20, Hitler's birthday. He would have been 81 years old on that day. The irony of it – I thought – and smiled. I suspected she still somehow marked the day. Well, so had I. And I smiled some more.

When I learned about the Third Reich and its part in German history my soul became mired in outrage and confusion, then pain and shame. I could not understand. I knew my parents were good and intelligent people – how could they ever have been the passionate Nazis they told me they had been. How could decent people ever allow to happen what occurred? Even though nothing indicated that my parents had been participants in atrocities or even condoned the holocaust, I perceived a conflict that bothered me greatly. Subconsciously I must have reckoned that I would solve my problem by running away and leaving things German behind me. I married an Englishman and immigrated to Canada. For years I never volunteered the fact that I was German. If Canadians wondered whether I was aboriginal, or Russian, or Slavic, I laughed and often did not enlighten them; everything was better than being thought of a German.

Almost forty years later I still feel good about being Canadian but I am now also comfortable with the fact that I was born a German. I do no longer feel a need to apologize for my father, my family, my people, my country of birth, for things that happened there before I was born and during my childhood.

Gudrun Moore

Chapter 1

A History Lesson

A short history of Germany is necessary to understand what is meant by the term 'Third Reich'. The First Reich existed in the middle ages when the German nation was called the Holy Roman Empire, the Second Reich came into being in 1871 after Prussia had defeated France, it was led by Bismarck. 'Both had added glory to the German name' (W.L. Shirer). A helpless Weimar Republic followed the disaster of the First World War and 'a Third Reich restored it, just as Hitler had promised'.

Martin Luther was a very important figure for the Germans not only because he started the reformation and not only because he translated the Bible into the vernacular, thereby creating a modern German language, but by expressing a hatred for Rome in his passionate sermons he awakened a budding feeling of nationalism in the German speaking people. Unfortunately, he sided with the rulers and not with the peasants in the peasant uprisings by emphasizing St. Matthew's admonition: 'Render unto Caesar the things which are Caesar's.' The uprisings failed and the masses had no voice during the time of political absolutism that followed. Then the tragedy of the Thirty Years War ensued.

It ended with the peace treaty of Westphalia in 1648 and confirmed about three hundred princes as absolute rulers of their small states with a German emperor largely in the role as a figure head. During the fifteenth and sixteenth centuries Germany had had many free cities without any allegiance to a ruler. These cities had been rich and commerce and learning and the arts had thrived in an era of peace and enlightenment. After the peace of Westphalia, serfdom was brought back, self- government of the towns was rescinded, the middle class almost disappeared, universities and schools were closed and the country sank into another dark age. Any emergence of German nationalism or patriotism was brutally subdued. Acceptance of autocracy and blind obedience became ingrained into the German consciousness. When in England and France ideas of democracy and rule by parliament rose and later manifested themselves, the many tiny German states, mired in backwardness and ignorance, did not follow. They remained static in their isolation.

The American Declaration of Independence allowed in 1776 that the 'free communication of thoughts is one of the most precious rights of man'. The French Assembly approved in 1789 the Declaration of the Rights of Man, emphasizing the equality of all men thereby repudiating the rule of the divine right of absolute monarchy and giving the people of France their freedom. These ideas naturally had a great impact on German intellectuals, but the public remained largely ignorant of these revolutionary thoughts for many more years because writers who espoused these ideas publicly were quickly seized and locked up. Many decided to leave their country and to live and write abroad.

By the early eighteenth century Prussia had become a state to be counted. By the time of Frederick the Great it had become one of the ranking military powers. The King ruled absolutely-aided by a blinkered bureaucracy and an army that enforced his laws ruthlessly. Obedience, work and sacrifice were the catchwords for the populace. "Gelobt sei was hart macht", 'Praised be what makes you tough', was the mantra fed to the people.

By the beginning of the nineteenth century voices for a unified nation became heard. The teacher F.L Jahn had witnessed the defeat of Prussia by Napoleon in 1807 and that became the spark for him to work for the unity and freedom of Germany. He became 'Turnvater' Jahn, founder and 'father' of the German Gymnastics and sports movement. His importance can be gauged by the fact that there are hundreds of sports clubs to this day that bear his name. Jahn believed that physical exercise was not only good for the individual but that gymnastics and open air games, including marching, could also be a patriotic exercise. Gymnasts and students came together in the volunteer Luetzow corps to fight Napoleon in 1813; Jahn was one of the commanding officers. After Napoleon's defeat at Leipzig, Jahn demanded freedom of speech, a constitution and the unity of the fatherland. Soon after the former members of the corps founded the German Student Society.

The following years were momentous years. The industrial revolution changed the economic climate, liberal revolutions and declarations of independence for many smaller states changed the face of Europe. Finally, in 1848 a constitutional Monarchy was declared by liberal representatives and a somewhat unified Germany established. But it fell to Bismarck, the Junker from Prussia, to finally unite all of Germany. In 1862 when he became Prime Minister of Prussia he declared, 'that the great questions of the day will not be settled by resolutions and majority votes – that was the mistake of the men of 1848 and 1849 – but by blood and iron.'

Bismarck built up the Prussian Army and had no problem dissolving parliament when they refused to allocate more funds. The 'Iron Chancellor' then went to war and Prussia eventually annexed all northern German states into the North German Confederation. The rulers of the southern states were still feuding with the French and definitely no friends of the Prussians, but Bismarck made deals with them and finally won them over. In 1871 the German princes offered the imperial crown to King Wilhelm I of Prussia and the Second Reich had begun. Austria was excluded.

A Reichstag was elected but possessed few powers. Not even the chancellor had to answer to it; he answered only to the Emperor, the King of Prussia, who ruled his militarist empire by 'God's Grace alone and not by parliaments, popular assemblies and popular decisions'. The state was glorified and hailed as the supreme power. The subjects were just that. One H. Treitschke, a professor of History, lectured in Berlin, "It does not matter what you think, so long as you obey."

By the time the twentieth century arrived much of the western world had accepted the ideas of democracy, but in Germany the ideas of the sovereignty of parliament and political freedom had not yet caught a broad foothold. The industrial revolution had made a prosperous middle class and they did not want to rattle the status quo.

Just before the First World War the Social Democrats despite persecution by Bismarck and the Kaiser had become the largest single party in the Reichstag and demanded parliamentary democracy. They were unsuccessful until after the disaster of the First World War. In November 1918 Germany under pressure from its military leaders had acceded to President Wilson's fourteen conditions of an armistice. Wilhelm II abdicated, and a German Republic was proclaimed on November 9, 1918. In February 1919 the National Assembly voted Friedrich Ebert as its first president. A constitution was written and the German Democratic Republic, also known as the Weimar Republic, was born.

The following years were tumultuous; the people found it hard to accept Germany's ignominious defeat and blamed their new government for the ensuing difficulties and problems. Different political parties and interest groups were feuding, armed veteran corps of different leanings overthrew local governments and each other; many political leaders were murdered. The Treaty of Versailles with all its restrictions and its reparation payments threw Germany into poverty and chaos. A galloping inflation and growing unemployment caused enormous hardship and discontent in Germany. The chaotic times were a fertile ground for a rising radical nationalistic movement.

In 1923 members of the National Socialist German Workers Party attempted to take control of the Bavarian government. Adolf Hitler, Austrian born and a former corporal in the German Army, started an uprising in a popular beer hall where a Bavarian politician was to make a speech. Hitler and General Ludendorff, a hero from the Great War, organized a march through Munich the next day but they were met with police resistance. Ludendorff was ordered to house arrest and Hitler was imprisoned. There was, however, much popular support for this new movement.

Hitler, a fiery speaker and a gifted orator, made good use of the Munich events and his ensuing imprisonment in later public speeches which were enthusiastically attended by ever growing crowds. He blamed trade unions, Communists, and above all the Jews for Germany's humiliating defeat in the Great War and for the social disorder and economic crisis the country subsequently found itself in. He stressed that he believed that it was Germany's destiny to rise again and lead all of Europe. He attracted millions of Germans with his promise of work for all and social justice.

A surprising development occurred in 1930 when the hitherto small National Socialist German Workers Party won 107 seats in the Reichstag, making it the second largest after the Social Democrats. During the next election the party garnered even more seats. Hindenburg was again elected president. His new Chancellor, von Papen, gained support when he succeeded in having the rest of the war reparations cancelled. Von Papen resigned but negotiated secretly with Hitler and exerted great influence on the eighty six year old Hindenburg who declared Hitler Chancellor of the Reich on January 30, 1933. The Third Reich had begun.

Luther had admonished the people to render unto Caesar whatever Caesar thought was Caesar's. Militaristic Frederick the Great, the philosopher king, flute player, music maker, and a friend of Voltaire, fondly remembered by the people in many tales and anecdotes as 'Der Alte Fritz', and autocratic Bismarck, the tough practitioner of 'real-politik', had both demanded subservience of Germany's citizens. Deference, obedience and unquestioning acceptance of their authoritarian superiors seem to have been ingrained in the people. Hitler found an unwary populace swept away by his promises for a great Germany unquestioningly ready to be led by their Fuehrer.

Chapter 2

ADOLF HITLER

He was born April 20, 1889, the son of a small Austrian customs official and the official's second cousin. Quite early he showed that he had a mind of his own. His father wanted him to become a civil servant. Little Adolf rather than submit to his father's wishes, decided not to study and eventually provided good reasons for his father to relinquish his ambitious plans for his son. After his father died his education was basically abandoned. At sixteen Adolf left school for good. For the next three years he lived the life of a loafer in Linz and Vienna, all the time supported by his family. His mother died in 1908 and the penniless nineteen year old moved to Vienna. After being rejected as an artist due to lack of talent, and from becoming an architect due to lack of education, Adolf, rather than studying the necessary courses which were made available to ambitious men and women by the Social Democrats and trade unions at that time, lived for the next four years as a penniless tramp, working at odd jobs, sometimes as a sign painter, sleeping in flophouses, eating in charity soup kitchens. He never attempted to get a regular job because he looked down on blue collar labourers. Convinced that he was destined to a higher calling, he suffered his vagabond existence experiencing misery and destitution with 'hunger as my faithful bodyguard'.

The large city of Vienna had great libraries and Hitler read voraciously, mostly German history and mythology and much about the now emerging Pan-Germanism. He became a devotee of Wagner's world of Germanic gods and heroes, and soon obsessed with everything German. He also devoured anti-Semitic literature. In his mind grew the conviction that the multitudes of Slavic races that peopled the Austro-Hungarian Empire and the Jews were subhuman and in his frequent angry outbursts he declared that he hated them all and that they had no place in a German speaking world.

He began to observe groups of people, unions, and political movements. He read political press, analyzed speeches and party organizations, studied its psychological and political techniques and he came soon to see what made a party successful. Hitler was a realist. He stated that a winning party must know how to create a mass movement; it must know the effective use of propaganda on the masses and it must know the use of spiritual and physical terror. These were all observations that he so successfully used later on in his own party.

Hitler, realizing that his life hitherto had been less than successful, left Vienna in 1913 and went to live in Germany. When the First World War broke out, he saw a chance to start anew. He petitioned King Ludwig III for permission to volunteer in a Bavarian regiment, the request was granted. Hitler became a good soldier and was twice decorated for bravery.

When the war was over, Hitler stayed with the army and became an education officer, euphemism for informer, a duty that required him to attend official functions of diverse parties which abounded after the war in Munich. On one of these occasions, he listened to a speech made by the founder of the German Workers' Party, an Anton Drexler, a locksmith by trade. He was intrigued and soon joined the party. He was member number seven. The other party members were a newspaperman, an economist, a poet, a journalist, and the war veteran Ernst Roehm. The party wanted to combat the Marxism of free trade unions and to agitate for a 'just' peace for Germany. Opposing the timid Drexler, Hitler soon took over propaganda. In a speech in the famous Hofbrauhaus, he outlined the 25 points of the German Workers Party. The first one demanded the union of all Germans in a Greater Germany. The second one demanded the abrogation of all the treaties signed in Versailles. Other points stressed that Jews were to be denied office, press and eventually citizenship. Other socialist points demanded abolition of incomes not earned by work, nationalization of trusts, abolition of land rents and land speculation, death penalty for traitors, usurers and profiteers. One point called for the maintenance of a sound middle class. The last point, number 25, insisted on the creation of a strong central power of the state. Not long after the party's name was changed to National Socialist German Workers Party.

Hitler organized the storm troopers, the SA, lead by Roehm, which protected his fledgling party at speeches and rallies. Looking for a symbol that would unite the masses he rediscovered the ancient sign of the swastika. Hitler himself designed the emblem emblazoned

In the summer of 1921 Hitler took over the leadership of the party. He quickly established the Fuehrerprinzip, the leadership principle, which was to be the first law of the Nazi Party and then the Third Reich.

The new party expanded quickly under Hitler's organization and propaganda. Herman Goering joined, as did Rudolf Hess, Alfred Rosenberg and Streicher, the newspaperman, later followed by Gregor Strasser and the fanatical nationalist, Joseph Goebbels.

Hitler masterfully used the destitution and the general discontent of a population stuck in economic hopelessness, witnessing at the same time the injustice of immense riches being accumulated by captains of industry who profited by the inflation that bankrupted the rest of Germany. The people became aware of the lack of power and direction of the Weimar Republic and became an easy target for Hitler's magnetic oratory and his fiery expression of his vision of a new Germany.

Hitler never left anything to guesswork as to what he thought and where he wanted to take the new Germany. He expressed all his ideas in his book "Mein Kampf" that he wrote while in prison in Landsberg in 1923. He always insisted that Germany must expand to the east – largely at the expense of Russia – in search of Lebensraum, literally 'room to live'. He blamed the economic and financial bankruptcy of Germany squarely on the Jews and he lay blame for the degeneration of German mores and morals on the "debauched and decadent" works of literature and the arts produced largely by Jews.

He wrote about his ideas on culture, education, theatre, movies, art, literature, history, marriage, even prostitution and syphilis. Marriage, he insisted, 'cannot be an end in itself, but must serve the one higher goal: the increase and preservation of the species and the race. This alone is its meaning and its task.'

Influenced by Darwin's theory of survival of the fittest, Hitler believed that 'this is a world where one creature feeds on the other and where the death of the weaker implies the life of the stronger.' And the stronger was, of course, the superior race of the Aryan, to which the German belonged. To Hitler the Germans were 'the highest species of humanity on this earth', the master race, 'which they will remain if they care for the purity of their own blood.' Hitler was obsessed with the notion of the 'Volk', a German word that cannot be translated just as 'folk', because it includes a deep and sacred connection to blood and soil. He wrote the 'Volk' must set race in the centre of all life.' 'The Volk lives in a state which is based on the aristocratic idea of nature'. This invariably led to the conclusion that democracy had no place, it was replaced by the 'Fuehrer Prinzip'. He explained that 'this principle – absolute responsibility unconditionally combined with absolute authority – will gradually breed an elite of leaders which is today, in this era of irresponsible parliamentarianism, utterly inconceivable.'

The philosopher Hegel and his ideas about heroes also influenced Hitler. He agreed with the philosopher that the 'will of the world spirit is carried out by world historical individuals", no doubt envisioning himself a member of the pantheon of greats such as Alexander, Caesar and Napoleon. Filled with a burning desire to lift Germany out of its morass and carry it to a glorious future, Hitler saw himself as the ruthless 'Uebermensch' of Nietzsche, the supreme leader for whom everyday morals do not apply. His Schicksal, or fate, that other German word with as loaded a meaning as blood and soil, or Blut und Boden, had led him at the helm of a new era, the Third Reich, which was to be the Thousand Year Reich. The self proclaimed master could justify all his ruthless deeds because they were done in the service of the greater idea. The withdrawal of freedom of the masses, introduction of slave labour, concentration camps and invasion of foreign countries were just realities that followed the granite 'laws of necessity'.

Hitler served only nine months of his five year sentence. When he came out, the party and its press were banned and he himself was forbidden to speak. But Hitler was not discouraged. He had had time in prison to find his own way and he had come to realize that the future of a new Germany was in his hands. He became the planner, organizer and master mover. He had the knack of attracting and singling out men who became devoted to him and who worked with him implementing his ideas and visions. By the time he was declared Reichskanzler on January 30, 1933, all of the administration and all of the institutions that were to govern the new state, were in place.

Chapter 3

HAEFNER FAMILY

There is a saying that to be remembered for three generations means immortality for an ordinary person. My father, August Haefner, or Gustel as he was called to differentiate him from his father August, was a passionate researcher of family history and dates and I have in my possession documents about births, marriages and deaths of the Haefners, going back to the time before the reformation.

There are no famous names to be found. I come across a judge and a seafaring cook, but most of my Swabian forebears were craftsmen, innkeepers or farmers living in small holdings in the Hohenlohe countryside in southern Germany. In 1811 a Haefner married the daughter of a cooper who lived in the city of Schwaebisch Hall. Five years later he took over his father-in-law's business and the house in the Gelbingergasse 39. Five generations of coopers were to follow in the house which is still in the possession of the family. For the purpose of this book, I will go back only four generations. I never knew my great grandparents, but my father did - the hands reach down through the generations and close the link. Immortality.

My great grandfather, Georg Wilhelm Haefner, was born in 1858, a grandson to the very first Haefner in Schwaebisch Hall. Like his father and his grandfather, he became a master cooper and wine merchant. Like his grandfather he married a girl from a family that was once associated with salt.

Since the early Middle Ages Schwaebisch Hall had been a famous city that based its wealth and political independence on salt. Stone Age inhabitants of the Kocher valley had already known the saline springs that welled up in the area. From the Middle Ages on, salt was produced commercially by boiling down spring water in large iron pans until only the white crystals remained. The burgers exported the commodity all over Southern Germany, even down to Hungary, and some amassed great wealth. The city was free and independent from any allegiance to a sovereign. Schwaebisch Hall even had its own coins minted, the 'heller' or 'Haller coin'. Hall is a word referring to salt.

In 1804 the salt springs became property of the King and the House of Wuerttemberg, who in exchange promised the families that had controlled the salt trade an annual stipend, the 'salt money', as long as the springs ran. As Gustel tells it with a grin on his face: 'The clever burgers of Hall set up the contract so tightly that even the Third Reich could not whittle away at it.'

Gustel also remembers quite well that he was often chosen by the Salt Committee to carry the special paper bags with the 'salt money' to the 'salt families'; a job he loved because it often brought him a tip. Years later, when it was Gustel's turn to receive 'salt money', he always donated it back to the committee because 'someone has to pay for the costumes and the dancing they do every summer.' Today our family's share of a few euros of 'salt money' goes to my sister Ingeborg while some salt shares are even sent to the United States.

The piles of wood used for keeping fires going under the large pans have disappeared and the Soleplatz, the 'salt plaza' is a parking lot. Tourists come in droves every year to observe the traditional customs and dances of the 'Sieder', the salt boilers. The main spring still runs but its waters are used in a resort and sanatorium. To this day the city still profits from its saline riches.

The house which the first Haefner purchased has not changed much on the outside. It still shows that it once was a church with a bell tower; a plaque explains the history of the 'Josenturm' as it is called. The chapel was built in the twelfth century when it stood outside the city of Schwaebisch Hall. It was dedicated to St.Jodocus, who became the patron saint against fire, thunderstorms, tough winds, and pestilence. He helped seafarers and protected cellars and pilgrims on their wanderings. I can still remember my father reciting a little tongue in cheek prayer that implored St. Jodocus 'to protect my house, but if a fire must be, let it be at my neighbours place.'

As the city grew, it incorporated the Westside of the chapel into its city wall. By 1582 it had become home and shop of a gun maker; then it housed a printing press. The great fire of 1680 destroyed the building and the tower down to its more than meter thick stone wall foundation. Both tower and house were rebuilt in 1686, each with two stories of timber framework done so beautifully that to this day they still catch the eyes of tourists and photographers. The building served successively as a fire tower, a German School, a warehouse and a fire hall before it became the shop of a cooper. The city owns the tower to which all access from the house had been walled in.

In 1883 when Wilhelm and his young bride, Marie moved in they found the building in deplorable condition. Gustel remembered his grandmother Marie reminiscing about the slatted floors which were so dilapidated that one could easily plunge through to one's death. They began to rebuild the inside: the ground floor was still the work shop. A first floor was built and an apartment with parquet flooring was constructed; a broad staircase led to the second floor with its living quarters. Wilhelm and Marie were modern. They installed pit toilets on each floor and brought water to the two kitchens. All was crowned by a large attic, with spare rooms and utility space.

Wilhelm was a good barrel maker, a good cellar master and a good business man and over the years he became well off. Marie was a good housewife and stern mistress to her maids. Marie loved money. By the time the First World War was over, Marie, who had become a widow in 1914, owned the large house and had no debts. It was also rumoured that Marie had a box under her bed with 30,000 Goldmarks in it.

Wilhelm and Marie had three sons. Their firstborn in 1884 was August, followed by Wilhelm, called Willie, and then Robert. August was an intelligent boy and he wished dearly to be allowed to enter high school. Despite his teachers' encouragement mother Marie insisted that he was the simple son of a simple craftsman and there was no need to aspire to a higher position in life. Marie's family had once been associated with the salt history of Hall, and included some illustrious personages, but as the salt treasury emptied, ambition and influence of the old family vanished until they were nothing but impoverished carriers of a once famous name. When August was ready for higher education around 1895, there was no money; he had to content himself with finishing grade school and then enter his father's trade just like he had done before him. That is just how it was.

Family tradition also told that mother Marie was once heard to mutter that August was actually an unwanted child and a real burden when he arrived in 1884. This must have influenced August in his attitude towards his mother. Later on, Marie tried to smooth this out but the damage had been done. There would always be a strain between mother and her firstborn.

As their business improved and the money began to accumulate, the family stature rose in the city; old family connections were renewed and the family enjoyed a good standing. Since there was also more money, the later sons Willie and Robert had a much easier life. Willie still had to apprentice with his father but Robert, the last born, went to high school. August never complained to his mother about the different treatment of her sons, but he did mention that he, because he had been bypassed in so many ways, felt that he had a right to inherit a larger portion than the others. These disputes came out when the war was over.

August finished his grade school and then apprenticed with his father. He worked away from home under different masters, as was custom, and then, in 1904, the twenty year old was required to join the military. To his great chagrin he was noticed as a soldier with potential and was sent – for another year - to Potsdam to a special battalion to which traditionally all the German kings sent one or two soldiers. When he had served his time, August had had more than enough of the military. He refused an offer to become a sub lieutenant in the colonial troops. Added to his dislike of the military was the knowledge that his then still secret fiancée had absolutely no intentions of becoming a colonial bride.

So, August went back coopering and eventually ended up in Switzerland at a large firm. He became a member of the local Musikverein, the band, in which he played the flute and the bass.

In 1911 he came back to Schwaebisch Hall to marry Emma Schweizer, his secret fiancée, who had grown up in the same street as he had.

August and Emma's Wedding Photo

He returned with his bride to Switzerland. A year later my father, August Jr. or Gustel, was born. Gustel loves to tell the only story he remembers – and that only second hand – from this time: 'grandfather Wilhelm had come to check out little Gustel, his first grandchild. One morning young mother Emma heated up a bottle of milk for baby Gustel on a kerosene heater. The bottle exploded and Emma, trying to clean up the mess of shards of glass and spilled milk, set herself on fire. Grandfather Wilhelm heard her screams and rushed to help her. Father August had a very fine boxer dog who, not knowing grandfather Wilhelm too well, charged to the aid of Emma whom he thought in danger, and defending his mistress sank his teeth into grandfather Wilhelm's throat. Now there were two people screaming at top of their lungs. Luckily Papa August appeared and greater calamity was avoided.'

Soldiers ready to go to war. Lined up in front of St. Michaels Church
in Schwaebisch Hall

There was not even time to move in properly before he had to leave. He spent the next four years and four months in France and Belgium as the driver of a horse wagon. Gustel wondered all his life that 'even though my father was a city boy and had no experience with horses – they chose him over farm boys'. August hauled ammunition and the Division minister but mostly he carried wounded back to the field hospital.

When he returned home in 1918, he brought back with him a small black notebook, the kind a soldier can carry in his breast pocket. In it he had daily recorded the main events of the day: the first year he noted the many marches, the battles, the ditches dug, how many weapons destroyed, which of his comrades had fallen. Later entries skipped days and became very short. He recorded his wages and how much he transferred to the bank back home. He jotted down the many letters from 'my dear wife, Emma' which arrived almost daily and the parcels with food from home.

The following are excerpts from his notebook:
1914
August 12: Marching
August 13: Marching
Aug 14: Marching
Aug 15: Marching
August 16: Marching

Aug 17: Rest day

Aug 18: Marching

Aug 19: Battle and heavy fighting

Aug 20: Continuing fighting

Aug 21and 22: continuing fighting

August 23: Break up in pursuit of enemy

Aug. 24: Heavy fighting at St. Blaise

Aug. 25: Crossed the border

And so it continues…

September 8: after weeks my first sip of beer – what a treat!

He wrote about spies they caught, the empty cities they marched through, the places where he went sightseeing, and the rain, the ever- pouring rain.

September 13: Sunday! Oh, what happiness. Today is a rest day. The first time after six weeks I have slept in a real bed and out of my clothes. What a treat! I am a new man. Sundays are usually the toughest days for us. Received 2.50 marks extra. At three in the afternoon was church service – no commandeering was necessary, the men came eagerly and voluntarily. 15 mark wages received.

Sept. 15: Received cigars. Letter from mother with the news that my dear brother Robert has fallen. Letter from my dear wife with the same news.

A week and many kilometers of forced marching later and he was in Belgium, in Flanders.

Sept. 24: Saw the comet with the parallel tail.

Sept. 26: Half past two in the morning pick up provisions in Mons. At noon in Valenciennes and after a seven hour trip in Cambrai.

Sept. 27: Sunday. Leave at three thirty in the morning. Two skirmishes. Marching on with unbelievable speed until nine at night. On the way we took much wine from a large farm, in the castle, 15 minutes away, much champagne.

28 Sept. Pursued the enemy. Overnight in the castle.

Sept. 29: Were pushed back in fierce battle. Heavy losses. Gained it back at night. Conquered Tierpal.

Sept. 30: Dug in up to our teeth. Poziers.

Oct. 1: Repelled two enemy sorties. Fortified our positions.

Oct. 3: This morning our general received the sad news that his son had fallen. He had joined only three weeks prior as a volunteer.

Oct. 4: Sunday. No news.

Later on in the evening he wrote that he got three cards and a letter and a parcel. One sausage, two cigars and a chocolate.

Oct. 6: Newspaper from Hall, Sept.22

In the evening drank two bottles champagne and six of wine.

Oct. 7: Another newspaper. Nothing new. Music – but without wine.

Oct. 8: Two letters from Emma. Evening piano concert in the inn across.

Oct. 9: Cards from Emma and mother, otherwise the fighting goes on with the usual fierceness.

Oct. 13: Beat back enemy attack at midnight. In the afternoon they almost trounced us, but we were lucky. Pancakes and apples.

He recorded the days where nothing happened, and days where friends and comrades got wounded and died. There were good days when he got letters and cards, cigars or a parcel with sausages, baked goodies or a knitted shawl and mitts. There was a day when he was able to save all except two horses from a burning barn, a day when he could clean a barrel at the place where he was quartered and press cider. Many days were spent digging ditches and cutting trees for their fortifications. On one day they dynamited a church tower probably to prevent it being used by the enemy for observation or a sniper's nest by the enemy.

Dec. 17: Enemy attack. Fierce. Bloody fight. A few hundred prisoners.

For Christmas he received many parcels and he listed each item and from whom it was sent.

The strength of the battles increased as did the quantity of the hardware to do it with.

1915 "With God"

August was not a religious man, he never even set foot in a church. So why now? With God. Perhaps he thought and wrote this for his own encouragement. It was the old German battle cry 'Mit Gott'. And it couldn't hurt.

And the litany of skirmishes and shooting continued. Almost daily he received a letter from home and at least once a week a parcel filled with goodies. The parcels were not all from his wife and mother; friends and neighbours sent so much. He had many true friends. He ferried goods and wounded and often ministers and priests, who were mentioned by name, with his horse and wagon to the field hospitals.

April 1: Pys. Courselette. Nothing new. A letter from my dear Emma, Gusti (Gustel) suggested that mother should go and buy a little sister for himself.

There were entries about attacks from the air with heavy casualties. He writes that he sees Zeppelins flying over them. But most entries throughout spring said: nothing new other than a letter from…and from…

He notes that reinforcements arrived frequently and on one occasion he has to transport an English pilot from Bayaume but he does not mention where he brings him.

On August 2 he travelled by train home to Hall for a twelve day furlough.

Aug.21: Grosser Zapfenstreich, (the German equivalent of a military marching band tattoo) to celebrate the victories in the east entertaining the troops.

In late November he caught influenza and was very sick.

Dec. 8: Fischer fallen. This had been his last day.

1916

The entries get shorter. There were no more notes about battles, or fallen comrades or rain. Only letters received are noted. There was one every day from his wife. He still listed every item in each of the parcels he received. He started noting what he ate every day – cheese, herring, sausage, rabbit, bacon.

Feb. 8: Willie and Berta are engaged. (Willie is his younger brother and Berta is the sister of his wife Emma.)

Feb. 14: Holidays until Feb.27 Wonderful days.

There was still an entry for every day, still a letter from his 'dear wife' and he mentioned what he ate - but nothing else. Not a word about what he did, what he saw; I guess it really did not matter. Nothing could have shown the futility of war and the monotony of its devastation. It was every day the same, the fighting, the killing and maiming, the misery and the deaths, the terrible, pointless and futile deaths of so many, of so many young.

During the summer months they changed their position frequently, names like Mashaing, Somain are mentioned, and his company advanced through Flanders. They marched through Wyngene, Thourhout, Wassigny, Moere. They marched in September, they marched in October and they marched in December again.

On August 5, 1917 he received the Iron Cross, II class, in the name of His Majesty the Kaiser and King. He never mentioned it once in his diary or ever spoke about it in conversation. In 2002, three years after my father's death, I found in his desk a small cardboard box with August Senior's tattered diary, the Iron Cross and other medals and ribbons. My mother had left my father's den with all its contents untouched. I took the little box back to Canada with me.

The arrival of 1918 was not even specially mentioned.

March 28: Sausages and much rain.

He marched to Dendermould, Gaurain. With the medics to Tortequenne and Lecluse .

In April he took his horses to Duri and marched on to St. Quintian. In June he was in Fremicourt and Grevillers, and in Bihuwurt.

In August he marched to Arleuse and Anhiers. In September we find him in Estrun then in Bouchain.

During October he moved through Eire, Vaziers, Vret, Tillay, then through Venilles, Rieuse, Peruwelz.

On November 6 he trudged through Stambruges then Thouricourt, and also Endingen.

Nov 11: FRIEDE - PEACE

Nov. 13: March to Roode

Nov. 14: Start to march home.

Nov. 20: Crossed the border

Dec. 10: Reported at 119th regiment in Stuttgart for demobilization.

Dec. 11: Discharged

And so he came back to Schwaebisch Hall and resumed his life. When years later I asked him to tell me about the war, he indicated that he did not want to talk about it.

"There is neither fame nor glory in the bloody business", he snorted, "only slaughter and carnage, and all useless and senseless".

He remained silent for a while but I could see that he was not finished.

"And there is so much blood - blood from my comrades, blood from other soldiers, blood from civilians, from women and children – but the blood of the innocent horses - that was the worst. You knew that I was the ambulance driver and I brought the wounded back to the field hospitals. It was bad enough to see the men die but it made me screaming mad when the animals got shot. They shrieked in their agony and then they went quiet and all was in their eyes –they were so quiet, and that, that really, really hurt. So much pain and so much suffering – for what."

He turned away from me and sat very still for a while and I could imagine that he saw horrific pictures in his mind. After some time, he looked at me and straightened up.

"And the big shots spout out their ra ra ra and remain safely far away from the action. It's always the little guy who gets thrown in and nobody asks him if he wants to go – they get foot rot or influenza, they suffer from giant lice and aggressive rats, and they are the ones to be blown up or gassed or burnt. It is always the little guy who does not get to go home anymore. He dies and the rats and the generals get fat."

The relationship between Emma and her mother-in-law during the time August was at the front, was all but happy. Marie had not welcomed her son's bride who had brought no money into the family and was considered a poor catch. Emma's father was no longer alive but he had once even become bankrupt. Imagine what the people talked! The many visits between Switzerland and then the move back home again had depleted whatever savings the young couple might have had. In those years the wives of soldiers received only a pittance in support from the state and so Marie had to help out which she resented greatly. Marie let Emma know at every opportunity, even publicly, that she lived on her, Marie's, charity. Emma had to swallow it because it was the truth. But of course, this did nothing to make her like the mother of her husband.

August came home to a business that had been greatly reduced over the last war years. His brother Willie had run it for a time and when he was drafted, Marie had run the shop with hired help. The cellars were empty and worse yet, there was no stock of dry oak planks which were needed to make new barrels or to mend old ones. August took over the house and put a mortgage on it so he could buy out his brother Willie. Robert had fallen in France just a few weeks into the war. All attempts in getting some of his mother's 30,000 Goldmarks failed. Marie referred to her notary saying he had strongly advised her against giving or even lending any of her money to August. That is what she said. He begged his mother for some of the money so that he could start the business again. But Marie refused. August did not get one dime.

So, August and Emma started from scratch. They borrowed from the bank, worked from early morning on, ate boiled potatoes and bread soup three times a day, together with their two journeymen, three apprentices and the maid, and scrimped wherever they could. August and his men made cider barrels and then also started to make cider. They delivered to inns and those bakeries that had a license to dispense cider and also private houses. In those days most people drank dark cider; only the rich could afford wine.

And then they got sucked into the devastating maelstrom of inflation. When a customer paid someone was made to run, literally, run to the bank with a suitcase full of paper money, because waiting till the afternoon or the next day would devaluate the money even more. Money became useless. August was soon forced to shut down the business.

He went to work as a cooper in a factory that produced commercial barrels. In this function he found himself travelling all over Germany, installing huge barrels and vats for wine, vinegar, spirits and sauerkraut. But times did not improve and the factory which was owned by a Jew - meaning a good business man, as Gustel always expressly mentioned - had to declare bankruptcy. August came back home and opened his business once more, there was no alternative. August again asked his mother for some help. She said she did not have a penny left, blaming inflation, her notary and two treacherous salesmen who had persuaded her to invest in shady stocks and bonds which left her penniless after the devaluation of the German money in 1921/22. August realized that he now had to look after his mother too.

Meanwhile his brother Willie had become a cooper at a winery and then bought the Gasthaus 'Harmony' located farther down the street. He boasted clear title to it. It seemed clear to August that his mother had in fact given Willie a portion of her 30,000 Goldmarks and kept it a secret. August decided to confront her and bitter fights and discussions ensued with the result that the rift between mother and son got deeper.

Gustel reminisces that 'whenever I came upstairs to visit my grandmother, she was sitting in her Trauerstuhl, the 'sorrow stool' – that's what we called a widow's chair. She sat still, her heavy figure ensconced in black, her eyes did not wander up and down the busy street. She did not peer into the windows across the street – she just sat there and cried. She always cried – tears rolling from her tired eyes, silently. The quietness frightened me very much. Only much later did I understand that she was mourning for her third born son, her favourite son, Robert, who had fallen in 1914 before Paris.'

As she got older, August had to provide for her going into an Old Age facility which cost him a heavy mortgage on his house. Gustel tells that 'after the loss of her money the old lady never smiled again. Her stout figure got stiffer and her jowly, fat face seemed to turn to marble that nothing could touch anymore.'

Grandmother Marie got sick with throat cancer and when she felt her end near, she asked that August would come and visit her. He refused to see her indicating that she had hated him all his life and had treated him unjustly and that he now saw no reason for any reconciliation. Young Gustel visited her a few hours before her death when she was barely able to speak. She told her grandson that during the last years she had finally realized that she sorry about that and regretted it so much. She cried bitterly. Sobbing she even mentioned those 30,000 Goldmarks that had caused so much misery. For the sake of peace, she said, she would never divulge the secret of what really had happened with the money and that she would take the burden into her grave.

And Gustel continues, 'Even though everyone knew what she had done with the money, Willie never owned up to having received a penny.'

August forgave his brother because he said he was entitled to get some money from his mother. What had bothered him was the secrecy with which it had been handled. He never blamed Willie for any unjust action.

Willie was not very industrious and was his own best customer in the restaurant. Some time after the war he was able to sell his business for a pittance. Family lore has it that he stored this money in a shoe box under the bed. August took him and his wife Berta, a sister to Emma, into his house while they were looking to buy a small house for themselves. For some reason nothing was suitable to the pair and they remained with August and Emma in the Gelbingergasse 39. In 1948 all German money devaluated from one day to the next – and Willie and

Berta now owned a box with totally valueless paper money. They remained in the Gelbingergasse.

This would eventually be the reason that in 1945 my mother, my sister Inge and I, and three years later on my father after he had come home from the prisoner of war camps, had to live in the barracks at the edge of town beside the Kocher River.

Problems later arose when in 1954 my grandfather sold the business to my father and he had to ask Willie and Berta to move out so that my father and his family could move into the house

Chapter 4

ERNST FAMILY

When I was nine or ten years old, I fell in love with ballads and became an ardent fan of Goethe, Schiller and Ludwig Uhland, the trio who had written thrilling rhymes about base fiends and true maidens, treachery and faithful friends, heathens and Saracens, cowardice and heroism, cruel kings and jousting knights. I knew how the poets looked because one grew up with the images of these literary icons on posters, in books and on playing cards. I also loved classical music and stern looking Bach and scowling Beethoven were included in my pantheon of great men. One day I realized that my grandfather, Opa Ernst, looked very much like Beethoven. That shock of hair, that scowling mien under those bushy eyebrows – just the same. Opa Ernst was special, just like the great ones I admired. Opa was a reader, I could see the stacks of books from the library next to his reading chair; and the library next to his reading chair and he even subscribed to a magazine with few pictures, the Reader's Digest. Opa was not your regular kind of grandfather, one did not fool around with him; he never humoured children and he never ever had a coin for them. He was firm and tolerated no nonsense. I was in awe of him and so I put him right up on the shelf with my revered heroes: Goethe, Schiller, Uhland, Opa Ernst, and Beethoven. This Opa Ernst was Herbert Ernst, the father of my mother.

The Ernst family lived in Silesia. From the thirteenth century on the Order of the Teutonic Knights colonized the country, bringing Christianity and agriculture to the Slavic population and many Germans had followed them. Family lore tells that a robber knight from northern Germany had killed another knight in a brawl and was forced to move east if he wanted to keep his life. He came to Silesia and became a tree faller and started a family. As the centuries passed Prussian Kings drained the huge swamps that stretched east from the Oder River and opened the land for further colonization. The Ernst families bought land and became farmers and later on rich farmers. They were hard workers and not sentimental and they cherished land and wealth.

My grandfather, Herbert Ernst, the oldest of four boys, was born in 1887, in Breslau which is Polish today but was then German. I am in possession of 300 pages of memoirs which he started in May of 1948 which are based on diaries of former years which he then destroyed. It was very difficult for me to read the old fashioned German hand writing, but I persisted, not only due to the obvious interest I had in finding out about this grandfather, but also I was interested in discovering his thoughts and positions about the Third Reich. I knew that he had been an idealistic member of the National Socialist Party; his son Manfred had told me that he travelled the region giving ardent speeches to gain the support of the locals for the party which he saw as the saviour of a defeated Germany. During the war Herbert proudly wore the uniform, he propagandized for the party and the Reich and eventually he acted as a deputy Kreisleiter, a party official in charge of a district. To my surprise and disappointment, he barely mentioned his political involvement in his diary – he bemoaned the ignominious demise of the Third Reich and he lengthily expressed his deep sense of betrayal – but whatever he had written before about his political ideas and life had been purged in this latest and 'politically correct' edition of his life's story. Was this a sign of prudence or was it cowardice? I am very sad to have to admit that after reading his notes he no longer shared the elevated place I had assigned him amidst my great illustrious childhood heroes.

Herbert grew up in a family devoid of demonstrative love and filled with strife. His introvert father did not get along with his extrovert mother. Both quarrelled a lot, in fact they separated for a while and then, for Herbert's sake, a fact the mother threw in her son's face on many later occasions when she blamed

him for her unhappy life, they came together again, making his father ever more bitter, unapproachable and brutal and his mother even more meddlesome.

His mother worked as a milliner during the time of separation, a trade she had worked at before their separation. She was an outspoken woman who loved fashion and society.

His father was a teacher and later vice principal at a large High School in Breslau. He was shy and quiet and very frugal, a pedantic little man who insisted on being recognized as an authority because of his position and status in life – and not because he commanded it through his character and actions. He was a man who insisted that institutions such as the state, the church, had absolute authority and to even question their actions was akin to criminality. He was a reactionary and conservative through and through. He did not drink, smoked only moderately, had no hobbies that cost money, he wore his suits until they could not be turned and mended anymore, his only frivolity was that he loved to change his socks frequently during the day. Herbert described him as a petty and small minded man, leading an unimpressive life, in fact a failure in his son's eyes because he did not even make it to become a principal. But Herbert noted also that he changed to an understanding figure when he was in the outdoors. Herbert's father loved nature and passed that love on to his first born son.

Herbert's grandfather had started out as a day labourer. He worked himself, his wife and five sons mercilessly in order to fulfill his sole ambition in life: to acquire wealth. He was hard as steel, brutal and cold; he knew no fun, no joy and no compromise. By the time the old man died he owned two farms. Each of his three daughters received 1500 Taler as a dowry when they married. He was able to send three of his sons to university. Eduard became a professor at the University in Godesberg, Ewald became a superintendent of schools, Emil, Herbert's father, became a high school teacher and vice principal, and the fourth inherited the farm. Ironically, Reinhold who took over the farm, was a poor manager; he became a drunkard and soon lost his farm, only to wrest a miserable living as a day labourer. One winter morning he was found, face down, an axe in the back of his head. His murderer was never apprehended.

Herbert was able to excuse the unbending, narrowminded and uncompromising nature of his father by explaining that his spirit had been broken by his severe father. He who had not experienced the kind guidance of a father was unable to give the same to his own sons. The only exception was Manfred, his third son, whom he spoiled and coddled and to whom he even sang.

Herbert's mother was very different. She was outgoing and noisy, she loved to talk to people and share her life and experiences with others. In his memoirs Herbert described her as selfish and thankless, as a tactless and interfering gossip, a know-it-all mother-in-law who found fault with everything her four daughters-in- law did, from dusting, to cooking to bringing up children. He missed warmth and motherliness in her, but acknowledged her intelligence, curiosity and industriousness.

Herbert recognized that the two so unlikely persons were not good for each other. He explained one of the curious reasons for their differences and problems by elaborating on their 'racial 'differences. He described his father as being of the 'Nordic' and more sensitive race and his mother coming from a line of the 'Westphalian race' a group he believed to be a more robust race.

The shy, reclusive and penny-pinching father provided no chance for the lively mother to experience society and the abundance of culture and entertainment the big city of Breslau had to offer. His enjoyment came from the outdoors, taken in moderate doses during Sunday afternoons or holidays. Herbert intimated that she filled her dreary days with idle gossip, quarrel, and interference in other people's affairs, blaming others when things went awry.

My grandfather Herbert was born in 1887; he had three brothers, Bodo, born in 1892, died of a heart attack in 1937; Manfred, born in 1896 fell 1914 at Binarvilles, in France, and Helmuth, born in 1901, ended his life in 1945.

The one thing Herbert thanked his parents for were the unforgettable and wonderful celebrations they made for their children at their birthdays and on Christmas. Herbert's Diary has the following entry:

"On our birthdays the number of years was indicated by a circle of burning candles surrounding the fat candle of life in the centre. A special birthday tray was brought to one's bed and the afternoons were open to having friends at our house.

Christmas was even better. On Christmas Eve nobody left the house after the noon meal. Everything had been organized and arranged before and we spent the afternoon in the most happy mood until a small bell rang and the doors opened to the room where the Christmas tree stood lit up with candles whose shine sank into eyes and hearts. Throughout the year the parents were more than frugal but on Christmas they splurged. They had bought between 140 and 160 wax candles and by New Year's Eve they were all burned. There were never less than twenty candles on the tree.

The cause of this light fantasy was my father who spent hours every year musing over the miracle of the re-appearing sun in the deepest dark of the year. Mother read the Christmas story, we sang carols, but the Christian aspect I considered more and more an add-on and not the essence and the real wisdom of the time. The old Nordic desire for light was personified in father. We understood him without words.

The last time the tree was lit up was always on February 17th, father's birthday. How shabby the brown tree top looked when compared with the luscious green outside. Despite that we sank into deep melancholy because something beautiful again had come to its end. We burned the tree in the stove. We never let a tree that had done its duty stand on the veranda or in the yard. When its duty was done it went back to the elements that once had given it shape. We never said these things in words but we understood and that was beautiful in my innermost heart."

Herbert was an intelligent boy but he had a problem with authority. Today a psychologist might diagnose him with having oppositional defiance disorder. When he was admonished or punished in school his behaviour did not change in the direction the authority figure wanted; usually the opposite happened. When his father beat him, he became only more obstinate and reticent. In school he did as little as possible for the teachers he did not like – and there were many. He excelled in the sciences.

Basically, Herbert was a book worm and a loner who did not easily make friends. He did a lot of hiking, alone or with like minded friends, or on holidays with his father and siblings. He roamed his beloved Silesian countryside, exploring hills and dales, ponds and rivers, discovering ancient castles and ruins or prehistoric sites and caves. He loved history – not the dates and battles and famous names he was made to memorize, but the living past that one could investigate and touch; he loved the past that came with stories and fables, especially everything that was connected to Germanic sources. He was an idealist and a romantic.

The family spent summer holidays in the country with family or renting rooms with farmers. Herbert wrote, "We lived with a family Jaeckel who had many children. They gave us their two best rooms for 24 Reichsmark for one week, the use of their kitchen and the use of their garden gazebo which was located under a huge walnut tree. The Jaeckels were people with whom even mother did not get into an argument. Those poor people, beaten down from too much toil and poverty, offered no opposition to anything we said or did or wanted."

"Three summer holidays we spent with them in the totally Catholic village, which had few farmers but many, many labourers, Jaeckels being one of them. The pictures of the saints that gazed from walls in garish colours and which had repulsed me at first, actually became good acquaintances because of the peace and harmony of the lives of the family. They became pictures which one greeted as friends when one gazed at them but without any desire to listen to the sermons they offered. They simply belonged to the lives of the Jaeckels and were accepted as they were."

In the fall of 1904 Herbert entered the seminary to become a teacher. He loathed the institution and its regimentation as much as he despised most of his self-righteous, incompetent and arrogant teachers who themselves were given orders by a black cassocked director and the church. He challenged them intellectually and academically and so he was not surprised when a trifling incidence became the cause for his dismissal when he was barely into his second year. The headmaster advised him to seek out another seminary and to make things easy gave him a report card with glowing marks and indicated that the reason for Herbert's dismissal was 'a high degree of nervousness that required a pause in his education.'

Herbert got a rousing send-off from his student colleagues which sweetened the unjust treatment he had received. The teachers were glad to see him leave.

At home he got into fierce arguments with his father who berated and belittled him and who finally slapped him in the face whereupon Herbert flung at him that he better never do that again or he would hit him back.

"I know that you were beaten as a married man by your own father. That was a shame for grandfather for what he did and for you that you tolerated it. You are not your father and I do not want to be like you!"

Herbert then stormed out of the house. He spent Christmas at a friends and the rest of winter at his beloved Field Mill, the farm where an aunt and uncle carved out a frugal life. It was an old and simple house and its hard working inhabitants lived in peace and harmony. For many years whenever he had the chance he came for a visit; here he was able to 'taste freedom and human kindness', this was his haven where he came to heal his inner turmoil with simplicity of life and where he knew he was welcome no matter what had happened.

At Easter he entered another seminary where he found a friend, Doebers, who was to become his lifelong comrade and with whom he was in contact until Doebers' death in 1951 when 'he had just received his first pension cheque from the State'. This institute was modern and not run by clerics, there was a stage and science laboratories, and a library with diverse newspapers. The students were allowed to leave the campus, to go to pubs and public events. Herbert cherished the liberty and became a very good and conscientious student. His spare time was spent not so much in the pubs, as he had only three marks pocket money, as he regretfully records, but hiking with friend Doebers through old forests, paddling up and down the river, playing his violin with much enthusiasm, and of course choral singing, often for the public or in fierce competitions.

I quote from Herbert's memoirs: "And then it happened again, I made decisions without considering the pros and cons and without using my head and giving in to my emotions." His friend Morgenstern had introduced him to a student fraternity, the S.V.L.V Riczyk and Herbert had joined that very evening. Herbert wrote, 'this was just what I needed. Away from the humdrum of life into excess and exuberance of youth....'

Joining fraternities was strictly forbidden to the teachers in training, and its Polish sounding name which came from a prehistoric fortification at an ancient crossing at the Oder River, made it later on even more suspect. Its members were young and enthusiastic about the origin of the name, they took it as an indication of a newly emerging Germanic time. Herbert remembered: "The history of our nation was our raison d'etre."

The young fraternity men listened to monthly lectures about German history, they drank beer, they hiked up historic mountains. Herbert exulted: "How we felt connected to the earth that had once drunk hot blood of men."
They built gigantic bonfires on hill tops and sang:
"I stand like a rock
Like the hinge on which the world turns,
Like a Kaiser for freedom and justice."

In his memoirs Herbert described these times as some of the best in his life, he enjoyed the camaraderie of likeminded friends who dreamt of a glorious future not only for themselves but also for their fatherland, their beloved Germany.

Herbert was elected president of his fraternity three weeks before his final examinations. A room patrol found a photo that showed him with cap and colours. Because of his rank in the fraternity, Herbert was immediately and without any recourse dismissed from school. The other students were allowed to continue but had to study another extra year because of their 'moral immaturity'.

Herbert took the train to Breslau and the predictable happened. His parents would not let him stay and threw him out. Eight days of walking and begging for food brought him to his true friend Doebers. The older Doebers had graduated as a teacher and had found a position. He was very poor too but he was able to make a few extra Reichsmark when he sang with the children's choir at funerals as was custom.

Herbert stayed with his friend for a few weeks. Even though he started selling insurance and had many odd and occasional jobs he got hungrier every day and more mired in misery, poverty and depression. In desperation he decided to flee to his old childhood haven, the Field Mill. He bought a train ticket as far as his last pennies would allow, then, playing his violin in the compartment and holding out his cap, watching carefully that the conductor would not catch him, he collected enough money to buy a full ticket for the rest of the journey.

In the Field Mill he was, as always, greeted with kindness. Here he was not judged or condemned, the family took him in as one of their own. A summer filled with garden and farm chores restored his balance and outlook on life. 'My dear aunt even bought me occasionally a bit of tobacco for a treat.'

In fall he reported, as required, to the military in Brieg where he arrived by train with his old suitcase that contained 'the second of my two shirts, a few handkerchiefs, a clothing brush and my coffee cup' and nothing else as he had not been home to see his parents who, he was certain, would not have welcomed him.

Service at the military meant moving and saluting from five in the morning until bed time when a recruit just fell into his bunk without any energy left for anything but sleep. The food was very basic and never enough. Light and coal had to be purchased by the men themselves. Most of the men received regularly pocket money from home and plenty of extra food. Herbert received neither money nor parcels filled with bacon and sausages like many of the other men. Nobody shared with him. He mentioned that most of the men were Polish and that he did not have much contact with any of his comrades most of whom he considered oafish and uneducated.

When Herbert arrived at his regiment, his Hauptman had received a letter from Herbert's father in which he was asked to watch out for the wayward, tough willed, and undisciplined son and to break his unruly spirit. Hauptman Schlimmer, and that name means 'Worse' in German, lived up to his name and the father's request and made life a hell for the young recruit.

But nothing is so miserable that good things cannot happen sometimes. One day in January 1909 when Herbert was out doing target practice, his instructor noticed that Herbert was shaking which was unusual because Herbert normally was a confident and good shot. He asked him about the reason and discovered incredulously that Ernst wore neither underwear nor socks – he had none – undergarments were not issued by the military and he had no money to buy any. It was minus nineteen degrees.

The Sergeant told Herbert about the letter his father had written to the captain and was very upset about the inhumanity of a father to his son. He gave Herbert 'the warmest of his own two jackets, a pair of underpants, a pair of woolen socks, one set of foot rags, a pair of knee warmers and a set of ear muffs'; he also spoke to his friends and from that day on many shared their goodies with Herbert. The kindness of strangers helped him survive; it did nothing to prevent further maltreatment from the captain.

In June he was reassigned to be the assistant to the company clerk and life became better. He was promoted to Private First Class and when he visited his parents on Christmas, he was welcomed by his father who was now proud of his military son. Upon return to the military, he advanced to company clerk. He handled all his duties in an exemplary way. Life had improved for him. He was inside and he was warm; he had better food and he was away from the clutches of his captain. And I am certain he had underwear now.

In fall he applied for entry into the Seminary at Bunzlau to complete his teacher training and this time he could include glowing references of his sergeant major, and consequently he was accepted. "Thus ended my time at the military that had started in such despondency and misery and concluded rather harmoniously so that in hindsight I can truly say that it was actually a good time. Memory has a way to distill things so that only the good remains."

He started his first teaching job in October 1911 in Gersdorf, a small village in Upper Silesia. Making the teacherage, which was actually still in the process of being built, into his own home with bits and pieces of old furniture he got from home or which he bought cheaply, was a real delight for him. He was happy to finally be the master of his own life. The actual school was in a wooden building some 100 meters across from his house. He roamed the country side and explored the area and became very fond of the sparseness of the Goerlitzer Heide. He began to landscape around the house, transplanting trees from the country side. He planted a large vegetable garden, many bushes and fruit trees; as well he constructed a gazebo with a fountain and a view.

On his first day in Gersdorf when he went to the local inn for his lunch, he collided with a young and pretty girl in the doorway to the restaurant. This was Gretel, Margarete Pohl, the not yet seventeen year old sister of the owner of the inn "Scholtisei" and the largest farm in the village. The two fell in love and a year later they became engaged. In the fall of 1913 Herbert applied to the authorities to take his final teacher's examination. His fiancé was expecting a child in spring and the wedding had been set for April. It would have been very unwise for a young teacher to marry before the second inspection.

This decision had to be made in haste and Herbert buckled down during the long winter months to study. He had worked hard with his students and he felt that he had been quite successful as their teacher. But the examination would also include methodology and pedagogical theory and history – areas he did not consider important and relevant for himself but he realized that his examiners did and so, with a heavy heart and somewhat unwilling mind, he sat down to study those subjects. He was not notified about the date of the inspection until a few days before. It was to be three weeks before the wedding with Gretel.

The inspectors arrived an hour before the announced time, but Herbert had presumed they would be early and was therefore present. He wore his best black suit and was secure about the outcome of the examination having prepared the students about the importance of this visit the day before. He knew he would not have any problems with his children.

He laid out all his books and charts and reports etc. before their critical eyes. They could not find any faults or irregularities. His lesson went just fine, the children were very well behaved and answered everything according to plan. He responded satisfactorily to all questions about method and theory of education, was well versed in its history and started to think that he acquitted himself rather splendidly. And then Herbert remembered:

"Then the inspector clamped his glasses on his nose and addressed me, 'after you left the seminary what did you consider to be your most important task?' The answer was supposed to be "to further my education". I knew that but I did not say it. Because everything had gone peachy up to this point, my old devil jester rode me again and idiot that I can be, I blurted out, 'to forget everything I have learned in the seminary'.

My ears were ringing with the icy comments that poured out over me and they rose to an even higher pitch when I tried to substantiate my claim with actual facts, I am sure they would have loved to fail me because of 'moral immaturity'. But by 12:30 it was all over. They did pass me – only with a 'satisfactory' – but they did. They sure gave me a rough time. Later on when I was part of similar inspection team I never put a candidate through what they put me through."

Herbert and his youngest brother, Manfred, who was visiting him, went to Pohl's Inn and they all celebrated into the early morning. Teacher Ernst had no class the next day; he had told his students the day before that the superintendent had given them all a day off for their good behaviour. He had not, of course, but

Herbert had known that they would be celebrating and that he needed the morning to sober up.

Gretel and Herbert married in April 1914; Irmgard, their first daughter arrived on June 4th and on August 1st came the call for general mobilization. The First World War had begun.

As a teacher he was considered an essential service provider and not required to join the military. He volunteered, joined as a non commissioned officer and "remained in this rank until in 1944 when 'they' remembered me and I had to join the Volkssturm, then they made me a captain".

Herbert was put in charge of training eight sets of recruits and quickly gained the negative attention of diverse superiors who were offended by his relatively easygoing ways. They would have rather have him treat his recruits in a more exacting and military manner and hand out discipline by the book. Herbert, although he was strict, preferred to lead by example and to allow the recruits some freedom and humanity.

He decided to take up quarters outside the caserne and had Gretel, his wife, and their daughter, as well as their German Shepherd dog move in with him. His meals came from the officers' mess and were delivered; 'often they were enough for all three of us'. The industrious and business minded Gretel baked and sold pastries and cakes made with potatoes. They were popular in some restaurants because one could buy them without food stamps. When spring came Gretel moved back to Gersdorf to tend the large garden and preserve food for the coming winter.

After two years in the military Herbert was diagnosed with heart insufficiency and declared unfit for front duty. In 1916 he moved back to Gersdorf and resumed his teaching duties.

But life in Gersdorf had become somewhat complicated. Gretel's brother, Erich, had entered into diverse business deals and tried to involve his sister and brother-in-law in them in order to improve his situation which had begun a downward slide. There was strife due to Herbert's political leanings; he had become a speaker for the Social Democrats, a party with ideas in contrast to the direction of the church and the mainly right wing and conservative population. There were never open disagreements but Herbert and Gretel figured it would be prudent to put kilometers between their present situation, their in-laws, and themselves.

Herbert traded his teaching position with a teacher in Leuthen. He writes in his memoirs: 'As I found out later the people of Leuthen liked me instantly because of my height. They expressed that it would look good at a funeral when such a tall teacher would walk next to the pastor, because by tradition the teacher had to assume a certain role at funerals.'

The small village of Leuthen was very isolated. Neither the school house nor the teacherage had electricity at the beginning, there was no store in the first years. The roads were impassable during rains or snow melt and the village was surrounded by ancient forests. In the village stood an old thirteenth century church, erected as a fortification with thick walls and a strong tower where in time of war the population could flee to for safety. Herbert was attracted by the freedom and independence he had been looking for. He was to spend fourteen happy years there. The school house was almost like a villa in size and appearance. Herbert improved the grounds by planting clumps of birch trees; he expanded the vegetable garden, planted fruit trees and a rose garden with a large gazebo at one end. He built a shed to house his bees; he had chickens, rabbits and the annual pig.

He wrote: "The greatest feast of the people of Leuthen was not the Christmas concert, as much as they loved it – but the day the pig got butchered. The people of the village, even the farmers, lived very simply and frugally throughout the year. But on the day the pig got slaughtered everyone dipped into the trough – 'the fat had to shine on all door handles' as they said. Because the people were all related a crowd of relatives always came together to eat and feast and everyone consoled himself with the thought that 'I will eat at least as much as you when your turn comes to kill your pig.' And eat they did as I have never seen the like."

"Early in the morning they started with boiled meat; at noon it was hot sausages; at two there was roast meat and at four there was coffee and cake. At six they munched on cutlets, at eight it was again coffee and cake and at ten they ate bread with cold meats. As long as someone was there, a meal was dished out every two hours. Some sat from morning till night at the table. As soon as a new dish was brought out, everyone dug in as if they had starved for days. I have never understood how this was possible."

"In the beginning we were invited three or four times to the pig feasts, which took place one after another throughout the fall, until I could hear the word 'pig' no more. We had to stop otherwise we would have become sick. Later on we went only to those families with whom we entertained social relationships."

As inflation sank over Germany the growing family increasingly felt its sting. Irmgard, my mother, was born in 1914, Erika three years later and Manfred arrived in 1924. As the girls needed secondary education, extra money was required for Irmgard's boarding school and later daily travel to a high school for Erika. Herbert's country teacher salary was never enough and had they not only eaten what they grew, the family would have been quite destitute. Gretel was very industrious and practical – she collected mushrooms and berries and had her regular customers, grocery stores in the city of Sagan, where she bartered her goods for items they could not grow themselves. For a while they canned and sold vegetables commercially; during the holidays they rented rooms to paying guests, and Herbert did custom photography for weddings and special occasions which also provided extra income.

Herbert discovered the 'magic' of radio. Despite their chronic lack of funds, he foolishly borrowed money to buy an expensive apparatus. Later on he tried to recuperate some of the funds by building and selling radios to other people. He became a 'radio nut', as he put it.

Herbert loved the rivers, the Oder and the Elbe, where he spent most of his summer holidays in his Klepper kayak. When the children were old enough, they took turns travelling with him, laying the foundation for cherished memories. Gretel was not fond of water and never accompanied him. She stayed home during the holidays looking after the huge garden and the ever increasing flock of fowl and other animals they raised for the table.

The school house in Leuthen became a place for many visitors whom Herbert entertained on many occasions. He loved having guests and his cellar was well stocked with home made wine and liquors which he dispensed liberally.

From 1928 on Gretel started losing weight, which was at first welcome because she had gained a lot after the birth of Manfred. Herbert explained it away by pointing out that Gretel smoked as much as he did and that cigarettes decreased the appetite. By 1930 she had become very thin but refused to see a doctor. On Christmas 1932 Gretel told her family that she felt this would be her last season with them and soon after she took to bed. A doctor who was called against her wishes, diagnosed cancer. He recommended a specialist. Gretel conceded to a further consultation.

Herbert noted in his memoirs: 'On the very hour that news flashed all over Germany that Adolf Hitler had become Chancellor of the Reich, Dr. Wagner informs me that my wife has inoperable cervical cancer.'

Radiation was prescribed and endured but ended after two months. In June the family moved to Heinersdorf where Herbert had accepted a position as a department head, which was a definite professional advancement for him. Gretel seemed to have improved enough to accompany the family on a small walk and hope for better health rose against all reason.

But it was a short reprieve and the next day Gretel took to her bed never to leave it again. Irmgard left her secretarial job in Sagan and came home; she cared for her mother until her last breath. Gretel was buried on the 29th of September 1933.

Chapter 5

GUSTEL HAEFNER'S EARLY YEARS

***The big plum tree in front of the window filters the sunshine and permits only little specks and dancing explosions of light inside the room where we, my husband Jim and I, sit with my father. He is going to tell us the story of his life.

My father, whom everyone calls Opa, works on genealogies; he has done ours and those of many local families and quite a few from overseas. His room is in the attic and most of it is taken up by a huge, ancient roll-up desk which is cluttered with papers, a pot of glue and a sticky brush. Opa usually writes his comments on the back of papers already used, 'there is no need to waste paper' he insists. His notes are a mess to read because pasted on papers stick together and sometimes he forgets to put page numbers on his writings.

A shelf above the desk is filled with history books about the city of Schwaebisch Hall and the Hohenlohe Region. The bottom to ceiling shelving next to it is stacked tightly with albums with an extensive international stamp collection. Opa spends most of the day up here – this is his refuge from the world or perhaps domestic demands to run hither and yon. Here he can listen to German folk music, waltzes and umpah, here he can read and putter and spend time organizing the family trees he investigates.

All the following chapters headed with Gustel's name are taken from tapes recorded up in his room in the summer of 1996.***

I was born in 1912 in Switzerland where my father was working as a cellar master and cooper; I was always called Gustel so I would not get mixed up with my father whose name was also August. I was just two years old when my grandfather Wilhelm died and my grandmother Marie called my father back to Schwaebisch Hall to take over the business.

One of the earliest memories I have is when one evening the lionhead knocker klanked on the heavy outer door. I went to answer and when I opened the door a bearded man stretched his hand out to me and I ran screaming back to my mother. That man was my father who had come home for a few days of furlough from the Belgian front and whom I, of course, had not recognized.

Once my father had returned from the trenches in Flanders in 1918, he and my mother worked very hard to make the business go. But times got very bad. Inflation became absolutely catastrophic. When it was all over, we had suitcases stuffed with useless coloured notes; we kept them for many years in the attic.

When I was twelve years old, I wanted to become a mechanic and my father finally acquiesced and through an old friend, who was a master at the company where I wanted to learn, secured me a place for a later apprenticeship. But times were becoming more and more difficult every year and one day my father declared he would not have the means to enable my future apprenticeship as a mechanic at the 'Firma Gross'. I was informed that I would have to quit high school after grade ten and then apprentice in my father's business to become a cooper and to learn the cider business. This was not at all what I had dreamed of – but there was little else I could do. My parents had no money, they lived practically from hand to mouth, and for them it was best that I apprenticed and worked for them.

So, until then I set out to enjoy school. I was good at mathematics and history. The school had the same disciplinary methods as my father: no questions, no arguments and the flat hand or the cane. Sometimes, I know for sure, I deserved it and sometimes, I know, I did not. We had an old Professor, Herr Gueterle, who was called the 'Eisbaer' (polar bear) probably because of his grizzly grey hair and the long Methuselah beard that rolled over his chest. He never allowed anyone to leave the classroom to go to the toilet and consequently it happened one day that my neighbour, a student called Greiner, peed on the floor, it ran under my desk and I was accused to having done it. Old Eisbaer left the class room with shaking hands, muttering threats against all students in general. Quickly after, young Herr Schurr stormed in, mustachios bristling, eyes rolling. He took me by the belt, smacked me down on my desk and lectured me with his cane. I took the dozen quietly because if I had pointed the finger at Greiner, I would have got it from my class mates too for telling on another.

I spent the summers being an extra hand at the summer festival theatre which was staged on the huge steps of St. Michel's Church on the marketplace. They had started performing theatre there in 1925. They played 'Everyman' and I loved being part of the excitement and the performances, even more so, since girls were also used as extras. Every one of us boys had a heart throb, of course. I still have a photo where I stand in front of the church, dressed in tights and holding a heavy standard up high looking quite like a man of the world.

We went to church, sometimes, as was the custom. My mother liked to go, especially on holidays, to take Thanksgiving cakes, Easter eggs and to have ashes smeared on her forehead on Ash Wednesday. I was more inclined to view church going as an occasion where all good families surveyed each other on Sunday morning and then had fodder for their Sunday afternoon 'Kaffeeklatsch' where everyone was discussed. My father was much drawn to what was known as the 'Nebenkirche', the church next door – that was the pub or inn closest to the church. He much preferred that place.

I was confirmed in St. Michael's Church when I was fourteen. After the ceremony in church, it was acknowledged in front of the whole congregation that

I was the only one who had replied in a loud and clear voice to all the questions and with the correct answer from Luther's Catechism. Of course, after the church we had a special meal at home with many relatives who had come especially for the occasion. My mother served marrow dumpling soup, pork roast, potatoes and vegetables and her wonderful gravy and for dessert we had a specialty of hers - Rheinischer Bund – a pudding cake which tasted of rum and was studded with slivered almonds. In the afternoon, of course, we all ate again, many cakes and tortes and good, rich coffee. We sat and talked, the men smoked cigars and then we sang, as was custom, helped along by cider and wine.

***In our family album is a large photo that shows rows of stacked barrels lined up against the house in the Gelbingergasse. Some barrels are placed end to end on the long handcarts standing on the street with which

they were brought to the shop to be cleaned and repaired. The apprentices, raw looking and young, stand still on the cobble stone sidewalk, glad for the interruption from their work. The small, skinny boy, almost lost in a heavy leather apron and dwarfed by the barrel next to him, is Gustel, my dad. His father half leans on a barrel in front of the open shop door. Opa Haefner has a bald and square head, a round and shaven face with a martial looking mustache, he wears the same leather apron as his son, only a larger one. He looks proudly into the camera; he is the master and two journeymen, two apprentices and his son work for him. A pretty young servant girl looks out of the window a floor above and out of the window one storey higher leans Emma, his wife, my Oma.***

I had become a member of the 'Turn und Sportverein', the sports club, where I spent many evenings. In winter we went skiing and there I was much envied by the younger crowd because I had such a selection of boards and staves, which, because they had just the right up-bend, made wonderful skis after being tied to ones' shoes with sturdy leather straps. Later on I had proper skis, but never the proper clothing – who had money for that anyway – and least of all I. My friends sang a little ditty about the fancy duds I wore:

'Haefner's Gustel, what a thrill,

Wears his tuxedo on the hill.'

We were very good at making up verse after verse on the spur of the moment- naturally they were never serious but poked fun at different happenings or people – and they added greatly to the merriment of the gathering.'

My apprenticeship at home began in 1927 when I was fifteen years old. The work was nothing new to me because I had already helped in the shop for many years. I knew how to sweep the wood shavings into a neat pile so shovel could pick them up for burning. I knew how to line up the chisels and planes, hammers and clamps by size and put them in their proper place. Because I was mostly the smallest boy, I had already cleaned many a barrel too.

Besides myself, my father had other apprentices who worked for free room and board and some pocket money while they were taught to become coopers. No longer did apprentices have to pay a master to teach them the craft as had been the custom until not too long ago. In fact, we were even paid: an apprentice was paid one Mark per week in the first year, two Marks in the second year and in the third year we felt rich with our twelve Marks a month. The boys lived in the attic and my mother took care of them, told them when to wash and change their clothing. She knitted socks and scarves for them for Christmas and told them to visit their mothers. At times we had a journeyman in the house too, but since his room was next to the servant girl's – it sometimes didn't work out too well.

My mother was a great cook and housekeeper. All of us and the servant girl took our meals together around the big table in the living room. Monday saw the leftovers from Sunday's pot roast, on Tuesday there was a stew meal, on Wednesday we ate one of her wonderful Spaetzle (German handmade noodles) meals, on Thursday she served a sweet meal, we always had fish on Fridays, on Saturday she served boiled beef with pickles and currant jelly, freshly grated horseradish and boiled potatoes. Ah – she was a grand cook. We had to eat fast, especially if one wanted seconds; the minute the master licked the spoon - that was the sign that he was done - we had to get back to work. Only he was allowed a rest.

My father rose at about six o'clock in the morning and after a breakfast of coffee, bread and jam served by my mother, he went to the barber. It was custom that the master artisans let themselves be shaved every morning by the barber. Everyone had his own bowl with his own shaving brush in it, properly lined up on a shelf. They were shaved with a straight razor sharpened on a leather strop.

It was back to work when the master came back and because his instructions were often stressed with the flat of his hands – son and apprentices waited eagerly for eleven o clock in the morning because that was the time when the master went for the 'Fruehschoppen' – his morning drink. That was a hallowed institution where masters, bankers and other worthies met according to a schedule every day in a different pub or bakery that had a license to dispense wine for an early morning drink. They sat around heavy tables, talked importantly of politics and fatherland, puffing huge cigars, sucking on bulbous pipes and quarter liter mugs of wine. No cider for them, oh no, dignitaries and men who had apprentices working for them drank only wine, and plenty of it. In my father's favourite place, 'Kronmueller's Beck', the baker kept tally of the glasses on the cellar door with white chalk. Once, my father must have left his money at home, or imbibed more than usual, when at twelve noon it was time for dinner, he got up, went to the cellar door, unhinged it, stuck it under his arm and proceeded to leave. When the baker wondered what August was doing, my father laughed at him.

"I just want to take my bill home with me."

I don't want to I imply that the master did no work. He did. Foremost he had to acquire work to keep the business going and then he had to teach the apprentices. First, we had to learn how to clean barrels: one of us had to slip in and if the door was too narrow, another apprentice or the master gave a good push to get you in. How often we lost all the buttons on our shirts. Then we had to rub and scrub, stave by stave, with soap and cold water, slimy, sour smelling strands of gooey mess dripping into our armpits and faces. I hated this job but soon learned to do it well, because when the master inspected and found it unsatisfactory, he helped you clean some more with buckets of cold water which he poured unceremoniously into the barrel with us in it. Once clean and dry the barrel was ready for sulfuring. Many customers made us take their barrels to our shop where we did the cleaning outside the shop on the sidewalk after we hauled them here on our hand pulled carts. Others had us clean the barrels in their premises. It was hard and filthy work.

The most hated work however, harder and nastier yet, was the pitching of the huge brewery barrels which could hold up to 3500 litres. We had to take them outside, no easy job either, pop out the doors and dry them. Inside the layer of pitch was cracked, allowing the beer to come into contact with the oak wood and absorb the tannin which gave the beer a bad taste. So we had to pour hot pitch into the barrels, light it with a glowing torch and roll the barrel to cover the inside evenly. This was very dangerous. I have seen a gigantic column of fire shoot out of such a barrel, sometimes they exploded and it could happen that one of the iron rings that circled the wood, flew off, decapitating the hapless man who worked there. We were lucky, we never had an accident. We got only stinking dirty, but then we could look forward to the good lunch that the breweries customarily set out for us, with lots of good beer, of course. We never drank when we worked at home, if the master had caught us he would have slapped us roundly.

Our days were usually twelve hours long starting before seven in the morning and finishing after the master completed his work. He went upstairs but we still had to put away all the tools on their proper places and sweep up. The shop had to be spotless. During fall, when farmers came with loads of pears and apples to be pressed into cider, we often worked till midnight on the heavy press, which was turned by hand. My mother did the counting of sacks and measured the litres of cider, with the farmers watching and complaining that not enough juice came out.

"Pull harder, boys, there has to be more juice in them!" They shouted.

And so we strained some more. Of course, mother had to feed all of them too. Once the cider was pressed, we hauled the full barrels on hand carts to the customers where we roped and rolled the barrels down into their cellars, or more often, siphoned the cider down to their barrels. But we never came home with full hoses as some of the cidermakers in town did. Later on we acquired an old Chevrolet which we fitted with a platform and once I had my driver's license, this job of delivering cider became much easier.

Later in the evening once my father had done his book keeping, he went out again to a pub, joining the circle of journeymen, salesmen and workers to talk and drink some more. All the while my mother sat at home, knitting or reading – my parents did not walk the same road; there were many differences between them.

My evenings and free time were filled with sports and friends. I played the violin. We sang a lot and we danced. At home I sometimes played the violin for my mother.

In the fall of 1929, I passed my journeyman's exam and kept on working for my father. He had in the meantime obtained a concession for wine and cider at the local fairs. We had a tent, tables and chairs, ice boxes and so forth – quite an enterprise. One day in summer when we were serving for a Singfest, I got into an argument with my father. I remember it so well. It was three in the afternoon, the place was already crowded. It was hot and noisy. Our words shot out quicker and quicker. I threw my serving tray on the table, turned around and stormed out. I marched home, stuffed some clothing into my rucksack. Naturally my mother wanted to know what had happened, naturally she cried but I left the house, got on my bicycle and pedalled fifty kilometers to Heilbronn to my uncle Doettling.

He was a cobblestone layer and I liked him. I straight away told him what had happened.

"Oh yes, my boy, you can stay and work for me."

And against the resistance of his unionized workers, I was able to work for him for a while. But heavens, those trade union boys did everything to make my work and my life miserable and I soon looked for work elsewhere. I was lucky and got a job in a winery in Feuerbach as jack of all trades: I made barrels, I worked in the huge cellar and later, because I was knowledgeable about new wine, I delivered truckloads of it all over the country.

I had started to get together with my cousin Eugen. He was 'jugendbewegt', that meant he was engaged in the youth movement which was prominent in this time. He was in the 'Turnerjugend' the sportsclub for the young and also the 'Wandervogel', the group which involved young people in wandering the German country side, they were into folk music and folk dancing. The movement had its roots in the Romantic era of the last century, when students and poets discovered a German nationalism, Germany having become a united country only in 1848. The young people celebrated its old songs, dances and customs. Eugen took me to the Hitlerjugend, the Hitler Youth, the movement that led me eventually to the National Socialist Party.

Young Gustel

In Feuerbach I had joined the 'Adler und Falken', the 'Eagles and Falcons', a group which had strong right wing tendencies. We thought that we, as a people, could no longer feed ourselves properly, that there were too many people crowded in far too little land and that in order to alleviate the hunger in the country, we needed to increase productivity. Granted, there were certain fantasies about the 'Raum im Osten'. The space in the East, but no one ever thought or spoke about conquering these areas.

We had a good time in that organization. We did a lot of hiking, played music and danced our folk dances for which I played the fiddle and we sang. I recall that I often pulled my fiddle out of its wax cloth bag and played to the folks in the train when we travelled to the old and abandoned farm house we had converted into our club house. What a wonderful time we spent there. Yes, we had a good and clean and orderly youth. The 'Adler und Falken' disappeared later; it was not forbidden, it just gave out – there were so many other things.

There was a great difference between the organizations 'Eagles and Falcons' and the Hitler Youth. In the first organization we had a lot of freedom in our activities and in what we thought and what we said. We were allowed to have fun and enjoy life with music and dance. No such freedom existed in the very strict Hitler Youth, which was very regulated and strongly in line with the National Socialist ideology and program. The boys' activities had a definite military flavour, for the girls the regulations steered towards the family and household, an idea which later led to the Arbeitsdienst or conscripted labour service for women.

In the meantime something had happened in Feuerbach which led me even more to the new movement. Feuerbach was a city of 40,000 inhabitants and at least 7000 of them were unemployed. The workers were affiliated with the trade unions and the communists. That these people became either communists or later National Socialists is really easy to understand because both these ideologies and organizations promised them work and food, justice and a future for their children.

I must have caught someone's attention with my Wandervogel ways, the short pants, the rucksack and the habit of leaving the city Saturdays after work to travel to our clubhouse. Perhaps it was also that I was neither a communist nor trade unionist, and because contrary to the communists who thought that everyone who had money is suspect of capitalist leanings and consequently was evil, I thought that a person who had more money than another was not necessarily evil – and because of all of that I became suspect. One morning at five o'clock as I stepped out of the house at Solitude Strasse where I stayed, to go to work, a group of drunken men strolling down the hill raised their fists and started coming towards me, shouting loudly.

"Let's go and finally kill that one!"

No time to dally around, I saw they meant business, so I ran down the street where at the bottom I saw the tramway. I flew in, the conductor, who had observed the chase, ripped the motor into gear and off we went.

This incidence gave me plenty to think about. Up to now I had had to be quiet about the things I thought and did. I had never been vocal either for or against the different streams of thinking. I knew what I saw and what I read in the papers. A short time later Hitler spoke at a rally in Stuttgart. I went and what I heard pretty much convinced me. So, that's how it happened. I became a member of the National Socialist Party, my number was 869 533. That was in 1931. I was nineteen years old.

During the autumn of 1931 I was very busy driving wine trucks, working many more hours than I was paid for. One day I approached my boss and spoke to him.

"Boss, I was hired for forty eight hours a week and not for ninety."

That is how many hours I had been working for him every week.

He looked coolly at me and replied, "You may go and get your papers. I was going to tell you that anyway."

I was not aware of any wrong doing on my part and I knew that I had done my work well. I said so to his wife when I went to get my papers. She indicated to me that it was not my fault that I had to go.

"I am sorry, but we have certain responsibilities and we had to hire another man for your job."

And then I found out that some poor sot with three little children at home had approached them and told them that he knew that they paid their driver 25.00 Marks a week and that he would work for 24.50 Marks. And that is how he got my job and there was nothing I could do. I took my papers and went on the 'Walz', that is I began to travel the country in search of work.

The 'Walz', an ancient word that implies walking, was an old, old custom where journeymen took to the roads and walked from town to town knocking on doors of masters of their trade, asking with the prescribed words 'out of town cooper asking for work' for a place. Work was always given, even if only for a few days. Free room and board was included and wages and the chance to see how diverse masters did things differently in the many regions of Germany.

I travelled through southern Germany, Lake Constance and from there to Switzerland. I had a cousin living in Zurich and this became a homing place before heading out through the rest of the country. I was offered the job of a cellar master in a large hotel but because I was not a Swiss citizen and could not get a permanent work permit, I could not accept the offer. I really regretted that I had lost out on that opportunity. I joined forces with another friend of the youth movement whom I met on the road and we travelled together. There was not much work.

The Swiss had a simple but important law: If the Swiss police found a foreigner with less than five Swiss francs in his pocket, they deported him straight out of the country. This was something I did not want to risk so I decided to cross over into Germany again. I was lucky and hitched a ride on a truck all the way to Mannheim.

At the first place I asked, I was given employment. But when mealtime came and we sat around the table and I watched the old, shaky grandfather slobber into his spoon before dipping it into the communal bowl that sat steaming in the centre of the table, I got up, excused myself and left.

Out on the street I remembered my father's old comrade, master cooper Heilig, the one who had been with him in the military in Potsdam. He was now a cooper in Heilbronn. I went to his house and introduced myself. He laughed and I had job.

By 1932 I was back home again working for my father, probably because there was no more work for me in Heilbronn. In Schwaebisch Hall I became heavily involved with the Hitler Youth, in fact, I founded the group together with another man. One night I marched my youngsters, boys and girls from twelve to fourteen years of age, when my dear friends, the communist lefties, threatened to attack them. I stopped, pulled out my .08 pistol and said, "Touch them and I'll shoot." After that we marched in peace. Later in 1933 the police chief of Schwaebisch Hall told me once, that he knew I always had a pistol with me when I went with my Hitler Youths, but that he was never worried I would misuse my weapon. I never had to use my pistol. I guess my friends knew I meant business.

I had actually also been with the SA, but only for a very short time, less than two weeks. They wanted to put me into things I did not like doing so I left. I also wanted more leadership, discipline and organization. I much preferred the Hitler Youth with whom I spent all my free time and weekends. I had joined the general SS. My number started with 109 thousand, the other three digits I have forgotten. They were men, volunteers like me, who worked in the interest of the party. We had a uniform and our main task was to police meetings, rallies and parades. But all our work was unpaid and after work.

The SS in Schwaebisch Hall was a regular 'Feierabend' or after work and weekend SS. Because I had motorbike, I was with the 'Motorsturm', the motorized company. I enjoyed moving around in an official capacity on my bike where I had to organize all sorts of things. For example, one day I was told I had to transport weapons to Schwaebisch Hall. I took our old Chevrolet, put a 300 litre barrel on the flatbed, took the lid off, filled the barrel with weapons, closed the door again and delivered them to the appropriate place.

The SS was well arranged. Groups of men were organized in a 'Sturm' or company that could be anything from thirty men in a small town to two hundred in a big city. Sometimes a 'Sturm' was a group of similar people, for example all butchers of the abattoir in Stuttgart, a large city, belonged to the 'Butcher Sturm'. Of course, this all evolved as the so called 'Ordnungsprinzip' the principle that brought order, became more prominent. This principle meant very simply that everything had to work – efficiently. In order to accomplish this, everything had to be tightly structured and there had to be absolute discipline.

We were present in our uniforms at large gatherings and whenever there were many people, we did what was necessary to keep everything orderly and peaceful. Before 1933 the public could disagree with speakers for example, after 1933 this naturally changed. Before 1933 the SS did their work on their own initiative, after that time they were mandated to keep order and peace, but it was interpreted differently.

In January 1933 Hitler became Chancellor of the German Reich. All public and important spots in town were occupied by SA and SS men. I was part of that troop too. Together with two other men I was stationed in the waiting room in the railway station. Our task was to be present and to prevent other- minded groups congregating and making trouble. It was quiet at all times at our station, but in town some Jews got beaten up and some vocal people of the left were arrested. Of course, I found this out only afterwards. I had no idea what had been planned from above. The only event that pleased me was that one Jew, a Herr Pfeiffer from the Gelbingergasse, got a good thrashing, but he really deserved it because he had a filthy mouth and he treated people like dirt. Well, that day was accounting day for him, not because he was a Jew, but because he was a very unpleasant man.

That was the first time for me that a person and a name actually had been labeled "Jew" in a specific way and for a specific reason. I never thought about them as being different. We had Catholics in Hall, and Protestants, and Jehova's Witnesses and Jews – that was simple. I had class mates like Salo, Salomon Schlachter and Heiner Wuerzburger. I went to visit Salo and his parents, but then I remember, I was told not to go there anymore. I realized that there were tensions between Christians and Jews but I was not really interested in those things.

After 1930 when the more and more repulsive paper of Streicher's 'Stuermer' appeared I got more interested in the matter. There were quite a number of Jewish business men in Hall. I particularly remember the old Herr Oppenheimer, a severely wounded veteran from the First World War. He owned a haberdashery. He was well known because he helped so many poor and little people in town. He was a very kind and generous man. His thanks from the German folk and the

German Fatherland was an end in Auschwitz!

Meanwhile I had become thoroughly tired of cleaning grimy barrels and when I found out that there was a call for volunteers to enter into a short military training program for the so called 'Politische Bereitschaften', or political readiness groups, something like the Reserves, I signed on. When I stood at the station waiting for the train, old Noodle Franz, the owner of the noodle factory, noticed me and came over. He inquired where I was headed to and when I told him he chuckled.

"Ah so, a bit of military. Look here, young man, here is something for you and good luck."

And he pressed five Marks into my hand.

Chapter 6

IRMGARD ERNST

***All children want to know how the world was when their parents were young and I was no exception. I grew up with my mother's stories and I was quite at home with her in the small village of Leuthen where she spent her formative years. She was well into her eighties when she finally sat down at the old type writer and shared with me – for the last time – the story of her life.

This what she wrote:***

I was always scared – all my life – and it started even before I was born. When my mother became pregnant, she was only nineteen years old. My father could not marry her right away as he was working on his second teacher exam, so she hid it from her parents. She was so scared – that is what she told me. When she became too big, she visited a favourite uncle and aunt. I guess then her parents found out. The wedding was arranged. I was born six weeks after they were married. That was in 1914. I believe all of my mother's worries about hiding her condition went straight into me.

I love to remember the village I grew up in. It was so small, just 250 inhabitants. It was called Leuthen and was in the Lower Lausitz, today it is in Poland. My father was the only teacher in the school and he taught children from the age of six to fourteen. Our house was large and new – one side of it was ours the other was the school. The school part was one very large room, a utility room and a large hallway. The toilet was outside, one for the children and one for the teacher and his family.

We had a huge garden surrounded by a fence hidden by bushes and flowers. Something was always blooming there. All we ate came from the garden. My father's salary was pitifully small. Across from the house was a barn where we housed our chickens, rabbits and our one pig. The house also included a large laundry room, which we called the wash kitchen. Water was heated once every four weeks in a large cauldron and all our linens, the bedding and the towels were boiled in it. They were then scrubbed with soap, rinsed and laid out on the grass where the sun bleached them.

I remember that Erika, my younger sister, and I had to go out every so often on sunny days with watering cans and we had to sprinkle water on the sheets so they would bleach better. Our weekly bath also took place in the wash kitchen. We had a large zinc tub which was filled with hot water. The first bath was for my father, next came my mother and then the three of us. We had to be so frugal because we never had a penny to spare. Even the wood that was needed to heat the water had to be considered – either it cost money to buy or it cost time to go to cut it and haul it home. The same copper pot that washed the laundry, that heated the water for the bath, was used in summer to boil jams. Hours and hours were spent stirring the simmering fruit with a huge wooden paddle. My mother never put any sugar in the jam – there was plenty of sugar in the berries, she would say, and all you have to have is plenty of patience. Erika and I spent hours watching the pot and stirring until our efforts turned out the sweet spread that would last us all year.

My mother used to love to tell this story about me: When I was only about two or three years old, I used to sit in front of the piano and 'play', accompanying myself as I sang full throttle 'The Black Rose from Istanbul'. Over and over again I belted out the melody – and nobody ever knew where I had learned that song. They all figured I had great musical talent.

My father built a little paradise for us children in the garden. He cordoned off a small square and then planted bushes around. He built a small table with two benches – this was our play room. We were so happy there playing with our dolls, or the cat, or reading.

Naturally we went to school and our father was our teacher. He treated us no different from the other pupils. He never checked our homework that had to be done after school. I can still hear him saying, "If you don't want to learn, fine, go and be a ditch digger or labourer – it is all up to you. I will not force anyone to learn."

As we got older our small world expanded and it started to include the forest. We loved to go there and play. We built houses and rooms of leaves and moss, made dolls and animals of pieces of wood and branches and twigs and dressed them in leaves and plaited grasses. We lived in a fantasy world full of play and games. Eventually other children joined us and we went into the woods with an old pram and we dug in the earth and carved and built and populated our world with dwarfs and elves, fairies and beautiful princesses.

Close by was an old quarry filled with water. We had no idea how deep and dangerous it was – we went there and learned how to swim. This bright idea came from me – I think today I must have had an angel with me during those afternoons. Later in life I must have always had an angel protecting me. I was totally convinced that whatever I started I would be able to succeed.

At least twice a year the gypsies came to our village. Everyone ran and locked up their chickens, grabbed the laundry from the drying lines, locked up everything in sight because the gypsies stole whatever they could carry away. They were bitterly poor. I often watched them, hidden behind some bushes, how they caught little hedgehogs, wrapped them in loam and baked them in an open fire. Once there came with them a young man who played the violin. I was bewitched and spent hours crowded behind bushes listening to his most wonderful playing. I was obsessed and spent every free minute listening to this man. I was heartbroken when my parents pulled me away – I think we left for a trip - I cannot remember – but I do remember how I missed the music.

Meanwhile our family grew to include Manfred, born when I was ten years old. I was not always happy about his presence because it was my task to look after him. Erika, who was three years younger than I was, was never asked to take care of him because she was always sick and miserable. When she was born, she was a real 'Sterbeling', that's what the people called a baby that was not expected to live. But she did and I am amazed that she turned out so healthy.

Our village had only one store and that was very tiny, it sold necessities like flour and sugar and oil. The next village was four kilometers away and the road led through a forested area. One Sunday afternoon we walked through that forest behind our parents. Erika and I, as was custom, wore our best Sunday dresses. I must explain that we never had any money to buy clothes because we were too poor. But we had aunts who were very well to do and they used to give their cast-off dresses to my mother. My mother was very handy with the sewing machine and she could take an adult dress and cut it and make it into a dress of dreams for a little girl.

On that Sunday Erika and I wore our best dresses, they were white and frilly and my mother had even embroidered them. We were on our way to the next village where a dentist couple had invited my father and family for afternoon coffee. Now the road had been covered with shards of glass discarded by the glass factory close by. Well, we could not leave those beautiful and exciting bits of colour on the ground. So, Erika and I began to collect the prettiest of them and soon we ran out of places to put them in. Quickly we gathered our skirts in our hands and used the created pouch to collect more and more of the pretty stones. We were ecstatic. We were going to use them for many jumping games at home. Suddenly my mother turned around and went white. My father turned also and then we were marched home without a word. I cannot remember if we were punished.

I still have to chuckle when I remember the summer when I was ten years old and Erika, who was seven, were in charge of our place when my father and my mother took a three-week holiday. We were in heaven. There was nobody to tell us what to do. We made raspberry pudding for breakfast, lemon pudding for lunch and vanilla pudding for supper. The only time we left our place was to go to the neighbouring farm for milk – we needed lots because we were only eating pudding! The eggs came from our hens and the lemons were stored in the pantry. We cleaned the house, we organized the attic, weeded the garden and were regular busy bees. Early on I noticed that one of our hens was broody. I searched for her eggs and found a big clutch. I took the hen and her eggs and made a nest for them in the barn. And one day we had little chicks peeping around. Then I really went into action: I collected stinging nettles and cut them finely and mixed them with ground grain and chopped hardboiled eggs. The little chicks grew beautifully. When my parents came home, they had to admire the clean house, the well looked after poultry and rabbits – but then mother saw the flock of chicks and she was less than pleased. She had not wanted extra hens for this summer.

One summer holiday, when I was just eleven years old, my father took a trip in our Klepper kayak down the Oder River to the Spreewald and I was allowed to go along. The vessel constructed of rubberized canvas with a collapsible frame was very light. We had little luggage with us: a tiny tent, a sleeping bag for each, one pot and one pan, two mugs and two plates and some cutlery. It was wonderful. Early in the morning my father, probably remembering his military days, bellowed, "rise and shine" – jolting me out of my sleeping bag. I jumped into the cold water of the Oder River for morning ablutions.

I loved the time with him. I did not have to wash all the time, or comb my hair and could just be the way I wanted to. A dip in the river was all that was necessary. For lunch we had pancakes, the next day it was boiled potatoes with butter and salt. And that's what we had for four gorgeous weeks. I remember that once on the river I told him that I had to pee. But he was wrapped in his own thoughts and would not steer towards land. I could not help it and I peed – and for the rest of the afternoon I heard the gentle slapping in the boat, back and forth. I added some river water but could still detect a faint odour. My father noticed nothing. That was his way – he was totally somewhere else. When we finally came home I looked like a savage. My mother was almost in tears and she chided my father for not keeping me properly.

"She will never ever be a real lady – what shall become of her?" She moaned.

Well, that was me and I did not change for many years.

Because my father taught music enthusiastically in school, he moved our piano into the school room. I spent countless hours there after class and on weekends, sitting in front of the piano, accompanying myself and singing at the top of my lungs. I was mostly by myself. I liked that. I was never bored. I read voraciously – at home I read just girls' books and Karl May, of course; we had all his volumes. Later on in boarding school I was exposed to the classics and grown-up books. I grew and grew – I was so happy.

I tried to pass the love for the written word on to my children. We sang a lot and when we went collecting mushrooms or nuts in my beloved forest, I told them stories about elves and spirits and the Heinzelmaennchen, those little legendary men who live under the caps of mushrooms. I did not want my girls to become 'Spiesser', philistines.

When I was thirteen years old my parents wanted me to enter a boarding school. I had to write an entrance exam. My essay was obviously so good that they printed it in the newspaper and praised what my father had achieved in his one room school. In fact, they used my essay to point out the results that could be achieved in a one room school.

I hated the boarding school. The noise, the many girls crammed into the large sleeping hall. I had no freedom, all day long I had to do what someone else told me. I was not used to that. For the first five nights I cried myself to sleep. I could not understand why my parents had sent me away from them. I was miserably unhappy. Because I was so deeply dejected, I was allowed to take the train home on the first 'open' weekend. Like a drowning person I clung to may parents when they picked me up at the train station. But I had to leave again. It was such a sad year but gradually I got better. Of course.

After one year the school was moved from Sagan to Bad Warmbrunn in the Riesengebirge and because of the distance I could come home only during the holidays. At home I still played a lot with my dolls up in the attic where I had a special corner for them, with a table, chairs and a closet for their clothes. I was sixteen years and I played – happy with my dolls. I had no idea about 'life'. I did not know about periods. When it finally happened to me, I wanted to die! Such a mess – and every four weeks. I had no idea about anything. In school whenever the girls whispered together and told their secrets, they immediately clammed up when I approached.

I hated mathematics, physics and science. What I liked was reading. Our school had a fantastic library and I made good use of it. I also loved sports. Once I took over spontaneously as 'teacher' when the real sports teacher became indisposed and because everything went so well on the fields, I was not punished. I entered competitions and I always won first prize.

I liked to be first. I liked the fact that nobody could tell me what to do.

Times in the late twenties were hard. There was massive unemployment in Germany; many people suffered daily hunger, some even starved to death. And then there were the stories about the rich who lived in opulence and decadence. I also listened to the stories told about the one man who would bring Germany again to the fore and right all the ills in this country. He promised he would provide work and bread and justice for the workers and the common people. He pledged to get rid of the rich parasites of society; he promised equal opportunities for all, especially the farmers who are the basis of a healthy society and he assured them they would get extra help and protection.

One night together with a dozen other likeminded students we climbed out of a basement window to listen to a rally organized by this new party. We did that a few more times until we were found out. From then on I was on the 'hit list' of my principal. One day she hauled me into her private apartment and instructed me to clean her silver. Oh – she did not get very far with that approach. I told her coolly that I had no intention of cleaning her silver as I was here in school to learn and not to be her servant.

That reminds me of the time in boarding school when we had fish for dinner, as was custom on a Friday. Well, I like fish, but I did not like this one – I found a worm in it. I refused to eat it. I was served the same fish for three more meals and refused to eat it each time. I telephoned my father and naturally my father came to my aid – as he had done with the silver. He had a big fight with the lady principal. She lost.

My father was wonderful. He was always there for me. I was never ever a doormat. People, especially those above me or in power could never ever make me do what I did not want to do. I was very headstrong and my sense of justice was extraordinarily well developed.

I should tell something about my grandparents. Herbert's father was a mean-spirited despot personifying the 'do as you are told attitude', not tolerating any questioning. My grandmother came from Posen, then a German city. She was the daughter of a painting master. Even as a young girl she was already emancipated – she became a hat maker and worked in a milliner's store. She often told me about those ugly young Jewesses. I never found out why she hated them so much. But even later I recall that she hated the Jews with a passion. She would never shop at a Jewish store. She preferred to spend more money to buy at a German store than buying it cheaper at a Jew's store. I was a child and really did not care and did not question a thing.

My grandparents lived in Breslau in a large apartment on the fourth floor. It had an extra music room with a grand piano in it. I still see my uncle Helmuth sitting on the grand playing Beethoven. All the children were very musical. I loved to go there in my holidays.

My grandparents raised four boys. Herbert, the oldest became my father. Because he was the first and there were three more to take care off, he was not allowed to go to university as he wished so very much. He had to go to Normal School to become a teacher. He never got over that. All his life he bicycled miles to go to libraries of the bigger cities and all his life he read voraciously. Once he was married his wife shared his love of books. Yes – she was much more than just a mother and wife and raiser of carrots and chickens. She had so much more to her.

My father's younger brother was Bodo. He was allowed to go to university to become a teacher. He had four girls. He was also a writer. He wrote a kind of 'Sachsenspiegel' a treatise about Germanic law and religion. He was widely known and quite famous. He was a dreamer and idealist just like my father. If you know the book by Felix Dahn, "Kampf um Rom", you will know Teja. When my father went to Normal School he was called 'the black Teja' by his friends with whom he discussed the nights away. Teja was the last king of the Goths in Italy. And now you do not have to ask any longer why I have this attitude. It came to me from my father and my uncles. I am proud of my heritage.

I am one hundred percent an Ernst – I dream and dream. I am an idealist and I have a great sense of justice.

The third son was my uncle Helmuth. He was the most intelligent of all. He studied engineering and he wanted to go to Russia as an engineer. Russia was his dream – as it was mine for many years. But then the politics changed and he abandoned his 'Russian dreams' and became a teacher at a high school. He also was a great pianist.

The fourth son was my uncle Manfred. He had just graduated from high school and volunteered for the front in August 1914. He was dead within two weeks. My father never overcame his loss.

My other grandparents, the parents of my mother, lived in Gersdorf. They owned the large "Scholtisei" which was a pub and a farm. The word 'Scholtisei" is an ancient German word, it once implied that the 'Scholte' or 'Schulze' as they were later called, had the right to speak the law and be the judge for smaller disputes. It was a position similar to the one of sheriff in the Old Wild West in the USA and a Justice of the Peace in England and Canada. Grandfather owned a large inn with many guestrooms and a large farm; he employed many servants. He had horses and coaches.

They were very well off. I can still see the buffet table laid out alongside the wall when they celebrated their fiftieth wedding anniversary. I believe more than one hundred guests came to celebrate the occasion with them.

The house was huge and had many rooms besides the guestrooms. The kitchen of course was gigantic and in the middle stood a large table. At mealtimes everyone sat around it and ate together. The whole house was modern and equipped with the latest; the kitchen even had a nook just for doing dishes.

Grandfather was a rather small man but my grandmother was tall and statuesque. She had such soft skin – it felt like a peach – and I loved to touch her cheeks. She told me her secret, 'wash every morning in ice cold water and your skin will stay young for a long, long time'. I still do this to this very day. Naturally we loved to visit them on our holidays. We lived so isolated away from the hustle and bustle of the world. That Gersdorf, the Inn, the farm and the many people we met there, were so exciting for us. It was so thrilling to be met at the train station by grandfather's coach drawn by two horses. We were such poor little waifs – now we felt like princesses.

I especially remember the Sunday mornings. The church was just across from their house. When the bells rang, we were ready in our Sunday best. Grandma pressed a coin into our hands. Erika and I walked hand in hand across the yard. We had been told to walk slowly and did so. Then the rest of the family followed together with most of the maids and man servants.

Uncle Erich, their oldest son, soon took over the operation of the inn and farm and my grandparents moved into the 'Ausgedingehaus', a house especially bought for them. It was large too with four rooms downstairs and three above. But grandmother could not sit around and do nothing. She needed animals and a garden. So she went and bought goats. Oh – how I hated those goats. They smelled horrible and I hated the stinking cheese and butter she made from their milk. I figured the whole house reeked of goat – so I stayed mostly at the main house with uncle Erich and aunt Trudel.

Christmas was a special time. Before everyone gathered under the Christmas tree, grandfather and grandmother walked to the barns each carrying a huge basket. They went to all the animals bidding them good tidings, giving them a pat and a treat. When that was done everyone gathered in the large room where the Christmas tree stood. It was always up to the ceiling and decorated with coloured ribbons, apples and real candles. We sang hymns together and then everyone received a gift. When the servants became too old for work, they still lived in their little rooms and they stayed on the farm, well looked after, until they died.

My grandparents did not have much education but they possessed and showed nobility of heart and I still admire them for that.

Uncle Erich was one of the first men in the district to own a car in the early twenties. Oh my – when he roared through the village that was quite a spectacle. It was one of those cars you had to turn a crank before it would start. I loved it.

Before the First World War a proper daughter's education included learning to cook. So my mother, because she came from a good house and was supposed to be someone respectable and also marry someone appropriate, was taught fine cooking in the kitchen of the castle. Gersdorf, the village where she had grown up, had a castle with aristocracy still residing there. After a two week apprenticeship she was required to take her first exam. Someone pressed fifteen pfennigs into her hand and she was told that she had to prepare dinner for everyone in the castle, the owners included. My mother was seventeen at the time. She thought quickly. She marched resolutely into the forest and gathered mushrooms of all kinds and the last hanging blueberries. A trip into the garden filled a basket with vegetables and the fifteen pfennigs were spent on a piece of bacon. She also gathered lettuce from the garden. For a light lunch she served vegetable soup, fried mushrooms and mashed potatoes crowned with brown bacon bits and a salad. Blueberries were dessert. A good thing she was frugal – it came in handy when she married – had to marry – the poor school master.

After a few years in boarding school, I began to tire of it. When I approached my father with my idea of leaving the school, he actually welcomed it because by sending me there at great expense he deprived the rest of the family of many things. I decided to quit and take a secretarial course at the commerce school in the nearby Sagan.

I moved home. The course I planned on taking was given only in the afternoon. Since the only train left Leuthen at seven in the morning I had to take it. My mother who was afraid that I would get into trouble if I had all the morning to myself without anything constructive to do, stuck me with a seamstress who was supposed to teach me how to sew in the mornings. I hated mathematics but I hated sewing even more. So, I mostly cleaned and did odd jobs at her place. She was understanding and I never learned how to sew.

Meanwhile I had become totally immersed in the new ideas and the new party. I was known to be a member and there were threats against me. One morning an SA man stood at the train station and walked me to the house where I spent the morning. In the afternoon when classes were done, he waited outside the school and accompanied me to the station again. There were many different young men who watched over me – not a problem because most of them were unemployed.

One of those men, I don't even know his name, gave me a book for a Christmas gift: Adolf Hitler "Mein Kampf" with an inscription in it: 'To the German girl in Germany's difficult time'. And there it was again – they helped me without pay, or reward, they were just good, honest men.

My father had read the book and became a Nazi too. Times in Germany were so brutal and here was Hitler. He became the light and the hope, the future and the promise for a new, clean, healthy and free life. Then came the political change and now pretty soon everyone had work, decent wages and even the poorest of the poor was entitled to a holiday. The farmers rose in status; they became important and recognized. Old people received their pension again. Germany began to grow healthy.

The war came. That was not good. Today nobody talks about the good things that happened before the war. What happened to the Jews was wrong – no civilized people should let such a thing happen. But it did and for all eternity we will be reminded and we will have to pay for it. There will be everlasting shame on our German name.

When my mother became ill with cancer in 1932, I quit the secretarial job I had found in Sagan and came home to take care of her. I stayed at home after we had buried her. Manfred was only nine years old when we lost our mother; he needed me. I ran the household for my father until he married a year later. He married a friend of mine, Trudel; she was only four years older than I was. I left home.

***These are my mother's words and that is where her story ends. She never told much about her life after that, the few stories I remember are included in later chapters. She never got over the fall of the Third Reich; the event smashed all her dreams and standards and so destroyed a very essential part of her being. She steadfastly refused to speak about the war, the Jews, her dashed hopes and dreams, her disappointments and disillusions – after the war she just kept going and did what she thought needed to be done. She never talked about my father's role during the war or the ensuing events and consequences.

In later years she was the first to see the need for recycling, she voted for the Green Party and she hoped for a united Europe. She was into her eighties when I gave her a copy of James Michener's "Poland". I knew she was not a friend of the Polish people. She read it and conceded that she did learn a lot and that she wished 'I would have known about many of these things before' but she gave the book back to me when it started dealing with the Jews, saying, 'I will not read this.'

And she didn't. ***

CHAPTER 7

ERIKA ERNST

*** Erika was my mother's sister. In 1948 she married US master sergeant Charles Vanek in Schwaebisch Hall. When he was called back to the States Erika crossed the ocean on the same military troop ship, but of course he had to stay with his unit in military quarters and Erika had different sleeping quarters, 'together with a lot of other girls' as she remembered with a giggle. They lived in El Paso before moving to San Antonio. After Charlie retired from the army, he tried to find another occupation. The early seventies were a time of great unemployment in the States, and since Charles was over sixty, he never found another job. He became very bitter and sick; he died in 1978 of Alzheimer's disease. His daughters Helga and Inga were still of school age. During the months he was at home Erika found clerical work at the Army hospital. Due to Charlie's error of choosing a single life pension from the US Army, his pension could not be extended to her after his death and the now penniless Erika was forced to keep on working. She sent her two girls through school and college and paid off a long mortgage on her house. When she finally retired from work at the age of 75, she was a systems analyst, and fortunate enough to be eligible for a good pension for herself.

Erika came for a visit to our place in the Okanagan Valley in BC in the summer of 2000. When I asked her to tell her life's story she agreed enthusiastically. This is her tale and our conversation. ***

When I was born in 1917 nobody was certain that I would live more than a few days or at all. I was what the Americans call a runt, I was small and sickly. Whatever love, good food and medicines my worried parents crammed into me didn't seem to do much good. I was a scrawny starveling and when I finally started to grow and thrive, the family was surprised to realize that I had been around that long already.

My father was a country teacher. He taught in a one room school for many years and he did not make a lot of money.

But let me go back to Leuthen where I grew up. You know that it was a very small village and the people who lived there were all very poor. Everyone ate only what they grew in their gardens. We had a large garden too. My father used to say that one reason for having a big garden was the economic aspect of it but he also said that it was good to eat what one grew – it was not only healthy but it also taught patience and thrift and respect for nature.

In some years my father even rented a large plot of land from a farmer and he grew potatoes. We ate a lot of potatoes – I can still smell the mashed potatoes or potato dumplings with a sauce made of dried mushrooms and bacon bits on it.

***I look at Aunt Erika who has closed her eyes in rapt remembrance. Since I have sampled this typical Silesian dish many times too, I know that what she remembers is the sweetness of the smoked bacon and the earthy, woodsy aroma of dried morels, yellow and red boletus and chanterelles blended together and slathered in a tasty sauce over the mountain of buttery mashed potatoes, turning it indeed into a dish for a king! ***

When harvest time came around the whole family went out to the field each one carrying a large fork with long tines. My father bade us to dig along the heaped-up furrow to loosen the potatoes out of the soil. I must have been six or seven years old and I much preferred to watch the water and the waves in the little brook that flowed alongside our potato field. Naturally it happened: I stuck the fork straight through my foot, close to my little toe. I screamed and pulled out the fork stretching my foot for-ward and then I saw the blood flowing out of my shoe so, so red. My father came, took the fork out of my hand and marched me to the water. There he washed my foot and took his large handkerchief in which he had just blown his nose, swished it around in the cold water, and tied my foot up. I was told to sit still and watch the family spade the potatoes out.

"He didn't take you to a doctor?"

"Oh, heavens no!" Aunt Erika laughs.

"There was a doctor in the little town four kilometers away, but that was not necessary."

After a while the blood quit flowing and when we were ready to sack the potatoes I was fine again and I helped too.

The doctor, by the way, was a friend of my father's. He used to come every Wednesday to our house when we had our musical evenings. My father played the violin, my mother the piano and the doctor the cello. They played Chopin and Beethoven and made beautiful music. For a while, we children were allowed to listen, then we were sent to bed and they sat and drank wine and discussed things. They talked a lot about books. My father read Schopenhauer and Nietzsche and many, many books. We had scores of books in our house, a real library. He also bicycled every week to the city and when he came home the basket on his bike was filled with books for himself and also for us children. Even though we grew up in the country, we were well read and educated.

Children don't worry about money. We didn't care that our clothes were second hand and changed and re-sewn by our mother. We had plenty to eat and we had the best parents in the world. We had a garden, we had books, we made music – what else could we need?

I had so many favourite places in our garden. There was the playroom our father planted and built for us. There was the pergola overgrown from spring on with flowering vines, I believe we called it 'Travellers' Delight'. That was the place where we had our daily coffee or tea in the afternoon. We watched the little hedgehogs coming out from under the hedges. They usually ran straight for the row of strawberries. Once I saw one scurrying home and its back was spiked with the berries. I am sure she took the berries back home to her babies. We hardly ever got any strawberries, I am sure, the hedgehogs got most of them.

But my very favourite place was the memorial my father had built for his youngest brother, Manfred who was only eighteen years old when he died in France in 1914. My father had a plaque made with only his name and the dates of his birth and death on it. There was an oak tree and a rosebush and a small bench. It was such a peaceful and quiet place, perfect for thinking things over and being alone.

My father never got over the death of his favourite younger brother; he also wrote a poem about him and set it to music. I cannot remember the words of course, but even then I wondered about the fact that my father almost envied his brother. He said that with his early death he was spared so much trouble, he would never have to experience futile dreams and fruitless hopes dashed and he was lucky not to have any more disappointments ahead of him, no more tears and sadness – he had rest now and nothing but stillness and peace.

We had a huge garden and after harvest the cellar bins were filled with sand into which we stuck carrots and turnips and beets. They kept beautifully. There were containers with potatoes, a barrel filled with sour pickles, one with sauerkraut, one filled with eggs in water glass, and another one with salted pork.

Sadness filled us all when pig slaughtering day came around. We all liked our yearly Rosie but when it was all over and done – we had so much meat to eat. We made sausages and my father even smoked some of it and the rest we salted away.

We also had honey. My father was a very good bee keeper. He used straw baskets turned upside down, as it was done in those days in Silesia. He loved his bees and he spent many hours with them. We did too and I cannot recall that we were ever stung.

My father made wine using all the fruit that was not boiled into jam by my mother. I can still hear and see and smell the bubbling vats and bottles in his wine room. He was very proud of the wine he made. But sometimes bottles would explode and the walls and even the ceiling would be coloured – then he was not so happy.

***Erika chuckled, lost in her memories. Suddenly a burst of laughter and she continued. ***

About not being happy I've got a story too. We had an outhouse which was about thirty meters away from the house. Since our house was the schoolhouse on one side, we had to share the toilet with the students. One side was theirs and one was ours. Of course, neither side had toilet paper. We used newspaper, neatly folded and cut with a knife. One time I had to go late at night, it was dark and I couldn't see. They had emptied the tank during the day but nobody had covered the hole. I did not watch out and fell in. I got very quickly up and then stood with my feet mired in stinking sludge, deep in the hole. I started screaming on top of my lungs. The family came running and they pulled me out.

They dragged me under the pump and I got cold water sloshed all over me. I shouted and I bawled, my father pushing the pump handle faster and faster with mother holding me tightly under the stream of water. But I still stunk. So they decided I needed a bath. I was marched into the wash kitchen, our laundry room. The big copper kettle, the one where the jam was always boiled in, stood on the stove and for some reason there was still hot water in it. Mother hauled in the grey zinc bath tub; I was undressed and then I had the luxury of my very own bath for the first time in my life. Normally I was number four on our weekly scrub downs, and by then the water was rather soapy. Manfred came after me but he, because he was the baby and the water was rather cold by the time it was his turn, always got half a pot of extra hot water.

Talking about Manfred – I have to tell you this. I remember it so clearly as if it had happened yesterday. It was in 1924 on a wintry and stormy February night. Irmgard and I had felt that there was something unusual going on in the house tonight. We had been told to go to bed rather earlier than we were used to. We also had been told not to go to our room but to the one we called the maid's room. Of course, we had no maid; we were much too poor for that. The chamber was under the attic; it just had a bed in it and not much else. We girls used the room as our play room and secret hiding place. On that night we were, for some unknown reason, told to sleep there.

We crept into the cold bed and listened to the wind rattling the tiles on the roof and whistling around the house. We felt curiously upset and scared and excited. We heard someone scream and then again and again and then we heard something cry.

"That must be a cat," said Irmgard.

But it didn't really sound like a cat, the meowing was somewhat different and then it changed to real crying. We huddled together and just could not explain the strange things that were happening downstairs.

Some time later we heard our father coming up the stairs. He opened the door and said, "Girls, you can come downstairs now."

We did. He led us to our mother's bedroom and there she was in bed with a baby in her arms. That was our brother Manfred. She smiled and looked at us.

"Isn't he beautiful?" she asked.

He looked all red and wrinkly like a weird little dwarf or overbaked monkey monster. Irmgard looked at me and I looked at her and we both said, "Yes, he is."

But we did not think so. Then the midwife came and we had to go to bed. Ours this time.

***I sit quietly giving Erika time for her memories. Suddenly she sat up and said from far away, "How I loved where I lived. It was paradise." And without stopping she added, "One day we heard a strange noise in the sky – and we saw our first airplane." ***

We had a small railway and the train took me to high school. I had to walk three kilometers to the station. Irmgard had been sent to Warmbrunn to a boarding school. But I had to get up at four in the morning to catch the train. In the train rode many women who worked in the factories in town. The way they talked was altogether different from what I had heard up until now. They were rough and of course they were poor. They were not the 'right' kind of women and I was not supposed to speak to them. I had to change trains so I could catch the train to Sorau where I went to school. This town was forty five kilometers away from home.

I think I was twelve when I was sent there to attend the lyceum, the academic school. I had to learn English – I remember that so clearly. It was very hard because my class mates already had had two years of instruction when I joined them. But my father helped me every day after I came home. It was tough but eventually I caught up with them. I loved school and I loved learning; I did well.

Our little village was set in a valley. One thing I remember so very clearly were the thunderstorms which broke out frequently around us. My father explained that one reason for that was the fact that there was lots of coal underground. The lightning storms lingered for hours around us and I can tell of horrific close lightning strikes.

When such a storm was approaching our father used to wake us. We had to dress completely and go down to the cellar. We were not allowed to eat anything because, our father explained, should lightning strike us with a morsel of food in our mouths you could choke to death on it. Besides, he used to add, 'I am sure you'd agree you'd not look a beautiful corpse with food stuck in your mouth!' We were always very much afraid. My mother used to take a box with all our important papers downstairs. There was good reason to be scared – many houses got hit and many of them burned down.

Sometimes we sat for hours in the cellar. I remember one particular building so close by that we could see it from our living room. The roof of the house and the barn was made from thick thatching like most of them were in our village. The barn was quite large and housed many horses. One night lightning struck. The farmer ran to let the horses out but they were so scared and confused by the light and crackle of the fires above them, they kept on running round and round in the barn – not one made it out – they all burned to death. I can still hear their terrified screams and shrieks. It was awful. I also knew of people who got struck by lightning and who died.

When I was twelve, I had to go for confirmation instruction. Twice a week I had to walk to a neighbouring village where we were taught the catechism of Luther. Two years after that we had confirmation in church. We had been taught to be good Lutheran Christians and after the ceremony we were considered adults in the eye of the church. At the service we wore young adult's clothes. I had on a black dress and a wreath of flowers in my hair and I felt very grown up. Of course, all relatives had been invited and after church was done, we all went home and the feasting began.

We had roast beef and then cakes and coffee. My grandparents on my mother's side had motored over from Gersdorf with huge baskets of goodies for all and a special gift for me.

This was also the time when many girls started their dowry chests. Good girls sewed their night gowns and petticoats and stitched their monograms into towels. From that time on girls were supposed to get 'serious' gifts such as linens and tablecloths and china and cutlery and such things which were placed in the dowry chest. I want to add that I did not have a dowry chest.

Here I remember a funny story: my grandmother really loved cats. She had one that always followed her and when she came to visit us, she brought that cat along. The cat was put in a large shopping basket with a net spanned over it so that kitty could not escape. One time when they brought me and my mother back from a visit and we were driving through the empty heather grandma felt the call of nature. Grandpa stopped the car and grandma got out and disappeared behind some bushes. And darn it – that cat managed to slip out of her prison and it escaped out of the car. We spent more than an hour looking and calling for kitty.

Finally, grandmother sat down on the roadside and started to cry. I was nine years old at the time and when I saw grandma sobbing, I sat down beside her and started to weep. My mother seeing me being so heartbroken started to sniffle too.

"Poor, poor kitty, left all alone in the wilderness."

The three of us made another attempt to find the cat but we were not successful. Finally, grandpa had enough and insisted that we drive on. So we did. And then something happened I cannot explain to this day. We arrived at our house, the grandparents retired after dinner to the inn next door. Next morning when we got up – what did we hear? 'Meow, meow! Outside our kitchen. We looked out and there stood kitty. She had walked all of six kilometers.

That was a wonderful event and naturally all the females of the clan cried once more – only now because of the wonder of it all, the miracle and the happiness that filled each and every one of them.

My grandparents had owned a large farm and a Gasthaus, an inn, which they passed on to their son Erich. They were very well off. But I think grandpa gambled, or invested badly, we never found out. When our mother died, we were supposed to inherit her share, which was supposed to be ten thousand Marks – a huge sum at the time – but all we got was three hundred Marks. My father was very angry with them after that.

I remember Uncle Erich well too. At the pub there was a large hall and he often held dances in there. The next morning Irmgard and I went there and picked up the coins that had fallen out of the pockets of the drunken men. We always found a lot. We spent most of our holidays at the Gasthouse. We loved it – they had so much food to eat!

Uncle Erich and his wife, Tante Trudel had twin boys, Wolfgang and Joachim, there was also Alexander, called Alex, and Johanna who married Erich Lang who was the teacher in Gersdorf. He always ate in the Gasthaus and that is where he met Johanna, Hannchen, as she was called. Their story predates that of my father and my mother. They were very, very young when they met.

When they were eighteen years old Uncle Erich's boys were regular Casanovas. They were always after cousin Irmgard who did not like their attentions, that naturally made them even more attentive and they tried to grab her and kiss her.

In the middle of their yard was the manure pile – their barn was filled with tethered milking cows. One day when Joachim grabbed Irmgard again, she gave him a push and he landed in the pool of liquid manure that spread below the high pile. Tante Trudel said that she was very angry with Irmgard and that she had really overdone it this time. Well, Irmgard did have a temper. I remember that one day she was sent to the store to get a bottle of vinegar. There was a fellow who followed her. She let him catch up and suddenly without a word she whisked around and cracked the bottle over his head. After that she was left alone.

Alex, Wolfgang and Joachim – not one of the three young men came home from the war; they all died at Stalingrad.

That just reminds me that all three daughters of my uncle Bodo, who died in 1937 of a heart attack, married American officers after the war and immigrated to New York. Sieglinde, Gudrun and Frigga – one of them is supposed to be on a portrait painted by Matisse that hangs in the San Antonio Art Museum, part of the McNay Art Collection. The girls became very well off – but sadly we lost all contact with them.

I was in school in Sorau, when one day I got a phone call to come home. There was no train at that time and my father told me he would be sending a car. I felt something terrible was going to happen – I, of course, knew that my mother was dying. The car driver had an accident and when I arrived home late at night, my mother was already dead. That was in 1933.

A year later our father married Trudel. Trudel had been a friend of Irmgard's and she had sometimes visited us. There I was – seventeen years old and had a stepmother only a few years older than I was. Irmgard did not take kindly to the marriage and very soon left home to work as a secretary on an estate. I felt like the proverbial fifth wheel at home and I hated it. I wanted to go to university badly, but Trudel told my father that it would cost too much money and that there was no need to spend that kind of money on girls as they would marry anyhow soon and then the money would be wasted. I wrote to Irmgard that I could not take the life at home any longer and Irmgard told me to pack my things and move in with her. I did and found myself a job and lived with her in Halle.

By that time, I had joined the BDM, the 'Bund Deutscher Maedel', the 'Alliance of German Girls', sort of the female equivalent of the Hitler Youths.

I was one hundred percent for Hitler. My father, who had very early on become a party member, had influenced me a lot. He was the local Party official or Ortsgruppenleiter at that time. Believe me, we all were for Hitler – everyone. I did not know one person who spoke against him. Hitler did so much for the working people, especially with his 'Kraft Durch Freude' program which could roughly be translated as 'Strength through Joy'. All workers got three weeks of holidays and they could go anywhere in Germany with their families. It is so hard to describe what a new and beautiful idea that was. And there were so many places and farms which the workers could afford and where they were welcome. There they were well fed and encouraged to have a good time with their children. They had been so very poor and neglected before – in those days before Hitler, they had nothing at all. Imagine, with Hitler now they had work, good wages and then three weeks of holidays – something unheard of until then.

Hitler did a lot for the youth too and the children and the orphans. Where there was hunger and misery before, now there were good homes for them, and schools and sports. Especially sports. When a child was known to be disabled or crippled, they were put into special homes where they eventually died. I guess they were not given any extra help to stay alive; perhaps they were helped to die. All the people I knew were aware of that practice and I never heard anyone disagree with it.

*** Erika got very quiet, and after a long pause she resumed, "And I never really realized at that time that it is actually a sin to kill disabled people and children."

I sit still – what I had just heard was overwhelming in its simplicity and sincerity and there was nothing that she or I could add. ***

But back to the Alliance of German Girls again. I loved it there. We had morally high standards; there were no cigarettes for us, no drugs. We read wholesome books and we lived a clean and healthy life. We rejected dirty stuff. We got up early and went to bed early. We did a lot of sports. And the men lived the same way. It is so difficult to describe. We were all such idealists – ready to give our all for these ideas and ideals. I loved it. Hitler was a god for me in 1933.

Hitler barely tolerated the church. My father had left the church in 1933. In the BDM one automatically became 'Gottglaeubig' that meant we believed in the old Germanic gods from Walhalla. I prayed to the Germanic gods, gods like Wotan and Odin. No Jesus, no church. Later on I worked for some time for the German Faith Movement.

When I lived with Irmgard in Halle, we were very poor. We had rented a tiny little room which was always cold. We had only cold water to wash with and we were not allowed to cook in our room. We did it anyhow on a small little electric plate. We had to – we did not have enough money to go out to eat. I remember those days well. One day I won 300 Marks in the lottery and we went out and splurged. I bought a swim suit and Irmgard bought shoes and then we went and bought our first not homemade clothes. It was fantastic.

It was there that I voluntarily joined the Arbeitsdienst – Labour Service. Like I have said before, I was an idealist, I believed what they told us and I loved what was happening in Germany and I fully supported the party. The Arbeitsdienst was good for me. We were sent to homes where a woman was needed, mostly to farms and large families where the woman of the house had fallen ill or was having a baby. Later on it happened that we were sent there to work on the farm because the men were at the front and the work load was too much for one woman.

It was often difficult. There was much work and I was not used to such hard physical farm labour. But my credo was: 'Gelobt sei was hart macht', 'Praised be what makes you tough'. And so I took discomfort, sore muscles, strange foods and customs and thought it would, if nothing else, serve to make me a stronger person. It was also easier to endure because I knew it was for the greater good.

Once I was sent to the Estate of Schlabrendorff near Zippau to work for the count. He was then fifty five years old and ancient in my eyes. He lived in a fairy tale castle with moats and fortifications, towers and crenellations everywhere. The big gate at the end of the drawbridge across the moat was closed every night.

I worked there in the library for about six months. I did not wear the official Labour Service uniform, just the jacket. He did not like the jacket. Count von Schlabrendorff was not a Nazi at all. His mother was a very old fashioned aristocratic lady, his sister, a spinster, was a bit more modern. The castle was filled with riches and treasures. Naturally the count had many workers and servants – but he did not do much for them. I remember his gardener who had a wife and two really lovely daughters - they all slept in one room. There was a cement floor and army cots. He did pay them well and he fed them well – but he certainly did not spoil his workers.

I, on the other hand, was allowed to eat with the family even though I was in a working position. When we went into the dining room, he always went in first. But at that age I was not very impressed by aristocratic tradition and I managed to enter first a few times, wearing my Hitler jacket, which, I knew, he hated. When the meal was served the count was served first, then his mother and his sister and I was served last. Of course, when the count put down his fork, we all had to stop eating. We had six different place settings; the cutlery was gold as were all the extra forks and the little plates. His highness ate very fast and since I was the last to be served, I never got to eat a decent meal. But I always went into the kitchen afterwards and there I ate my full.

The count was not married. I always felt that something was not quite right. One day, I recall, the butler showed me his sleeping chamber. The huge bed stood right in the middle, it had gilded posts. The walls were painted with nothing but naked women. Some were very beautiful but some were in very strange positions and some were even disgusting to me. Remember I was very young. I thought he was odd. The count drove every Saturday to Breslau. I did not know what he was doing there.

My father was rather worried about me working at this place because I worked for and lived with an unmarried man. My room was on the third floor in the attic and I shared it with a servant girl. So one day my father arrived and inspected everything. The count greeted my father very politely when he saw the swastika on his lapel but he said nothing else. He ordered his butler to ready a meal for us. We enjoyed it very much.

The library in the castle was huge and I figured it would take years to catalogue all its contents. I remember those books – many so old, so thick, so precious – many bound in leather.

Later I found out that he was imprisoned before the war and taken into custody. I don't know why. A worker talked about it. The Gestapo came and took him away. The old castle is in what today is Poland. It was not far away from Leuthen and it was famous and very ancient and beautiful.

I know they used his castle to house children that were evacuated from Berlin during the bombing raids.

After working for him I was sent by the Labour Service to many different places; I worked in Leipzig and in Vienna, but mostly in Silesia. Often we lived in camps and took the train to wherever we worked. One year I lived in a camp where I had to get up at five in the morning so I could start at the farm at six.

There, one day on the train, I met Konrad. It was love at first sight. We exchanged addresses and we got married on April 15, 1941. He was in Russia and I was in the registrar's office, beside me a chair with a steel helmet on it. I got married by proxy. I don't think my father ever met him. A few months later he came to Berlin, where Irmgard was living, and we went on our honeymoon to Vienna. The three weeks went by so fast and we went back to East Prussia where he had been the teacher. He had a little house there – no furniture in it – but we bought some and soon we had our very own little nest. It had been arranged that I would take over his teaching job when he had to go back to the front.

I wanted to have a baby so badly. In order to speed things up I even went to a doctor to ask for advice. The doctor just smiled and said to me,

"Frau Loeffler, you won't ever get pregnant you are much too thin."

I weighed 98 pounds. Soon our time together was over. He went back to the front and I went back to start my career as a teacher.

Chapter 8

MANFRED ERNST

***Uncle Manfred is my mother's brother. Today, in his eighties, he still rides motor bikes, sails, walks his beloved dog, and works during the summer running a camping ground on Lake Constance. He still remembers everything that ever happened to him, he can still speak Russian, some French, some English and even Hungarian which he learned when he was together with a lady from Pecs. Uncle Manfred is a bit high strung and passes that energy on to a succession of Dachshunds who are nervously watching his every move. At home they shift their ears to the tic toc of dozens of self-made clocks that adorn his walls; all chime and whistle at the same quarter, half and full hour, setting some of his dogs howling along.

When he visited us a few years ago he fulfilled my wish to know the story of his life. His greatest wish was to drive through the Rockies and to go dancing in a western type saloon in Calgary. We obliged of course, but once we were through the snow sheds at Rogers Pass heavy grey clouds started dropping down to the road and he never saw a snow covered peak and when we went to a saloon it was on a Monday night and the anticipated volleys of 'yeehaw' did not quite materialize even though there were a few cowboys in press button shirts, jeans and cowboy boots swinging their similarly attired girls to a country two step – Manfred was satisfied. He mused.

"I've driven through the Rockies, I've sat in the hot pool in Banff, I've eaten ribs in Calgary and I have danced to cowboy music – life is good!"

This is his story as spoken on a tape recorder.***

I was born on February 8, 1924. From my sixth year on I went to my father's school. I was not a scholar and found school difficult. I remember that I never grasped that words come on their own. I used to hang one word on to the other and make a long snake of letters across the page. By the time I figured out how to do it correctly a whole year of school had passed.

My grandparents from Breslau spent all their summer holidays with us. One day my father and mother took me along to travel with them back to Breslau. I think I was three or four years old. I recall that my grandfather always had very cold feet and that he had the habit of changing his socks every half hour. Grandmother always carried about six pairs of socks with her. A few kilometers before Breslau he went to the toilet to change his socks. When he was doing that, he always placed his shoes on the toilet seat. Unfortunately, the train leaned a bit too heavily into the curve and the shoe dropped into the toilet and down to the tracks. Grandfather came back to us with only one shoe and one black sock on the other foot. He was very mad because he had lost an almost new shoe and he wanted to pull the emergency brakes. But it was pointed out to him that that would not be a good thing. He desisted but was angry and bemoaned the loss of his shoe for the rest of the trip. In the station he took off his one shoe and walked in matching socks as he left the train.

We took the electric tram to get to our destination. My father had lit up a thick cigar after we had settled down. Suddenly I felt very thirsty. The tram conductor came along in his spic and span uniform and I thought him all powerful. I tugged at his sleeve and asked politely, "Could you please stop the tram at the next pump, Sir, I am very thirsty."

He looked at me and said with a huge grin on his face, "I am sorry young man, I cannot do this."

I was so dumbfounded and disappointed by his answer and then suddenly I remembered that I had not seen one single pump on our whole way. And I blurted out in frustration, "Don't they have any pumps in this crummy village?"

To understand my reaction, you must know that in Leuthen we had no running water in the house or in the school. We had a pump outside and used a hollow tree as a pump handle. That is where I washed myself every morning and that is where I got my drinks. I knew nothing else as a child.

One of the most exciting things I ever got was a Billy goat. I named him 'Karle'. The local shoemaker fitted him with a harness and my father made me a small wagon which was pulled by Karle. Like a little king, I used to sit in the wagon and proudly drive him through the village where we lived. That was the time before there were proper sanitation institutions and pipes in the village. People used outhouses and when the tanks were full they used large dippers to empty them. The contents were chucked onto the village meadow where after a short time all had disappeared but the small rectangular pieces of newspaper which had been diligently cut by someone in the household and equally diligently used as toilet paper. These small shreds stayed for a long time on the meadow and I remember that a few times, when Karle was being driven through the village, on a sandy road and not on asphalt mind you – and he spotted those white flecks on the grass, he resolutely and in total disregard of my yanking on the reign, veered off through the ditch, spilling me out, and then proceeded to eat the papers on the grass.

Karle was my friend who protected me from other people. Strangers or bullies from the school were his favourite foe. When he decided that he did not like them he first spiralled his head upwards, riveted his yellow eyes on them, then bent his head and charged towards them ramming his horns in their behinds. He was better than a watchdog for me. Billy goats have a horrible smell and my father used to joke that 'the smell of his friendship hung heavily around me.'

There were strange customs in our village. For instance, my father had to go to every funeral because it was tradition that the school children sang. The dead body was laid out in the living room and the wake was in the next room. Imagine – all those flies marching from cake to body and round again. I never ate anything. When the body was finally carried out of the house the feet had to go first. And when the feet were outside but the head still in the house, the four men who carried the coffin had to lift the coffin three times up and down – in the doorway. The people in the village believed that this prevented the soul of the deceased from coming back into the house.

The people there were also very superstitious. There was an old woman and everyone believed she was a witch. She lived in a small cabin with a huge roof made of straw. Under the gable were two holes – one to the left and another one on the right side – holes made for the owls. The floor of her home was just packed loam. She used a broom she had made herself of birch branches. She always sprinkled the floor with water before she swept. In the middle of her room hung a black iron chain from the ceiling with a heavy sooty pot suspended from it and that was her stew pot. She cooked all her meals in that pot over an open fire. In the roof was a hole for the smoke to escape. I still feel the goose bumps I used to get when I had to go and see her. My mother sent me there sometimes to bring her vegetables from our garden. All the children were very much afraid of her. There were many stories told about her. One said that she went in the forest, chose a nice tree then sank her ax into that tree and that milk came then out of the axe handle. That is how she got her milk, they said. The villagers explained that that was the reason sometimes their cows ran dry and gave no more milk.

Once I remember a man had died. We had a carpenter in our village who made coffins. When he was done the widow came with a wheel barrow, placed the coffin on it and went home. We all saw that. The bottom of the coffin was covered in wood shavings. She laid a sheet over it and placed her husband into the coffin. Then she realized he was too big for the coffin. So she placed the body in the wheel barrow, drove into her yard to her big wooden block that she used to split firewood, placed his head on the block and cut off his head. She put the body in the coffin and laid his head into his arms.

It was custom that a certain woman washed the dead bodies and for payment she received the sheets and bedding in which the deceased had died. Frau Schneider came to wash the body. The widow told her that her Gustav had wanted to fit into the coffin and therefore she had to hack off his head. But don't worry, she assured her, he did not feel a thing he was dead already. And she swore her to secrecy. Nobody found out about the story until eight years later when the widow died and Frau Schneider told the story, adding that she should by rights actually have her head chopped off to as she had done to her husband – and that is how the whole village found out!

The widow was buried next to her husband - but with her head on.

We all believed in stories. When I was just five years old my favourite was my book about the Heinzelmaennchen – the little people or fairies. Behind my grandmother's house was a pond with many bull rushes in it. It looked just like the place where the goblins of my book lived. I knew that they were living and working underground because one always found little mounds of earth. Following the pictures of that book I went to my mother and told her that those goblins were working very hard and that they were wearing out their clothing rapidly. I asked her if I could have some pieces of material that I could give to them so they could mend their pants. Naturally my mother obliged. I ran to the pond and placed little swatches of material all around the water between the bull rushes. Erika, my beastly sister, went out at night and collected them. I did not know that and next morning I was overjoyed that I had helped the little people.

Once I went with another boy to a meadow where cows were grazing. There was a huge bull with a shiny ring through his nose.

"Well, Fritz, how about we let him out." I suggested.

And we opened the gate. The bull charged through the open gate and his cows came after him, udders swinging.

We got scared and ran into the forest. When I came home my father looked at me. Then I knew. He did not say a word but handed me his pocket knife. I knew what to do. I went to the back of the garden and cut a good switch from the hazelnut bush that grew there. Yes, I knew what I had to do. Then I was placed across a chair and got six good ones applied methodically and slowly across my rear.

I knew I deserved it. I never let another bull out again.

In May of 1933 the family moved to Heinersdorf, near Gruenberg because there was an occasion for my father to advance in his profession. But the move made me very sad. I was nine years old and had just realized that my mother was very, very sick. It had started the year before, and I remember that at Christmas she had said to me, "Manfred, the next Christmas I will no longer be with you."

She had cancer. She had been often in the clinic in Breslau where she received radium X-rays, but nothing helped and she came home again. Irmgard was nineteen years old and she looked after her.

My father became a Hauptlehrer, a department head, and had four teachers under him. I went for another year to school there and in my tenth year I entered the Real Gymnasium in Gruenberg. I got a bicycle and had to pedal three kilometers to school. That was such a huge change for me. I had grown up in Leuthen, a small village in the plains with only 250 inhabitants, and now I had to get used to the city, to traffic and so many people.

There was also much excitement about the new government that had taken over in January of 1933. Mind you, that was politics and as a ten year old I did not understand or even care about it at all. When I became ten years old, I joined the 'Jungvolk', an organization set up by Hitler for young people from ten to fourteen; after that one joined the Hitler Youth.

In my new school I was in a class with thirty seven other students. We started to study Latin and French. The level of academic expectations and achievement in school was very high and we had to work very hard. Classes went daily until two o'clock. I found French rather difficult but my father helped me after school and I worked hard as I did later on for English. I had always very good marks in the languages and only passing marks in mathematics. Little did I know that I would later on make my living using nothing but numbers and formulas – then I rather fancied myself as an interpreter. Consequently, when reaching the upper levels where one is streamed into either sciences or languages, I opted for the latter. My choices were Hebrew or Russian. I certainly didn't see a point in studying Hebrew because I had no desire to live in Palestine, and so I chose Russian. Little did I know how I would much later benefit from that choice.

Every year at school, on the second day of September, was a celebration in remembrance of the victory in the battle of Sedan in 1870, the famous battle where the Germans beat the French. This was a favourite day because we did not have to go to school. The students, wearing white shirts, blue pants and white school caps with different colour visors which indicated the grade they were in, joined the city band of Gruenberg and together we marched. We were good at marching because in the Jungvolk and the Hitler Youth, we marched a lot. We marched fourteen kilometers down to the Oder River. There was a large place and a pergola made from branches and young oak trees housed the band. Athletic games and competitions were held later on, followed by beer and sausages roasted on large grills – we had a fun day. In the evening buses came and brought us back home.

Before I continue with the events in 1938 I have to explain the situation in some parts of Germany and the East. Before 1918 there was no country Czechoslovakia. The areas of Bohemia, Moravia and Slovakia belonged to the Austro-Hungarian Empire, which had collapsed at the end of WWI and had broken up. The Czechs and the Slovaks joined and became a new country: Czechoslovakia. They did this over the protestations of over three million Germans who were living in these regions and who did not want to be ruled by the Slavs.

In the thirties not only the Slovaks but also other small ethnic minorities had begun to resent Czech dominance over the economy and government. A very vocal group of Germans, the Sudeten-Germans, began to feel that they were not heard by the new government either and they began to protest. Hitler encouraged them to demand self-rule and he threatened to declare war if tdemand was not met. In 1938 Britain, France and Italy signed an agreement with Hitler that forced Czechoslovakia to give the Sudeten territory to Germany. Later in that year Hungary and Poland also claimed parts of Czechoslovakia. On October 1st, 1938, German troops marched into the Sudetenland and Czechoslovakia ceded the area to Germany. In March of 1939 German troops invaded Moravia and Bohemia and set up a German protectorate. The Hungarians occupied Ruthenia. On March 15th, 1939 Hitler entered Prague, the capital of Czechoslovakia.

I was fourteen years old at the time and I clearly remember that suddenly the reservists were drafted, they had to undergo a refresher course and then they joined the army.

Then came the first of September 1939 – and I can clearly remember it, it was a Friday. I can recall that the radio reported that Poles had invaded the radio station in Gleiwitz – whether that is true or not, I do not know, but I know for sure that on September the third the Poles had murdered about three thousand Volksdeutsche, that is ethnic Germans, in the Polish city of Bromberg. This had happened before the German army got there. We knew about the events from some refugees who escaped and travelled through our region. We also read about it in the newspaper. Later it was never mentioned again that it was the Poles who massacred the Germans before the arrival of the military troops.

***These incidents did in fact happen. On September 3, 1939, Poles shot a number of German civilians without any provocation. The exact number of victims could never be verified. This was the 'Bromberger Blutsonntag', the 'Bloody Sunday' of Bromberg. The occupation of the Gleiwitz radio station was staged by the German SD, the German security service. This was an idea that had come from Heydrich who was looking for reasons to invade not only Czechoslovakia but also Poland. Men of the security service, who spoke Polish, were dressed in Polish uniforms, they stormed the station and even managed to shout some Polish anti-German slogans into the microphone thus lending apparent truth to the invasion. Another of these pseudo aggressive actions of the Poles included the destruction of the Customs buildings at Hochlinden. This was the incident Gustel, my father, was involved in and which earned him the Iron Cross. Basically, these and a few other staged incidents demonstrating Polish aggression were the brain child of Heydrich. 'Operation Himmler' provided the rationale and gave the impetus for the invasion and the war with Poland. ***

Another bit of history background to explain the situation: after the defeat in the First World War in 1918 the Treaty of Versailles stipulated that the Republic of Weimar, that is Germany, was only allowed to have a standing army of 100 000 men, and no planes or tanks. Reservists were continuously being trained but they were always discharged because of the imposed number restrictions. Stories circulated that these forces used tanks made of cardboard; tanks that were moved by men riding bicycles inside the contraptions. Rumours flew that the French and the English assuaged Polish concerns of a built-up and powerful German army by telling them about the cardboard tanks. So when things got serious and the Germans really invaded Poland, the Polish cavalry, thinking they were attacking cardboard tanks, went for the German tanks with lances and bayonets. All were shot, the brave Ulans and their fine horses. This is not a joke – it really happened.

*** Actually this never happened. What had occurred was that a Polish cavalry unit got trapped within a German tank unit and in order to escape the men had to ride through the enemy with catastrophic results. ***

The Polish were no hindrance to the Germans and on September 18th, they signed their surrender to Hitler.

Meanwhile in school they worked us dreadfully hard. In the morning I left my house at six thirty and I returned at half past one. My father had remarried a year after my mother's death. His new wife, Trudel, came from a family of innkeepers from a village. Naturally I found it very difficult to have a strange woman in our family. I maintain to this day that a mother can never be replaced – never. I had to battle for about three or four years with the pain about the loss of my mother. I found it so very difficult to get over it. I was only nine when she died. I was ten when my father married again. He was forty seven and she was twenty five. She was nice and tried to be good to me and make me like her. She helped me with memorizing those endless, long tables of verbs in the languages I was studying and slowly she did win my trust and respect. I could see that she was trying her very best to be a good mother to me.

Before we had moved to Heinersdorf my mother had stayed with her sister, my aunt Else, who had cared for her so very well. I remember now that after we had moved to Heinersdorf and mother was with us again, one day she went for a little walk with us. She was so pale and could only walk so slowly – one could see that she had not much longer to go. One afternoon in September, by that time she could no longer walk, my father and Irmgard stood by her bedside. Suddenly my father who must have seen things that I could not see, asked her.

'What do you think, mother, should we call Erika home?'

I can still see my mother's face as she slowly shook her head, a tear sliding ever so slow down her cheek, then her head fell to the other side and she was dead.

I hurt so badly. I tended her grave every day for such a long time. I used to love to come to the cemetery.

Of course, when I was eleven, the pain was not as acute as it had been two years before and my friends and I did a lot of nonsense there. The funeral chapel had window shutters made of wood. Because they were quite old the knots had fallen out and the shutters were riddled with nice round black holes. One day we had a bright idea. We decided to use the holes for target practice. Armed with pebbles we began to throw stones through the holes. Suddenly a swarm of hornets shot out of one hole. They pursued us, but we were hightailing away from the building. But they flew faster than we could run and one stung me in my ear and another was sitting on my neck and got me there. It felt as if the devil was riding me, jabbing me with a red hot iron pick. It hurt! I was bolting towards the school, yelling and screaming on top of my lungs. My father came running out. Once he had assessed the situation, he revved up his motorbike, sat me on it and we raced to the doctor in Gruenberg where I had to suffer two needles administered into my neck.

One of our favourite pranks was smearing soft soap on the rail lines of our little train station. Freight and passenger trains stopped very often at our village because it was here that they were shunted onto different tracks. We greased the iron lines with the soft soap and when the locomotives wanted to pull the wagons, they couldn't move them. The lines went a bit uphill at the station and that aided our efforts. Then the locomotive engineer climbed down from the hissing engine to investigate. It took a while but eventually he saw the slimy mess in front of the engine. Oh boy – did he holler. They had to go and get sand and rub the soap off with it. Naturally we boys were hiding in the bushes not too far away, trying to stifle our laughter. We enjoyed ourselves and our feats immensely.

I got great pleasure from the things we did in the Hitler Youth. I was fourteen and I loved the sports and the marching and quasi military exercises, the uniform and the camaraderie of us young boys. At one time we made model airplanes. During the fall of 1939 we had to go out to the big farms and pick potatoes – they were picked for the military.

My father often took me camping. He had a boat and we visited many lakes and paddled down many rivers. Once, when I was thirteen years old, he planned to row all the way down the Oder River to Stettin at the Baltic Sea. We had a small tent with us, a kerosene stove, a pot and all the stuff one needed for camping. One day after some hours on the water my father said to me that it was time to halt and he added, "Get out at the left side." I was so used to immediate obedience that I stood up and jumped out without a moment's hesitation. I dragged our little sail with me and then disappeared like a rock. The river was flowing very swiftly. But I managed to disentangle myself from the sail and swim in front of the boat and get to the other side of the river. My father maneuvered the boat back to the bank, got out and ran alongside the river trying to fish his sail out of the water that was flowing swiftly toward Stettin. He must have run over a mile but eventually he had to return without his sail that we saw bopping further and further away in the distance. He was rather sour with me for a while.

Unfortunately, our holiday was cut short when my father received a telegram announcing the death of his father. He decided to go back to Breslau and to leave me at the camp ground. He talked to the guard there and left me with some money so I could buy myself some bread.

He went home, buried his father and then returned together with his younger brother and we continued our trip to the Baltic Sea. We spent another three weeks there and then took a tug boat back up the river. That was interesting as they sometimes pulled twenty smaller craft behind them. Those were the boats that brought coal from Upper Silesia to the harbours on the Baltic.

My father, meanwhile, had become the principal of a sixteen-teacher school in Gruenberg. There were eight classes of boys and eight classes of girls in the school. My gymnasium (high school) was right next to his school. By this time I had abandoned my plans to become an interpreter in the Russian language. I wanted to become a Forstmeister, a forester. This probably came about because I had four uncles who were Forstmeisters. I visited the families during the holidays and I loved their way of life.

In January 1940, when I was fifteen years old, I said to my father that I was fed up with school and studying, that I did not care for all the languages and the math, the sciences and the sports – and I finally spilled out to my astonished father, that I did no longer want to go to school but that I wanted to be a forester.

It was a long struggle to get him to agree with my plans. He so very much wanted his son to get the Abitur, matriculation, and have an education. But eventually he gave in and we took the train to Breslau where the department of forestry was. Because of my appearance and earnestness, and also because I had decent report cards, I was accepted in the forestry program.

There were two ways to become a forester: one was to sign up for twelve years with the military who would then afterwards provide a free education and training. This was not the route I had chosen.

I got my first posting as an apprentice in the Goerlitzer Heide, about sixty kilometers south of Gruenberg. And what a coincidence – the neighbouring forester was my uncle who had taken over because the original forester had been drafted to the military.

One of the chief duties of a forester was the marking, numbering and measuring of trees destined for cutting. When the timber was sold and hauled away, the numbered trees and their measurements were compared with the list the other party kept. It was one of my first jobs to shout out the number of the tree, its length and diameter, so my forester master could check it off the list. Exact records were kept.

The following year I was transferred to another place. Two small fish ponds were connected to a canal and my main task was to shoot pike. I had acquired a small caliber rifle, a Mauser, and because money was scarce and we had little to eat, I learned to shoot pike with the gun. When you hit them, they come up and their swim bladder explodes; then they are easy to catch and I always went home with at least five or six fish. We ate a lot of pike that season.

This was also the time I shot my first deer. I believe I was almost seventeen years old. My forester master told me that there was a doe which was quite old and that I should get her when I saw her. One day I got her into my sight, she was about twenty five meters away, and I aimed and pulled the trigger and I dropped her instantly. I was a very good shot – but this was my first live target and I was quite proud of myself.

In March 1941 I applied for a position in the Riesengebirge, a huge plot of land that belonged to the Graf von Schafgottsch, said to be one of the richest men in Germany. I wanted to learn how a private forest was run and managed. I also had to attend the institute of forestry in Reichenstein. The course was shortened to only two months because of the war. That actually was a splendid time in my life. I joined the local band because I was quite good at the horn; there were thirty two men in the band. I wore my forest green uniform with shoulder epaulettes like a lieutenant and had my pants tucked into the boots. We were certainly a fine looking bunch when we marched down from the school to the market place, playing "Alte Kameraden". We could all march because all of us had been in the Hitler Youth. In the marketplace we closed ranks and gave the population a concert. I am telling you – the girls were all over us, but we were kept like monks – girls were 'streng verboten', not allowed in our school.

There they worked us hard. We had to memorize the Latin names of all the flora and fauna of the local forests. Luckily, I had had some Latin and so the names were much easier for me than for many of my colleagues; I felt sorry for them sometimes.

Following the course, I had to go back to the Riesengebirge. Our forest bordered on the Sudetenland which by that time had become German. Many Czechs lived there too and many of them came over to our side to poach game. Our forests housed many wild sheep and they were much prized. My master was a very stern man, a Rittmeister from the First World War. I had to address him as captain and only in the third person just like I had had to address Count Schafgottsch. Today I shake my head, but then I had to step back three steps and call him 'Durchlaucht', 'Your Highness'; his daughters were addressed as 'Comptesse'.

I must tell you how that noble bunch hunted: A rope was strung in an area of about one square kilometer where the elks had been fed special feed for quite some time. Heraldic flags and banners were fluttering from this line indicating the illustrious members of the hunting party. The flags had been drenched with a chemical that attracted the game. Outside of this demarcation line shooting stands had been erected which soon housed the aristocratic sporting crowd, the Fuerst von Ratibor, Count this and Count that and their excited female counterparts.

I had to be there in my best uniform. The drovers then chased the elk just in front of the shooting stands from where volleys of shots were fired. No wonder they could bag over eighty magnificent elk in one season, thirty deer and countless wild pigs.

As an apprentice forester it was my task to open the game. For this we wore heavy, long gloves. The animal had to be slit open from a specific point between the hind legs and we had to make a clean cut all the way up to the chest. Then we had to cut the throat and lift out the tongue. We had to open the carcass with one deft movement and then with one swing lift out the intestines, liver and stomach. Woe and behold if only one drop of blood was on our uniforms!

Once it happened that I stepped on one of the elk's legs. My Rittmeister was standing closely by watching me. Count Schafgottsch was there too. Without a moment's hesitation my good Rittmeister grabbed his riding crop and whacked me viciously across my back.

"That is something you will do only once and never again!"

"Only a butcher does what you have done."

I never forgot his words and I heeded them. Yes, he was a tough task master.

One time, I remember, he had sent me up to the old Czech border to walk a certain old path and do border patrol. And he distinctly instructed me not to turn around. I was on a pair of old skis, so old they still had brass fittings, they had originally belonged to my sister Irmgard.

I did as I was told. But I must admit that I was curious as to why I wasn't supposed to look around – and the devil pinched me and after I had passed the 'Witches Stand' under those old and black and gnarled spruce trees, I looked back – just a bit, mind you. And there I saw the old Rittmeister following me in the far distance and checking up on me if I really did use that old path which he had ordered me to take and not made a short cut on another path which would have been much more convenient and easier to traverse.

After a while I could not see him anymore and I skied down the hill, as I had been instructed. There he stood, watch in hand, checking my time and arrival place.

Life was certainly tough at his house. I had to be up in the morning at five thirty for a breakfast of flour soup and a hunk of dry bread – that was all. Then I was ordered to go into the woods to cut trees. I had to go with the regular forest workers and the wood cutters so that I would learn to appreciate their work. It was very heavy work indeed. We had to cut the trees, drag them out and de-bark them. We had to take especially good care with the bark of the fir trees which was rolled up later to be used for tanning leather. I was only seventeen and that was heavy work for me.

One day in winter I had to leave with my master, the Rittmeister, at one thirty in the early morning hours. We arrived at a clearing. Suddenly two persons appeared on their skis. They were wearing heavy back packs. They were probably packing poached game. One of them must have noticed us. The forester was standing next to a fir tree and observed the two men through his field glasses. Suddenly a shot rang out and the forester collapsed.

One of the two men had shot him in the knee. Richard Kittelman, that was the forester's name, yelled at me.

"Shoot him! Shoot him!"

Here I was, seventeen years old and that was the first time I aimed my gun at a human being.

I quickly pointed my Mauser towards them and got the first one under the jaw. The second man wanted to hightail but Kittelman ordered me once more to shoot. I did as I was ordered and got him in the arm. When I got to the man he was sitting in the snow. I tied his legs together so that he could not get away and sort of bandaged his arm where I had smashed his bone. Then I laid the Rittmeister on his skis, tied him down and dragged him up with a rope to the nearest mountain cabin which was luckily only three hundred meters away from where this incident had taken place. I could establish radio contact and I was able to get a rescue team into the mountains which took him back down. They also took the wounded man and the dead body. This event haunted me for many days. I was only seventeen – and here I was and I had shot a man.

When I came home again, I was given the administration and management of a certain parcel of land by the forest overseer. I was allowed to sleep till ten in the morning but everything had to run ship shape. I had to do all the forestry tasks and was even trusted with the payroll. We employed about two hundred prisoners of war, they were French, and about thirty German forestry workers. They had to take care of about 40 000 cords of fir blown down in a storm.

In February of 1942 I had to get back to forestry school and take a condensed version of the normally much longer course. I took my final exams and passed with flying colours. April 30th was the last day of my secondary education. I was eighteen years old and a certified forester. I went home for a few days. Not long after I received a letter. I was ordered to join the army.

I did not have to join the Arbeitsdienst, Labour Service, because in 1939 I had volunteered for the military. I was just young and crazy then. I told myself that the war against Poland had lasted only two weeks, the war against the French would perhaps be four weeks, and Holland and Belgium – pshaw – how long could it take to take those small countries down – and I wanted to make sure there would still be some war left for me – remember I was just fifteen then and my attitude was rather lackadaisical.

Chapter 9

GUSTEL IN THE MILITARY

We began our military training by rebuilding our premises which were in an old dilapidated work camp associated with the Mauserwerke in Oberndorf am Neckar where they had not produced any weapons, except in the original factory halls, since 1919. We learned 'Ordnung' (that most beloved word of the Germans meaning orderliness with a system). We learned how to handle a rifle, to march and salute and whatever else was deemed necessary that would quickly turn us into soldiers. When I returned home it was obvious that a co-existence between my father and myself was impossible. I wanted to do things my way but it was still his business and as for handing it over to me – he was still not old enough yet and besides he would not have been able to afford that. And so, with his approval, I signed up with the military in Ellwangen where more reservists were organized.

Here life began to get more serious: the marching and training with weaponry became more detailed and we learned marksmanship. They started to introduce military terms and regulations, soon we had companies and battalions. Men from the Wehrmacht and police battalions had begun to arrive and before I knew it I was working as a Kompaniefeldwebel, or sergeant major, even though I was in reality only an Obergefreiter, or corporal, and regrettably also received only this salary. In my company there were men who had twelve years service under their belts and they did not like this. They complained and one of them replaced me. I was made deputy Zugfuehrer, that is platoon leader, and was in charge of thirty to forty men.

The real Zugfuehrer, Lieutenant Goesele, was supposed to teach these men. One morning Goesele did not show up for instruction. Some of our superiors were known to drink a lot, and he was one of them. It was seven o'clock. I was here, the men were here and I knew he would not show up because he was once more sleeping off his hangover. I started lecturing. Suddenly the door opened and the commander of the battalion entered.

"Where is the First Lieutenant?"

"Not arrived yet, Sir."

"What are you doing?"

"Teaching the class, Sir."

"But this is not your job."

"Yes Sir, but what else could I do?"

"Carry on."

He sat down and listened while I carried on with instruction. When I was finished, he barked, "Well done."

An hour later came his order that I was now officially the platoon leader. That's how you stumble up the stairs. It happened to me a few more times.

I was in regular military service until 1935. Once or twice I attended a Reichsparteitag, those huge political rallies in Nuremberg where the Party, officially and ceremoniously and for all the world to see, met and spoke. We were dressed in black uniform, shiny high boots – these things were worn only for parade purposes, otherwise we wore field grey, in fact later on we wore nothing else.

***My sister Inge and I loved to hear the following little story which predictably was part of the Nuremberg Rallies' tale. One of us would ask, "Wasn't that an exciting event, Papa?"

"No, not really. It was a job for us. We had to march long and then we had to stand for hours without moving as much as a muscle. These events always took place in summer when it was hot. It was even hotter in our uniforms."

"Didn't you ever have to go pee?"

"Aber Kind, but child, that was impossible. We were on parade."

A long pause followed, and we waited for that boyish grin to spread over his face. "But sometimes we did. You know girls, sometimes we just peed into our pants from where it ran into our boots. It was all black anyhow and nobody could see anything."

Inge and I erupted in delicious giggles.

"I bet the other soldiers envied you."

He chuckled, "I know they did." ***

In 1935 we became officially part of the Wehrmacht as Waffen SS. All rules and regulations of the Wehrmacht applied to us from now on. This was just the time when I was performing the duties of the 'mother of the company', a sergeant, even though I was only a corporal, and therefore I witnessed the change very conscientiously. I also witnessed how we were transformed from a wild and free bunch of men into a disciplined military unit.

The Waffen SS Regiment 'Deutschland' was put together in Munich in 1936. It's fourth battalion was Ellwangen and that is how I came to Munich. My good Obersturmbannfuehrer, Lieutenant-Colonel Steiner, was already commander of the regiment. When I arrived in Munich, he sought me out and for more than half an hour he walked with me across the training yard. Then suddenly he said, "Haefner, I need you as a sergeant major."

"But Colonel, I am only a corporal and would like to keep it that way."

"Nonsense, I need you as a sergeant major; officially this time."

I really did not warm up to the idea, but then I thought that on the other hand he could have just ordered me to do what he wanted me to do and here he is trying to persuade me, quite a difference in approach, and so I finally agreed. That was how I officially became a sergeant major in the summer of 1936 and that is what I was until I quit the Waffen SS in 1937.

Ten other men were transferred with me to the Ellwangen battalion, all corporals and sergeants, and there together with another ten men from the local unit we were assigned 150 recruits whom we were to shape into a company. This actually went quite well. The recruits were men who had served in the work service for the state, the Reichsarbeitsdienst, and they knew a few things. Sometimes I was very strict but there always was a reason for it.

I was a terror with my inspections. I checked my men not only for creases and buttons, rifles and mattresses, but also for fingernails and combs; even handkerchiefs were on my list. These boys never knew beforehand what I was going to check and when; I became very devious in outsmarting their anticipated expectations.

You must know we were a proud bunch, we, the men of the Waffen SS. Three thousand men were in barracks, a whole regiment. So, when on Saturdays and Sundays not only the sergeants but also the officers checked to make sure the men were dressed according to regulations and were presentable to the public, dozens of men were regularly sent back and denied leave – but never ever one of my company.

My rank was Stabscharfuehrer, that is what a sergeant major was called in the Waffen SS. Some of my friends had shortened that to 'Staberl' and that is how they addressed me but the men were not allowed to do this, they had to use the proper address of my rank. My men soon realized 'der Alte', that was me they meant by 'the old one' was alright and they came to appreciate that my controls served them well indeed.

As the weeks went by cars had started to line up in front of the gates of the barracks. There were cars from the smallest to the fanciest limousine filled with young ladies eager to pick up their beaus. And, naturally, for this the men did not mind being in ship shape. Speaking of girls, I am reminded of a certain corporal who once asked me for leave on Saturday night. When I laughed at him that he didn't have a dime in his pocket, he laughed back at me.

"Well, true enough Sergeant, I don't have a penny right now, but if you need some tomorrow night just let me know."

One of my corporals, unfortunately he fell in Russia in 1942, used his good connections to get access to a cabin in the mountains. Every Saturday at one o' clock a train left from Munich heading southward towards the Alps, filled with people and their skis. I was informed about this and let it be known to my men that it was possible to get ski holidays over the weekend – it was in my power to hand out short weekend passes. But regrettably too many men failed inspection on Saturday and the train had to leave without us. But to nobody's amazement the 'Appell', that is inspection on the next Saturday, found everything in order and absolutely spic and span, and forty men could haul their skis into the train and head south towards the mountains for fun and snow.

The cabin was more like a barn but we did not care. We piled our rucksacks and sleeping bags on the straw and in the mangers; wherever we found a spot to sleep we spread out – we did this all winter long. Sunday afternoon at two we headed back to Munich.

One night while out on the mountains my buddies jumped on me and I noticed they were half naked.

"Staberl, get up! Put on shorts! Get up! Get up!"

I didn't really want to but they did not let up and so I finally gave in seeing that there was nothing else I could do. When I got outside there were a dozen of them hopping around in shorts, rolling down the hills, screaming and hollering like children. It was warm! Something interesting was happening here: in the morning at about four o'clock the so called Inntaler, that warm wind that came up from Italy through the valley of the Etsch River, slipped over the tops of the mountains and then slid down the valley of the Inn River. This balmy breeze blew for about an hour and then it was gone. Disappeared. Icy mountain air fell down over us like a curtain, it grew very cold and we quickly crept back into our sleeping bags.

One day as we were leaving a snowstorm surprised us. It was so thick we could barely see two meters ahead. We had just started on our way downhill to another cabin further down, where we always had our customary 'snow water', which was a hot raspberry drink, before heading to the train, when we noticed a girl standing quite forlorn in the swirling snow, sobbing quietly. She had lost the courage to ski downhill in this weather. The wind was by now howling and swishing snow around in a wild and white swirl. We had to bring her down, and I roped her between another man and myself and then started off. We skied downhill on an old logging road which was none too wide, but we went slowly and carefully. Suddenly we heard yelling and screaming from behind us.

"Watch out! Clear the path!"

I shouted, 'down', and we had barely folded ourselves onto our knees down to the skis, heads bent, arms close and angled, don't forget we were tied to each other and there was no time to undo knots, we merely tried to make ourselves as small as possible, when a group of men came stampeding down the hill. When they noticed us they gave one blood curdling yell, then jumped over us and hollering and laughing disappeared around the next bend, one of the fellows waving a good bye with his sticks. Those were men! That's what they enjoyed!

We made it safely into the valley and sampled another 'snow water' before we boarded the train back to Munich. Of course, I was a gentleman and decided to get the lady safely home. But she declared as we were leaving the station that she wanted to have a drink. Well, in Bavaria a drink is always beer, and beer comes always in a 'Mass', that is a one litre mug, also called a Stein. Good. I ordered two drinks.

I was really very thirsty and it would have been so easy to let that lovely brew slide down my parched throat, but I thought, if I do that, she'll think me not a proper gentleman but a drunkard. So, I drank slowly only half the mug and then slowly and very regretfully I set my mug down on the counter. The girl meanwhile had emptied her Mass in one long draught. She sat her 'Stein' down, looked at me and smiled, "are you sure you wouldn't have rather had a milk?"

I escorted her home; she was the daughter of a professor from the University of Munich.

One day in the spring of 1937 my corporals and sergeants came to me.

"Staberl, we want to go to the Bieranstich at the Nockerberg."

That was the place where at this time of the year the newly brewed beer of the famous brewery was sold and all of Munich went there to have a good time, listen to umpah music, and drink Stein after Stein. I did not need much persuasion, one does, after all, have to experience local customs and when in Rome do as the Romans do.

Right outside our barracks was the stop for the tramway. We just about filled one wagon. By the time we arrived at the Nockerberg the police had already been warned that a wild bunch was coming. We had been quiet and orderly in the tram. At the Nockerberg we drank our beers without drawing undue attention to ourselves – but on our way back we went through some of Munich's pubs, singing and marching over tables, playing 'Simon says', and nonsense like that – all the time followed by the police who were watching us carefully. They escorted us into the tram and back to the barracks.

We were lucky no one found out about our escapades. Our commander would not have appreciated our unbecoming behaviour. On the other hand, other than making a lot of noise and behaving like a bunch of silly adolescents, we did not damage anything besides, perhaps, our image. I would not have allowed any destructive or serious misbehaviour of my men. I would have stopped real misconduct in a flash. Marching over tables is stupid but harmless. We surely had a wild and wonderful time at the Bieranstich at the Nockerberg.

My sergeants and corporals approached me one day with complaints about their lieutenant who treated them unfairly. I tried to get to the bottom of it but everyone involved clamped up and I got nowhere. Not long before, the commander of the battalion, with whom I had a very good relationship, had told me if there ever was a problem not to hesitate but to come to him. Consequently, I went to him with the accusations the men had laid on their leader. He investigated and found out the truth. The two officers were found guilty of their charges and received a severe dressing down and an official reprimand. This caused the officers and other superiors to get very upset with me because I had not followed procedure but had gone over their heads and directly to the top. When it had all blown over, the commander told me that he had wanted to recommend me for the Officers school.

"But", he said, sadly shaking his head, "you have loused up your chances to get the approval of these officers and they will never recommend you. Haefner, you have come to a dead end. There is no future with you here anymore. Really sorry."

So, I quit the Waffen SS even though I had a four- year contract.

And what to do now? I had two possibilities: I could go to the Gestapo or to the Grenzueberwachung, the frontier police. The Gestapo had a certain tinge and taste to it – it was not an organization I wanted to be part of, so I signed up with the SS frontier police. They welcomed me with open arms because they loved to get people who had experience and were knowledgeable about what was happening. My first placement was in Kiefersfelden, opposite Kufstein.

Frontier police guarded the Austrian and Czechoslovakian borders, and they took in refugees from both countries. The National Socialist Party was forbidden in Czechoslovakia and was not very popular in Austria and sympathizers of the party often got into trouble in these countries; often they were persecuted and so many escaped into the Reich. You can see that the SS border police were very politicized at this time.

*** Ernst Hallerwedel, whom you will meet later on in the chapter 'An Austrian Connection', was one of these men who escaped from his own country, Austria, into the security of the German Reich. ***

Our job was to take these people in and prevent their falling into the hands and bureaucratic net of the regular border police who might have treated them not with as much understanding as we did. We did not ask too many questions but passed them on to the SS from where they were usually assigned to a certain camp and then quickly released. Older defectors were integrated into communities, the younger ones usually joined the Waffen SS.

We were supposed to aid the German border guards. They gave us field grey uniforms, but of a different hue than theirs; ours was smoky colours. Then we worked together with them. Not much was happening on the roads; we were mostly on the railway stations where we did passport controls. An agreement with Austria allowed me to travel to Innsbruck and check passports on the train until Kiefersfelden – in other words we checked passports in Austria. I did much travelling during this time.

I filled my post to the best of my abilities. I had acquired a St. Bernard dog, Rigo, who went on patrols with me. The very first time he had accompanied me, he took off and galumphed into Austrian territory. That could have led to problems. After that I always kept him on a leash. Rigo was a huge hound. He could pull me along with the energy of a steam engine – my tongue hung out further than his after such a race. He looked gigantic but he was one lionhearted softy. What he liked most was riding with me in the sidecar of my motorbike. We made quite a pair!

Of course, we were instructed about border legislation and conditions. Perhaps at the beginning we were too strict and too harsh in adhering to all the rules, but then they told us, not to forget that we were not only officials but also humans. We were told never to forget to be a 'Mensch', a human being, at all times. I have always tried not to forget this bit of very good advice and to do my work accordingly.

In the fall of 1937, the frontier police were dissolved and absorbed into the German border police. I kept my rank since the police were organized much like the military. I was now a Kriminalangestellter, a criminal officer, occupying the lowest position as a civil servant in the bureau of criminal investigations. I had an arm band on my uniform which said 'Grenzpolizei' or border police.

When the year 1938 came around, the number of border police and also its powers increased because there were now radically different conditions at the border. Times had also changed in the Reich where everything had become tougher and more tightly organized. The border police were taken into the jurisdiction of the Gestapo – and this is how I ended up taking orders from the Gestapo after all.

The Grenzpolizeischule or academy for border police had been founded in Pretzsch at the Elbe River. Because I had already experience at the border and a certain rank, the commander ordered me to transfer to Pretzsch. There I worked first as a Zugfuehrer, platoon leader, which made me responsible for thirty to forty men. I was in charge of their general training. I specifically did the weapons training which included theory and practice with the pistol, the rifle and automatic weapons. There were four such training groups at any one time at the school. The man in charge was an SS Obersturmfuehrer, or First-Lieutenant. He was not really interested in the practical side of the school, so in short order I was in charge of arrangements for food and lodging and the daily odds and ends not only for my own platoon but for all four.

The school was a regular police academy. The men had to learn theory about the law, criminology, about arresting people and how to do specific policing. A course lasted three months. After the men passed the exam they were Kriminal Assistant, this was the lowest rank of the police. They were now civil servants. From Pretzsch they were sent to positions at the border or to a post of the Gestapo – since everything was now within the jurisdiction of the Gestapo.

Meanwhile I had also inserted an ad in the newspaper, indicating that I was interested in making acquaintances with young ladies. A girl responded to the ad. Her name was Irmgard; she worked in an office in Halle. When I met her for the first time, her sister Erika was also present. I rode my motor bike to visit the two girls.

*** This young lady was to be my mother. As a youngster I could not hear enough about the courting of my parents. Naturally my dad was not so forthcoming but invariably my mother would offer two stories: 'Both your father and Rigo, his huge St. Bernard dog, were wild about riding the motorbike. I would sit behind Gustel, arms closely wound around the driver, and Rigo sat in the sidecar, eyes closed in absolute ecstasy, fur, ears, lolling tongue and slobber drifting in the wind behind as the machine barrelled down the roads. What a chaperone we had! I was so in love. It happened that your father had visited me one evening. When I got up for work the next morning, I did not feel like eating anything, my head was still in clouds; I was dreaming about every word he had said to me. I put on my coat, I got into the tramway and drove to work. I arrived at the building, I entered the office, I took off my coat to hang it up – and there I stood in my slip. In my dreamy world I had forgotten to put on my dress.'***

One day I got the order to get my men ready for a different assignment away from the school. We prepared, took live ammunition. Next morning, we were loaded into trucks and off we went. I had no idea about where we were headed. During the day the drivers let us know that we were off to Austria which was about to be integrated into the German Reich. I was glad about that because I have always thought that the Austrians were Germans like we were but they never wanted to admit it. I figured they were no different from the Bavarians who had not wanted to be German either for the longest time. The annexation of Austria was to take place on the next day, March 14, 1938, and the Wehrmacht was on its way into Vienna.

It was a long and circuitous route we had to take – we were held up for a while somewhere – and there, suddenly right in front of us, Hitler drove by in his car and waved to the excited masses.

Once we had crossed the border into Austria we were warmly and noisily welcomed by the population. The people cheered and waved, they threw flowers and gifts into our cars and trucks. I saw one car filled to the top with gifts.

The Wehrmacht arrived in Vienna with planes at three o'clock in the morning, and we were there at four o'clock; we were the first ones in Vienna. After a good night's sleep we were assigned to guard and security duty for all the offices and all of the official buildings of the Sicherheitsdienst, the security service. My group was split up and the men were posted all over the city wherever we were needed. Once I had to bring a prisoner to Dachau. I did not know the man or the reason why I had to bring him there – that was none of my business; my task was to deliver him there safely – and that's what I did.

Slowly some of my men came back to me and our group increased in strength. It had become apparent that Jews who escaped from Austria to Italy, Yugoslavia, Hungary and Czechoslovakia, were plundered in the trains they rode. The new regime did not condone such actions; it frowned on hoodlums and theft. Whatever the Jews were not allowed to take, the border police officially took away from them. I was ordered to control the trains and make sure that the shady characters who were working in fake SS uniforms or were otherwise harassing passengers, were apprehended. I had to ensure that 'absolute Ordnung', absolute order prevailed in those trains.

I searched out which were the most important trains and not long after, my men, proudly wearing their field grey uniforms with the large arm band 'Grenzpolizei' written on it, controlled the trains leaving Austria. That is what we did for fourteen days – for the protection of the Jews when they left Vienna. Of course, from the minute that we were in the trains no transgressions whatsoever happened any more.

In October 1938 came the annexation of the Sudetengau. I cannot remember exactly where we were ordered to do security service but it was along the border close to the famous Spas of Marienbad and Karlsbad. When we were ordered to go to Karlsbad we found accommodation in a Czechoslovakian police station which was abandoned. We had no orders. After a day or two I told my men, "We cannot just sit here without doing anything. Many Jews are leaving the cities in a hurry, we are going to check their houses and apartments and secure them." We took some paper and wrote on it in large letters 'Gestapo' short for 'Geheime Staatspolizei", Secret State Police. Then my men went into the homes as far as they were open. They closed off water and heating systems, windows and things like that. When they left they hung our paper on the closed doors and affixed a large seal to it. After two days of that someone remembered us and we were ordered back to Pretzsch. Many particulars of that time are forgotten, but this incident I remember, because we had nothing to do and I had ordered to check on the homes. Securing the abandoned homes appeared to me the right thing to do at the time. It was a matter of bringing 'Ordnung' into a confused state of affairs.

In Pretzsch I resumed being the 'mother of the company' at the police school. I also got married at that time. Once I had a company from southern Tyrol who liked to sing a lot. They knew a wonderful song, 'Oh, how beautiful she is' with which they celebrated the beauty of their homeland. One day when I marched my men through town, they started to sing this song and it was close to where our apartment was. Your mother looked out of the window, blushing like a rose.

*** My mother tells me with a sweet smile on her face that from that time on suddenly most of the marching drills went past the house they lived in – and that the men turned their heads towards her window in salute and sang enthusiastically up to her. ***

Once I had a group of older gentlemen who had come for a refresher course. I remember I was given instructions to assign appropriate exercises and so I had made the hurdles lower and the races shorter. They all survived it very well. It was a busy time for me; new trainees coming in every three months bringing with them many problems and much responsibility. There were many challenges to my resourcefulness. Once we had to bore through the walls surrounding the moat in which the castle sat. The walls were two meters thick. At another time we had to construct a new ski jump which would pass the new safety regulations.

The first commander, a Standartenfuehrer, or Colonel, D'Angelo, was replaced by Colonel Dr. Trummler, who was not a military man but a very good manager. Trummler loved to drink after work. Your mother can tell you how many nights I did not come home because I had to go somewhere with him.

*** Aunt Erika had visited a few times in Pretzsch and she remembered with amusement that 'Life was darn hard in Pretzsch because when one came home late in the night after having had a good time, it was very, very difficult, to find one's house as they all looked alike in that subdivision – and sometimes Gustel, who really liked to have a good time, ended up in another house and they had to help him to his own home."***

Trummler told me that I was indispensable and that he wanted to have me around at all times. In 1947 he had to face a British Military Tribunal that subsequently found him guilty and condemned him to death. He was later executed. From what I have heard he was accused of giving orders to shoot down airplane personnel that bailed out from planes that were shot down or burning, but I don't know any details about it.

At the police school the candidates were trained to be border police, but of course the successful candidates could later join the Gestapo. The Gestapo's mandate was to ferret out people and organizations which endangered the security of the state. The men who worked as border police, because they were now under the jurisdiction of the Gestapo, had to discover enemies of the state and that often involved informers. When informers had fingered a person, we had to discover if the accusations could be substantiated or if they were without foundation. Often enough informers brought us people and we could find nothing. The police also had to find out groups who were not in line with the official directions. Often when people talked too loudly or too much, they were given a warning. They were hauled before the Gestapo and told in a stern voice that what they were saying or what they were doing, was wrong and could get them into serious trouble. Naturally they were also informed that a repeat performance could get them into a concentration camp.

Contrary to general belief, we, that is the Gestapo, could never bring anyone into the camps. Whoever was in a concentration camp was there because the State Prosecutor or the State Security Bureau or the Minister of the Interior, had put them there. The Gestapo could not do this on their own. But many cases bypassed the state prosecutor because the state did not have great confidence or trust in the existing justice system. Men in power handed specific cases over immediately to the Bureau for State Security and not to the justice system, and then the accused ended up quickly in the concentration camp.

Meanwhile the Germans had marched into Prague in March 1939 where they were not welcomed like they had been in Austria or the Sudetenland. Slovakia became an independent country, a protectorate of the Reich, which really meant we had our fingers in everything. The German invasion was not an action against the Czechs but rather an action against the Russians, who had started to rattle their sabers at the eastern border of Czechoslovakia – or so it was presented to us. The new protectorate was called Boehmen – Maehren, or Bohemia-Moravia. Of course, our police were there and because one could not demand that the Czechs not to be against us, they found plenty of subversive activities and there quite a few problems.

One day we were ordered to drive to the State Security Bureau in Berlin. I stood next to the door among other uniforms. I recognized quite a few of the many SS leaders who came together for this occasion because I had met them on previous visits to Pretzsch. And then Heydrich entered.

We were informed that the conditions along the Polish border had become untenable because the Polish continuously committed border violations and also because strong propaganda was in effect spreading the news that the Poles wanted to march to Berlin.

Of course, the real story was different: The Poles were very strong because the English in their fight against Germany had promised them unlimited help. We thought that the Poland problem was totally different: from 1918 to 1921 one and a quarter million Germans had their land expropriated by the Polish government. Originally these Germans had settled in areas where the Poles could not or did not want to live, many having settled there in the times of the Teutonic Knights, the Order of the German Knights, who drained the wild marshes many hundreds of years ago. Many of the Germans and also many of the mixed population were descendants of artisans brought to Poland by the Polish aristocrats and princes, this also a few hundred years ago, at a time when Poland's population was predominantly rural. And in 1918 the Poles took the properties of these people and sent them out of the country that they had considered their fatherland and home for hundreds of years. And they had to leave everything behind just as it was repeated again in 1945 where they had to flee once more with nothing but a packsack on their backs. With a background like this, we figured we had a legitimate bone to pick with Poland.

In Berlin they did not speak of war but it was strongly suggested that increased vigilance was advised along the border and that special preparations should go into effect to prevent further border violations. It was also agreed to have a contingency plan in readiness for possible new German refugees.

And suddenly Heydrich saw me and exploding in red rage he screamed,

"I have ordered explicitly that the lowest rank present today must be a captain, how come there is a sergeant major present?"

Poor Trummler who had asked me to accompany him got it with full barrels. Then Heydrich positioned himself in front of me and hissed with an icy voice full of fury in my face.

"You were privy to secret and classified information. I want to tell you that if you are not quiet and if you open your mouth, the way to a concentration camp is very, very short for you. And you had better believe me when I tell you, you won't live there longer than an hour."

I believed him.

From that day on my name was on the list of special 'watch-out-for-men' of the Gestapo – forever.

Chapter 10

HERBERT AND TRUDEL

Herbert married Trudel in November 1934. Trudel was five years older than Irmgard, Herbert's oldest daughter. A few years prior she had come into the teacher's house as Irmgard's friend. After her mother's death Irmgard had continued to run the household and look after the family. Tensions arose quickly because Irmgard and Erika could not get over the fact that their dearly beloved mother had been replaced – and replaced by such a young woman. Trudel received the full support of her husband in matters relating to the running of the house, the domain that Irmgard had held for more than a year.

Irmgard found employment in an office and left the house; Erika followed quickly after. It took some time before the girls returned again to their father's house.

Herbert became very involved in his new job as a principal of the large school in Heinersdorf. He became actively engaged in matters of the Party and rose to the position of a deputy Kreisleiter or district leader. His summer holidays were still spent paddling the rivers on his boat and camping, mostly accompanied by Manfred.

In the summer of 1937 his holidays were interrupted by a telegram that announced the death of his brother Bodo from a heart attack at the age of forty five. Bodo had been teaching mentally challenged students (making much more money than Herbert – as he mentioned in his memoirs!). Bodo had been a leader of the German Faith Movement, a religious faction which was rooted in the ancient Germanic Gods.

Herbert described his funeral in his memoirs:

'There was a large delegation in the Great Hall of the Concert House in Breslau. Everybody rose as we entered the hall and walked past the front seats. The high coffin rested on the podium. The SA did the honour guard. Behind the coffin a tall metal bowl held the flame. Behind the flame was the symbol of the German Faith Movement – the golden wheel of the sun emblazoned on a dark blue background.

We were moved as we listened to speeches, which in the face of death said so much more than the foreign Latin words could ever accomplish. Here spirit spoke out of our spirit. The sign of language is truth and draws with much respect and homage the veils of deepest feelings, more than could ever be expressed with words. A life is completed and returns to where it came from, the beginnings of all being. It is not the years that put value on a life but what it had contained. This is the reason that the life of the departed had been a full one even if though his years had not been many.

When the service was over everyone rose when we left the hall. The funeral cortege drove through pelting rain to the crematorium in Graebschen. We drove through the long street and past house # 85where he was born, past the house from where he made his first steps, past the house from where he went first to school, past the house where he lived when he left school. We moved so often during our childhood – always from one apartment to another. It is as if he had wanted to greet his childhood once more. Memory ran deep on this last trip.

Finally, all words were said. We stood with a raised arm to give the last greeting and salute to a tireless fighter for 'Germankind' and the German Man. I was shaking. The coffin disappeared – soundlessly closed the portals of eternity behind his coffin. It was done. Now he belonged to us only in memory. Soon fire will consume his body. Wordless we drove home.'

In July of 1938 Herbert and Trudel expected their first child. Herbert bemoaned the fact that the happy event would take away his much deserved recreational paddling and camping trip but Trudel talked him into leaving anyhow. He set out with Manfred and their Faltboot 'Edda' for a trip to the Schlesiersee, a large lake and Herbert's favourite.

They set up camp close to a youth hostel in order to be in easy reach for telephone messages about the forthcoming event. Herbert backtracked by train and returned on his motorbike so as to be independent and quickly mobile. But plans went awry and by the time Herbert received the phone call and raced on his motorbike to the hospital, it was two in the morning and his twin baby girls had already been born.

Manfred meanwhile had once more been left alone in the care of the camp guard. Herbert returned to continue his holiday the day after he saw Trudel and the babies, but was called back again the following day. One of the baby girls had died. Herbert lamented the fact that the birth had taken place in a hospital and not at home and that therefore not sufficient care had been extended to the premature infants. He thought that homecare would have been better for the babies. But little Sigrid, the survivor, thrived.

And then, as he sadly noted, there was not much time left for holidays…

Chapter 11

GUSTEL IN POLAND

Preparations started towards an offensive at the Polish border. I was stationed together with my men at a place which was called 'Drei Linden' (the place is called Hohenlinden in some reports, Hochlinden in others) which was the location of the border post. It was pointed out to me that we could expect incidences which could involve us in active combat. I thought that sounded serious enough and we prepared for military actions. Generally, that was a time when frenzied activity could be observed from commanders down to the men, nobody really knew what was being played out and all pretended to be preparing according to a definite plan.

Suddenly many men from Upper Silesia were conscripted. Upper Silesia was an area where for many years back in history conflicts had been played out between Germans, Polish and Austrians, each ruler of these nationalities claiming ownership in many a lost and many a won battle. These men spoke next to their native German an excellent Polish. The Wehrmacht took some of them, dressed them in Polish uniforms and equipped them with Polish weapons. They were slated to be used in a special offensive in this region.

I recognized some of the officers despite the smart and thin moustaches they had grown and despite the sideburns which were all supposed to make them look Polish. One day when there was a great inspection, they all lined up, all those many Polish officers, then they opened their rucksacks and pulled out woolen blankets which were inscribed with large letters: RSHA – Reichssicherheitshauptamt, the Central Security Main Office of the Reich. I can still hear the laughter that rose into the air. And then, strangely, they weren't used after all.

Our quarters were at an estate in Upper Silesia that belonged to the Count of Hohenlohe, its Polish name was Slavisziztsch, the German name of the estate was Ehrenforst. From there we went immediately on a foray to the border to find out about the place and situation. On the German side the land fell in a gentle twenty degree angle towards the valley where a little river flowed at the bottom. There was a bridge and the German border post and customs house. On the Polish side the land rose steeply. When we entered the German border house we saw it had been vandalized. A customs official, to whom I spoke later on, told me that Polish troops had frequently come by and when the German officials, for security reasons, withdrew to the hills, they had entered the house and destroyed everything within.

My task was to occupy the post and should Polish troops come by, to defend the house and its position. Now I knew: war games were on.

German military was already present everywhere. Then suddenly came the order to retreat because there had been a complete change of plans. A lieutenant-general told me that a retreat had been ordered because a huge area of the border had not yet been reached by German soldiers and it would take them another day to get here. Evidently, the war had been postponed.

In reality all actions had been delayed due to last minute discussions in Berlin with England concerning Sweden and Poland. Whatever the reason, I cannot tell and we were never told. Anyway, it all started in earnest the next day.

I was notified that another troop of border police was marching toward us and that they were to make contact with us and then to withdraw again. And so we set off. Well, I thought, now I am going into war; it was a peculiar feeling located mainly in the stomach area. My commander who was not a military man insisted on being part of the action. We moved down from the hills toward the border post on a road which was lined with trees on either side. I had given orders to march in the ditch; my commander was leading the way. I had sent some of my men to the left and some to the right, just to be extra cautious; nobody knew what was taking place down in the valley at the post. And suddenly, without a reason, and I have never, even later when I tried to understand it, understood why, I yelled, "Take cover!"

Instantly we were in the midst of a barrage of fire from the Polish automatic rifles with volleys of bullets whistling over us. I know if we had been marching upright, we would have all been dead – I ascertained this afterwards once it had become quiet again, by studying the trees; the bullets had hit exactly at the heights of our heads.

My commander was pale and shaking but by the time we entered the post he had composed himself again. Another troop of Polish soldiers must have entered the customs house since we last had seen it, because it was now totally demolished. Meanwhile the other group of border police arrived and after an exchange of pass words they left as ordered. At three in the morning, I received orders to clear the post and to withdraw to the right. I sent my men away, but contrary to orders, I myself stayed behind because I felt responsible for what was happening here.

And then I noticed that men were dragging figures towards the border post. I crept closer and noticed that the men from our security police were supporting figures in Polish uniforms, bodies that stumbled along on wobbly legs like drunken men. They marched them down into the valley, shots were fired, bodies slumped to the ground and were left there. Later I learned that the security police had taken inmates from concentration camps, dressed them in Polish uniforms, injected them with a sedative on top of the hill before marching them down to the post where they were shot. This action was named 'Konserve' or 'canned goods' because people were used like canned material, something that was canned and therefore dead.

The Press came and took pictures of the 'Polish bandits' that had been caught and killed as they were once again crossing the German border, providing explosive material and gruesomely realistic and discriminating photos that without doubt were adding fuel to the already emotionally charged situation. The Germans felt truly that the Poles were out to invade their country and even with only thirty or forty million people against our seventy million, including the Austrians, we considered them a serious threat, especially with their promised support by the English.

Of all the people involved in the incident I knew only the driver of the truck, but he just loaded the corpses up after the photos had been taken and drove them away. They were needed for later presentations. I knew the doctor whom I saw giving the injections, I saw him again in Patras, Greece, in 1944 where he was a medical doctor for the Wehrmacht. I never spoke to him about this incidence.

It was very unsettling watching these goings on. I saw that it was intended to dupe the German population and rile them up some more, but, remembering the perceived Polish threat, it was enough to make a clearly thinking person very confused. I said nothing because I was, after all, not supposed to have been present, I had witnessed the whole clandestine affair only by accident.

Meanwhile morning came and the truck with the bodies had disappeared. The Poles who had shot at us at midnight didn't stir. They were probably deeply asleep in their bunkers, believing they had scared us away. By now I had been informed that officially the war was to commence at five o'clock. I was ordered to leave the place at five. The first German tanks had arrived and driven down into the valley but they could not cross the bridge because it had been blocked by the Polish with all sorts of obstructing barricades. The drivers stopped their tanks and watched me twisting and ripping the whole mess apart – the taught wire was squeaking and snapping, metal pinging on metal, it was amazing how much noise it made. But the Poles in their hide-out slept through it all – lucky for me too, for if they had woken up they could have shot me like a clay pigeon on a platter. The bridge cleared I went back to my men and then back to Pretzsch.

Due to the successful action at the border post, I was promoted to SS Untersturmfuehrer, a Second Lieutenant – now I was an officer. I was also decorated with the EK II, the Iron Cross second class – but I am not quite sure for what. I did nothing extraordinary; it was strictly police work. We secured the house, took up connections, and that wire on the bridge – well I was a soldier what else could I have done? I was not ordered to do so, but it was something that needed doing and I did it. All was my duty.

I would have never told of these events at the "Three Linden", nor about the conference at the RSHA with Heydrich, if these topics had not been exposed already to some extent by the press and the radio.

*** The events my father told about are corroborated in Heinz Hoehne's book "The Order of the Death's Head" in the chapter 'The SS and Foreign Policy'. He names the place 'Hohenlinden', my father speaks of 'Three or Four Linden', but notes that he was not too clear about its name. The actions at the border posts were all staged by the Germans, but of course my father had not been aware of that at the time. ***

After my return to Pretzsch, I resumed my job as a sergeant major but I now had to look after a different kind of clientele. The security police had decided that in view of the war they needed to train more men for leadership positions at higher levels. For this purpose they started special courses to select personnel suitable to be trained for these positions later on in Berlin. Officers and superiors were invited to suggest suitable men for these courses, but high school students could also apply.

Applicants had to come to Pretzsch to sit for oral and written examinations. Out of 1000 men only 100 were usually chosen. To make a long story short – one day my superior suggested that I take the course myself. I went to the commander, gained his approval and was promptly accepted. I passed oral and written exams and was then ordered to go to Berlin for further studies. In my class were only eight men who did not have their high school diploma. I don't know how I was chosen to go to university with all these doctors and lawyers that were in the class. I had had only six years in high school. I was very proud.

I would like to add that we did have a fair share of men who applied for these courses in Pretzsch and who thought they could pass by saluting, klicking their heels, and shouting 'Heil Hitler' after every sentence – not one of them made it. So in January 1940 I went to Berlin to complete my high school matriculation and at the same time take my first semester in the 'Fuehrerschule der Sicherheitspolizei' the 'Academy for Leaders in the Security Police" where they trained criminal commissaries. I got myself a room and then hit the books. I sat for my commissary's exam and my high school matriculation; the latter was quite interesting as it had to be done in front of people of the Ministry of Education and they strongly resented giving the diploma to us men who received what they considered a condensed and shortened high school education. We took subjects considered necessary for modern general knowledge such as politics, history, civic education, mathematics and of course, literature. There was neither Latin, physics nor chemistry for us – which I regretted very much.

When we appeared for our oral examination in fall, the examiners approached the questions in such a negative way that finally the dean of the University of Berlin protested about the inappropriateness and unfairness of their line of questioning. Despite all the bickering I received my matriculation.

In the meantime my family had also moved to Berlin. We lived in Tahlmanstr.6, in Charlottenburg in a block where thirty to thirty five families lived. I took courses at the university. We had additional courses where experts from all over the Reich came to lecture. I studied hard. I had to write many papers (***one of them the famous one on 'Camels as Important Trade Routes' which appears in a later chapter***) and I did much sport. Sport was part of the course which was named officially " Lehrgang Anwaerter des Leitenden Dienstes" a course that prepared candidates for leading positions in the security police. Many of the other candidates were men with Ph.Ds, lawyers, Kriminalraete, a senior rank in the police, all of whom had been selected in Pretzsch. For the Kriminalraete this was an opportunity to climb to a higher level.

1940 passed and the spring of 1941.

Suddenly all candidates were transferred back to Pretzsch. I went back to being sergeant major with extra duties in other towns. More than two thousand

men had been brought together from all branches of the security police. We did our regular duties. We were not told anything but we gathered that preparations were leading to another military offensive. Generally, I was too busy to take part in guessing games as to where we were to be put into actions. Even the generals, whom I all knew personally and with some of whom I had very good relationships, volunteered no concrete information. One of the stories that circulated with excitement had it that we were to march through the Balkan, across the Bosporus and wind our way to Turkey and eventually end up in Egypt to make war there. Well, I thought, that sounds interesting and I left it at that.

One day mass vaccinations of all troops started. It took about fourteen days to give the necessary needles to all the men.

Slowly detachments were put together and larger units set up. It was all very secretive and nobody knew anything concrete and those who knew were quiet. Two days before this offensive was to start, I was ordered to Schmiedeberg, a small town not far away. One of the generals came to me and whispered in my ear that I was to guard the door. I could not understand why this was all so hush, hush. I was not allowed to let anyone other than certain people, which I knew, enter, under no circumstances because a very important conference was about to take place. Only then did I notice that guards were everywhere in place – it was a strange atmosphere. All was quiet as if holding its breath.

I have no idea what was discussed behind that door where I was standing guard but I never forget when the men came out into the daylight, their faces were white and like masks, they expressed incredulity, horror and shock. They had just learned that they were to be the leaders of the Einsatzkommandos in Russia.

Chapter 12

MANFRED AS SOLDIER

I remember my first day in the garrison so clearly: they made us wait three hours before they gave us something to eat. We were in the washroom to clean out our mess kits when suddenly the sergeant stormed in. Someone yelled: "Achtung!" and we all fell into military stance. I had a cigarette dangling from my mouth and abruptly he turned towards me. He was a brute of a man, someone we called a 'twelve ender', a veteran from the Reichswehr, his gut was hanging below his belt and his notice pad was stuffed in his breast pocket. He immediately hauled me to the company commander and told him of my indiscretion.

The Hauptman asked me, "How long have you been a soldier?"

I looked him straight in the eye and answered, "Three hours, Herr Hauptman."

"Oh man, get lost. Eventually you'll learn it."

A couple of days later when we were quartered in barracks, the sergeant came looking for five men to unload clothing from trucks. We were ordered to empty the vehicle which stood outside the supply room, not the one that stood right beside the ramp. That we did. We opened the doors, took the clothing out and piled it on the ground. The driver got into his cab. He drove away and we took off. A few minutes later the sergeant came towards us, hollering and swearing.

"Where are the idiots?"

We quickly vanished, hiding behind closet doors and under the table fearing that now something was really amiss.

"Where are the Schweinehunde?"

Well, we had to show up. He razzed us down royally.

"What idiots are you! What the hell do you think you are doing, depositing the clothing in the yard?!"

I looked him straight in the eye.

"Sergeant, you ordered us to unload the truck. You did not order us to bring it in."

He glowered at me, the red rising up his neck and face.

He never asked me for anything like that again – he gave very precise orders from then on.

But he did have it coming: I once had asked him why we newcomers were always ordered around so much and he answered, 'Well, you have to learn to take orders and you have to learn to take orders the way they are given. Don't ask, don't think, just follow orders. Leave the thinking to the horses – they have the bigger heads.'

I had remembered.

After about four weeks during which time we did practically nothing else but march; we were allowed out of barracks. There was a little village about three kilometers away. I had acquired a small NSU Moped, 98 cc. Curfew was at ten thirty. On our first free day I loaded a comrade up behind me and we drove to this neighbouring village and by three thirty I had consumed about ten pints of beer. At ten at night, I started to look around for my buddy but couldn't find him. I thought he must have left already and walked home.

So, I thought 'what the heck' and went and enjoyed another beer. Then I hopped on my moped and drove off. About two hundred meters before barracks I had to answer a call of nature. I laid the bike into the ditch, pulled down my pants and leaning on some bushes I did what I had to do and then I must have fallen asleep.

At seven in the morning, I was wakened by harshly shouted orders. There I sat, I had no pants on and the 180 soldiers of the company marched by, laughing at me.

Then the sergeant approached.

"Get up on the double!"

And I couldn't get up because my legs were entangled in the pants. The lieutenant strode over and pulled me up.

In front of the grinning soldiers, I had to pull up my pants and push my moped twice around the exercise yard around the whole company – running on the double! This done I was ordered to get back into barracks and change into working fatigues and run out to the shooting range. He did not forget to bellow at me that my punishment would be three weeks of confinement to the barracks for not being in at curfew.

The shooting range was three kilometers away. I changed, slung my rifle over my shoulder and ran all the way there, pushing my moped all the while. The lieutenant was right behind me.

By the time I arrived at the range I was totally out of breath. When the captain who was a perfect shot who always got his fifty seven rings without fail, saw me coming, he barked, "This man is next!"

He probably figured that I being so totally out of breath wouldn't be able to shoot straight.

I was going to show him something!

I shouldered my rifle, I held my breath and pulled the trigger.

First shot: eleven

Second shot: eleven

Third shot: a twelve

And then one more shot and after yet another one I had more rings than the captain.

He exclaimed, "in light of your shooting prowess, I will give you only three days 'confined to barracks'!"

In front of the gate leading into the barracks lived a jackdaw. She had learned all the parade commands barked out there. As we were marching by one day, eyes peeled to the centre of the exercise yard where the sergeant gave the commands, the bird sat on the roof of the small building. From the right came the order, "Company Halt!' and naturally we instantaneously and naturally stopped. Our drill sergeant was not amused and chased the cheeky bird away threatening it with dire consequences should it happen again.

One day our drill sergeant decided we had not sung loud enough during marching exercises and he figured out that it was me who did not give his all. So he drew me out of the marching column and ordered me to climb one of the trees that lined the exercise grounds outside of the wall, where the population was promenading and taking in the fresh air. Once I was up I was ordered to sing "Es ist so schoen Soldat zu sein", "Oh what joy to be a soldier."

I sang – what else could I do.

"Es ist so schoen Soldat zu sein..."

"Sing louder. I cannot hear you!"

"...Rosemarie..."

"Louder, I still cannot hear you!"

"... nicht jeder Tag bringt Sonnenschein..."

"Louder. Verdammt noch mal!"

And in desperation I yelled,

"Yessir. Rosemarie..."

And I heard the tittering of the perambulating crowd.

I was also one of those poor devils ordered to scrub the hallway with a tooth brush.

In the spring of 1942, the English Air Force dropped Czech partisans with parachutes into their former homeland. Not long after the hated Heydrich, who was the protector in charge of what was once Czechoslovakia, was driving in his car when he was wounded with a hand grenade by resistance fighters. He died a week later in hospital. No one was sad.

My first deployment was in the massive manhunt involving more than 20 000 German soldiers and the local police forces trying to find the assassins of Heydrich. Many days we searched and inquired fruitlessly. Eventually someone squealed and we received our first useful tip of their whereabouts. One interrogation led to another and eventually we found them hiding in the catacombs of a church. But we got only their dead bodies out – all had committed suicide.

My next assignment was in the Lueneburger Heide where we were trained in the use of antitank bazookas. That machine was a real Schwein, a real pig. The left and right tires of this weapon were of rubber and they were hellish things to pull and drag through the sandy soil on a run. And we got so little to eat! One small piece of fish next to three small half potatoes and a dab of mush and that was all. We never were able to eat our fill – and I was only eighteen years old – I was always so hungry. Luckily my aunt Tilchen, the wife of the forester, sent me bread. After four or five weeks of training we were sent to France.

I was sent first to Normandy. We had to cross a river in a rubber dinghy. A group of five men was pulling it with a rope across the water, another group of five was pulling it back again. We were eleven men in our group. I was gunner that day and I jumped in last. By that time the group across the river had begun to pull the rope which was moving the dinghy; I fell into the water. I was wearing a heavy steel helmet and cradling the very heavy rifle and I sank like a rock. But then I surfaced and with the boat far out of sight, I swam back to the bank and tried to pull myself out with one hand by grabbing some bushes and roots, the other hand of course hanging on to my rifle. I had just heaved myself clear of the water and straightened up when the commander suddenly appeared in front of me.

"Man, why don't you shoot?"

I tipped the weapon over and water and mud came pouring out. This made him realize that I couldn't use it as it was and I was ordered to clean the MG. Just at that moment a soldier passed by on a motorbike and yelled, "Hello, Unternehmen Seeloewe, Operation Sea lion, has started!"

That was the password to indicate that enemy forces were landing on the coast, in Dieppe.

We were loaded into trucks and roared towards Dieppe. About 30,000 Allied troops had landed, and it was there that I received my war baptismal.

We poured into the city through its narrow streets. My first posting was on a balcony and from there I could look down on my first Sherman tank advancing in front of soldiers wearing those flat helmets brandishing their bayonets. The driver of the tank noticed the fire my rifle made when I fired it. He aimed his cannon towards me, but the shot did not hit me but went through the door downstairs where it exploded. The blast downstairs was followed by a ceiling crashing to the story underneath, then the balcony followed when the ceiling collapsed and shortly after I found myself sitting on the street. The flat helmeted Canadians locked us in the cellar.

We could hear plenty of fighting outside. I believe our troops had entered our street when I heard boots marching.

"Hit this soldier on the carotid with the flat of your hand," I whispered to my buddy. "I'll take the other one and then we'll split."

Just when I was going to give the enemy a mighty whack, the door got pushed in by a troop of German soldiers. Our two Canadian soldiers raised up their hands.

I yelled, "Don't shoot! Germans!"

We took the two soldiers prisoners of war. That was the end of my time in Dieppe.

On my next deployment I was the second gunner and my task was to feed ammunition into the cannon. Gunner one pressed the trigger and gunner three was responsible for the supply. One day during a break from the weapons training, gunner one was smoking a cigarette. Halfway through it he handed it to me saying, "I don't feel so well – you can have the rest."

That little cigarette butt almost cost me my life. Next morning I woke up with a furnace blasting in my head and a throat lined with sand paper. The physician informed me that I had caught a goodly dose of diphtheria and that I would have to go immediately to the hospital.

By the time the ambulance had deposited me in the hospital I was almost delirious with fever and I only vaguely remember that someone rammed a needle into my posterior. I woke up two days later with a tube down my throat – the only way my air passages were kept open. Without it I would have suffocated. The good part came afterwards – I was sent home for three weeks convalescence.

During the time I was at home, my company had been transferred to Russia. It was March already, March 1943, when I again joined up with them. There had been fierce fighting; a whole division had been deployed here. So many soldiers of the Wehrmacht had just run away. They had suffered through the winter and then the muddy and cold spring and they were plain worn out.

We moved north and soon the biggest battle broke out at Kursk. 6000 tanks and 4000 aircraft and two million soldiers were thrown into the field. Stukas were diving and dumping their bombs then flying back to load up again. We advanced fifty kilometers every day. That was shortly after Stalingrad. After five days all came to a halt. We had captured Russian tanks and took them and other armoured vehicles with us. We painted swastikas on them and flew our swastika flags behind so that airplanes overhead would realize we were German.

We were ordered to attack again. We had modified their tanks by building flame throwers into their backs. They could spit out fire for 200 meters at a temperature of 2000 degrees. The Russians had dug themselves into holes. When a tank with a flame thrower saw such a hole the gunner aimed and the flames travelled into the hole and everything in it was burned, absolutely everything. This way we drove back the Russians another 150 kilometers. You must realize that the Russians when they saw their own tanks coming always thought it was their own and by the time the realized that we were German it was often too late. We took few prisoners; most were just shot, as did the Russians to our men.

Then all came to a halt again and we were ordered to retreat. This most horrible of all battles cost more than one and a half million soldiers their life.

Later in the summer at Maximovska, we had to comb the forest for partisans. There we did take some prisoners. One day I was in the tank with four other men. When we stopped I climbed on top of the tank. Next to us was a burnt-out Russian tank. I saw four dead bodies on the ground. I knew that there are always five men in a tank but somehow I didn't react to that. And here I stand on top of the tank and see a Russian not forty meters away. The moment he aimed at me my brain kicked in, and registered that there was one Russian missing. I threw myself off. But he hit me, just underneath the clavicle; and then another one right next to it. Blood poured out of my mouth and nose. Our driver bandaged me immediately with an airtight bandage because otherwise I would not have been able to breathe. And that is how I got to fly in a Fieseler Storch to the field hospital.

The hospital was in a huge tent. There were about thirty or forty patients, and doctors and nurses moving about. I got placed right away on the operating table and before I blacked out I heard the physician asking,

"What is the matter with this boy?"

I was just nineteen years old.

On awakening I heard above us the drone of a BE2, a Russian Doppeldecker, a bomber. Those bastards used to shut off their engines when they were going to drop bombs. They were able to glide quite a distance before dropping them. Done that they dove quickly and steeply down and used the rushing air to start their engines again. This one unloaded about twenty small bombs and one of them hit the operating tent and exploded about three meters behind the doctor who had just operated on me. He reared up and dropped dead. And I, half out of my mind because of the anesthetics, jumped off the table, ran about one hundred meters and then I collapsed.

A medic had run after me, picked me up and I ended up being sent by train to the hospital. There were about two dozen other patients stretched out on the straw in the freight car they used to haul us there. The worst was that there was nobody to bring us something to drink. Just imagine, it was July, it was bloody hot, and we all had lost blood and were very ill. When we arrived in Kiev on the station a fat purser showed up. We told him that we had been travelling all day and that we were dying of thirst. There were two medics in this train that carried about 2000 wounded. He just waved us off.

Finally, in the hospital we not only got enough to drink but also were put into a bathtub which we urgently needed. After that I went to convalesce in Eichstett in Bavaria.

In Eichstett they fitted two small hoses into the holes under the clavicle where the bullets had entered and slowly the pieces of the bullets drained out. They had tried to remove the remnants of the bullets but were unsuccessful. After all was done still two pieces were left behind and the doctor said that he would leave them there in the hope that it would in time become encapsulated – which it did. I still carry two bullets with me to this day – they give me no trouble as they are nicely encased. Only whenever I have an X-ray taken I always have to explain my souvenir from the war, my two bullets in my chest.

*** Here Uncle Manfred opens his shirt and proudly shows us the scars under his left clavicle. ***

Three weeks later I was able to walk again, the hoses were removed and the wounds were stitched and everything was healing nicely. I got bored and thought I should give soccer a try. On my first try-out I stepped on a pebble, not bigger than a chicken egg and I tripped. That resulted in a broken ankle and ripped tendons. Four men carried me back to the hospital. By the time my doctor looked at me, my foot was swollen like a devil's egg and my good boot had to be cut off. I had to remain for a few more weeks but eventually I healed and was ready for some more war.

Nuremberg, where I was sent next, saw me stuck in barracks from November till February doing book keeping. In March of 1944 I was sent to Estonia. We were bivouacking next to a river across from the Russians on the other side, when, at six in the morning a buddy declared that he felt like having a swim.

"Are you nuts?" I yelled.

"There are Russians over there and they are going to pluck you off the water like a sitting duck!"

We were safe in our ditch but the river was open and he would have been an easy target.

"Bah, this is too early; they won't shoot." He shrugged my warning off.

I was worried. He went cockily ahead and had a good swim. I saw the Russians on the other side and they, just like he had predicted, did not shoot at him.

After his swim he explained it to me: "It's like this, Manfred, from six in the morning until six in the evening there is no war for a very good reason: Behind our line is a huge swamp, a very treacherous swamp, and behind their camp is also a very dangerous swamp. Every day at eleven the food is carried through the swamp. Every man, be he Russian or German wants his dinner – so the Russians don't shoot us and we don't shoot them – heaven forbid we should hit the pots and have nothing to eat. That's what we soldiers have settled for."

We shouted greetings across the river to the Russians and they shouted back. We watched them build a bunker during the daylight hours and no shots were ever exchanged during the day. When night time came it was different – there was war – but never during the day.

All this came to an end when someone decided that dams and paths built from wooden beams would make traversing the swamp much easier. Some of us were sent back to headquarters. It was a long twelve kilometer march, especially the last eight which went straight through the wettest part of the swamp and if there would not have been corduroys laid already the whole area would have been impenetrable.

To make matters worse, during the night we got lost and suddenly the five of us entered a clearing with a huge fir tree in the middle of the place and a log house close by. We heard voices and saw some light and carefully crept closer and hid behind the fir tree. Someone opened the door and we could make out about twenty men inside the hut. We were definitely outnumbered and so we stayed quiet. After a while one of them came out. He was stone drunk and could not walk straight. He staggered to our fir tree and pissed – pissed straight onto one of my boots. Luckily it was dark and perhaps in his stupor he would not have noticed anything anyhow. We closed our eyes so he would not see the white. He saw nothing, zipped up and went back inside.

We left the place and were only half a day late to our destination. We had a field telephone with us and one morning it would not work. We had no choice but to use the field radio which was strictly forbidden because this way the Russians could pin point our position. We sent a message out letting them know that we were unable to use the telephone. I took off with two men, a machine gun and rifle, to find where the cable was broken.

I found where the wire was cut. Suddenly a moose came crashing though the bushes, snorting and with its head down. My two comrades hightailed and climbed the next tree. But I, a woodsman and hunter, knew about game and shooting. I stood behind a tree and shot, but in my excitement I missed. When I shot the second time the moose was only about seven meters away from me. I hit him in the top of the head and saw the bullet exit below. The moose ripped around and stomped back about two hundred meters and then went wild. He had wrapped the telephone cable around his legs and of course he snapped it. We raced after him; I knew he would not last much longer and I did not want to chase him through the bush. I told my buddies we would fix the telephone wire and wait. This done we looked for the dying animal. We found him shortly. I gave him a last shot and he was quiet.

We skinned it and cut it up and telephoned back reporting our luck. They came with a wagon and the whole company had good meat for the next two days. I felt so good and everybody congratulated me and made me feel like a real hero.

I had the huge antlers sent to Gruenberg. They weighed about fourteen kilograms. My father had a silver plate engraved with my name – ah – it is all gone now – only the memories are left with us – everything else is gone.

One day we had to go and get radios. We were sixteen men. The machines we used were quite ingenious. There was one that looked like a type writer, in which we could insert a cylinder which contained the code. When we got a signal, it contained the code. The code, by the way, changed every two hours. Two men took up the coded message when they saw the letter S lit up. The radiograms were transmitted by the code converter who dictated it to another one that typed it out. There was no talking involved. Another man had a larynx microphone into which he just mouthed the words without ever a sound being heard. These messages could be printed. It took about two minutes to decode a message. We even had direct access to Hitler's field headquarters in Eastern Prussia. Whenever I did the specified code, SSd, SSd, all radios had to get off the line. In case of an emergency, we had been ordered to swallow the code. When we wanted to send a message, we quickly put up the twenty meter high antenna, send the message and then took the antenna down again. We knew the Russians were on to us and quite able to intercept our messages.

We were ordered to pick up new machines which were better and wireless. We flew in a U52 from Reval, today's Tallinn, to Koenigsberg in Prussia. On the way one of the three motors of the U52 caught fire. The pilot declared that the extra three men had to jump to abort the flight. It was night and we were about 800 meters in the air and it was raining. We put on the parachutes and were pushed out. I almost shit my pants – I was that scared. I had never done that before. I somersaulted a few times until the line was straight and the parachute opened.

After what seemed a very long time, I landed in some bushes. I assumed my buddies were somewhere too. I noticed that there were little frogs in the water and around the bushes and they let out a tiny 'tac tac'. I copied them and it was not long before I heard the same 'tac tac' a few bushes away. We crept carefully towards each other, mindful of the many partisans we knew to be about in this area. The three of us re-united and I felt much, much better.

We snaked our way towards the highway and planned to flag down a car with our red flashlights. An officer stopped and after we showed him our papers which spelled out that we were to pick up the instruments in the Wolfschanze, Hitler's field headquarters. He realized that we had to pick up important communication devices and he aborted whatever mission he was on after he radioed to his own commander, telling him that we had to go to the Wolfschanze.

One day we drove to Memel. I was sitting in the jeep and because it had been raining in the night, the canvas above us was very tight. The driver decided to open the roof. He climbed out and started to fold it down. He fiddled with the metal rods on one side and I was on the other. Suddenly one of these confounded rods jumped and I found my finger jammed between the hinged tight rods. I pried it out but had to leave my nail behind.

See – to this day the finger has only a scrap of a nail.

*** Manfred sticks his finger in the air – "See - it still has only a scrap of a nail!" ***

I screamed like a banshee and bled like a pig. We put a bandage on because I had to take turns driving. Only by whacking myself in the back of my neck could I control the bleeding.

In eastern Prussia, I believe it was called Deutsch Hassenwitz, we came to the river Rus. The Russians felt so cocksure and safe that they went to bed at night in their pajamas. We thought we'd get them and planned a blitz offensive for half past three in the morning. With drawn bayonets and without a sound we ran towards the village at the planned time. They must have had some guards because suddenly shooting greeted us. We saw figures in nightshirts hurdling themselves out of windows and bolting off towards the fields. We were after them in hot pursuit, shooting with our machine pistols. I don't think many got away.

It was there that I threw up for the first time when I saw what bestial creatures the Russians could be. I have seen many dead bodies in my life, but that was different. There was a saw mill used to cut railway ties to their appropriate lengths. There was a huge saw blade and there laid a woman who they had sawn in half when she was still alive. But first they had cut off her breasts. I moved away and my stomach heaved and I vomited my guts out. There and then I swore that I would never take a Russian prisoner. From that day on I shot every Russian soldier – and I don't mind telling you that.

When I was a prisoner of war a Jewish commissioner asked me how many Russians I had shot and I answered him that I had not bothered to count.

No, from that day on I shot them all. They had killed so many people, old men and women, hundreds of them. I saw them there, hundreds of them and we have photos. It was awful. But I have proof.

We were moved to Silesia about twenty kilometers away from where my uncle was a forester. I had to take a four week course to become a corporal. The testing was done on January 6th, and by six in the evening I had holidays. I walked the twenty kilometers through the heather, a pistol with me, a rucksack with some provisions and my shaving kit. I followed the lines I had drawn in my map until Heiligensee where I had spent so much time as a child. It was half past one in the morning when I silently entered the barn. It was January and it was crackling cold. My aunt had one cow, she mooed and that felt like a welcome to me. There I lay down, drew some sweet-smelling straw over me and slept. I slept well.

In the morning when my aunt came to milk the cow, her little dog sniffed me out immediately. She was more than surprised and very moved when I told her that had I slept in the barn with the cow because I had not wanted to bother her at such a late hour.

I spent four wonderful days there and then drove to Gruenberg to visit my father. Another few days were spent with an uncle and we even went hunting. The idle days did not last long. On January 20th I received a telegram ordering me back. That was in 1945.

My company had already left when I returned to barracks and I had to join another one to catch up with mine. We got to Oppeln and the Russians had already crossed the Oder River and we saw action right away. The Russians had surrounded us in Landsdorf and our losses were heavy.

In March I had to cross a river which was chock full of ice. I had my steel helmet on, and loaded down with weapons I waded into the icy water. It was deep in places and I had to swim. With chattering teeth and shaking with cold I pulled myself onto dry land.

About one hundred meters away stood an old farmhouse. I marched quickly towards it. I knew that the population had fled from the Russians in great haste leaving most of their belongings behind. I thought I could perhaps find some dry underwear in there. I went into the living room. Suddenly I heard two Russian talking. I quickly jumped to the side thinking those bastards would shoot through the door and that is exactly what they did. They were scared to open the door so they just shot through it. Across the door was a mirror and that got shattered. I scrambled out of the house and through the barn into a small outhouse. As they came bolting out of the house, I aimed my pistol and shot them dead.

I went back into the house and looked for dry and clean underwear. I fitted myself out quite nicely with civilian clothing – my uniform was dripping wet – and left the place as a private citizen with a steel helmet on. I also took some beautifully smoked sausages with me.

My next order was to take my men and break out of the area we were. I led them along a clear cut path in the forest which was about eight meters wide with a ditch on either side. Half of my men walked on the left in the ditch the other half walked in the right. I spotted a man standing about two kilometers ahead of us. He yelled at us in Russian, asking for smokes. I answered him back in Russian – momentarily forgetting the fact that I was wearing a German helmet. He lifted his pistol, fired in the air and ran off into the forest. And then the shooting started.

There were about fifty Russians twenty meters away from the road. I collected all my men onto the right side of the road. The Russians threw a grenade which I caught and promptly hurled back. It exploded nicely among them. Good thing it didn't go off in my hand or else I would not be able to tell this story today!

When the melee was over, I counted seven of my men dead. I had been shot too, but only grazed. There were a couple of holes in my helmet. When I figured the skirmish was over, I crossed the street and damn fool I am, I tripped over a root and fell on my back. When I looked up there was a Russian standing over me ready to ram his bayonet into me. Well, I shot him before he could haul out for the deadly swing. He dropped dead nailing my jacket to the ground with his bayonet. I pulled it out. The Russians took off when they saw how many we still were.

We had to get back to the German line. We were carrying five badly wounded comrades. Some Germans hid in the forest but because it was getting very foggy nobody was shooting because they did not want to shoot their own men. We were about one hundred meters away from our line when they started shooting at us. They thought we were Russians coming out of the forest. I yelled at them that we were Germans and then they gave us fire protection left and right and we made it out.

I reported to the commander.

"Twenty two men reporting back, seven dead, five wounded."

"Alright," and then with a look at me, "Ernst, you look a mess."

"Sir, we were engaged in hand to hand combat."

Only then did I look at my clothes which were bloody and in tatters. And only then did I become aware that I was bleeding too.

I was always lucky. Here I had got myself into automatic rifle fire and not one had hit me.

We eventually broke out of our enclosure and were moved to the Hirschberg area. We were in Langendorf about eight kilometers north and stayed there until May 8th. We built trenches and on May 7th we were told to kill a pig.

The farmer said, 'The Russians will be here pretty soon, so let us slaughter the pig because if we don't, they surely will and this way at least it will be us who get to enjoy it'.

Neither my buddy nor I had ever slaughtered a pig but we certainly were game.

The farmer tied the pig's hind legs and my buddy held it. I took my rifle and shot it between the eyes. I got it in there quite nicely but then the bullet came out at the bottom of the head, the pig took off like an arrow dragging my buddy, who still held the rope tightly wound around his arm, behind. The porker knew nothing better than bolt straight though the manure pile. Some fifty meters away was the garden and the critter started rooting around for vegetables. But her joie de vivre was short lived, I quickly mounted my bayonet onto my rifle and with my buddy still holding on to the pig and urging me on, I bayoneted her through the heart. She dropped dead. We stuffed ourselves with roast meat.

The next morning, we destroyed all our vehicles and organized some horses. The locals had long fled and their houses stood empty. We hung mines in doors, put them in stoves and wherever we thought the Russians would touch it. Safely at a distance we watched many blow up. On May 8th I rode with eleven men through Warmbrunn and on.

At twelve o'clock we heard of Germany's capitulation. We took a rest – but we got no joy from it. We rested and spoke of all the many dead and wounded comrades, of all the hardships and losses – all now in vain. We were very disheartened. Now the real Huns are coming we said. We said they were not human beings, more like animals: cruel and brutish. That was our opinion of the Russians.

I remember once I met a wagon with refugees heading west. An old man was driving, a young woman with two children sat in the wagon. Suddenly a jeep with two Russians drove up. They stopped and one of the soldiers swaggered up to the wagon and dragged the woman from the wagon toward the ditch. He didn't make it very far – my bullet got him square in the head. The second saw it and wanted to run away. But I got him too. The children were screaming and the old man was shouting and thanking me with tears streaming down his old and wrinkled face. The woman kissed my hands.

This happened in March of 45. There still was war. After the war they were not much different. One day as we were riding we met a train filled with refugees. The Russians stopped it, swarmed in to rape the women and rob them of their last possessions. By that time our troop had grown to 150 retreating men and we attacked the Russians. They took to their heels. We were mad and we were desperate and we hated them. The train collected its passengers again and rolled off to the west.

Chapter 13

ERIKA TEACHES SCHOOL

Konrad, my husband, had been a teacher in a small village in East Prussia. He also had a little house there. He wanted me to go there to teach in his stead. Such things were possible during the war. He made the necessary arrangements and I went with him when we came back from our honeymoon. Our time together was soon over and he had to leave to go back to Russia and I prepared myself for the classroom.

The student population had actually increased because children had been evacuated from Berlin to places all over the country. This village had received some too, some of them were big boys – they were taller than I was. I still remember my first day – I was scared stiff!

When I entered the large classroom, the students rose and blared, "Good morning Mrs. Loeffler."

I marched to the desk, took the register and smacked it down on it's top.

"Ruhe! Silence!"

They sat down and remained quiet.

I was trembling in my boots. My voice settled down as I was reading the names from the register and the children rose and sat down again.

I had to teach grade one to eight and I got better at it by the day. The kids were good and I started to love my new job. We had a sports club and we went swimming and we marched – of course.

When we marched, we sang: "Heute gehoert uns Deutschland und morgen die ganze Welt!'

'Today we own Germany and tomorrow the whole world'

That is how we felt – and I did too.

One day the superintendent, who knew and liked Konrad, came for an inspection. The children behaved themselves and all went well.

At the end he said to me, "You know, Frau Loeffler, perhaps you lack the formal education and training to be a qualified teacher, but you teach by instinct. I recognize you have the inner qualifications and know how to be a very good and successful teacher. Keep up the good work."

That made me immensely proud.

On our marches we often marched past a prisoners' camp. Many of the inmates, prisoners of war, were from England. During the day they had to work in the fields but at night they were locked up in fenced- in barracks. I had a little dachshund who always marched with us. Naturally she was very nosy and inquisitive. I guess the prisoners liked her and eventually she dug a hole under the fence and visited the men. One day she returned with a bar of chocolate tied to her collar. Imagine – a Hershey Bar! After that she became somewhat of a friend of the prisoners and went visiting quite often.

One day the Ortsgruppenleiter, the local Party official, found out. He called me to his office.

"If your husband were not a lieutenant in the army and at the front in Russia, I would arrest you and haul you to the concentration camp," he barked at me.

He accused me of fraternization with the enemy.

I tried to tell him it was only a little dachshund that crossed the fence of the prisoners' yard and not me.

He told me that if he heard about one more such incident he would 'personally shoot the damn cur!'

From then on I locked my little Dachsi up whenever I went to school – and that was the end of the lovely chocolate bars!

I taught for three years in that little school in Neudorf.

*** Then suddenly Aunt Erika becomes strangely quiet and we can see that she has slipped away from the present and entered some place and time far back in her life. Her eyes focus on her cigarettes; she lights one and resumes her memories.***

There are many things I don't understand – there is the supernatural – I know there is something there: One day I was replying to Konrad's letter I had received the day before. He was near Stalingrad and he had written to me that they would start the offensive. I had a premonition and I sat down and started to write to him – and suddenly I put down my pen and started to cry and I couldn't stop. I got up and marked the calendar. Two years later when the major of his company found me, he told me that Konrad had been badly wounded. The field hospital where he was taken to was soon surrounded by Russians. Russians were known never to take prisoners. The major told me with a face of stone that the Russians were known to take patients from the hospitals, throw them on the ground outside and then drive over them with their tanks. Konrad had told me in one of his previous letters that he would commit suicide rather than fall into the hands of the Russians. That is what he had done. The major could not tell me an exact time but he could tell me the date – and that was the very date I had marked on my calendar. I had just known.

I also knew when my mother died. I had dreamt the night before she died that I was in the funeral procession in Heinersdorf – where I saw myself walking behind the coffin, crossing the rail tracks. It was raining and Manfred was by my side. And that is what happened a few days later.

I believe that we can feel if someone we love is in danger.

We had so little time together, Konrad and I. Perhaps three months. I don't think my father ever knew him. But your mother did. He visited once in Berlin and he brought her a small gift – a silver sugar spoon with a handle that held a piece of oval amber.

*** I hold my breath, get up, open the glass door to the book shelf and hand Erika a little spoon, blackly tarnished silver with a piece of oval amber in its handle. Erika looks at me with huge eyes.

"That's it. Oh my God! That's it!"

My mother had given me the spoon for a keep sake the year before but never told me it's story.

Erika takes it gently and cradles it in her hand.

She is very silent – and so am I.***

Chapter 14

"THE FATEFUL YEAR"

This is the title given by Herbert to this chapter in his memoirs – and regrettably the first three pages of his handwritten notes are missing. Here is an excerpt.

'…Especially the old Germanic sacred place interested me. Here, near by in the year 9 A.D. had been the battle of the Teutoburger Forest where the Germanic warriors defeated three Roman Legions. Many years later Charlemagne, the Saxon Slayer, had destroyed the ancient symbol of Germanic belief, the Irmin Column, in his quest to christianize the heathen Saxons. Today a stone relief stands here telling the tale. It depicts the standing cross next to the Germanic sacred column.

Shivers went down my back when I looked at the seven hundred year old stone. Deeper than his creator had imagined, it told of the past and it foretold the future. Then he had thought that the cross was victorious over the heathens. Truth is deeper: Christendom which is foreign to the Germanic nature, was victorious over Germanic faith, turned over all old values, and taught to appreciate 'verartetes', that is degenerate and unnatural things; it taught the people to despise the ideas that had been valued. It taught humility instead of manly pride, submission instead of freedom, it made the faith surmount the ties of blood, taught the unimportance of the beautiful world and focused on the dream of eternal happiness of the soul. It elevated the sense of a servant and broke the sense of honour of the free man.

This is how Charlemagne and the cross of Christianity broke not only the Irmin column (author's note: the Irmin column was a sacred tree trunk venerated by the old Saxons) but also our innermost beings. This is how it had for centuries emasculated and murdered our Volk which really only today, after the misery of the total collapse of our people, shows clearly how far it has progressed.'

In the year 1939 Herbert had to interrupt his paddling holidays once more to attend the funeral of his father who had died of tuberculosis in his 79th year. A day later he joined up once more with Manfred who again had stayed behind, and both resumed their holidays.

On the suggestion of his superintendent, he applied for the principalship of the Pestalozzi School in Gruenberg, a large industrial city in Upper Silesia; he assumed the post in April of 1940.

One of the main reasons he was glad to relocate from the small bedroom community of Heinersdorf to the city was the fact that the leader of the local branch of the Party, an uneducated and pompous man and also the mayor, was the cause of many disagreements and problems. Both his sons played large roles in the Hitler Youth. Herbert recalls that they damaged and destroyed school equipment and furniture during some of their meetings and Herbert, in the capacity of principal, withdrew the permit to hold gatherings at his school which did nothing to endear himself to the bureaucratic Party official.

On his introduction by the Superintendent to the teachers of his new school, Herbert was faced by a wall of faces who, he felt, were forecasting his failure to do justice to administering such a large school. After all, here was a principal who had taught in the country for twenty nine years in small schools only, now presuming to be head of sixteen teachers. They were anticipating an unavoidable disaster. But Herbert proved them wrong. He was a very capable principal who introduced many new ideas and methods including the unheard-of innovation of ongoing inspection and evaluation of the staff, a notion which was originally much decried. His school became a well run and a very good school indeed.

The government soon rewarded him and offered him the position of superintendent despite the fact that he was a few years above the specified age limitation and installed him in that position in June 1944. He notes that the only drawback of the new job was the fact that he now could no longer enjoy the long summer holiday a teacher was entitled to. A superintendent got only three weeks – barely enough to go paddling or camping.

Trudel's parents had taken over the restaurant at the railway station in Birnbaum and they did very well financially. Herbert praised his parents –in-law for their generosity in supplying the teacher's household, he wrote: 'So much food such as butter, bacon, meat, flour, sugar, geese, ducks, chicken and what not came our way from Birnbaum from 1940 to 1944. One cannot imagine how those extra supplies improved our life in Gruenberg – in fact, I must confess, that we lived better during the war years than many years before.'

Trudel and daughter Sigi even stayed at a Spa with money provided by her generous parents, the Haemmerlings. Herbert visited them there and wistfully described its luxury, a luxury which in earlier years he could never afford due to of lack of money and which he now would not afford for ideological reasons.

He noted in his diary: 'There is one thing I regret today: During the war the population was exhorted to buy only what was absolutely necessary. Slogans like 'Do your duty to the fatherland and don't go shopping. Put your money in the bank instead' were printed and broadcast on the radio. We were told that to buy unnecessary things increased the general lack of goods and impoverished the people in general. So, I did buy only what I needed, with the exception of the clocks. I was a clock nut and I bought parts for dozens of clocks which I put together and had ticking away in every room of my place.'

'I put all our money in the bank. The girls were long on their own and my payments for Manfred stopped in 1942. We had two savings books and we watched our accounts grow and dreamed of all the wonderful things we would be able to buy once the war was over. I watched in fascination how I was making money by having money, without as much as moving a finger to work.'

'How we were betrayed. After the collapse of our fatherland, I lost everything, every penny was gone – and what made me bitter was that the people who had gone and spent their money and bought furniture and jewels or art or whatever, still had these goods. I feel they laughed at me then and they laugh at me again today.'

Chapter 15

GUSTEL IN THE EINSATZKOMMANDO

It was early in the summer of 1941 when we were informed that we were to leave for Russia as part of our practical training. The war against Russia had already started three days before and we were soon on our way. I was in the Sonderkommando 4a, with commander Standartenfuehrer, Colonel Blobel. I was the designated transport officer.

I had of course no qualms about a war against Russia – that was for me an ideological necessity. The National Socialist Party opposed communism. The reason for the war was that we wanted to avoid the spread of communism in Europe. We were taught that the goal of the communists was to move westward. The communists had vowed to stop only once they reached Gibraltar - and since Germany was on that path they had to be stopped. For us, communism was a non-issue; we had studied it long enough and in detail in the university courses I took in Berlin.

We pushed forward with our two trucks and cars towards the East. We were about seventy men, members of the Gestapo, the Kripo, or criminal police and the SD, the Sicherheitsdienst or security service. We had extra personnel like truck drivers, cooks and other helpers who did not belong to the Gestapo but were necessary for our actions, they had been hired especially for this event. Most of them were German but a few were what we called 'Beutedeutsche' which translated means 'Loot Germans'. These were German men who had lived previously in Poland or Czechoslovakia, and local jargon had affixed that name to them. They were good orderly men who did not live up to their uncomplimentary nick names.

The roads to the east were plugged with marching troops, wagons, supplies, and a lot of motorized units. Often we came to dead end roads because the field police had blocked off cross roads. Despite the traffic and the problems on the road, we succeeded in overtaking a complete German Infantry Division on the road into the region of Samosh, in Poland.

After Samosh I talked with Colonel Blobel, my commander, whom I knew quite well and with whom I had a good relationship. Blobel explained to me that we had to take harsh measures against communist functionaries, and that we had to proceed against them not with the regular and recognized criminal and judicial procedures. And then he told me also that 'der entsetzliche Befehl' and he used those very words, the heinous order had been given that all Jews had to be shot. He made it very clear to me that he was totally against the action and that he had the greatest unwillingness to do what he was told to do. There were many more that felt the same way and did not want to do what they had been ordered to undertake. For example, the director of the Higher SS and Police leader of the SD who had Kommando 6, did not want to do it either. But they were put under pressure. There were so many men who thought it was wrong and a bad thing to do.

When we arrived at our destination, we first reported to the general whose army was there. In our case that was Wehrmacht General Field Marshall von Reichenau; he was in charge of the 6th army. The Russians also had a sixth army stationed there. I was ordered to accompany Blobel, maybe because I had the best military background, the longest service record and that little black-white-red ribbon attached to my uniform. After introductions and other niceties were taken care of, Blobel informed von Reichenau about our orders and that our position was to be in the rear of the army. This is how it had been planned: Einsatzkommandos were put in the rear.

"Well," said Reichenau, "Fine and dandy, but I do not need you in the rear, I need you in the front."

Then we knew. And von Reichenau also told us in no uncertain terms, that "I am one hundred percent responsible for everything that happens in the total area where my army is located."

This was something that was very important to me later in my trial. Some did not want to remember those words, but I had not forgotten them.

Reichenau explained to Blobel that because he was the Commander-in-Chief, he was responsible for everything and that he would therefore order us to be active in the front and execute there the normal tasks of the security police. He also added that as far as the shooting of the Jews was concerned, he was to be notified about any larger action.

I think this is the place to explain why we had come to Russia and what we were supposed to be doing. Our task was twofold: firstly, we had to find out who were the partisans and prominent functionaries in the different regions and where they were. If they were present, we had to apprehend them and deal with them. We had to investigate if cells of resistance were forming and then we had to stop them. The Wehrmacht did that too, but they were only interested in the military ramifications, whereas we had the military as well as the political resistance in mind. And then, of course, we had been ordered to deal with the Jews.

Reichenau told us to keep up communication with his communications officer, a Hauptman Lulai, and this is how I became liaison officer between the army and our operational group.

Since we were supposed to be stationed in the frontal region of the sixth army we packed up and moved forward. First, we came to Sokal, that was the border between the former Poland and Russia where the war had started four or five days ago. I should add that Poland was under German governance as Generalgouvernement Poland. My duty was to report to the local commandant who informed me that in the last five days more German soldiers had been shot than had fallen when they crossed the border. It was our task to find out who had shot these men and because there were no longer regular troops present, because it was now our territory, it was concluded that the actions were most likely committed by communist functionaries.

I had to travel south to the head of the Einsatzgruppe C, Major General Dr. Dr. Rasch. Einsatzgruppe was the collective name for the detachments 4a, 4b, 5a, 5b and 6. My job as a liaison officer required that I had to report to him the order given by General Reichenau with reference to our placement in the front rather than in the rear of the army because this opposed orders previously given and was therefore of considerable importance. I also had to communicate to him where we were stationed at the present time. Upon my return to Sokal, I was informed that thirty persons had been arrested for the killing of the German soldiers. The Wehrmacht ordered them to be shot. The order required these prisoners to be executed by the Einsatzgruppen.

We had a rule that each and every officer of the different units had to give the order to shoot at least once so that afterwards nobody could say, 'I was not there and I had nothing to do with it'. So, my turn came too and I had to give the order to shoot. I also had to check afterwards if the men were dead or required another shot.

In Sokal, when I was at the Higher SS and Police Leader South posting, I found out that the Russians had caught four German airmen who had jumped out of their burning plane and had them massacred in horrible ways. According to the Wehrmacht there were witnesses to the atrocities who later reported the incidence. One of my colleagues had to report to Reichenau. Reichenau ordered that in retaliation 3 000 Jews were to be shot.

Here a little bit of background on Reichenau. Perhaps because of my professional background or because I am just a sociable person, I have always talked to all the people I have met. Rank did not mean much to me and I have heard many a great story told by men of all ranks. Once, some of them told me that when they were crossing a border river, the soldiers suddenly saw a man standing in the middle of the river, rifle in his hands, and that man was wearing a uniform with red stripes, in other words, he was a general. When they had started crossing Reichenau had taken a rifle from one of his men and waded through the river together with his soldiers, right in the front line. His soldiers were, of course, mightily impressed.

Reichenau was not your typical general – he was not a paper pusher, he trained and was a very physically fit military man. One winter when he exercised in subzero weather, he suffered a severe heart attack. It was decided to fly him back to the Reich. On his way to the hospital his plane crash landed and he died.

Soldiers told me how surprised the Russians were at our sudden advance over the border. They knew that something was about to happen. There were after all enough troops and machinery in action and movement for a long enough time not far away from the border. It is impossible for people not to notice something like that. However, when the final attack came, they were totally unprepared and so it happened that Russian tanks still sat in their garages in a town fifty kilometers behind Sokal – a very easy target for the advancing Germans who could either destroy or take them without much resistance.

A German tank division was ordered into action at Charkov. Again, the Russians were not at all prepared for such a blitzkrieg and only after our men were far behind Charkov could the Russians muster any kind of organized resistance and could fight back.

Blitzkrieg sounds really impressive, and it was, but it was not easy, especially once we had to support the troops which were so far advanced. We actually had a lot of problems, our motorized units were always far ahead, but the foot soldiers were very slow. The SS Leibstandarte, for example, was fully motorized, in fact they had so much power that they continuously ran out of ammunition. The SS was motorized but there were still divisions who moved only on foot or with horses – again the logistics were difficult because horses needed extra rations if they were to be kept moving at top speed.

Our next stop was Zhitomir. First, I had to go south and liaise with Major General Rasch. Rasch himself was a dreaded man. He was extremely disciplined and expected absolute obedience from every man. He made it clear to his men that he expected all his orders to be executed without question and in case of any doubts, he would certainly see to it, that pressure and force would be applied so that the order would be carried out. I knew him from the Poland offensive. Here he was commander of Einsatzgruppe C. These units were units of the security police and as such called Sonderkommandos in contrast to the complete unit which was called Einsatzkommando.

Rasch ordered me to carry on and see the Higher SS and Police Leader South. This was the head of the combined police forces; it included the security police and their Einsatzkommandos and all the police regiments. We had regular police regiments. They were former regular police taken from their posts in towns and cities together with other people who were put into these regiments. There was one more – the Police Regiment Russia South. The leader of this troop was

SS Obergruppenfuehrer Jaeckeln. He also had the absolute command over the Waffen SS here. I saw him only once. This was the place I had to go to and take up connection with the liaison officers of the security police. I cannot remember the reason for it. Well, on my way there, I heard that this police regiment had been ordered to shoot 42 000 Jews in Broskorov. Unfortunately, it was the main task of these men to shoot Jews. At another place they had to shoot 36 000 Jews. Later in my trial they were trying to implicate me in these actions, accusing me to have been the officer in charge but I was able prove them wrong.

Russia South was an area that encompassed a southern strip of Russia, all of the Ukraine but not the Black Sea region.

Having fulfilled my task in the south I went back to Zhitomir. We did not relish ferreting out Jews of which there were relatively few. Meanwhile Generalfeldmarschall von Reichenau had made his quarters in Zhitomir and I was hardly needed as a liaison officer anymore, whenever there were things to be discussed, Blobel himself went to Reichenau. I was given other duties.

One day in July or perhaps August, a dirty and tattered looking Ukrainian man in bare feet came to our office. I asked him what he wanted – of course we had an interpreter with us.

"Well, Sir, it is time for the harvest. The wheat is ripe but we have no one who will give the order that harvest may begin."

I asked him where he came from and he told me that his home was ninety kilometers away from Zhitomir.

I was ordered to go and check it out.

With a driver and an interpreter, a 'loot German' who had been a lieutenant in the Polish army and who spoke perfect German and also Ukrainian, I boarded our fancy car that had been built for the Autobahn but definitely not for Russian country roads and drove out to the village of this peasant.

On arrival we were informed that only an hour ago the last Russian troops had left – our German troops were still another ten kilometers further west. Between the driver, the interpreter and myself we had two rifles and one automatic pistol – not a lot to make war.

The elders of the village showed up. Much talking established the fact that, yes, it was time for the harvest.

"Good, it is time for harvest."

"But what about the order?"

"What do you mean – order?"

"We need an order to cut the grain."

"No problem. We will give you the order to cut the grain."

"But how are we going to cut the grain?"

"What do you mean?"

"The Russian soldiers have unscrewed the jets of the carburetors of our tractors and thrown them away. Now we cannot use our tractors anymore."

I sympathized with them and told them so. I also explained to them that we were in no position at this time to help them with spare parts, repairs, or good new German tractors. We told them that they would have to harvest their grain just like they had done it in the old days, with scythes and sickles. I appointed an elder as man in charge and ordered the rest of the population to obey his instructions.

I inquired if there were any Germans living in the area and was told there was one living outside the village. A German woman lived there with her children, the village did not think much of her and I did not inquire anymore. There was also a teacher. To my amazement I discovered that here, in this poor little village, ninety kilometers away from the nearest city, the local school offered German as a foreign language.

The teacher spoke a pretty rough German, but she was easy to talk to and very willing to do so. I asked her to show me her books and was surprised to see that they were written in quite acceptable German, of course, the contents were totally in the communist line. Reading about German capitalists and imperialists poked my sense of duty. As a member of the security police, I had to do something about further dissemination of such subversive material in this school.

From Blobel I received permission to see Reichenau. I gave him a report about the tractors and the wheat harvest.

"Well, something has to be done about that," he said and gave orders to his troops to do what was possible to help the Ukrainians to get their harvest in. We had special orders that allowed troops to be deployed in special cases to help the local population.

Blobel was informed about the teacher who taught German in that small village. Blobel in turn reported it to the Minister of Education who consequently ordered that a sample of those books be sent to Berlin. This meant that I had to travel back to the village to collect the offending books. The poor teacher cried and pleaded with me until she understood that I was not going to take away all of her precious texts but only one of each.

The official line with the Ukraine was that it should be free of Russia and that we were to do everything to enable a good relationship with the Ukraine. When the region became a civil administrative unit and the Gauleiter Koch of East Prussia was installed, he did exactly the opposite of what we did for the local population. In Rovno he was known to have hit Ukrainian men in the face with the riding crop. Heinrich Himmler himself tried in vain to remodel a Ukrainian town into a German one. At university where we had discussed such issues at great length, it was always pointed out that the Ukraine was the homeland of the Ukrainians, and that they needed room to live and the opportunity to grow the foodstuffs for their existence. We always discussed the reality of the present and if change occurred what would be the consequences for the future.

I learned from the Ukrainians that some of our soldiers behaved like rogues towards the Ukrainians causing them harm and much grief. Once a beekeeper came to me and complained that some soldiers had willfully destroyed all of his hives.

"If they had told me they wanted honey, I would have given them some," he cried.

I also discovered that some Germans stole chickens, or geese and even calves. These small animals were the property of the individual peasant and not property that belonged to the communal farm, so the loss of this livestock was grave indeed for a peasant family. I also learned that some soldiers had shown requisition papers, in fact, I am sorry to say, I have seen very many of them that had been signed with a swear word or a curse. It was upsetting to my sense of order.

I marched immediately to Reichenau and informed him about this unacceptable behaviour of these soldiers. He got very angry and gave the order that the paymaster had to go to the villagers and reimburse them honestly with the full amount of the requisition if the villagers could prove that livestock had been stolen.

As a police function, I considered the upholding of good order a very important task. I was relieved when Reichenau put it right.

Things were happening at this time in Zhitomir also. An old communist functionary, who was hated by the population, had been found and taken into custody. This man was hanged in the presence of a couple of hundred Ukrainians and about two hundred men of the Wehrmacht. Afterwards 150 Jews were to be shot. They had been brought by trucks and they were made to walk about 400 meters to the place of their execution. This was my second time I had to witness an execution. I had to watch how people were lined up and how they had to wait for their shot. As they were arriving, I noticed that they were bloodied and seemed to have been beaten. The soldiers had torn off branches from trees and as the Jews were walking towards their place of execution they were beaten by the soldiers; hardly anyone arrived who was not bloody.

I again went to Reichenau and reported what the men of the Wehrmacht had been doing to those Jews. Reichenau gave orders that from now on neither civilians nor ordinary soldiers were to be present at executions.

This event came up in my trial too. The chairman of the trial rose and said, "Herr Haefner, this execution happened not because of an order from Blobel, this was an execution ordered by the Wehrmacht." That is how it was. That was another execution ordered by the Wehrmacht.

I was often absent due to my being a communications and liaison officer. The execution of Jews was not a mandated task of the Wehrmacht, but here they did it anyhow. Shootings had even been announced with placards and posters which informed the population that an execution was about to be taking place and the reason for this action. This I had not known until the judge told me at the trial.

The Wehrmacht gave the orders for execution and we had to do it. They did not shoot them – we had to. One example is the so called Kommissarsbefehl. This command ordered the Wehrmacht to find out which of their prisoners were Russian or communist functionaries (Kommissare). The Wehrmacht took many prisoners and it was not difficult to find out who was a communist functionary because they were usually well hated by the population. When they were pointed out to the Wehrmacht they were seized and we were ordered to shoot them.

About ten kilometers from Zhitomir was a place where a police regiment shot about ten thousand Jews. Our detachment was not involved, but I knew about it because I had to go there as a communications officer.

In the area where we were stationed the water was not safe to drink. Our men suffered from diarrhea and therefore truck-loads of mineral water were brought into our camps. One day I drove past a truck and trailer filled brimful with mineral water. The truck would be parked there for a long time; all four wheels had been removed and the truck was blocked up on stones and lumber. I investigated and was soon enlightened by grinning soldiers, that they had to look out for their own spare tires and wheels, and so consequently, whenever they came upon a vehicle without a guard, they quickly helped themselves to the required parts.

I have seen many German vehicles with four or five extra wheels securely tied to the top. Once Rasch's car was stripped when he was in a meeting. Rasch expected not only absolute obedience, absolute perfection and efficiency from his men; he was also mean. I pitied the driver.

The end of August (1941) had come and it was obvious that Kiev was ready for occupation. Some of the troops were already hundreds of kilometers ahead of us. I got the order to set up a small detachment and join with the Wehrmacht in order to be present at the occupation of the city. We moved east and took up quarters at Belaya Cerkov. I reported to the Wehrmacht field commander, an Oberstlieutenant from Austria and inquired about my task in Kiev. He stared at me and thundered: "Here are a lot of Jews, and as everyone knows, your job is to shoot all the Jews. I give you the order to shoot all the Jews of Belaya Cerkov!"

We had absolute order from Rasch to do whatever the Wehrmacht told us to do without hesitation or delay. The order of the field commander was relayed to Blobel. Blobel did not want to shoot Jews. He, a good man and a veteran soldier from the First World War, found it incomprehensible to shoot civilians just because they were Jews. In his distress he went and he did the one thing that soothed his brain – he got totally drunk. In this state he threatened to shoot the first Wehrmacht officer who crossed his path. My colleagues alerted the doctor of the Wehrmacht who quickly came and gave him an injection to quiet him down.

On returning from my trip, this was the first thing I was told. I realized in what dangerous situation Blobel had got himself into and that I had to do something to get him out of it. While I was there Blobel regained consciousness and immediately demanded to have his pistol back. He shouted, "I'll shoot the first Wehrmacht officer I meet!"

I tried to calm him but had to ask for the doctor to administer him a second sedative. I put Blobel in a car and after getting into contact with the Wehrmacht, I drove him to a sanatorium. We had a special field hospital that dealt with psychological and mental cases. Many soldiers who had experienced shooting and blood, had seen comrades smashed and torn apart and die, could not handle it. Many suffered severe traumas from it and many just could not take it anymore. That was the place where I took my commander. I did it on my own because I thought it was necessary.

On my way back I drove through a small town. In the market place was a huge excavated ditch. I asked what that was for and I was told that Jews had been shot there. Then I could see it for myself. A Hauptman of the Wehrmacht and a few soldiers were walking alongside the edge of the ditch. The Hauptman was walking like a demented automaton, a heavy rifle in his hand directed straight down into the ditch. A voice came from the ditch. A Jew who cried out in German - they all spoke German.

"Gebt mir noch ne pulle!"

"Give me another one!"

And the soldier aimed at the spot where the voice came from and fired another volley. It became quiet. I left quickly after that.

Back at the office I learned the following: After I had, left my colleagues had telephoned Dr. Dr. Rasch and told him what had happened with Blobel. Rasch called me and said to me with an icy voice, "The order of the Wehrmacht is to be obeyed and the Jews have to be shot. If you will not do it, I will organize that you will be shot by your own men and if they refuse, I will get the police to shoot you. If they refuse, I will get the Wehrmacht and then I will know for sure that you will be shot."

Now I knew. We had to do what the Wehrmacht ordered us to do.

Colonel Blobel had to face the military tribunal in Nuremberg. The

Americans condemned him to death. He was hanged in Landsberg in 1951, together with Braune and Ohlendorf. Those three men followed one conviction: we will not implicate anyone else. An honest and orderly German does not pass blame on to another. So they were quiet. Blobel never exposed that the order to shoot more than 33 000 Jews in Kiev came from Reichenau, that is from the Wehrmacht. Braune did not talk and neither did Ohlendorf.

When I asked him in Nuremberg why he was quiet about this he answered me, "If I speak, all the generals who were down there in the area would have to face the tribunal."

That's how naïve he was. The Wehrmacht got away with everything they had done. One process took place – and nothing else, nothing in all these years. The SS were singled out as the scapegoats.

I want to give just one example to show how the Wehrmacht was involved and how they were never made responsible for their deeds. One day the Rumanians decided to rid themselves of their Jews. They rounded them up and 40 000 Jews, men, women and children, were locked into seven large Russian freight trains. The trains were pushed over the border into the Black Sea region which was at the time occupied by the Wehrmacht. There was not a police regiment or SS within ten kilometers of the borders. Someone on that side decided that they did not want the Jews either and pushed the trains back into Rumania. Naturally the Rumanians did not want the trains back. The locked trains sat on the track in boiling August heat.

After twelve days water from the decomposing bodies started to run from the wagons. I was not a personal witness to this event but soldiers, that is soldiers from the Wehrmacht coming from this area up to Zhitomir, men I did not know, stopped me when they saw me and told me about this.

Later on, I inquired if that tale was true. My lawyer affirmed it. I spoke about this incident in my trial but not one word is in the written record of the trial, not one word. Every word that could compromise the Wehrmacht had been expunged. Anything that I have said that could in any way implicate the Wehrmacht was swept under the rug. Notable though is that in my trial a Wehrmacht lieutenant made this statement: "Yes, our commandant ordered that in every village that we entered, all Jews were to be shot."

Back to the events in Belaya Cerkov: one day I was ordered to shoot the Jews of Belaya Cerkov. This was one thing I did not want to do. I phoned Blobel and he threatened me with military court, something he would probably not have been able to enforce, but he used it nevertheless. We had a long discussion and in the end we agreed that his company of Waffen SS together with my thirty Waffen SS would do it and report daily back to me. Bluntly put, it was the job of the

Waffen SS to shoot the Jews. This was communicated to the field commander and all went as planned.

The next day I meet the field commander on the street.

"Lieutenant, the male Jews are all gone now – that's finished. Now it is the women's turn."

"Sir, I wouldn't touch the women."

"Haefner, those women have to go."

There was nothing I could do.

After a few days I met him again. He was very upset.

"The women are gone but now I have more than a hundred children on my hands. I don't know what to do with the children."

"Have you asked the locals to take them in?"

"Yes, Haefner, I have tried that – but they all refused. They don't want to have anything to do with them."

I told him that I could not help him and I did not want to help him. He had brought this on himself. He found a place to house all the children and three men of the Waffen SS had to guard them. Of course, it was not long before those children began to cry and sicken. There was nobody looking after them and they were scared, and thirsty and hungry.

A church minister of the division happened to come by and he found out about the situation. He immediately went to the Division headquarters and reported the incident blaming me as the man mentioned by the Waffen SS as being in charge. Of course, he was unaware that these men were 'on loan' and under orders from the Wehrmacht field commander, neither was he aware that the children were there on orders by the field commander and not on mine.

As this was happening, I wasn't even in Belaya Cerkov. Rumours had been circulating that in an unoccupied area between Zhitomir and the Dnieper River Russian troops had been sighted. I wanted to find out what was going on and since the Wehrmacht knew nothing I decided to investigate myself. My driver and interpreter refused to come along so I went alone. But I could not find out anything and returned not much the wiser.

Upon my return I was immediately summoned to the Division office. I went and was instantly berated because of the children. They also told me that as we were speaking, the children were being shot. I retorted, probably in the same rude voice they were using, that I had the permission but not the command to shoot all Jews, even Jewish children but that I had not given any order to shoot the children. I marched out and went to the place the shooting was taking place. There, the men from the Waffen SS were shooting the children. I stopped it immediately.

I went back and notified Blobel about the happening. The Wehrmacht had reported in a letter that the SS officer – that was me - had let one hundred children starve for days and then had let them be shot. Naturally Reichenau called Blobel. Blobel listened to my side of the story and then went to Reichenau.

Reichenau called a conference. Blobel, Lulai, another officer, the field commander and his communications officer were present. I told them the whole story. The field commander glowered at me as I disclosed his part in the sordid affair. His communications officer received a severe dressing down from Reichenau.

"Such a situation has to be taken care of in person and not through letters. Letters will be kept and become a record and then everybody will know."

Reichenau ended the meeting by stating that in view of the awkward affair, there were still twenty or thirty children alive – that is what he called an awkward affair – they had to be dealt with in a suitable manner. That meant of course, someone had to shoot them.

Reichenau ordered us to do it. Blobel said to me, "Obersturmfuehrer Haefner, see to it."

"Colonel, I cannot do this. My men of the Waffen SS who are supposed to do this are volunteers, men seventeen or eighteen years old. I do not want for them to have on their conscience for the rest of their lives that they shot little children."

This caused another lengthy discussion.

Blobel asked me, "Do you refuse to execute the order of Reichenau?"

I answered, "Let the men who captured the children be the ones to shoot them."

That was accepted by all.

We had learned that the field commander had engaged a number of Ukrainians as police aides. They were the ones to do it. I was to be notified when it was to happen.

The time came and they told me to be there. I went all by myself without my driver and translator. At the place there was a small ditch. Then the Wehrmacht came with tank cars loaded with the children. The Ukrainians came – and they were shaking too. And I had to be there and watch it. The children cried and screamed. When the men started their shooting, a little girl with dark hair, as old as you at that time, my daughter, came to me and took my hand. I needed all my strength. And then I had to check that all the children were dead. When it was over, I had to report to the division that it was all done. I would not wish this day on my worst enemy – never – never. I am still not over it – 55 years later.

*** My father was twenty nine years old on that day in 1941. Today, as he tells the story he is eighty four years old. Tears are rolling down his old face and he covers his eyes. Tears are rolling down my face too. There is nothing I can say. Absolutely nothing.

After a long, long pause be breathes deeply and continues. ***

Well, I had to go on. We had to explore the area. Here and there was oil. Oil was interesting to the Wirtschafts-amt, the department of economy. We sent off reports. One dealt with an experimental station that grew tomatoes. Well, all just ordinary SD work.

While we were still waiting for the occupation order of Kiev, I took the new colleague who had joined me recently and we went on a foray to the front. We motored towards Kiev until we reached a large artillery position from where Kiev was bombarded. We drove further until we reached the main fighting line where we parked on a spot which had a great viewpoint to watch the action. The first post warned us that if we would venture over there, we would have to count on being shot at by the Russians.

"Thank you, we are aware that this is the war."

We carried on beyond the German post. To the left was a little forest which the Russians had under fire. From the right a German reconnaissance troop appeared. I commanded the officer to move his men down to the road to benefit from the tree cover. At that moment the enemy fire stopped. I said to my comrade, "Time to leave, they are rearranging their aim." We weren't gone fifty meters when the first barrage hit exactly where we had been a few seconds before.

We went into a small village for some rest. Outside the settlement we sat down besides the car to eat our sandwiches. I started munching wondering about the horrible sweet and rotten smell that surrounded us. It was a hot day and the flies were buzzing crazily. It did not take me long to realize that a dead Russian soldier lay close by.

Two days later the occupation of Kiev began. We were ordered to enter the city only when it was cleared for all administrative units. One or two houses were burning at the outskirts of Kiev; the rest of the beautiful city was unharmed. We made our way down to the Dnieper River because we heard shooting. The Germans were shooting across the river, the Russians were shooting back, but neither one bothered us. We had a look at the buildings that we were assigned to later officially occupy. We made it safely out of the city – no one stopped us or asked questions.

The next day I officially entered. First, we moved into our quarters and then the men did. Outside the city on a hill stood a palace which we requisitioned for the Higher SS and Police Leader. I told my Waffen SS to move up there to guard the place.

The house where we were quartered was previously the residence of the Russian Secret Service. They must have shot many people down in the deep cellar, because along the wall, just at the height of human heads; were deep runnels imbedded in the cement, the place where the bullets had broken the cement.

The following day I reported to the commandant of the city, a general hailing from Wuerttemberg by the name of Eberhard, and started to confer with him about the job we had to do here. Then something else happened: Kiev started to burn. Eberhard was very upset, he had a lot of water, of course, but very few firemen and he desperately needed equipment like hoses and pumps.

"These are the winter quarters for the German troops," he said. "They cannot burn down. We have to do something."

He immediately requested urgent help from the Reich. Regiments of firemen were sent with trucks and equipment from Frankfurt and many other German cities back home.

Kiev kept burning.

In the afternoon I wanted to enter a certain part of the city but the Wehrmacht stopped us explaining that a row of houses had to be dynamited to make a fire guard. We complied, of course, and waiting for the explosion to happen, I noticed about one hundred meters away a group of order police transporting a group of men, some of whom carried gasoline cans. Later on, I discovered that the police had caught the men red handed as they were emptying gasoline cans and then threw matches on it; they were Jews. The Jews had caused the fires in Kiev. What happened to these people, I don't know. I'm sure I can guess.

Meanwhile, Eberhard had long given the command to shoot all the Jews of Kiev. I did not want to have any part in it but could not get into contact with Blobel who was still back at Zhitomir. Eberhard summoned me and read me the riot act.

"If you do not make sure that your commander gets here soon, I will haul you before the military court."

There was nothing left to do but get into my car and get Blobel by myself.

Upon our return we saw that Dr. Dr. Rasch and the Higher SS and Police Leader had arrived with two battalions of order police. There was a conference which I did not attend. When the upper brass talks, a little lieutenant is not asked for any input. Interesting was that the superior of the commander of the city had sent only one officer. He clearly did not want to be involved in this business with the Jews. Eberhard, on the other hand, was gung ho on it. Together they decided that the Jews had to be collected and transported to a designated place where they would be shot. Posters were printed and distributed. They called all Jews to be at a certain place at a certain time, to bring papers and travelling provisions. The posters also indicated that non-compliant persons would be shot. I couldn't help myself thinking that if they just knew – either way they would be shot.

Rumours had been circulated about a possible relocation of the total Jewish population and they believed it. The collection points were close to railway stations. The people came quietly and orderly. On arrival they had to leave their suitcases and bundles, they were made to take off their clothes – these things were collected to be later on distributed as Volkshilfe, the aid for the poor Germans. Then the Jews were moved to the deep gorge through which a small creek ran. The walls either side went steeply up. That was Babi Yar.

We, the SD, had one troop for shooting. They were men from the Waffen SS. New methods had been developed to shoot the victims. No longer were they made to line up to be shot on command simultaneously, now they were made to kneel at the edge of the ravine, one closely next to the other, and the men walked by and shot each and every one with a pistol shot in the neck. The victims toppled over and down into the gorge. The order police used ten troops of police to shoot.

I watched it from a distance. I listened to the screaming and crying and the shouted orders from the police. We were strongly forbidden to interfere with the order police and we wanted to avoid trouble because even though the organization of the whole affair was done by the Sonderkommando 4a the actual shooting was done by the order police.

This went on for three days. Three long days. The brook at the bottom of the ravine ran red with the blood of the people killed. It really ran red with their blood. More than 33 000 human beings were shot there. At the end the bodies were laying, stacked six to eight meters high. The next victim lined themselves up without a fight close to the edge of the ravine, they knelt down and bent their heads and waited for their shot. The police stood waiting for the next victim to get into position.

I had nothing to do with the actual herding and shooting – everything went according to plan. I could not take any longer what was going on and I went as far away as I could.

'Was soll's, was soll's'. What could I do, what could I do?'

When mealtimes came a small troop of security police took the place of the Waffen SS so they could go and eat.

Rasch appeared on the second day with his entourage. Luckily, I got wind of it and was there, because if I would not have been there, for sure Rasch's first question would have been, "Where is the supervising officer?" Officially I was not the supervising officer. Blobel had said to me, "Go out there so you can get used to it."

I reported to Rasch and then tried to step back and disappear again.

Suddenly the high pitched and shrill voice of Rasch cut through the air.

"What is happening here – they are still moving - you have to finish them off!"

"Major General, these people are all dead. Nobody survives a shot directly into the neck."

"I give you the express command!" shrieked Rasch.

*** As my father is telling the story, his face changes as does his voice which mimics the screeching and threatening voice of a mad man. ***

What could I do. I took my pistol and gave each one of the two dead Jews one more shot in the neck. I could see that Rasch was at the edge, he was shaking and as pale as a ghost. This was the first time that he saw in reality what he had ordered us to do. It was so simple to give orders from behind the safety of one's desk – and now he could see how it was for those men who had to do the dirty work.

Something I have often thought about: I found it difficult to understand the meekness with which the people suffered their fate. Very few escaped. One woman escaped by faking death. She crawled out in the night and escaped. She eventually ended up in Norway and came from there later on to appear at the trial.

Two days later we were ordered back to Berlin again. We all were. We were informed that the experiences in Russia had been part of our 'practical training'. The purpose of the events we had participated in was that we were supposed to prove ourselves.

We had been ordered to do things which, under normal conditions, we would have never done. We had been trained to obey orders even though we personally might have thought them repulsive and disgusting, unpardonable, unjust and just plain wrong. I did many things which I did not want to do. I must admit that I always tried to remain far from the field of action and not to get involved in certain activities and I certainly did not volunteer.

*** I have read accounts of the events that occurred in Belaya Cerkov and in Babi Yar and I realize that the tale my father shared with me was a very considerate and much sanitized version in which the brutality of the murders, the anguish and despair, the suffering and pain of the hapless victims took up little place. It was after all a father who told his daughter of his part in these most horrible and heinous events. ***

Chapter 16

GUSTEL IN THE GESTAPO

Our studies had been only temporarily interrupted by 'Operation Barbarossa' and now it was back to the books again. We, who had been split up into different detachments, all came back together at school.

So I went back to the books for another year. In the fall of 1942, some of the candidates were pulled out of the courses and put into regular service. I was one of them. I had become Kriminalkommissar (the lowest rank in the upper officer class of the criminal police). I was again a first lieutenant and my first posting to the Gestapo was at Innsbruck

Work at my assigned field which was 'Heimtuecke', or homeland security, started with a bang. One day the Gauleiter, who had a direct telephone line to my desk, called me and said, "There is still one Jew in the Gau. (a Gau was the main territorial division of the Nazi Party. There were 42 Gaue in the Reich) This Jew must be done away with so I can finally honestly say my Gau is free of Jews."

I informed him that I was new at the job that I came fresh from school and that I needed a bit of time to become acquainted with the local conditions. This I was granted. I went to my superior who warned me to treat the Gauleiter carefully because he was a stickler for details. My boss explained to me that he knew the Jew who was the highest decorated Jew from the First World War.

With unmistakable sharpness in his voice he said, "He is a hero. He was decorated for great valour – are there any more questions?"

"Nein, captain."

Then I learned from my colleagues that my superior, the captain, had brought this Jewish man from Berlin, he was a so called 'Schutzjude' a protected Jew; of course, he was protected only by an ordinary person and not by the highest leaders.

Finally, I had to let the Gauleiter know that I would take care of this business. I seesawed back and forth for about six months. I pleaded with the Gauleiter that I needed more time or had some other excuse. In all honesty I could not tell him that my superior did not want the man killed. I protected my boss and took a lot of flack for him – and that wasn't always easy. I once asked the Jewish man to come to my office. I wanted to talk to him but unfortunately on that day something very important had come up and I never got to speak to him. I regret that to this day.

Later I was posted to another place, but whenever I could manage to come to Innsbruck I inquired and was always told that the fight for this Jewish man's life was still going on. Only now the Gauleiter had become nasty. One day, late in fall, my boss phoned me and informed me that he had been forced to shoot his friend, the Jew. The Gauleiter had put so much pressure on him, and as we know the line from a Gauleiter to Himmler is a great deal shorter than that from my superior to Himmler, that he had to do something. Because he did not want his friend to go to a concentration camp, he had him committed to a Arbeitserziehungslager, a camp where people who had gained the attention of the Gestapo were held for some time for work and re-educational purposes. That is where he had him shot by the camp director.

This story became public after 1945. My superior, a captain who by then had become a major, had to face his judges. He was sentenced to life in prison. A few years later he hanged himself in an Austrian prison. The camp director, the man who had shot the Jew, a man whom I personally found very unsavoury, had to face his court in Germany. I contemplated for a long time whether I should come forward and speak to his defense and explain that the guilty person in all this had been the Gauleiter and nobody else. But then I learned that the camp director had shot a seven year old Ukrainian boy for very minor reasons and then I was quiet and did not speak up for him. I have no idea what happened later to the Gauleiter.

Kreisleiter Primms was another official the Gestapo got involved with. He had reported to us that people had broken into the cabin he owned near Innsbruck and more or less destroyed everything inside. This actually was a matter of the criminal police, but because he was a Kreisleiter, this became a case for the Gestapo, and as it could be tied to homeland security it landed on my desk. The Gauleiter gave me instructions on how to treat this affair and the Kreiseiter in turn gave me instructions as to how to proceed. This did not have the anticipated impact on me but I realized that I had to be doubly careful so as not to step on the toes of these two high gentlemen.

We started to investigate. The first thing we found out was that the Kreisleiter had had a party with his girlfriend in this cabin. This was not good because the man who had a lovely wife and three children at home, had sworn to the Gauleiter that he would quit his philandering. Evidently, he had forgotten his oath and the Gauleiter got extremely angry.

Then we tried to discover how the thief had gained entry into the cabin – there was no sign of a forced entry, we could not get in and we were stumped. Meanwhile the case had made such waves that two civil servants from the Reich Security Headquarters came to investigate the affair. They immediately involved the criminal police who were able to force an entry and once inside they recognized the very personal style of a notorious burglar whom they consequently caught.

The whole affair put me into a bad light. The Kreisleiter was annoyed with me for exposing his dalliances with his girlfriend, the Gauleiter was displeased with me because the seamier side of some of the party officials was being made public and the population could now gossip about their superiors.

In March of 1943 the Gauleiter phoned me.

"Comrade Haefner, in this village is a woman who has torn a picture of Hitler off the wall. She rages against him and she calls him names. I instruct you to do what is necessary. Bring her down and lay charges against her. Such behaviour cannot go unpunished."

I called the local policeman and ordered him to be at my office the next morning with the woman.

She was an old and shrivelled up peasant woman, bent over from the hard work she had done all her life.

I had not even time to greet her when the gendarme bellowed at me: "Herr Obersturmfuehrer, Lieutenant, Sir, I never want you do give me another assignment like this."

"What is the matter?"

"It is simply this: The woman received a letter yesterday informing her that her fourth and last son had fallen."

The woman was crying pitifully and the gendarme was red with anger.

I called my secretary and I told her, "I have a woman here who needs some care."

I asked her to go to the cupboard in the back room where for occasions just like this, bottles of good red Tyrolean wine were meant to give solace, and I asked her to give the old lady a glass. She did, but the woman kept on crying. I could see that she was not approachable. I was in a real quandary. I knew I could not just let her go, which is actually what I felt like doing, but justice must be seen to have been done.

So I spoke to the gendarme.

"I will state that the woman deeply regrets what she has done and in order to make amends she will pay fifty marks."

The policeman burst into laughter.

"Are you crazy? This woman has never seen that much money in one lump in all her life!"

"Does the woman have milk and butter at home?"

"Yes, lieutenant, that she has."

"What is the price of butter on the black market in your village?"

The eyes of the policeman seemed to be popping out of his head.

"Sir, the pound is twenty five marks."

"Well, my good man. You will now pay the fifty marks for the woman and then you will go home with her. Make sure you sell the butter for a good price so you can get your money back."

With an open mouth, eyes bulging, and swallowing hard, the gendarme stared at me. He shook his head like a dog coming out of a deep lake. Normally the police arrested people who sold goods on the black market – and here he had orders to sell butter on the black market – from the Gestapo.

We wrote something up and the woman signed. The policeman signed. And so it came about that the gendarme could take this little old woman back to her lonely hut in the mountains and nothing happened to her.

Hergottsakrament! God Damn it! Sometimes there are situations where you just cannot forget that you are a Mensch and not only a uniform.

I followed up with a call to the Gauleiter who thundered at me.

"But I wanted you to arrest and charge that woman!"

"On the contrary," I addressed him back. "That would be much more deserved by the person who had reported her."

And I put the phone down.

I knew that the Gauleiter etched another notch on my slate.

At another time this phone call came from him.

"In St. Anton in a hotel is a man, a half Jew, who has drawn unnecessary attention to himself again with his talking. Take care of him."

I went to St. Anton and met the man. I asked him what the reason was for the complaints.

"Everyone treats me as if I was Jew," he said.

"I am a German, a regular, ordinary German and I want to be treated like one."

What to do. It is not the man's fault that he was categorized by the National Socialist laws as being half Jewish. I tried to impress on the man not to talk so much and not to blow up every time and not to draw unnecessary attention to himself. But he would not listen to me - he was too agitated to listen to reason. Then I had to tell him that I would let him go today with an official warning but if he would make another ruckus again, that I would have to arrest him and that next time he might be sentenced by a court to a concentration camp. We, the police and the Gestapo could not take anyone to a concentration camp. All such referrals came only from the courts. Naturally, we could recommend that a person be sent to a camp and the powers above would quickly consent.

Again, the Gauleiter was not very happy with me.

One day the phone rang.

"Comrade Haefner, you will accompany a Ministerialrat (a senior councilor in the civil service) through several towns in Tyrol."

When I asked about the details, the Gauleiter told me that it had become known that workers and soldiers who had the right and a need for holidays and who had the proper papers, had to be turned away because other people, that is civilians without the proper papers, occupied these places. He told me that Goebbels himself had insisted that we investigate and straighten this mess up. The Senior Civil servant was to check hotels and rooming houses and in case of trouble – well that is where I would come in.

First, we drove to St. Anton and checked a few hotels. Everything was fine. In one very large hotel a friendly soul let me know that in this place at five in the morning a trumpeter blew the signal 'back to your own beds'. One night I checked a lieutenant. His papers were in order but the girl, who was in his bed, had none. Well, I had compassion and ignored it. Poor sot, I thought, a few more days and then you have to go to Russia into mud and hell. I tipped my hat and left.

At another time we discovered a pretty girl who had no holiday papers. We kept on meeting her between one and five in the morning in four different rooms. I did talk to her and told her that she better be smart and pack her bags and leave. I hope she did.

We did wait for the famous 'back to your beds' call in the morning, but it never came. Someone must have tipped the trumpeter off and he was smart enough to be quiet.

Then we went to Zuers, high up in the mountains. One approached it on a high grade which stretched like a narrow backbone from one mountain to another. I lugged my typewriter in my backpack and I carried my skis. First my driver and I walked and then we clamped on our skis and slowly negotiated the pass. We skied very carefully. On some places we could walk, on some we were able to ski. On some spots we had to sit on the ridge, legs with attached skis dangling either side down into the abyss, creeping forward on our rear ends. It went down very, very down either side. But we made it. Our Ministerialrat, of course, had hired a taxi and was there long before us poor foot sluggers. I should have taken that route but I liked skiing better.

The 'Rose' was a first class hotel with 260 beds. It had a fancy suite for our Ministerialrat, but all they had left for us was a bed in the servants' quarters up in the attic. Our controls always took place in the night when normal hotel service was over and it could be assumed that people were in their beds. After one o' clock in the morning we went from room to room. "Geheime Staatspolizei, your holiday papers please."

The rooms were filled with contented factory workers and soldiers who all had their papers and everything was fine.

A holiday pass was an official holiday pass issued either by the Wehrmacht, or the factory or other place of employment. It had to be an official paper with stamps and signatures on it, without such a paper it was difficult to obtain a place in a hotel, especially in later years.

Real trouble we had only once with a lady in Kufstein. She was a Fuerstin von S., an aristocratic lady, who lived in a beautiful apartment. It is important to remember that in 1918 the nobility and the use of titles were abolished in Austria. But she, because she was the descendant of a very influential and historic Austrian family, was still addressed by everyone as 'Fuerstin von S'. She lived in that place without a holiday pass and this was against the rules and therefore she had to go. I asked the Ministerialrat to speak to her and to explain to her that she actually – I could not even finish my sentence when the Ministerialrat interrupted me sharply, "what - explain to her? She has no pass, she has to go."

Tears and crying did not soften his heart and she had to leave.

Meanwhile the Gauleiter of Munich and a few other party officials had become involved in the affair. They were making a lot of noise and insisted also that the good lady had to go home. This was actually none of their business because this took place in Austria. Many of the letters and calls arrived at the Gauleiter and he, again, saw me causing a lot of trouble.

As a Kommissariatsleiter I had my own office in Innsbruck, the head of the regional headquarters for the frontier police. I had two or three men working for me and sometimes extra personnel such as interpreters whom I borrowed from another office. The Gestapo got involved in a variety of things – so much could be cloaked in the term 'Heimtuecke', 'homeland security'. Everyone who said anything against the Reich, its ideas or leaders was suspect. There were cases where we had to get tough with people. Loudmouths and show-offs who really drew too much attention were given time to cool off in an Arbeitserziehungslager, a camp for work and re-education. I recall one case where a young colleague had to go and arrest a rich farmer who had mistreated a conscripted worker in a particularly offensive way. The farmer was put into a labour camp for a while to give him time and the opportunity to reflect upon his behaviour and, primarily, to work at hard labour.

But actual events that brought people to court never occurred in my district. Most of my cases were small and I always tried to mediate and not to forget that I was a Mensch, a human being, who could have compassion for his fellow man and their foibles. There were so many cases like the one with the little old woman and the Hitler picture – and I know that so many of these persons were sentenced for five to eight years once they had been pulled into the system. This is a heavy punishment, especially when one remembers that the actual punishment was only to be started when the war was over.

One day a little man entered my office and greeted my secretary in a very friendly manner. She responded with a smile.

"Gruess Gott, Herr Pfarrer, Hello Vicar, nice to see you again."

When I wondered about him my secretary told me:

"A few years ago we had to give the local minister a warning because he talked unwisely and too much. Since then, he comes in regularly to inquire if there is anything against him here."

Then my secretary chuckles, "And he always remembers that we have a tumbler of good wine for him."

And true enough, the little minister asked me if there was anything against him here. No, there wasn't, and yes, he would be delighted to sample another glass of our very good red wine.

What a kaleidoscope of people and stories and events were brought to me. I often worked very hard to prevent an injustice, to swing something so that men and women did not have to go to court. Once there, I could help them no longer. The system had a way of swallowing people. I experienced a lot of good things, but don't think for a moment that I did agree with everything I had to do.

"Genosse Haefner, Comrade Haefner, there has been trouble in Kitzbuehl. A man insulted Hitler and caused a commotion in the village. Take care of it."

The local police brought the man to me. We talked. He admitted to have sworn and cursed. I thought he was hiding something. I summoned the Ortsgruppenleiter, the local Party representative, and spoke to him. Then something clicked in my head and I asked to have the delinquent brought in again. Alone. This time he talked. The Party man wanted a piece of land that he owned and the Party man had provoked him and done his best to get him into trouble so that he could get his fingers on the property.

I gave the culprit an official warning and then he could go home again. I warned him to watch his temper and his mouth in the future. Unfortunately, I could do nothing against the Party official except report him to the Gauleiter and explain to him that he had misused his office and position to threaten and put pressure on a man.

Again, the Gauleiter was not happy with me.

I think I acted correctly. As a National Socialist one does not condone such blatant abuse of power. As National Socialist one is on the side of justice and one does things right. Always.

The Church was part of what I was supposed to watch. One day I approached my secretary.

"I am now here for four months and I have not heard a thing about the church. How is it? Do we have trustworthy people?"

"No, we don't…"

And before she could utter a 'but' I ordered her to go to church next Sunday and report back to me with some information.

The region was very Catholic. Nearby was a small nunnery. Their priest wanted to visit his nuns a few times during the week but he felt that to be seen in his black habit would cause too much curiosity. But he must have figured that if one dressed up as a chimney sweep nobody would notice how often he visited the nunnery. That is what he did and he visited his nuns secretly as often as he wished to. But someone must have been watching and seen him because I found the following entry in our files: 'Father X. visited the nun's cloister today to sweep their chimneys.'

One day the Gauleiter demanded that we legally claim rooms in a cloister which we were using already. I discussed the problem with my superior. I pointed out that there existed contracts between the Reich and the church and that we could not legally hand those rooms over to the Gau. I explained that they could be used as leases but not expropriated.

I explained the situation to the Gauleiter. I believe I even wrote a letter explaining again the legality of the situation. He was highly displeased with me because he realized that with my being involved, he could not think of expropriating the rooms.

Another notch on the slate.

Wild stories were buzzing: the Kreisleiter had raped his secretary. I contacted my superior. He warned me.

"This is a hot iron. Don't burn your fingers."

"You know that I am a civil servant and as such it is my duty to see that the law is upheld."

That was my position and I made that clear to him.

I phoned the Gauleiter. He was less than pleased about my zealous behaviour and used nasty words towards me. But he did have to give me his permission to start an investigation without which I could not have touched the Kreisleiter.

I first spoke to the secretary and I learned that more people knew about the case. After I talked to the Kreisleiter who, more or less admitted his guilt, I contacted the Gauleiter and informed him that I would refer the offence to the prosecutor.

"Oh no, you won't!" threatened the Gauleiter.

"I will," I replied. "You cannot expect me to break my oath of office."

He told me that I could do what I felt I had to, but that he would also see that nothing would happen to the Kreisleiter. And that is exactly what took place. The file was put away and nothing ever happened to him.

Much later I once discussed this case with the Gauleiter and he told me that he could not afford to lose the Kreisleiter at that time because he had nobody to replace him.

One day our office received a memo that a woman had tried to commit suicide. I was told that her husband was in the concentration camp in Dachau. It had become known that a group of men was unhappy with the Third Reich and that they held weekly meetings in a restaurant. The police went and arrested the men and also the people who had been sitting at the next table. One of them was the husband of the distraught woman; he was an electrician and from Innsbruck.

I heard about the incident in the evening. From our office a report had to go each evening to Security Headquarters, the RSHA in Berlin, noting the events of the day, listing arrests, names and numbers of the people involved. In the ensuing investigation it was ascertained that the electrician was neither a member of the subversive group nor was he in any way against the Reich and that he had just been at the wrong place at the wrong time.

Wheels started rolling to free him. But he was caught in a bureaucratic tread mill from which he could not escape. I approached my superior who in turn went to the Gauleiter. Finally, another memo arrived and my boss told me to drive to Dachau myself and see if I could do something. I did and spoke to the electrician who was working in the office there. He had no complaints about his treatment there.

I had to tell him that his wife had tried to commit suicide. I felt very uncomfortable about the whole thing. I knew that the man was innocent but nobody in Berlin would listen to anything we had to say. The poor fellow had to remain in Dachau until he was freed by the Allies. In a way he was lucky, because due to our intervention he was kept working in the office – and I feel that was a great sight better than being a foot soldier on the steppes of Russia.

One day my boss approached me, "Comrade Haefner, the French Fremdarbeiter, the foreign conscripted workers, are on strike on a dam in the Vorarlberg. Go, check it out and make sure they get back to work."

2500 meters high a dam was being built to contain and regulate the water used for a hydroelectric station further down. I took a French speaking interpreter, because I did not trust my own French capabilities. The work camp was high up in the mountains. I inquired of the guards what had happened and was told that the workers had gone on strike and that the guards had locked up eight of them.

I told them to release the eight workers and then I went and searched out the men.

They were men from Marseilles. They had been brought up here in their flimsy city clothes, thin socks and poor shoes, to work on moving earth with picks and shovels. Up here high in the mountains it was always wet and foggy and this year it was a particularly wet summer and it had even snowed.

"We cannot work under these conditions, we'll all get sick and die."

The men told me they never got dry.

They also told me that they were housed and fed very poorly and in their desperation they had decided to refuse to work. Imagine – in the Third Reich – conscripted workers on strike!

I ordered all the French workers to line up in the yard. I told them that they had legitimate cause for complaints. I assured them that I would attempt to improve their working and living conditions, but that I would expect from them in return that they would go back to work. They agreed.

I phoned the Gauleiter and let him know what I thought about the whole mess up in the mountains. I told him that one can't expect more from the local police but that a few Party boys had done a miserably poor job organizing the work camps up there. Men who are expected to work must be fed and clothed and housed properly. I also told him that I thought it ludicrous that the Poles and Russians, used to cold and usually in possession of warm and sturdy clothing, were employed by the farmers in the valleys and housed warmly in barns and fed well at the farmers tables, whereas these French boys in their thin socks were freezing up there and became more and more unable to work. Poor organization all around!

Then I put the phone down. Immediately I knew this was something I should not have done. It is one thing to describe conditions but to tell a Gauleiter that he had not done a good job or telling him what should have been done – that was definitely too much. I realized that I had accumulated too many notches on my slate.

Back in Innsbruck I found out that a transfer was imminent and while waiting for what higher powers had in mind for me, I carried on checking out factories and businesses under the watchful eyes of my superior.

Once I had to check an armament factory and to my great delight the manager spoke a beautiful Swabian dialect – just as I did. He told me that he was controlling everything in the factory and that I didn't need to bother because everything was ship shape. When lunchtime came and the women came from their working posts – I could not believe my eyes, they walked arm in arm and singing to the lunch room. Imagine! Singing! They were Ukrainian and Russian women, conscripted workers, and they were singing. I am sure the manager was very pleased with my report.

At another place in Tyrol the working conditions were far from satisfactory. Here they were making parts for airplanes. But something was definitely wrong because whenever the new parts were delivered, they had to be scrapped because they were already outdated. Worker morale was very low and the local Austrian workers blamed the conscripted foreign workers for sabotage. I had to be very careful and not give advice to some official higher up and so I reported only what I saw without any interpretation. That I left to my superior. Luckily, I had by now learned to keep many things to myself.

A few days later I was informed that I was to go to Kiev to join Einsatzgruppe C.

Chapter 17

GUSTEL IN THE EAST AGAIN

When I arrived in Kiev the Major-General let me know right away where I stood.

"You will be transferred to a police regiment. Let me tell you that if you make trouble there too, something unpleasant is going to happen."

After a few days I was ordered to take a Fieseler Storch and fly to my new command. The area was known to be full of partisans and driving on the roads was considered to be too dangerous and if a tank protected convoy was not feasible, it was preferable to fly. Our aircraft flew high enough to be out of antiaircraft artillery range. The pilots usually nosedived and leveled them just in the last minute – and they really enjoyed doing that when they knew they had a greenhorn on board. These planes did not need a runway only some flat ground. My green face must have caused some mirth when they saw me hopping out of that infernal machine.

I reported to my police regiment, a regiment from Hamburg. I became the 1C, that is the officer in charge of reconnaissance of the enemy. They could actually do that job quite well by themselves but for some reason they had asked for a man from the Gestapo. My first task was to get to know the regions, its roads, towns and settlements.

This is not an easy task in an area that is crawling with partisans and where there was much resistance by the local population. Many of the Party officials had not exactly understood how to treat the locals; they had threatened them or had treated them often unfairly and they had succeeded in making the Ukrainians resent us and making them our enemies. The region was no longer under military regulations; the military had advanced into new territories and the area here was now under civil administration. The objective was to get the most out of its agricultural potential, in plain words, we wanted to get as much grain and foodstuffs out of it as we could.

A Russian officer, the leader of a group of thirty or so partisans, had fought his way through to the far south, his main goal being the oilfields of the southern Ukraine which they planned to sabotage. Few things could hurt the Germans as much as blowing up oil wells. They depended on their continuous supply to keep running the thousands of vehicles they had brought into Ukraine. The partisans had already dynamited a few wells and everyone was alerted to catch them, and new rumours had them moving further north into our area.

The regiment had cordoned off some areas. I had been given a company and after we had ascertained the Russians' position in a small forest, I took up my position there. It was night. One of the commanders was in a weakened position and I offered my support but was denied. He was worried that too many of our men would be shot in the dark night and so I had to retreat. And, of course, that is exactly where the Russians broke through. Command came quickly to make a new offensive line to catch him. I had the outer line with twelve men. On our way to our new position by hand we had to move a tank that stood in the middle of the road, hindering our sight and possibly providing too much security for our enemy. It was to be a quiet night, with shots that were heard, but no action for us and soon we were called back. The Russians had broken through some five hundred meters further west with no casualties on their side.

One day I was informed that a leader of the Ukrainian resistance had been spotted in a certain village. I received an exact description of the road, the village and even the house where he was holed up. We went with two motorbikes with sidecars and a jeep. And as was custom with the Ukrainians, as soon as they saw Germans approaching, they ran to their churches and rang the bells, informing the whole village of our impending entry. We came to the edge of the village. I ordered the jeep to remain and with the other motorbike we drove up to the house. We surprised the man in his kitchen, apprehended him, tied him into the sidecar of one of the motorbikes and roared off with the church bells still clanking. All happened so fast that not one person interfered with our kidnapping of the partisan. Of course, we drove like devils on our machines.

When I delivered the man, I learned that people captured this way were treated as prisoners of war and not as partisans and so the case was out of my hands. At this time of the war there had been contracts worked out between nations that laid down laws about the treatment of prisoners of war. Gone were the times when the Germans, like the Russians, took no prisoners of war but shot them. And I know that the Americans did the same; they shot prisoners of war in 1945. Often, I knew, it was the men who were quick with their bullets. Some officers were like that but it was mostly the subordinates. They had to be watched closely. It was always up to their superiors to see that they did not abuse their place.

I witnessed once on my first run in Russia, that one of our drivers painted a Jew's face with black shoe polish. I dressed him down and reported him to the commander. As a superior one has to watch one's people, this is so important. I have always done that.

I believe it was already in the spring of 1943 when a larger action was being prepared. A group of partisans was to be closed in on and captured. I had a driver and an interpreter and we left in our jeep. First, I had to check on the Wehrmacht who was supposed to cordon off certain areas in order to prevent the partisans from breaking through. I quickly found out that they had not done so but that the partisans were close and outnumbered us by far.

I decided to pull back. We drove down a road at high speed and I noticed a small path veering off the road. A thought flashed in my brain and nestled in my stomach: not long ago there were barriers here, where are they today? My driver hit the brakes but it was already too late; we plunged over the broken bridge down into the river below. My beautiful Mercedes jeep had its radiator deeply bored into the ground. Luckily the river was only two meters wide and not deep at all. I hit my head. The steering wheel rammed into my driver's chest, the interpreter was thrown out of the vehicle and I was out cold.

I woke up in hospital. Apparently, my men had heard the impact at a two kilometer distance and rushed to our aid. The driver and the interpreter had managed to crawl out. I had been still in the car, unconscious. Meanwhile the partisans had also been alerted and the situation was becoming dangerous. My men quickly moved tanks to the bridge and down to the river to block and secure the area. Then they came for me and hauled me to the hospital.

I woke up to a discussion between the nurse and the doctor whether I had had a tetanus shot or not. The doctor ordered me to stay in bed for twenty days as I had incurred a severe concussion. On day twelve I found out that my driver and interpreter were in the same hospital. I found them in a large hall where the ordinary soldier was looked after, in bunk beds which were crammed three tiers high into the room leaving little room to walk. The patients lay on dirty and moldy straw. I was ashamed to remember that I lay in a smallish room, with lots of air, in a single bed and had white sheets which were changed regularly. Even with the white sheets we suffered from lice and fleas and I figured that the men on the straw suffered even more than we did from those pests. Of course - that was the Wehrmacht. I was the only SS officer there. We, that is the SS, would have never had a hospital like this one. When we were in action, we always shared with our men whatever we had. We ate the same food and we had the same blankets.

Meanwhile as I was starting to feel better, I noticed the nurses around me. I saw they liked me. One nurse, the daughter of a prelate from Potsdam, was very reserved and very proper; but even she sometimes blinked at me. There was another one, a plump and pretty girl from Eastern Prussia, who always stopped to chat with me. I think she liked my stories too. One day she cried, "Oh God, this is not fair! I finally find a fellow I like and he is married!"

We were six men in our room. The worst casualty was a Hauptman who had been the pilot in a plane that had been shot and consequently had caught fire.

He had remained long enough in the cockpit in order to give his men a chance to bail out over German territory. He must have had horrible burns under those bandages. I spent much time with him. One day he looked at me with his red rimmed eyes and pleaded, "Comrade, please, no more stories, you make me laugh so hard that my skin cracks and tears apart. It won't heal and I'll never get out of these bandages."

The second time I visited my men the doctor caught me. He thundered at me that he had given me twenty days of bed rest and what in heaven's name was I doing up and about. I informed him that I was feeling fine and ready for further duty. He shook his head but still issued me a paper, 'Haefner released on his own wishes. Ready for front duty'.

When I returned to the office I was ordered to go to Warsaw. Waiting on the station with my suitcase – yes, I went to war with a suitcase, besides the grey field uniform, I had to have civilian clothing and then, of course, my parade uniform – I watched the bustle on the station. It was a huge place with trains departing for Upper Silesia, to Warsaw and to the East. I believe it was Stolbunov, on the Polish-Ukrainian border. They were able to send a train off every five minutes because up to fifty locomotives were constantly under steam, ready to be exchanged and ready to leave at a moment's notice.

Outside the station were long rows of earthen hills, neatly smoothed out, two meters high alongside the tracks. A station attendant explained to me that here had been a huge prisoner of war camp. Typhus had broken out and the prisoners, mostly Ukrainians, had died by the thousands and they were buried under those mounds.

The train was filled with soldiers who did not seem to mind their dirty, smelly and often bloody uniforms. They were tired and worn out but many were in high spirits; they were going home, to a bath, clean clothes, to a wife or a mother. The officers mingled with them and their uniforms were as badly in need of changing as was mine. In one compartment sat a lone figure. Heavy eyelids in an arrogant face, his uniform was immaculately clean and his boots shone with polish. He had involved himself in an argument with the men who had henceforth left him and he had all the seats to himself. He was an administration officer, a paymaster.

I was riding with the men. Many of them had thought about bringing a souvenir back from the front and they had organized chickens and geese, I even saw a duck and some hams. The fowl, some of which were already plucked, the others still in their natural plumage, were slightly frozen swinging in the cold wind outside the windows. They brought happy smiles to all the faces that looked outside.

I almost regretted to have to leave the train after some hours, but they travelled west and I had to change trains to go to Warsaw. The station was deserted and I found out that no train was to leave for Warsaw within the foreseeable future.

"Ask an engine driver, we have many who drive to Warsaw," the attendant told me.

And that is what I did. I found one who would take me in his locomotive to Warsaw.

The huge engine hissed and steamed over me as the driver leaned out beckoning me to throw my suitcase up to him. I packed my suitcase and tried to swing it up to him but neither my neck nor my hand would obey. I had to have some men lift my baggage and then me up into the cab.

It was a memorable trip. Alongside the tracks were the twisted and burnt-out carcasses of many wagons that had been dynamited by bandits and partisans. Often the locomotives pushed one or two empty wagons ahead of themselves because this way the locomotives could take the impact of the exploding mines on the tracks and lessen the impact to the locomotive and on the train.

On arrival I phoned my office for a taxi to drive me straight to the hospital. The doctor looked me over and then grinned.

"Thank God for easy cases."

When I asked him what he meant by that he explained that on the previous day a train filled with soldiers going home had been hit and that he and his colleagues had been busy stitching all too many wounded together through the night.

"Explosions have a nasty way of tearing whole bodies apart," he smiled sadly, "so thank God for an easy case."

It turned out that I had a cracked vertebra in my neck and a broken bone in my hand, neither of which either my doctor or I had been aware of. I was lucky; I was sent home for three weeks of R&R. So, I took the train to Lindau where my family was living now after having been evacuated from Berlin where the heavy bombing had begun in January of 1943.

My command had been disbanded and I sat in Warsaw waiting for orders. The commander of the local security police was Colonel Hahn. He seemed genuinely happy to have someone to talk with.

"There are parts of Warsaw where no German ever dare enter. If we want to get in we have to have three divisions of infantry otherwise we won't be able to. The Polish have become very powerful here already." Referring to the Jewish ghetto Hahn said that there were fights to this day due to the underground passages; he also mentioned that there were not many more people alive.

When I walked through the area, order police were continuously busy checking the underground sewers. They explained the situation.

"The resistance is very tough here. On one day we had forty five Germans shot. They were men who had come from the front and become careless here. Following these incidents, we captured fifty local men and held them hostages. The population was told that these people, their names were all mentioned on placards which were publicized, would be kept as hostages and they, should just one German be shot, all would be executed. That happened once and then never again."

For the few weeks I stayed in Warsaw I did little else than visit with Hahn. He seemed glad to be able to unburden himself to someone and share his load of sorrow and grief with someone, even a little lieutenant. He often used harsh words when he spoke about his superiors.

"They seem to do little but sit together and cook up dangerous mixtures of orders and commands which they hand down without a thought as to their practicality or consequences. The order with the hostages did not come from me – someone up there figured it out – and I had to be the one to shoot civilians."

One day Hahn said to me, "Well, Haefner, enough of sitting around here and doing nothing. Here are your new orders. You are being transferred to Greece."

That was in November 1943.

Chapter 18

GUSTEL IN GREECE

I took the train to travel to Athens. It was an uneventful and quiet journey; only in Yugoslavia did it have the potential to be dangerous due to the partisans there. Tito had organized the men and was waging fierce resistance to the Germans.

In Athens I took quarters in the beautiful Hotel Britannia, one of the two hotels which were reserved for the SS alone, the other one, where Wehrmacht officers were quartered, was the Angleterre.

My area of work was the 'Bandenreferat' that meant dealing with partisans. Resistance and partisans were a complicated affair in Greece. First there were the national partisans who had full co-operation from England. They had British uniforms, ammunition, and money, especially money - that was more important in Greece than weapons. Some of these national partisans worked together with the Germans against other organized groups of partisans who were communist. The communist partisans were naturally supported by the Russians. They were fighting against the national partisans and the Germans. They were not that important as they did not have the same support as had the national groups.

It was sometimes tricky to figure out which of the groups or which faction of any one group were with us and which were against us. It was somewhat easier once I had interrogated my first prisoner who had been caught by my predecessor; there and then I gained much valuable information.

Germany had gone into Greece only because the English had tried to get to Germany from Cairo through Greece. Strange conditions if you think about it. One day I had a chance to speak with a minister in the government and I recall that he was rather hesitant to agree to something and I told him that I understood that he was not able to decide something unilaterally because he had to contact the exiled government in Cairo which in turn had to contact Churchill in London – a rather time consuming task. He was somewhat embarrassed.

One aspect of Greece that I quickly learned was that whoever greased the hand of the police most had easiest access to whatever he wanted. The little farmer on his donkey cart bringing vegetables or oranges to market had to wait a long time to get entry into the city, whereas the large trucks, after a quick handshake, were waved through in no time by the police that controlled the in roads. Once I mentioned this to a Greek official and he smiled sadly.

"We are aware of the problem but our civil servants cannot survive if they don't do this."

When I pointed out to him that our German civil servants receive a good salary and a good pension upon retirement, he replied, "Our men have to rely on this extra money, this is their pension for their old age."

As is custom I had to report and introduce myself at many places. Outside Athens was a steep hill and on top of it was a winery, 'Weinhaus Claus', that had been founded by a German. During the war it was alternately occupied by the National partisans or us. When I was in Athens, it was occupied by the Wehrmacht who had a flak battery up there. I reported to the officer and told him my business. He called a man, whispered something to him and not long after I could hear two salvos fired off in my honour. Imagine! What a welcome!

During our occupation there were three regiments of Efzones in existence. They normally serve in their traditional pleated white skirts, white tights, pointed shoes with red pom poms on them. They told me it takes them an hour to get dressed and requires the help of another man. But during the war they were wearing British uniforms and they carried British weapons and ammunition. One regiment was stationed in Athens, one in Patras and the other was in Thessaloniki. I had to communicate with them also because they were fighting against the communist partisans. We actually had a good relationship with them.

One day something very unexpected happened. It snowed. It snowed in Athens for the first time in twenty five years. Outside the government building were ministers and civil servants, laughing and hollering, engaged in a snowball fight. The only ones I felt sorry for were the Efzones standing on guard. They shivered mightily in their tights and short skirts. But the inclement weather had another effect: it cancelled the war. Our German troops who had been equipped with uniforms and gear for the tropics – and that is another story yet! - huddled in their mountain hide-outs close to the fires and showed no signs of entering into any offensive whatsoever. Their main interest was to stay warm. They had to be watchful only that the other side did not surprise them with an unexpected attack.

Actually, the war did not touch us at all. We were a group of likeminded men without much to do. Consequently, we had a roaring good time. We learned to sing a few Greek love songs. One, "Agapimu parnassiee" comes especially to mind, something with darling and lots of love. One night after we had celebrated the good life with plenty of retsina, we moved into the elevator in the Hotel Angleterre and rode the elevator up and down, singing on top of our lungs. An old and very stuffy captain of the Wehrmacht wanted to use the elevator at the same time. Naturally he could not because we occupied it singing 'Agapimu parnassiee' and plenty more of all the lusty and bawdy songs we knew. We knew a lot of songs. We did get a lecture the next day.

But it was not all retsina and song. One day I was ordered to arrest a man who was known to be a communist leader. I gathered together a squad from other jurisdictions, men who had been part of the Waffen SS, who had left and joined the frontier police school in Pretzsch. We drove to the outskirts of Athens into a poor quarter where many impoverished peasants that had fled to the city lived in shacks hammered together with plywood and cardboard and cut up oil drums. I had an exact description of the place I had to find. When we arrived, I sent an advance man in. As he proceeded down the steps into the cellar, I followed him immediately, against all instructions and common sense. On entering I saw in a flash that the rope of his grenade had become hooked on the edge of the table. I let out a yell, my man and the Greek froze, I stepped forward towards my man, undid the rope from its table corner – it slipped back. A sigh of relief escaped from three throats. We arrested the man who did not resist.

We left this quarter of Athens and ran into a barrier of German tanks. When I wondered what was going on and asked a driver, he knew no particulars.

"Just following orders, Sir!"

When I reported to the commander upon completion of my mission, I asked him about the tanks.

"That is very simple," he replied. "We were expecting a riot in this quarter following the arrest and we were going to make sure we'd get you out come what may. That's the reason we had moved the tank in."

"Thank you, Sir."

I had so much luck in the war. So much luck.

One day the Greek city administration came to the office and complained that there was a soldier who did not pay his taxes.

We were dumbfounded. What was that – a German soldier not paying taxes to the city of Athens? Our combined investigations revealed the following: Some German soldiers took from property of the Wehrmacht whatever they could lay their hands on and then sold it. With troops who sit around with not too much to do such things are always to be expected. They sold their loot for good English Gold Pounds. And then they went and bought houses. We found one who owned six houses in Athens. He was smart enough to accumulate so much real estate but not smart enough to not be found out for not paying taxes owed. Of course, he had to face a military court. I did not know the outcome of that because it was a Wehrmacht affair.

A similar event involved not men but officers. Some of them were wheeling and dealing to the extent that they brought in merchandise from Paris. They brought it with planes from Paris to Athens! They were found out and I am sure there would have been a bad ending if it would not have been for the fact that one of them was the bearer of the Knight's Cross. Such a man could only be touched with the knowledge of Adolf. It probably got hushed over. The big ones always get away. It was an affair of the Wehrmacht and not really in my domain of activity.

At the coastline of the Adriatic Sea was a regiment 999. Regiments with that number were the punishment regiments of the Wehrmacht where they put the rag tag, good-for-nothings and riff raff – you get the idea- and where they were given a last chance to better themselves and do their bit for the fatherland. Their commanding officers usually did not choose these particular assignments. In Africa, for example, where one such regiment had been deployed, the men had shot each and every one of their lieutenants and sub lieutenants and then gone over to the English.

One day the commander of the regiment had to see me in Athens and he told me that the men of his 999 took and sold everything that was not bolted down.

"One day they even sold their antitank cannons to the Greek resistance."

I don't think they appreciated the chance given to them to improve themselves and become accepted members of society.

At that time Athens was one gigantic market place. Everything could be had there – if one had the money, English Gold Pounds. The newest cameras, the finest British cloth coming from Cairo; radios, technical products, things produced in Germany in 1942/43 which were not to be had in the Reich, but here they could be bought. I bought gifts for my two little girls too before I left for a holiday back home.

*** The gifts were 'Marlene' the beloved little turtle and two garishly coloured house coats. Sister Inge and I were extraordinarily proud of these garments and I always imagined they had been bought in a bazaar straight out of 'One Thousand and One Nights'- one of my favourite books later on. We adored the masses of exotic looking blooms and curlicues that flowed on the fabric. We had our 'Turkish' coats for years. ***

One day a sergeant approached me and told me that much trouble was brewing in his unit. He had been told by one of his men that a troop of Wehrmacht was going to arrest his commander. When I investigated, I found that the captain of the company and the major were both vying for the favours of the same Greek woman. The major had threatened to arrest the captain to get him out of the way. The captain had threatened that his men were prepared to fight for him to prevent an arrest. It looked very much as if the two men were going to wage their own private little war. The sergeant had come to me to prevent bloodshed.

What to do? I could have gone to the commander of the regiment or even the division but I did not want to do this. Then I figured that I would get the 'bone of contention' out of the way. I went to the Greek woman, a very beautiful young woman, and arrested her. She was officially arrested by the Gestapo for some unwise comments she had made in public. She went to live with my woman interpreter. I did not want anything else for her, she knew that she had been apprehended on trumped up charges, I only wanted her out of the way of these two men.

Unfortunately, the problem had not completely disappeared. The commander from the regiment visited one day.

"Herr Kamerad, I would like to know the absolute truth about that affair."

I thought it seems that some people have talked and rumours had reached the commander's ear. Of course, if I had told him about these two men, they would have ended up facing a military court because it certainly could not be condoned that a company had been alerted to fight against another leader. I swore a holy oath that I had arrested the woman because of her loose tongue.

After the war I met the commander in a prisoner of war camp and then I told him the truth. Shaking his head with a slightly amused mien he said to me, "I thought you were hiding something."

I had to tread very carefully with the Wehrmacht and I did not want to get into trouble with them myself; on the other hand, I did not want to get these two cockerels into trouble either because of a woman.

Later on, the Greek lady went with the lady interpreter to Germany; that is, I took both of them with me when we left Greece. I just could not leave her behind because the Greeks did not look kindly on those who fraternized too much with the Germans. And I certainly could not report to the Efzones that she had done absolutely nothing but that two German officers had behaved like besotted idiots because of her.

At that time Greece was administered by a military administration from the Wehrmacht. We could not do very much without their input. They had to give the orders for large actions, something they did not want to admit later on. For example, there was a list of names and when the commander ordered so many persons to be shot because he wanted to teach someone a lesson or he wanted to deter future agitators, names were plucked randomly from the list containing names of men and women who had incurred the negative attention of the people in power, and he had them shot without any qualms. Once I had to interrogate a man and halfway through the investigation, the man disappeared. When I asked where he was, I was informed that his name had been on the list and that he had been shot. There were names of people on that list who should never have been on there. But the Wehrmacht was not very fussy. Many mistakes were made.

You ask me who shot the people? They were men who worked as the driver or the cook. Men like that - they were always the ones who had to do the shooting.

One morning I received the order to report to the deputy commander.

I did and was told I would be transferred the next day to Patras. I was baffled. I had done nothing wrong. My conscience was clear. But orders are orders and so I packed and went to Patras. Pretty soon I got excited: I finally got to see the Greece from high school, not only Athens but also the Gulf of Corinth and the Peloponnese.

I started my work in Patras by making the rounds to the important personages to introduce myself and to state my business there. Outside of Patras lived the director of the electric works for the whole region. His wife was German and he himself spoke the language very well. He had a nice son and a pretty daughter. This was the man who was the go-between I had mentioned before. Every Saturday evening he hosted an open house for all the officers. Some officers from the navy showed up, but mainly the officers of the Jaegerregiment 749, which was positioned in the region, and they were there as his guests. I always went there with my interpreter. Of course, my driver was there too, but he had to wait outside.

I learned that the commander of this regiment, Colonel Sonntag, due to his fear of partisans always drove through the countryside with a sizable armed entourage, a large military vehicle in advance and another large one bringing up the rear. I was amazed at this show of strength, because I drove into the countryside only with my driver and my interpreter and between us we had one carbine and one pistol. I had made sure beforehand that the locals were aware of that. I did not want some partisans to throw a handful of grenades onto our vehicle. I did not want to topple off the narrow road that hugged the rugged coast and end up at the bottom of the Mediterranean or the Gulf of Corinth.

Nobody ever wanted anything from me, ever. My predecessor had to watch out continuously and the partisans were continuously harassing him. I had heard that sometimes they marched right into his door. Partisans dressed in British uniforms and carrying British weapons marched to his door. What cheek! They were communist partisans who got the uniforms from the times when the English still were in Greece.

My predecessor drank too much. On one of his drinking bouts he lost all sense when he and a few drinking buddies, officers from the navy base, took torpedo boats and cruised in the sea. He was transferred due to the trouble he caused and because his relationship with the Wehrmacht was deteriorating rapidly. I was put into his place in the spring of 1944.

One night we decided to get out into the Straight of Corinth. We knew that partisans were moving under the cover of night. We were sitting in a small boat when a large sailboat glided past us, quiet with the exception of the soft 'swush' it made as it cut through the jet black water. It made no sign that it understood or had any intention to follow our signals to stop. We had only a carbine and a pistol and they were much bigger than we were. I decided this was not the time to start a war. We were quiet, watched the moon rise out of the still and dark waters until it was high above us and then we quietly went home.

One day I took the boat out into the sea, dropped anchor and swam. There were four kilometers of sea on either side of me and I felt like a dolphin, able to swim forever and ever. Then I spotted a sea turtle and I climbed quickly back into the boat again. I knew the power of the jaw of these creatures from an encounter with local fishermen who had caught one in their nets. The animal had tried to fight its way out and ripped the net to shreds. This is one reason the fishermen do not like to catch them even though they appreciate their delicious meat. The turtle was still alive when I got there and the fishermen asked me to shoot it. I was on patrol with my translator. I shot but of course the bullet veered off its thick shell and the head retreated quickly into the protection of its carapace. In the end we had to shoot it with a carbine. But before it was shot, the fishermen showed us the strength of its jaws by shoving a stick between its teeth. The turtle simply snapped it in half.

One day the local commander sent a messenger to me with a written order.

"Order from the military commander of the Peloponnes. Tomorrow two ferries with about three hundred Jews will arrive and you are to see to it that they are being fed."

The military commander of Corinth was responsible for everything that went on. He was accountable to the military commander of Athens. Up to this day I had not been involved in any tasks with Jews in Greece.

I called my superior in Athens, SS Brigadier-General Blume and filled him in. He answered back.

"Thank heavens that we have nothing to do with the whole affair. This time it is all done by the Wehrmacht."

The Wehrmacht had caught the Jews on the mainland and brought them on the Canal of Corinth to Piraeus, the harbour of Athens. I was informed that according to international agreements that had been hammered out between Athens, Cairo and London, the feeding of prisoners of any kind was the responsibility of the Greek Red Cross.

It happened that the director of the Greek National bank was the director of the Red Cross. He was informed about the arrival of the Jewish people. I took my quietest and most reliable man for this assignment. The ferries had each between one hundred and hundred and fifty Jews on board and they had Wehrmacht guards. The ferries docked, my man went on board and returned after a while reporting that the people were being fed. But he admitted that some of the young women had complained that the German guards bothered them too much. Immediately I commandeered two other men, one a 'Loot German' and the other a driver, the usual men in my detachment, to go on board and prevent the Wehrmacht from bothering the Jewish women. I figured the presence of these two men with their visible police stripes should quiet things down. More I could not do.

Since this ended my involvement with these people, I did not give it another thought until one day, as I was walking with my interpreter, I met a sailor from one of the ships, I believe it was the captain. I asked him what had happened to the Jews on the ship.

"Well, they probably were shipped to Auschwitz and sent up the chimney."

I want to show that when higher officers and soldiers, and for that matter ordinary people, say they knew nothing about what went on with the Jews, they are lying. Here, in far away Greece, a sailor of a ferry knew exactly what was happening. His language was coarse – but it was the truth. They all knew.

In all my years I took it only once from a man that he did not know what was happening. He was a judge of the Supreme Court, the highest court in the land. He talked to me during my process in Karlsruhe.

"I must tell you," he said, "I was an officer at the frontline for the whole duration of the war and I did not know."

I believed that. Officially, of course, the officers or soldiers were not informed; nobody was told what was happening at the rear. He could have listened to the men talking, because they knew, and they did talk. But men are hesitant to speak about these things to a superior or their commander. In the Wehrmacht there was a much greater distance between the ranks than in the SS. We talked much more. I never hesitated to speak to a general.

The Jews from the ferry were probably transported with others to Germany and ended up in the concentration camp in Mauthausen.

The time came when it was obvious that the Russian Rumanian front was broken. Of course, we got wind of it. I could see that the Russians would be at the Hungarian border in short order and advance through Bulgaria putting us in the grave danger of being cut off in Greece. It was time to retreat.

First, we looked around for vehicles and soon realized that we did not have enough of them. But somewhere in Patras we found a truck which our drivers were able to put back into driving order. We got ready to leave our place. One of my men did not pull his weight and I told him without mincing any words that

I personally would shoot him if he would not change his attitude because it was my task to take the rest of my men safe and sound back home. The next day he came to me.

"Lieutenant, Sir, I had received very distressing news from back home and was totally confused. It will not happen again."

I told him to forget about the incident.

We drove off with two trucks and two cars, one of which I drove. I can't say that we were nervous but we did proceed with increased vigilance and caution on the road back to Athens. We had to negotiate the coastal road up to Corinth, a stretch were the partisans ruled because they had the advantage of the rugged land. On one side they sat deep in the Peloponnese where nobody could reach them and they could quickly ferry to the other side with a boat. But nothing happened; finally, we drove over the bridge that spanned the Canal of Corinth into Athens.

The excitement of departure spiced our discussions and speeded up our preparations. A detachment of about three hundred men was put together and I, of course, was to be transportation officer. First, we were instructed to leave Greece by truck but meanwhile another troop of German soldiers had been caught in heavy fighting with the partisans and it was then considered to be safer if we left by train. We took the train to Saloniki. Once there, I would have preferred to carry on by train but for some reasons, which were not proffered to me, this was not possible and we had to disembark men, equipment and vehicles, and we were to drive to Belgrade by ourselves.

I had again a motorcycle with a sidecar, a very heavy machine but I cannot remember whether it was a BMW or a Zundapp. Someone had to sit in the vacant seat on the motorcycle. I asked for a volunteer and one man put up his hand. He drove with me for one day and then refused to get on the machine again. A renewed request for a volunteer to drive with me netted me only the refusal of three hundred men.

Not much happened on the road, only I wanted to push our unit forward by overtaking a regiment that was marching before us, the commander told me in no uncertain terms to stay behind the police regiment which was moving like a cumbersome caterpillar, slowly, much to slow for my taste. It made me very impatient – but I had to follow orders.

Sometimes the problems on the road were purely logistical. The deputy commander drove in a 360 horse power Mercedes; that meant he could move at a speed of 200 kilometers an hour, but behind him came the supply truck which could only do twenty kilometers an hour. And between those two extremes I had to keep our troop together. That meant that I was forever driving forward and backward, no wonder that none of my men wanted to drive with me. A certain danger of losing control and plunging down into the deep valleys which wound around the mountains paralleling our road, was always present too.

Suddenly at one stage the national partisans appeared and got into a shooting skirmish with the regiment in front of us. I was grateful for them being ahead of us. We were three hundred men but only twenty or thirty had any kind of military training and I was responsible for them. This area was not easily travelled because it was rough and rugged mountain country. Later, much later again, when we had again a German Film industry, the famous Karl May films were filmed here in the empty wilderness – which looked just like the Wild West in America.

Once when the road dipped even more steeply down around a rocky promontory before gliding into the valley, I sent a small troop of men ahead to make sure the road was clear. It was very narrow and the corner was very sharp. They gave me the signal, 'all clear' and I started my machine. That very instant a large Italian truck rounded the corner and hit me head on. I was too shaken up to worry about the scrapes and nicks I sustained, but my motorbike was totally wrecked. We loaded it onto one of our trucks and we carried on.

Another time I must have fallen asleep on my machine and was heading straight towards the side of the road where I would surely have fallen to my death, but someone noticed and drove next to me and pulled me back. The valley floor was about eight hundred meters below.

Once we were out of the mountains a good road led us straight to Belgrade. My job was advance reconnaissance (Rollkommando) and I had to lead the way. We had one car with fellows who had been in the Leibstandarte (a SS regiment). They were as wild and adventurous a bunch of men as one can imagine. The second of our cars had been badly damaged and was tied to the lead car with a three meter long rope. Since not one man volunteered to steer that vehicle, I could do little but do it myself.

The first car started driving, some men turned around and smiled at me and waved. I steered but the car was weaving from left to right all over the road. Then the bandits laughed some more and drove faster. I swore and threatened them with my fist. They drove faster, I swore more, and sweating blood and water, cursing the whole bunch of them, I hung on to my steering wheel as they drove faster and faster. They just guffawed and waved at me. Finally, they came to a halt. I stormed out of my car and thundered at them about responsibility and told them they were 'Schweinehunde', endangering all our lives and more of the same. They just laughed some more and stated, "We knew you could handle it!"

Chapter 19

THE END OF THE WAR FOR OPA ERNST

The government decided in the summer of 1944 that fortifications were to be built along the Oder River with the intended purpose of preventing the Russians from crossing that natural and vital border between east and west. Enormous amounts of money had been earmarked for that project and the Reichs employment ministry had instructions to draft men to work on that project. Herbert noted in his memoirs that 'amazingly there were suddenly all sorts of supplies available that had not been obtainable before and warehouses filled with pots and pans, dishes, bedding, blankets, work clothing and boots were thrown open to facilitate the new projects.'

The Kreisleiter called Herbert and informed him that he would be recruited to work on the planned fortifications along the Oder River. Herbert phoned his office and told them that he had been conscripted and would not be available to do his job as superintendent for the time being. He was to be in charge of provisions and shelter for about five thousand workers. The men and women were put up in private houses and hastily constructed barracks. All teachers under the age of sixty had been called up, that meant that most schools were closed and some were used to house the workers. Herbert looked after his charges very well, made sure they had decent places to sleep, warm and waterproof clothing to work in and most important, that they had enough food to eat.

After about four weeks he received a new assignment which made him responsible for a certain aspect of construction. He was provided with a tractor, two trailers and was ordered to procure the posts for the twenty mile long construction. The trees to be used stood still in the forests.

He noticed quickly that the population did not think much of their Party superiors. They had caught them time and time again only preaching and not practicing what they ordered the rest of the folk to do. While the locals had little food or goods, the Party functionaries had plenty of everything; there were excesses of eating and drinking, stories of improprieties with employees abounded, criminal activities even were observed – but when they were reported to the Kreisleiter he did nothing about it. The local people talked about the 'death dance of the Party'.

In the middle of December the first refugees from Silesia and other places in the east arrived with tales of deprivations and horror. Herbert perceived the influx of these people as another kind of 'Voelkerwanderung', a modern migration of thousands of people from one end of Europe to another. This time they were trying to escape the threat of the oncoming Russians. The refugees had little, they were cold and hungry and they were not welcomed by local Party officials.

At the end of November 1944 Herbert was sent to an eight day crash course to become company leader for men of the Volkssturm or Home Guard. The demands were very high and Herbert did not feel up to the challenge for psychological and physical reasons, he was after all fifty seven years old and his arthritis was painfully acting up, but he remained because as he said, 'after five years of war there was just nobody else left to do it.'

The newly drafted men of the Home Guard were all employed during the day and training took place on weekends; their leaders, who were also employed during the day, had to spend extra long hours pouring over orders and planning the training tasks for the newcomers.

Herbert became quickly aware of the increasing breakdown of the system. There were neither weapons nor other materials. The battalion leaders overwhelmed the lower leaders with a mountain of demands, new companies were formed, dissolved and reformed and former training had to be repeated. He wrote that it was 'like carrying water in a sieve'.

Another problem was the condition of the drafted men – whoever had been willing and able had long been deployed in the war effort – men that remained were not necessarily either tough or willing for the assigned tasks.

His diary showed that he was again working during the week days as a superintendent during January 1945. On Sunday, 28th, a very cold day, as he was doing shooting exercises with his men, he heard for the first time cannons and artillery fired by the Russians. When he returned home he was informed that an evacuation order had been issued for women and children and men not drafted by the Home Guard.

He and his twenty eight men were in charge of departure of the evacuees at the station. He made sure that the seats in each wagon were filled only with women and children and that any man who wanted to enter was drafted, if it was at all possible. Prams and overlarge bundles were not permitted. He did not know where the trains were headed.

Among the refugees on the first day were his wife Trudel, his daughter Sigrid and his in-laws. His father-in-law who had been told to report to the Home Guard, tried to sneak into the wagon while Herbert conveniently looked aside, but he was noticed by a Party official and ordered off the train. The man then persuaded his wife to stay with him. Understandably they did not want to be separated. Both stayed with Herbert for a few days. One day when he returned home, they were gone.

Herbert spent the next days destroying notes and files in his office (he does not elaborate in his memoirs what papers those were and what was the function of his office – were they Party materials??), he also supervised trains and continued training the men in the Home Guard. At home he hid belongings in the cellar, observing regretfully the rows of preserves that had to be left behind – but still in hope that Hitler would be able to stem the 'red tide' and that they would be able to return and claim their possessions.

When after a week resting at home with a sprained ankle sustained when he fell off his bike, he returned to the station he was astonished by the demeanour of the men who acted surprised to see him. They had assumed that he, like so many, had run off.

Disgusted with what he increasingly observed he noted in his memoirs, 'I see healthy men, able to fight in the reserves, young soldiers, loaded down with loot from deserted German homes, pushing themselves in increasing numbers into the trains, pushing women and children aside; they would often only relinquish those seats when I threatened them with my pistol. They had no scruples about taking their seats and condemning the women and children to fall into the filthy hands of the Soviets. Our wonderful Wehrmacht! The guarantors of victory!'

His memoirs continued, 'Those guarantors themselves went pillaging through German villages. When they travelled in trucks, they threw away their rifles and ammunition and loaded their vehicles up to the breaking point with goods they robbed.

But I still remained blind and explained their behaviour by rationalizing they had become demoralized through the years of war and repeated withdrawals. But they still are loyal men and when the secret weapons come out – they will use them.'

Another entry: "Sunday, February 11th,1945 arrived. Our companies were to be deployed for the first time with antitank weapons. Suddenly we were ordered to hold our fire. Leaders of the various companies were drawn together and ordered to retreat with their companies behind the line of the Neisse River. Before that they were to sabotage the existing factories and render them useless."

Herbert spent the next days with the company training the former workers of the destroyed factories. They had ten French military rifles without ammunition and ten grenades. The men who had worked in the factories and who had never held a grenade in their hands were the new fighting force. Herbert's hopelessness and dejection increased by the day. He himself had a pistol, Manfred's Mauser and a Russian MPi.

Two days later he received the order to depart with his men. They had blankets and foodstuffs for two days. A last pig was slaughtered and they had a feast. At midnight they moved out to join with other companies at a place near Gruenberg. A roll call revealed that instead of one hundred eighty men only eighty had shown up.

During the night he witnessed the approaching Russians, observed the night sky turning red as the cities burned. The men heard the firing and watched the retreating soldiers in columns of trucks and cars followed by the local inhabitants who start fleeing in whatever vehicles they could find.

Finally he received orders to march out with his men. Off and on he got new orders about where to advance, but he never received any provisions or shelter. The men had to fend for themselves. Often they shared space in a gymnasium or school with other refugees, sleeping on straw or the bare floor. One night someone stole Herbert's wallet with all his papers and the last of his money.

Four days later he received orders to move his men into abandoned and damaged factories and restore them again to functioning order; it had been decided to open them up and to produce goods again. Then suddenly all reservists were sent home.

Herbert then found out that parts of Silesia had not been overrun by the Russians and he decided to return with a group of like minded men. On the train they met up with SS members who spoke of a plan to back-track and to cut off the Russians from their own rear. They also talked about the secret weapon that was still to appear and that would set everything straight.

When he reported to the Kreisleiter he was dismissed from further military duty and he received permission to join his wife and daughter who, he knew from a letter that had been delivered to their old address, had found a place near Chemnitz. He took the train and reunited with them in Breitenau.

Herbert and his family, which soon was also to include his mother, moved into two rooms in the house of the manager of a chicken factory. They were able to use the family's kitchen and they were very grateful that they did not have to provide the normally carefully doled out wood for cooking. To heat their living room they received every two weeks two hundred pounds of firewood – but this was never enough to warm up the large room. His mother slept there on the couch and Herbert and his family slept in the other smaller chamber. After some time Herbert was re-hired as a second teacher and received some salary.

He reported back to the Home Guard that came to include fewer locals and ever more refugee men. Herbert commented sourly on the fact that the homeless refugees now had to fight to keep the land of those who still had some. Herbert did not feel welcome by the local population and he grumbled about the lack of help the refugees received in the village from people who still 'had so much'.

Chaos spread, as no one seemed to be in charge and conflicting orders rained down on the men of the Home Guard. They built more barricades and Herbert trained the men how to use automatic weapons. More refugees arrived daily from the east. Air planes rained bombs with stepped up frequency, littering the country side with increasing numbers of burned out vehicles and dead bodies.

The cold spring weather caused his arthritis to flare up painfully; it almost crippled him. On April 28th, an attack of tonsillitis caused a doctor to declare him unfit for further military duty. Herbert became very depressed. Not only had he lost his position as a superintendent, his home and all his possessions, he now had lost his job as a second teacher because the schools had closed in March. On April 30th the family received the last letter from the barely twenty one year old Manfred. It was to be almost three years before he would receive a card from him – sent from Siberia.

Herbert noted in his diary that 'Hitler said in a speech on April 16th, "The wave of the Bolshevik flood will crash at the gates of Berlin'. Herbert's comments to this statement was 'thus spoke our leader just before the last. Did he not see we had nothing left to fight with? Was he such a bad leader? Did he lie to us? If so, when had he started to lie to us? We still believed in the justice of our fight, in its purity. We still believed the government edicts, even though our troops had been forced to retreat for the last three years and we still believed in the mystery weapons. They were planned to come from the north and wreak havoc with the advancing Russians from behind.

Rarely did a nation believe and trust as we had done in this war and rarely had a nation been lied to and been betrayed as our nation was.'

May 7th, 1945 arrived. Since early morning tanks and trucks rolled through Breitenau pursued by the quickly advancing Russians. Cars and wagons pulled by horses or bullocks loaded with refugees and their belongings rumbled along between them. Often the roads became clogged and the movement came to a standstill. Everyone was heading west. Even Wehrmacht vehicles were loaded up with private citizens and goods.

Herbert had linked up with two other families, and together they had decided to join the exodus to the west. They had an oxen pulled wagon loaded with their belongings and their families. But before they could head west Herbert had to fetch his mother who put one obstacle after another in their way. By the time they were ready to roll they could hear gun shots, and exploding grenades. The Russians were near.

The road they travelled on was rough and steep and soon they had to prod the oxen to keep on moving. The men walked behind picking up the boxes that kept on falling down. They could hear the Russians approaching behind them, their shooting and yelling coming closer. They decided to let the animals rest in a forest where they met a group of young Wehrmacht soldiers who urged them to press on.

Herbert sat down on a log and ripped up his party book which indicated his rank and standing in the army, into small bits and hid the pieces under the roots. As he was contemplating what to do with his pistol and the revolver he had on him, he looked up. A dozen Russians stood about thirty meters away from him. With his boot he ground a hole into the soil and dropped his revolver in it and covered it with soil. Then he got up slowly and ambled towards the wagon scratching his back all the while with the hand that cupped the pistol. Trudel had been standing at the wagon and watched him approach. She quietly offered him a sandwich, at the same time gently taking the pistol from him. She tucked it in a satchel and hid it under some boxes at the bottom of the wagon.

More Russians drew near, watching them closely. They surrounded the small group of people and fleeced them of anything they fancied: rings, watches, wallets, everything of value was taken away. With much chattering and laughter they disappeared back into the forest. When Herbert's group got back onto the road again, they soon noticed that they were completely surrounded by Russians. Broken boxes and suitcases, a lot of clothing and bedding, mattresses and the odd corpse littered the side of the road. The group decided to get to a smaller but safer side road.

Night was falling when they got stopped by another troop of Russians. The soldiers searched the group again and took what they wanted out of their already diminished possessions; the result of their search did not please the Russians too much. They took their time searching the women. One of the Russians noticed that Herbert carried a whistle on a ribbon around his neck; his old teacher's whistle. Probably thinking that this was a token of some officialdom, the soldier hit him in the face and bellowed 'Nazi'. He then grabbed him by the lapel, shook and threatened him with a barrage of Russian words. When he released Herbert, he rummaged through his pockets and emptied them of everything they contained: matches, the pipe, his handkerchief and some tobacco got thrown on the ground. Having emptied Herbert's pockets which flopped ridiculously flaccid out of his pants, he positioned himself in front of Herbert and slowly and with a nasty grin on his mug stuck his pistol at Herbert's face. In a flash little Sigrid jumped in front of her father, screaming, "Nein! Nein!"

The Russian seemed bemused by courage of the small, blonde girl. He patted her on the head and very slowly he packed his pistol back in its holster and stalked away.

Everyone had been watching in frozen silence. Little Sigrid earned much praise and admiration for her brave deed.

There are many stories about the Russians in my grandfather's memoirs: How the Russians discovered pipes coming out of the wall that delivered water when one turned a handle. They ripped them out and stuck them into another place wondering why now no water came out. They did the same with electric switches and with lamps. Upon discovery of flush toilets, they practiced flushing and then rushed into the cellar to see what was happening. They drank not only all available alcoholic drinks in uncontrolled amounts, they drank cleaning fluids, antifreeze and perfume.

But not all their discoveries of a modern world made for an amusing anecdote. They were very cruel too. Herbert wrote of the multiple rapes that took place, where no female was spared whatever her age. Some of these acts were so vicious that many of the victims died. Men who wanted to help the women were made to watch or shot point blank. On their way to the west they come across villages where the whole population had committed suicide rather than fall into the hands of the Russians. Dead bodies are everywhere, many hacked to pieces, some crucified naked on barn doors.

At some time Herbert decided to head back to Breitenau. The Russians did not stop their wagon. They moved into their previous place in the chicken factory. On June 16th he opened a school in another village; in the capacity of principal he hired two other teachers. On June 23rd the district commissioner informed him that no refugee teacher would be allowed to teach. The new and acceptable teachers had undergone a six week crash course and they replaced all teachers that were refugees or had been Party members.

Herbert was now unemployed and towards the end of summer real hunger set in. He had to feed his wife, his daughter and his eighty year old mother and because he was not working he received only two pounds of bread a week per person. There was little else available. The family did what everyone did – they went to the fields and the forest and gathered mushrooms, berries and leaves. Herbert noticed that some chickens escaped during the day, he caught them before night set in. He wrote that he 'wasn't even ashamed of it'. A few weeks later Trudel obtained work at the chicken factory and with her wages she was able to purchase eggs and even milk.

During harvest time the family went out to the fields gleaning heads of grain and even grain kernels. Herbert dried them, packed them in a sack and threshed them by walking on them, winnowed the result by blowing on them and then exchanged the clean kernels for precious flour at the mill. But other families were out there too and one had to start early in the morning or else all was picked up. Wet days meant disaster because the grains sometimes started to sprout or they spoiled and rotted if kept wet too long. Despite all their efforts they were always hungry.

The farm they lived on was right beside the railroad going from Chemnitz to the east. After the overthrow countless numbers of trains, filled with Polish men and women came from the west. The travellers had the trains bedecked with green branches and red flags – they were going home and they were jubilant. Again and again the drunken travellers shot from the trains and when the trains stopped they poured out and plundered what they could. For weeks, whenever a train appeared from the west, the station emptied quickly, and people close to the trains hid in their houses.

When the populace went to the Russian commanders complaining about the behaviour of the soldiers, the thefts, the rapes and the killings, the commanders listened – but nothing ever was done. Local communist leaders established themselves quickly in the villages and towns, local bureaucracy spread like a fungus – and the refugees were always last in line.

Former members of the Party were deprived of their homes and their possessions without much formality and these confiscations were made official. Police with red arm bands roamed through the streets and appropriated what they wanted. Goods and services were provided preferentially to the locals. Nobody wanted the refugees; in fact they were looked at askance and they often heard insinuations as to why they didn't go back home.

This threat soon became reality when refugees were told they would no longer receive food stamps from their local administration and they were thus forced to leave a town or village. After some initial hesitation Herbert moved his family to Herreden, a small town in Thuringia, he wanted to get away from the Saxons whom he had not found welcoming at all. They remained there in the Russian occupied zone, the future German Democratic Republic, for another two years until his daughter Erika enabled Herbert to get to the American occupied zone in the west.

Life in Herreden, even though it was in the Russian occupied zone, started out not too bad. They located two rooms and because he was unable to find a room for his mother, which he would have preferred because he did not get along with her, she lived with them for the as long as they resided there. Initially they received more food stamps than they had before but that soon stopped. Because Herbert did not work they got no stamps for either meat or fat for two months. He used this time to scrounge the garbage dump for wood and odds and ends that could be used for their new home; from the found scraps he made furniture such as an easy chair and shelves. He re-discovered that cherry leaves made an acceptable, albeit very evil smelling, substitute for tobacco. Trudel spent her time working in farmers' fields and standing in line for hours to receive the two loaves of bread, the odd carrot and potato, or the much coveted sausage water that had to do for soup stock.

Herbert tried, again unsuccessfully, to get back into teaching – but former Party members were excluded. He finally landed a job with a threshing crew and later on as a forestry labourer which allowed him a few more food stamps. The pay was very small; the only benefit he saw were the free pieces of firewood he could carry home every evening after work – an old local tradition.

Their first Christmas as refugees was filled with memories and sadness. They knew nothing of the where-about of Irmgard, or Erika or Manfred. On December 27th a letter arrived telling them of the suicide of Helmut, the last and youngest of Herbert's brothers. Helmut had left his home in search of his wife who had ended up in the British sector of Germany. He had been robbed of his last possessions by some Poles before he showed up starving and destitute at the end of summer, on Herbert's door steps. He stayed with them for few days and then left because he believed that he would not be given any food stamps, as he had been threatened by local authorities. His brother, Herbert, who could not envision looking after yet another person, also encouraged him in this endeavour. Desperate because of the unsuccessful attempts to cross the border, he swallowed cyanide in early September. He was forty four years old.

Herbert notes in his memoirs that he was amazed about his brother's decision to end his life because he thought 'my brother would be more robust and tougher than he showed himself in the end too be. He had been a member of the party only since 1941 because he had to be. We both had great differences of opinions; he was in definite opposition to the fascists and he did not withhold his ideas…. perhaps he was the more intelligent of us and he took the one path which leads to peace for which I yearn… perhaps I would have thrown this life away too, this life that has no goal anymore if it would not be for my daughter Sigrid. My goal now is in her life.'

A deep depression engulfed Herbert and he admitted that if he did not have his young daughter, only seven years at the time, he would have ended his life. In his darkness he saw his life as unfulfilled and wasted. He had to acknowledge that all his dreams had been dashed, not only had all his possessions gone, but his professional life had ended for him. The fatherland for which he had had such high hopes had been conquered by men he did not understand, whose communist ideals he loathed and whom he hated. He saw not only the demise of Germany but a future where all of the western culture and civilization was destined to be overrun by the Reds from the East. He had read Spengler's "Untergang Des Abendlandes", "Decline of the West", and had been deeply impressed. In his notes he wrote that if he had read the book in his youth he might not have become a follower of National Socialism.

Herbert wrote in his memoirs: 'What is left of all my dreams, my hopes, my battles and beliefs? Nothing is around me and nothing is in me. Nothing brightens my darkness today. The worst of old age is when others show you that everything that you had believed, everything you had fought for with all your strength and power, that all is a phantom, a dream, even a crime. Even a criminal is looked after and provided with the basic necessities of life. Nobody does that for me and that proves that I am even lower than a criminal. Could the difference between my existence then and my existence today be any greater? Then I was free; full of self confidence. I was a man with a good and secure profession, a man whose opinion meant something, a free man, open to the beauty of the world. And today? I am a person in the lowest class, everywhere unwanted and in the way, broken and not free. Today I am that. I am a man who plunders through garbage hoping to find something useful in the trash others have thrown away. It weighs like a mountain on me.'

'I sit and think that in my life I was often short sighted or even naïve. When I was working on the fortifications along the Oder River, I remember wondering about the ridiculousness of the enterprise. I was so sure that no Russian would ever venture that far west. Our Wehrmacht, I knew, was our bulwark against that.

Did I not know that after Stalingrad our Wehrmacht had been retreating, abandoning one region after another allowing the enemy to come ever closer? Was losing the war not the logical outcome of all of this? But I was blind and involved only with my heart and not with my head and intellect.

The dominance of the heart over the brain is my strongest characteristic. I could name hundreds of incidents where I have suffered because of this, my nature.'

'It was in the very same vein that I joined the National Socialist Party. I was driven by no intellectual consideration or the wish to gain certain advantages – it was only a matter of the heart. Whatever people say today about the inhumanity or the cruelties that were committed in its name, I did not know then or later.

Yes, there were several things, as small as they were, that I did not agree with, especially during the war. Once I said to my Kreisleiter, "It might be well and good for you that you only have to press a button and men will hop and dance to the melody you choose. Perhaps this condition is called for by the fact that we are in a war. I do not wish that these things remain like that afterwards. Once the war is over, I want these things to disappear. This is not National Socialism; this is a dictatorship, which differs from Bolshevism only in their goals and not at all in their methods.'

'When an acquaintance, who witnessed my words, said to me, "You will keep on talking until they will come for you and put you in a concentration camp." I replied that I would always speak my mind and that nobody could take that freedom away from me.

Should someone make me silent because of my words this is evidence that the movement, which had called for personalities without blind obedience and submission, had deviated from its goals. That, I will promise, will come back and haunt them with a vengeance.'

'I have had no personal advantages during the time I belonged to the Party. It was not just a slogan but a duty and condition that I, as a member of the Party, had extra duties and more obligations than the others. This is why I have sacrificed more time and energy and health for what I had once valued as something that could fulfill the dream of my people, a dream that had started a thousand years before.

Was the path we were led on wrong? Were the hands that led us not clean? Were the hearts not pure? Were the German people already so degenerate that they could no longer carry an idea and that the awakening of our dream was so unbelievably horrific?

I do not know and I do not want to judge – how could I – I was part of it. One thing is certain: history has found against us and that is hard to bear.'

'It is also true that others cooked their soup with the fire that consumed us. They have long wolfed down their meal when we arrive and announce that we are hungry too.'

'Perhaps not only I, but the German people as a whole, lack a sense for the reality of the practical life. How else could one explain that German immigrants everywhere in the world do the hardest pioneer work, but that when that is accomplished, practical men, who know reality, come and take over and bring in the richest harvests into their own barns. Why did the French and the English and the Italians succeed in establishing unified states which was denied to Germany?'

'We, who dreamed of freedom while others divided the world among them, were the procurers of culture for many peoples, and have been, not only since the last debacle, their slaves who have worked and are still working for them? It was not only I that missed out on advantageous conditions. The history of our people is a history of missed opportunities.

There is only one real and effective law that one has to accept, even if it destroys one, and that is the terrible law of necessity.'

Chapter 20

GUSTEL IN AUSTRIA

From Belgrade we drove on to Neusatz or Novograd, the border city, where we were loaded onto the train heading towards Vienna. We passed through villages where all the population was German. These were people whose ancestors had been brought here by the Austrian Kaisers, especially Maria Theresia, to be a protective live wall against the Turks and their influence. They were lovely villages where milk and honey were still to be had. We ate in one of those places and were served freshly baked bread, good butter and thick lard with bacon bits in it. It was a paradise we did not want to leave.

Conditions in the station in Vienna were not what they usually were. We had to push and shunt wagons by hand. There were too many men milling around, there was too much equipment and it happened that one empty wagon started to roll and pushed a man against the buffer of another wagon and killed him. Since I was in charge I was worried they were going to blame me for this very regrettable incident, but my commander said that the guilty party was the man who emptied the wagon and thus caused it to start to roll.

"An officer cannot be responsible for a place here and another one five hundred meters away."

I was cleared of any wrongdoing but it was still on my mind for some time. The detachment was disbanded and I sat in Vienna waiting for my new orders.

Along the German-Hungarian border, in the Burgenland, the Wehrmacht was building huge defensive fortifications with placements for artillery and infantry; they built especially endless ditches to trap the anticipated Russian tanks in. The whole enterprise was administered by the military, but the work and the workers, their shelter and food, was under the auspices of the Gau, in particular the local district where the actual construction occurring. The people working on the fortifications were conscripted workers pulled there together by the individual Kreisleiters, the leaders of the districts, from farms, factories and camps. Whoever from the local population could be spared from a job was moved to the area. An additional 30,000 Jews who had just been captured in Budapest, were provided by the SS Ministry of Economics, the same people who ran the administration of the concentration camps; they in turn lent the prisoners to the Gauleiter and the mandarins of the districts.

Freight trains brought the Jews to the border where they were received by the guards that the party had provided. From long experience I knew that the Austrians generally did not like Jews. There were many women and children in the trains which pulled up. I thought if they were distributed around the towns, there would be too many problems. I went to the Kreisleiter and suggested that there would be rape and killings if we accepted the women and children. I could not say any more; he was an Austrian and they did not want to hear the truth. He answered, "Good, we will not unload the women and children. They will stay in the train and the party will have to look after them."

I was glad to have lessened my problems. I then checked the accommodations for the Jewish workers. They were put up in barns and sheds and whatever else was empty and could be used to house men. Huge ditches were evacuated to make sleeping quarters for them. At first, I was apprehensive but when I saw that they were lined and covered with bull rushes that grew abundantly along the lake here, I was satisfied that they would make an adequate shelter.

I was policing the area of work with six to eight men and my task was to intervene when problems arose whether they involved Austrians, Jews or conscripted workers.

My first district was close to Vienna. When I went to see the Kreisleiter I found him to be the most arrogant of men. I introduced myself and stated my business here. He snapped at me, "I don't need this. I do all that myself!" And to myself I thought, "Alright, there are no Jews up here. See how you'll get along with the conscripted workers, loudmouth."

Further south were very few Jews and the Kreisleiter was a very reasonable man. I can only praise him. He was such a change from the other Kreisleiter who was furious because the Gestapo was now checking up on him.

And then the problems started. The first district Kreisleiter had taken Jews to work for him in his office. One day when I spoke to the Kreisleiter one of the two girls present attacked me immediately and insulted me. Next day she was gone, the Kreisleiter had transferred her to a job in the ditches. With her outburst she had forfeited the chance to sit warm and snug in an office and exchanged it for a job digging ditches in winter. She had not used her head. The other girl was pretty and she was pleasant and quiet. Later I learned that she was the niece of Weihman. Weihman was a Jew, a pharmacist from Budapest. He was an intelligent man and a good man – we will hear later more from him.

First, I had to make it clear to the Kreisleiter and his closest associates that I would not tolerate any maltreatment of the Jews. I told them that the Jews were here to work and not to be badgered, mistreated, or killed. If someone had to be shot, this order had to come from higher up and not from us. I knew my people. I know that if I had not intervened right from the start and had explained that they could not expect any leniency from me if I heard of ill treatment of the Jews, many would have been shot. That happened often enough in other places.

About two weeks after the Jews arrived, typhus broke out. I informed the Kreisleiter and warned him to be careful, because this infernal disease did not only attack Jews. By that time some Jews and at least ten guards had already died. An empty hall was found and as the Jews fell ill they were put in there. Sometimes the hall held up to two thousand persons. We were ordered not to enter the area because of the high danger of infection. But I went there anyhow; I had to see what was going on. I did notice that the hall was heated. The sick were lying on good and clean straw. The locals did what they could. My friend Weihman was there too. I shook his hand and wished him speedy recovery and all the best.

One day some Jewish doctors approached me.

"We have good medicines against the disease. Let us get it from Budapest."

I went to the Kreisleiter and pleaded with him to let the Jewish doctors go and get the medicine. I also volunteered to supply a detachment to fetch the medicines from Budapest.

"No," he barked at me. "That is out of the question!"

And that was the end of it. Slowly the disease disappeared. The party never published exact numbers about the deaths and I did not work together with the party. I had to use my own resources to find out that about 1500 people had died.

One day my men come back from the outside – we had to spend much time listening and observing to find out what was going on, we had to have our ears to their mouths and we had to feel the pulse of the population – and they told me that there was a problem. "We have got to know some women and they have called us every name under the sun. They said we were a despicable and miserable bunch of men."

The men had no idea what the women referred to. I had to investigate.

I sent my men back to the village and told them to make the women talk, even threaten them they would be hauled to my office if they would not speak.

They opened up. The following had transpired. The local Party had found accommodation for the Jews; some of them were quartered in a cellar and they had been supplied with straw. Meanwhile the rainy time had started and ground water was rising in the cellar. Someone had the great idea to move the straw higher. They made the Jews throw stones and rocks onto the floor of the cellar, cover them with some planks and then pile the straw on top. The Jews were expected to wade through the water on the cellar floor after many hours of hard work in the ditches, climb onto their rock pile and sleep on the straw. There was no possibility of the people ever getting dry – the damp and wet around them was bound to make them sick very soon.

The population was upset about this inhumane treatment. Some church ministers became involved. The women had told my men that the local political leaders were spreading the rumour that all this had happened on orders of the Gestapo.

This made me angry. That had been the doing of the party and not of us at all. I sent my men out to the place where the Jews were labouring and ordered that all work had to be stopped immediately. I told the men in charge that the Jews would have to be put up properly. I instructed my men to stay with them until they could be sure that the last Jew was properly housed.

And that is what happened. With the co-operation of the population and against the will of the 'brown shirts' all Jews found proper and dry accommodation with plenty of straw.

Then I started to think –what I had just done went far beyond my mandate. I would have never been allowed to give orders to stop work or to enforce that the Jews had proper warm shelter. I went with great trepidation to the Kreisleiter. I explained to him that I put great emphasis on the importance of keeping the Jews, the workers, healthy in order to fulfill the assigned work load in as short a time as possible. I suffered no repercussions for my handling of the event. The Kreisleiter did not report me to Berlin as he could easily have done.

I was glad that peace had returned and the work could resume. Our good name was again restored when the population was made aware who the real guilty party was. It had not hurt our image either to stand up for humane treatment of the Jews against the machinations of the Party.

We never had any problems on the construction site with the Jewish men or women. The only ones who caused trouble were the conscripted workers. Those problems were mostly harmless. These men constantly tried to run away and get 'home' to their factory, or farm or wherever they had been taken from. We simply caught those fellows, gave them a stern lecture, threatened them with the most horrendous punishment and then sent them back to work. There were so many of them. Mostly they attempted to run away in the evening after work. We had the same rounds every night. They just would not give up.

One day the postman complained that they had so much to do with parcels and letters to the conscripted men. "All of Austria is writing to them," he whined.

I decided to control for one day what was sent to these men. It was in my power to do this. What a surprise: the parcels were filled with cookies, bacon and sausages and the letters were filled with endearments and longing and promises. It was remarkable what a relationship some of these men had with the Austrian women. They obviously filled a husband's role not only at the place of work, such as their farms or business where they had been conscripted to, but also in their beds. Under normal conditions I should have done something about this, but I thought – they are all content, the men and the women and the husbands are far away and know nothing about what is going on at home. I know most husbands would have had a different opinion about it and even fewer would have condoned it – but I still kept quiet about it and changed nothing. I thought what they don't know won't hurt them and then – all is fair in love and war!

One morning as I was travelling around the area I came to a site where nobody was working. I saw no Germans, only Jews. I did not know the men but they knew me.

"Herr Kommissar, the political leader who is in charge of the plans here has not shown up for work today. We want to tell you that if we had the plans we could continue with the work even without him. We want to defend our Hungarian homeland from here, even if it is on German ground. After all, the Russians are about to enter our homeland. We do not want the Russians to win. We want a free Hungary."

What can one say to that. They worked.

There was trouble with the Jews only once. One day I noticed that here and there tall, tough and healthy looking Jews were not working. Naturally I asked them why they were not at work.

"My shoes are at the cobbler's."

All Jews had been issued some kind of clothing for their work. Their shoes, often only slippers, were not very tough and I could understand that they were frequently in need of repair. But I kept on noticing again and again that seemingly the same able bodied men were lounging around. One day I took Weihman with me because I wanted to find out what was going on.

Weihman went with me to the cobbler's shop. The shelves were filled with lines of shoes. First the cobbler did not want to talk, but eventually he did. He told me that whoever put money in his hand did not get his shoes repaired. The result was, of course, that the poor Jews had to work and the rich ones could spend their days in idleness. Hearing this made me very angry. I struck the shoemaker a few times across his legs with a stick I grabbed from his shop. He limped for a few days but I never felt sorry for him. So eine Affenschande! What a dastardly thing to do!

The result of that was more harmful to the Jews than they could have foreseen. We now realized that they still had possessions as far as they were able to carry them. I went to the Kreisleiter and reported the incidence and consequently the Jews had to hand over all of their wealth. Some of them had large sums of money, especially gold pieces, which they had sewn into their clothes.

One day Weihman came to see me. He hummed and hawed until I was sure there was something he wanted me to know. Finally he opened up and told me that in a village a political leader had raped a young Jewish woman and then shot her.

I thought if I let this slip we'll have a catastrophe on hand. I went to the Kreisleiter and reported the incident. To my greatest astonishment he told me that he knew about the rape and the murder but that he had made no efforts to have it made known to me nor, for that matter, had he done anything about it.

I organized a vehicle for myself and drove to the village. I could not find the man who had killed the Jewish girl. He had already been transferred to another area and so slipped through my fingers. Now, much too late, did the locals and the present political leader corroborate the sordid story. But now it was too late to do something about it.

One day we drove to Oedenburg on the Hungarian side. On our approach a formation of bombers came flying exactly towards the city. I decided to wait out the bombing outside of the city. And wouldn't you know it, the bombers emptied their hatches exactly over the railway station and surrounding houses. The bombs rained down like a plague of satanic eggs and exploded on the station that was crowded with trains filled with soldiers. I had a look at it when it was over and the fires and the dust had settled. Dead and wounded were everywhere. Craters six meters deep dotted the station, or what was left of it. Freight trains were hammered with one end into the ground, the other end stuck up into the air. All I did was file a report – I had become immune to business that did not concern me.

The Russian troops had entered Budapest and we knew that a critical time lay ahead of us. The first preparations for the future were taking place. I had been ordered to take my men to Vienna and three days after – as I was to get to know later on – the Russians had reached the border. During the time I was waiting for new orders, I was called to my superior.

"Sorry, Haefner, but we have to send you back where you had just been. Ten thousand of the Jews are to be moved away and the Gauleiter has asked especially for a man who knows how to deal with the Jews and who will be able to police the columns on the way."

Again, I was given a motor cycle with a side car and I went off to intercept the marching people. I met them. And who was marching in the front row? My friend, the pharmacist from Budapest, Mr. Weihman. We greeted each other and he expressed his happiness about my being there. When he informed me that they had stopped marching because there had been shooting in the back, I decided to turn around and investigate immediately. I drove along the column of ten thousand marching people for about two kilometers until I entered a village.

Marching columns have very distinct patterns: they are tight and quickly moving at the head and by the time the tail end is reached, the people are drawn out and they end up running in order to catch up. Exactly that is what was happening here. As the column was moving through the village, some locals saw the last ones running to catch up.

Some busy body yelled, alarming the village.

"The Jews are escaping!"

That is when the guards and soldiers had started shooting. It was pitch dark and the little cone of a flash light that was allowed to penetrate the darkness did not much to illuminate anything.

"Hold your fire!" I roared.

Meanwhile the last of the dawdlers had arrived. Because they had had a relatively good life at the fortifications where they had worked, many had been able to organize bundles and boxes which they carried along. In their fear to lose the column or to be shot, some had thrown away their bundles. And I had to stand and witness that a tracked personnel carrier who had followed the rear, drove over such a package and I heard bones cracking. For the rest of my life I will remember that sound. Some human being must have been in that bundle. And I stood by and could not help.

One hundred and eighty men were guards for the column, but as I quickly noticed, no one in particular was in charge and there was no organization. The guards were a motley crew. Someone had given them a stick in the hand and told them, 'Now you are a guard.' Since I could not discern a leader of the whole enterprise, there was only one man I could talk to and that was Weihman. I was so glad he was with me.

Eventually we arrived at a large meadow. A train with fifty two wagons arrived. They were small with overhanging roofs over the platform at either end, they must have been built around 1890. Somehow I understood that five thousand of the ten thousand people who were just standing around were supposed to get on that one train. I knew how that would happen; I had seen it often enough. The guards would scream at the people, they would hit them because they would never move fast enough for the impatient guards who yelled themselves into a frenzy. I had seen it before and I hated the picture.

"Stop! All stop!"

I had the one hundred and eighty guards line up.

"Which one of you is from Upper Austria?"

This was a region further west from us. I chose two times eight men of those who had not raised their arm. The other one hundred and sixty four stood wonderingly in front of me.

I dismissed the men.

"Men, you may go. You may go home."

They did not hesitate but marched off eagerly, not quite sure if I was not playing with them and call them back any minute now once I had come to my senses.

As I watched them disappear I hoped fervently that nothing would happen or else I would have to pay dearly for what I had done.

I kept the sixteen men because I had found out that another train was on its way for the remainder of the Jews and I wanted each train accompanied by eight guards.

Then I addressed Weihman. Easily and quickly, without any screaming and hitting, the first five thousand people were loaded onto the first train without any incidences. Weihman and his men organized it all. They were fantastic. I remember them so very well. They were doctors and lawyers, so many educated people, and the others listened to them and followed their instructions without a word. I ordered a row of seats to be kept free for the guards and told them to look after the Jews. In truth, if the Jews were going to do something against them, what could the eight men have done?

By now I had heard that the trains were to travel to Mauthausen. There was a large concentration camp. Looking back – it is hard to believe but I actually knew nothing at that time. All I knew is what the train engineer or Weihman told me. And so the train left, filled to the rafters with five thousand people. They were crowded even outside on the open platforms and crammed into toilets. One hundred men and women in each small wagon, but all went well.

The second train arrived. It had twenty two modern wagons. Again, Weihman organized an orderly entry of his people into the train and they left with their eight guards.

I travelled on the road following the trains. A bombing attack had demolished the station in Krems. The railway officials informed me that it would be at least two days before the tracks would be fixed and we could travel on. So, here I was, with a train full of five thousand Jews and eight guards. I needed food for them. I went to the Kreisleiter and he told me that he had absolutely no reserves left.

It made my blood boil. No one from the Party cared – some idiot had sent the Jews away without any thought of consequences; had not thought of bombing raids, or guards or food. I went back to the train and told the guards not to let the local population get to the Jews. I knew that the people here did not like the Jews and I did not want a tragedy to happen. Then I went to Weihman.

"I am sorry, I tried to get something for you to eat. There is nothing. But back there alongside the train are gardens. Take down the fences and make a fire and perhaps you could still find some potatoes, or turnips or carrots in the gardens you could eat. I know it is spring – but go and try it".

I left them and motored to Mauthausen. Before I reached this town I encountered a road barrier. I guessed that whoever had no valid travel permit landed on the huge tree at the road side; I could see bodies dangling from the thick branches. There were many.

I got stopped. My arm flew up in military style – but the body in front of me could not have cared less. A voice barked at me.

"Permit."

"I don't need one."

In the next moment I could feel already a rope coiled around my neck. It was a really greasy rope.

"Listen. I am here on business and I have a train with five thousand Jews waiting."

Maybe then he realized that I was not a deserter, neither Waffen SS nor Wehrmacht, but that I was police. Slowly, ever so slowly, he removed the rope from my neck and waved me through. I was very much relieved. Here, in the middle of nowhere I was totally dependent on him and he did not seem a man to be reasoned with. His 'Kettenhunde', his 'chained dogs', as his men were called because they had a sign hanging around their necks on which 'field gendarme' was printed, were standing around us, watching it all carefully. It looked to me that they would not have minded in the least to string another one up and see him hang.

I arrived at Mauthausen and went immediately to see the camp commandant.

"You have to be bloody kidding. Yesterday I got a train with five thousand and we were already short with rations for the people I have, and now you bring me another five thousand. I do not know what to do anymore."

This was such a terrible event. In the last days of the war the camps were overrun with inmates. They were never announced to a commander. The Jews were sent in ever increasing numbers, but food was not, and that is why so many died of starvation. This was not the fault of the camp commander. This was the fault of the bureaucrats in Berlin who just ordered the Jews in.

When I came back, unfortunately empty handed, I asked Weihman, if they had been able to find something in the gardens.

"Sir, we did not get anything out of these gardens – we couldn't do it. They weren't ours."

And they had not had food since the day before.

Then Weihman and his men started to prepare the locomotive which was already under steam for travelling. They took buckets and carried coal from the tender on the station to the locomotive. With buckets they filled it up. What could I say? What could I say?

We resumed our journey. We came into a bombing raid but stayed in the tracks outside the station. I had gone to the train conductor and that is what he had advised. We were safer out on the tracks than in the city.

Waiting out the air raid I started thinking. The people had not even been able to go to the bathroom since the toilets were stuffed full of people. I talked to Weihman.

"Tell your people that they all have permission to leave the train and walk around in the open within a distance of one kilometer. Tell them also when the locomotive whistles three time it is time to come back."

And that is what happened. After two hours the loc blew the whistle three times and all went quietly back into their wagons. I did not know if some of the Jews absconded during this time. I did not care. On the outside they were probably not very safe because, as I have mentioned already, the population, which were mostly farmers and very Catholic, did not like the Jews at all.

We came to Mauthausen and the guards were already waiting for the newcomers. The dreaded routine began again. They screamed and yelled and beat on the people and it was awful. I tried to swing my weight and ordered one especially brutal guard to behave himself. He turned around and told me that I was not the one to give him orders. And he carried on with his stick. I was quiet because if I had made waves, everything I had done during the last days would have come out and I would have been in serious trouble. So I said nothing.

And suddenly Weihman and two other Jews came towards me. One was the owner of a construction company in Budapest and the other was an older, rabbinical looking man, probably a rabbi.

"Herr Kommissar, we want to thank you in the name of thirty thousand men and women for what you have done for us."

I started to swallow. The three men fell on their knees before me.

"Lieutenant, Sir, in the name of thirty thousand human beings, we ask you to please stay with us."

All I could say was, "I could help you up to here but now I cannot do any more. I do wish you all the best."

I had to swallow hard. I turned and walked away. There was nothing I could do for them now. Nothing on God's earth. Nothing at all.

The commander in Vienna considered a Russian occupation a rapidly approaching reality and he prepared for the oncoming event. He asked for a volunteer for a special detachment. Of course my hand went up, even though I had no idea what I was about to be doing. More than three hundred criminal police sat around as he answered with a nod towards me.

"I knew that you'd volunteer."

I was an officer and I always thought that the uniform demands a certain responsibility. As long as I thought I could do something in the interest of the people and the fatherland, I was going to do it. Or else one is a 'Hosenscheisser' a chicken shit. I was quite aware that at that time the war was practically lost – but maybe – somewhere in the back of my head was still the hope for the wonder weapon they had promised. But this was today and I still had work to do. As officer one has a duty and responsibility towards the state and the people.

I was given a dozen men and I was told that I was to go to the Wehrmacht on the front and join them there.

The sixth Panzerarmee under SS General Sepp Dietrich could not free Budapest from the Russians because his generals and the generals of other SS tank corps could not agree on a common line of action and instead of uniting to attack the Russians, they attempted to reach Budapest on their own on different days and consequently they were soundly defeated. The German troops, that is foremost the men of the SS Panzerarmee, fled in an unorganized fashion towards the German-Hungarian border. I have seen myself that German units of the Wehrmacht crossed the border and when stopped by General Dietrich, who asked them why they were retreating, replied to Dietrich that they were retreating on orders from their superiors.

These troops, so it had been planned, were supposed to hold the stations of the fortifications which had been built in the Burgenland, the flat, open land east of Vienna. But as they were now in wild retreat, these positions were not manned. In fact they were totally open, there was not a soldier to defend them. The SS troops marched over them to regroup back in the hinterland. Of course, now the Russian tank corps could easily surge forward, disregarding fortifications and antitank ditches – and so the front unravelled without any resistance right up to the Danube River. The odd small troop that tried valiant resistance had not a chance in hell.

The Russians were now able to move forward without any resistance right up to the Semmering Pass. This was as area of sanatoria and hospitals where more than three thousand soldiers were recuperating. One lieutenant put together a troop of volunteer soldiers from there and tried to put up some resistance to the Russians. If it was not for him, we would not have had one hero here.

The office Security Service was already further west, no longer in Vienna where already vicious battles were fought. The military teaches one thing very quickly: the safest place is the place furthest away from the enemy, and by enemy in my case I mean the commander of the security police. The further I was away from him the safer I was.

I went with my men to the furthest corner of the Reich and that was the Semmering, along the ancient road from Vienna to the south, over the Semmering Pass, down into the Steiermark and into the border region with Italy and Yugoslavia. There I reported to the local commander, the only one there. The

Waffen SS was somewhere else. I told him that he could use me and my men for any special task he wanted to be undertaken.

My first assignment was to investigate frequent break- ins and robberies in farms and small holdings in the hinterland. It was thought that the perpetrators were either conscripted workers or deserters who broke into the premises to get food. We went into the mountains and started to comb the barns and sheds were straw and hay was kept. It was not very long before we found two deserters who had originally come from this area. We took the two down with us. But desertion was the business of the Wehrmacht and so I handed them over to the local commander. I asked him to give me a receipt for the two men. I had learned to be rather careful. I knew that prisoners sometimes disappeared, I was also careful with my own men. I trusted nobody anymore. It was totally within the scope of events that men were killed because that was easier than to transport them. Subordinates did not always do as they were told.

Towards the end of the war the Wehrmacht, in desperation, looked for anyone who could be put into a uniform and hold a rifle. They collected them in the Volkssturm, a Home Guard battalion, Germany's last hope. The commander in the village led such a battalion, but he himself, a forester in peace times, was a military man.

He had one look at the two and said quickly, "They will have to face military court."

"Sir, what have you to gain if these two get the death penalty for desertion?"

One of the men was a high school teacher, he was pale and fearful. The other one seemed not to be intelligent but he was afraid too.

The commander insisted on bringing the two to justice because now he was scared that I would haul him in front of the court if he would let the two go. But eventually he believed me that I did really not have an ulterior motive and genuinely saw no benefit from handing over the two to the authorities.

He contemplated for one long day. Finally he asked me, "What shall I do with them?"

"Send the teacher home, and the other one – well, keep him for yourself. He will be very grateful that you spared him and you can use him to run errands and messages, carry food and ammunition and what have you. This is better even for you, than to have him shot."

And that is how the two escaped an otherwise grim fate. I had by now come to the conclusion that after a certain limit, all toughness and show of power was no longer of any use.

When the front stabilized the former forester came with his Home Guard battalion and established a front of resistance. One morning when I came to report to him again, as I always did, the man sat in his office and cried like a child.

Something terrible has happened. Something that should never have happened. And it is all my fault."

He told me that a certain unit had been badgering him for days to be deployed at a strategic point on a mountain from which the Russians had a commanding position over a wide area. This unit was the former bomber squadron General Weber, 'on foot', as he sadly pronounced, a heavy sob shaking his body. There was no longer an active squadron as all of their planes had been shot down but the men had been transferred to the front here.

"They were honest, decent folk, good soldiers, there wasn't one of them who did not have a medal for his many front deployments. But they were not infantry and they had absolutely no experience in that field of action. This is the reason I always refused their demands to be sent into action. But they kept on asking me and yesterday I finally agreed to it. This morning they stormed the mountain and of course, it was foreseeable, they were repulsed with very great losses.

"So many dead. So many dead."

I commiserated with him. He felt responsible for the dead.

The back country was swarming with deserters, absconded conscripted workers and also Russian volunteers on the German side. We were not aware at first that they were Russians, we thought they were simply soldiers in German uniforms. The commander of the section wanted that something be done against these men. It had been agreed with the Wehrmacht that they would cordon off a certain section and that the search in the country and in the mountains, the barns and farms, would be done by my men. A Volksdeutscher, a Staff-Sergeant, who was a decent and reliable fellow, was to be the leader of the expedition. He came back in the late afternoon reporting that they had found these people in the mountains He also reported the German deserters and the conscripted men were much smarter than the others and most of them had been able to escape from the search party.

To our amazement we found out that the men in German uniforms were actually Russians. When at the end of the war the tables were changed, they figured it would now be to their advantage to be fighting on the Russian side again. But when they tried to rejoin their Russian units, the Russians did not want them and sent them back to Germany. Some of the men must have found out that they would be shot immediately after being taken in. Of course, now they were scared to admit on the German side that they were turncoats again and so they fled into the mountains where they had to rob farms to stay alive.

The Staff-Sergeant reported that they had shot a number of these men rather than bring them down. I did not like what I heard. I'd rather they would not have shot them. But since I had not been out there with them I had not been able to have any influence on their actions in the field.

For some time we had taken quarters in a private house. One day I thought that something was just different. The housewife never met my eyes and avoided speaking with me. Next morning I discovered a deserter, a Sergeant, had been hiding behind the tiled oven. The lady of the house, a refugee herself, had stowed him there. She was frozen with fear. I interviewed the fellow who stuttered and stammered some crazy story about some reconnaissance he had to undertake for his superior. But I knew that the SS Regiment Leibstandarte, from which he was deserting, was stationed about twenty kilometers further north. He did not change his story and so I had to hand him over to the Wehrmacht.

There he immediately admitted to his desertion. I was not really interested that something drastic should happen to him. Actually I was quite angry with him. If the nincompoop would have opened up to me and have admitted that he had deserted I would have told him to join my men, to come with me and the case would have been closed. He must have been very scared of the Gestapo. As it was, he had to go through the courts but with me and a few other men speaking up for him, he was only sentenced to a time punishment. That was on a day when some judges condemned six other men to death for desertion.

Sometimes I could help a person. Especially now, I thought, as things were coming to an end; I felt much more lenient towards people and more understanding about human nature and could even condone some of their foibles and infractions.

My men, as was their job, took up connections with the local population and especially the female part. There weren't too many men left anyhow. One day they came back and reported that they had been malingered. When I investigated it came out that people were talking that men in uniforms, uniforms like the Waffen SS, had come, apprehended a man and shot him. The people said that it had been the Gestapo.

We denied any involvement but they did not believe us. In the meantime, the war came to an end. Much later I learned that there had been a court case about this incident and that the Austrian justice system had caught and sentenced the real culprits. I was glad that we, in the end, had been cleared. Some men had probably stolen uniforms or bought them – they may also have been privately sewn.

I had started to send my men out periodically to find out how far away the Russians were. Once I sent them out to climb a mountain. When they had almost reached its peak; they had just time to observe our German defenders dropping their weapons and hightailing down the other side of the mountain. My men quickly realized that the Russians were approaching from the other side and then they took the weapons which had been thrown down, and welcomed the very much surprised Russians with volleys of shots.

The Russians had occupied a position from which they deployed seventeen centimeter artillery guns on a mountain. I sent my men there to scout out if there was possibility to get to those weapons or at least destroy them. As they were marching halfway up the mountain, the usually not very watchful Russian soldiers noticed them when they were half a kilometer away and started to shoot at them. Luckily my men were not walking in formation but were spread out and by the time the Russians had organized and trained their heavy artillery on them my men had disappeared. The only damage the Russians did was that they succeeded to set the mountain on fire. But it was spring and it was wet so the fires soon died out.

And then came the end of the war.

As usual I reported in the morning to my commander. As I was there my office phoned and I was instructed to leave immediately with my men and go to a city on the river Murr. When I told the leader of the Home Guard battalion of my transfer, he almost wept. He had got to know us and he recognized that there were still things to be done which he could never accomplish with his Home Guard battalion of old men or green boys.

When I arrived at the city I was told that the war was over. That was on May 7th, 1945. This shows they knew what was going on in Berlin. I was glad about that because otherwise I would have become a Russian prisoner of war. The area where we had been was officially declared the Russian occupied zone. I took two cars and loaded up my men and off we drove westward, away from the Russians, into the mountains.

Chapter 21

Erika And The End Of The War

You ask how much I knew about the Jews and the concentration camps? I must say that I really knew nothing about the camps. But I had seen what was happening. Once, when I visited my sister in Berlin, I saw the Gestapo pull an old man and his wife out of their store, a jewelry store, and then they threw them into a car. I had no idea what was going on. And then I saw another, similar incident. I asked your mother what was going on and asked her what the police were doing with these people. She said that they would take the Jews and put them into concentration camps. I never understood the reason behind that and I never knew why they did that.

I am not a friend of the Jews. In my experience the Jews do not know a fatherland and money is their main interest. But it shocked me to learn what the government did to them. I did not know anything about concentration camps. Nobody talked about them. Nothing was on the radio or in the papers. People just did not know about these things. I am convinced that had the general public known about what was going on, there would have been an uproar. Germany is not a big country but there were many people who would not have tolerated what was going on. But most people just did not know. When after the war I learned about the gas chambers and about Buchenwald I thought these tales were lies. I could not believe that a German would do that or would allow such things to happen. Then I saw the pictures and was horrified.

What I did know, though, was that we had conscripted workers, foreign workers. We had lots of them in Gruenberg. We saw them at work and we knew they marched to work in factories or on farms and I knew that after work was finished, they marched back to a camp where they were locked up. If you remember the Hershey Bar and my little Dachsi – that came from inmates of such a camp.

I have to tell you of the end of the war for me: I remember even the date, it was January 22nd, 1945. We had a Nazi meeting after school and we were told that the Russians were coming close but that we as Party members could not leave; we were to stay and defend our fatherland. That is what the Ortsgruppenleiter, the local Party leader, said. At two o'clock that same night the sirens wailed. I jumped out of bed and when I looked out the window, the sky was red with the flames of burning houses. I could hear artillery and I knew that was the doing of the Russians; they were about ten miles away.

I dressed warmly in pants and boots, grabbed my knapsack, stuck my dog in it, my papers, a few clothes and left my house. I also had a pistol with me. Konrad had given it to me and he had trained me how to use it. He had told me that when you have a pistol you can defend yourself or even shoot yourself. He had warned me never to fall into the hands of the Russians, who were cruel beyond belief and who raped everything female they could find.

The main road was already clogged with cars and wagons. I took a side road and by the time I got to the edge of town we were a troop of twenty three women and fifteen children. Our group had not been planned, we had just left and sort of found each other and now stayed together. It was twenty eight degrees below and we trudged through deep snow. We came upon a farm house; it was empty, the owners having left already. We moved in and stayed there overnight. In the bigger houses we often found food: canned fruit and vegetables in the cellar, and sometimes smoked or salted meats and sausages; we were happy about that. The small crofts were mostly bare of food. We just marched and marched. It was very cold and the snow was very deep. We stayed away from the big roads and found very little to eat in the few houses we passed. They were all empty. Some had burned them to the ground. We saw many dead people and animals. Our group started to get smaller as some became too weak to go on.

My best friend was also with us. She had had a baby just four weeks before. It was not long before she could no longer nurse her baby and it died. She walked for many hours with the dead baby in her arms. I noticed at one point that she started lagging behind. Then she took her pistol and shot herself. We did not talk. We could not cry anymore. We laid her out beside the road with her baby underneath her coat on the mother's body, covered her with pine boughs and marched on.

Once in a while when we came closer to the highway we went into the farmhouses. We could see that the Russians had been here before us and they had left heaps of dead bodies behind; all of the women raped to a bloody mess. Often we found little children with their heads bashed in on walls and bedposts. Once we found a woman with her abdomen slit open and the unborn baby pulled out – it was still connected to the mother. It was horrible. The children with us died because we had no more food. They just sat down and froze and died. Many of the women gave up when they lost their children. They no longer wanted to live – they just stayed behind, stopped walking and fell in the snow. Freezing to death is a sweet death. That's what they say.

It took us three weeks to get to Stettin. When we got there we had two children left and of the twenty three women four were left.

I saw so much death and horror and pain – and I did not understand it. I think my brain must have shut off and stopped registering anything. I believe that is how I survived.

In Stettin we decided we had to get onto the train. We stood on the platform and when a train came, we crammed in. The washrooms were full with wounded. We drove for eight hours then the train stopped. It was the middle of the night and it was pitch black. A voice walked along the train.

"Women to the right. Men to the left!"

All passengers that could walk poured out and we could finally relieve ourselves.

I don't recall how many hours it took to get to Berlin. Often the train stopped and we could hear bombs and see the flames of explosions. We scrambled out and laid flat in the fields. But we were lucky; after a while the whistle blew and we piled into the wagons again. And on we rumbled.

So I came to Berlin. Your mother had long ago been evacuated to Lindau. I recalled that I knew a lady from the Arbeitsdienst, Maria Huber. I thought I would look her up. I remember I was so tired, I think I was sleeping on my feet. In the subway the people moved away from me – I think I stank so much. I came to her house, I walked in and collapsed into her arms. She didn't talk. She took off my boots and bedded me on the couch. I slept. I slept for two days and two nights and then I washed. I still had my little dog. They had tried to take him away on the platform in Stettin but I would not let them.

For some reason I could not stay any longer with Maria. Then I remembered Frau Wolf, the mother of Hubert Wolf who had fallen in love with me in 1936 when I visited the Olympics in Berlin. I knew where his mother lived. I went there. She was kind to me and let me stay with her for the remainder of February. I slept in the bathtub because she had no extra bed in her tiny apartment.

Every night the English bombers came – we saw an awful lot of people running down streets in flames. They came every night. At the end we did not care anymore we were no longer afraid. There comes a point when it gets to be too much. We had become numb. Frau Wolf had bad legs and I went shopping for her and that meant that I had to stand in line sometimes for four or five hours for a few potatoes and a turnip. It was not much but we managed. Flour soup and a potato with salt was a delicacy. And once, I still remember, I came home with two eggs. We made eggs sunny side up and I think we first drooled over them and admired them and then took a long, long time to eat them. We wanted to make them last really long. I am not sure we did not lick our plates when we were done.

The time came when we were told to leave Berlin because it was close to being conquered. I got a ticket for Lindau where Irmgard was. I had to leave my little Dachsi behind. Frau Wolf promised to look after my beloved little dog. We were not ten miles out of Berlin when suddenly the train stopped and we could hear the sirens of the air raid warning. We spilled out of the wagons and spread out in the field before us. It was a potato field and we laid flat in the cold furrows for about an hour. Luckily they did not hit the train and after a time we were told to get back in and then we drove off.

There is much time in a train to start thinking. I did not dwell on the fact that all the promises given had come to an ignominious end. I had always been somewhat realistic and only cautiously swallowed the political swill we were fed. But still – here I was, a widow at twenty eight. I had nothing, even my little dog I had to leave behind. Where was my father? He was such an ardent patriot and he hated the Russians so deeply. I am sure he had decided to stay behind to defend his beloved fatherland. I had not heard from him in such a long time. I did not know where my young brother Manfred was; he was only twenty one years old. Was he even still alive? The only safe bet I had was my sister who lived in that lovely town on the shores of Lake Constance. There had been no bombings. In Lindau I looked up Irmgard and then I found work in an army hospital.

Chapter 22

GUSTEL AND HIS END OF THE WAR

I sent two scouts out and when they returned, they reported that we were actually in the American occupied zone but that they, the Americans, would not allow any German soldiers to drive through because they had been told that the Russians were driving their tanks over the fleeing German soldiers and shooting them on the road when they encountered them.

I immediately changed my direction. I planned to veer south, make a detour but head back to the American sector. We turned our cars around by hand on a very narrow strip of road under the astonished glances of German soldiers who were clogging up the roads. We moved south and then west until we reached the American zone again. Then I spoke to my men.

"We now have to get rid of our weapons and anything that could identify us."

We entered a small side road and behind two small sheds which were filled with hay, we collected all our weapons, grenades, ammunition, all our papers and passes, we ripped off our insignia and signs of rank and threw them in the ditch we had dug. One had to camouflage oneself.

It was not difficult to see where we had to go. American soldiers stood on the side of the road and pointed with their fingers where they wanted us to go. And on we went, through the last Austrian villages where, for the last time, we were greeted and welcomed with gifts of flowers, not unlike in 1938 when we had marched into Austria and where the people had greeted us tumultuously with gifts of flowers and many hurrahs. Near Braunau at the Inn River we were collected in one huge camp.

And wouldn't you know, the first people I saw there were the soldiers of the Jaegerregiment 749 which had been in Patras the same time I was stationed there. I found their commander and asked him if I could hide in his troop and he gave me permission. I felt that I had to disappear as a person. I was quite aware that I would eventually get into trouble due to the events with the Jews in Ukraine and I wanted to lay low. After two days the lieutenant colonel told me that his men were wondering who the stranger in their midst was.

"Comrade, I can hide you no longer."

I accepted that. I told my men that with the war being over they were free to do as they wished to.

"I am no longer responsible for you. From now on you are on your own."

Some time later the call came for all SS members to step out. We were moved into a different camp. All in all we were 40 000 men in the camp near Ebensee. All SS men. There were the troops who had fought at the end of the war against the Russians at the Hungarian border, the Yugoslavian and Austrian borders, and they had been collected during their retreat.

On one side of our camp was a small brook that carried the effluent of an abattoir that handled dead horses, cattle and other cadavers. That was the water designated for our drinking and washing. We were lying on the naked ground and it rained most of the time. A border line was drawn out with a thin rope and we were told not to cross this demarcation line or else we would be shot.

One day there was a crowd surging towards the rivulet for drinking or washing and one impatient man slipped underneath the rope to get faster to the water. We yelled at him to get back to the rope. But he kept on going towards the water. One step, two steps and then the guard who had his rifle already aimed, cocked the trigger and shot him. One of our men, our spokesman because he spoke perfect English, negotiated with the Americans for permission to get the dead man's body back onto our side. This took more than three hours.

For the first twelve days the Americans gave us nothing to eat. The last dog was long gone and the last shred of tobacco was chewed. We were very hungry and wet and cold. One day the Americans drove up with trucks filled with a few sides of beef and halves of pigs. They piled the meat before the gate, poured diesel fuel over it and lit it.

"So – now you can taste how it is to be hungry too. Now you can feel how those Jews felt when you let them starve to death."

Back in Patras when the Germans prepared to retreat, the warehouse was opened and we were told to take what we wanted. In this way I acquired a pair of night vision binoculars, the kind the navy used. I still had them with me. In this camp we had black guards one day and white ones the next. One day a black guard started to talk to me. He gave me permission to trade the binoculars with a man outside the camp. They were worth a few thousand marks. The German received permission to come and trade a kilogram of ground whole wheat meal for the binoculars. I handed him the glasses and he gave me a tin can of flour full to the brim. In short time I had eaten the flour which I had mixed with water. This is the tin can that I used later for grass soup.

We ate grass and dug up roots and plants. I had eaten all my precious flour and was horribly hungry again. I thought I'd get more value out of the grass if I boiled it. I shaved a piece of wood into match size slivers to heat the water, next I had to get some grass because by now the ground of the camp was bare. I approached the rope which was our demarcation line. On the other side were

American soldiers. I asked one of them if I could get permission to get some stalks of grass. I was on my belly with my hands reaching out from under the rope onto their, the American, side. I showed him my can and told him that I wanted to cook some grass soup. He did not agree immediately but after some time he relented. I crawled on my belly to the rope, extended my hand and filled my can with grass.

But one thing I did not and could not see and that was the line of men behind my back who also wanted to have some grass. The American granted it to one and then to another and then three more. As the sixth prisoner stretched his hand out underneath the rope for some grass, the American, der Schweinehund, the bastard, lifted his automatic pistol and emptied it into his body. The man was a meter away from me and, of course, he was dead. The guard started waving his pistol which he had loaded again and made threatening gestures towards us. I quickly crawled out from underneath the rope and went back to where the men were watching. Each time one of us came close to the rope he lifted his pistol and threatened to shoot.

It took many hours before we were allowed to take the dead man back to our side. Yes, it was bad there, very, very terrible.

And then, one day, they started to feed us. I cannot recall how many men were fed on one loaf of bread as daily ration. Of course, that led to many problems too. We had to divide the bread among ourselves and that sometimes caused difficulties. On one of these occasions a man was beaten to death because he had taken a slice of bread to which he had not been entitled to and another had to go without. Tempers flared easily. We were starving and counting the crumbs of bread doled out to us. Nobody got blamed for his death – he just disappeared. We were such a huge mass of men, all looking more or less the same to the guards, dirty and unshaven. We had neither name nor number. The Americans did not know that a man was missing.

Conditions in the camp went from very bad to unbearable. We had people who tried to make the Americans understand that if they wanted men to survive some things would have to change. One day General Patton, the High Commander of all of Southern Germany, came to inspect the camp. Later we found out that some of our men in the camp had succeeded in alerting the International Red Cross in Geneva about the conditions persisting in the camp and that is why Patton came.

We had to assemble and many men dropped to the ground as they were lining up to greet General Patton. They were too weak to stand.

Double rations were immediately ordered. That meant double rations American style, not just two loaves of bread for a bunch of starving men, but food, real food. Naturally this brought up another no less dangerous problem. The older men had warned the younger men to be very cautious and not to eat too much. But many of the younger men, and we had plenty of seventeen and eighteen year old men who had joined the Leibstandarte just before the end of the war, and who were the most starved, just could not resist the food and they ate. They got very ill.Their systems could not handle the overload and many were in grave danger of dying. The camp guards quickly realized in what danger many of them were and in what serious state of alarm the camp was. The Americans used trucks and ambulances around the clock to drive the worst cases to the hospital.

Once Patton had been here, the Americans could no longer run the camp as they saw fit, but they had to obey orders from above. Times got better. We got fed; we got shelter and we were looked after. The relationship between us and the Americans had improved so much that the Americans took our men to act as guides and carriers. They had discovered that there was much game in the forests. They did a lot of hunting and collected many trophies.

A former civil servant of the criminal police was in the camp; he had gone over to the Americans and had helped them a lot. One day they called me and when I reported they addressed me with my name and rank, thanks to the turncoat. The Americans wanted me to deploy my criminal and investigative skill and use them in the camp. I complied, somewhat halfheartedly and they got some names from me but not many. I discovered that they were mainly interested in 'the spoils of war'. They wanted not names or men, they wanted valuables, like art and gold and old treasures. Again, I was somewhat helpful but not too much. Sometimes one gave them a little in order to avoid having to show them the really great stuff. There were enough German soldiers who pointed the finger to sought after treasures and happily took what the Americans doled out as thanks.

This was about the time that I noticed that many of the Austrians did not want to be Germans anymore but again only Austrians. But some of the Americans did not take this kindly. They explained to them, "Well, back in 1938 you were yelling 'Sieg Heil', here is your chance to yell some more now with the rest of the Germans."

Not all, of course, denied to have been German friendly, but there were many. In contrast to the Austrians, the men from Alsace that I met, always considered themselves German, then and now again. I was actually amazed at their attitude and behaviour.

The attitude of the Americans changed when the CIC, the Counter Intelligence Corps, came to do its work in Germany. The CIC had now started to ferret out war criminals. Of course, the CIC was a Jewish run concern. It seemed to us that any important position in the States and especially in the field of intelligence was occupied by Jews.

At the end of the war, at the offensive in the French Ardennes, where German troops, especially SS units, were to repulse American units – it happened that American soldiers got shot. The CIC was informed about that and because the Leibstandarte was involved, they scoured the prisoner of war camps to find out men who had been involved in these events. Here, in my camp, they found a Sergeant whom they first beat up mercilessly and then took away. I quickly figured out that the officers of the American Army did not think too much of the men from the CIC.

We were allowed to improve the shelters for ourselves. One day, I believe we were building another barrack, when our men, as they were digging the foundation, came upon a cache of ammunition, rifles and other weapons. Obersturmbannfuehrer Sonnenstuhl, lieutenant-colonel Sonnenstuhl, I shall always remember his name, immediately halted the digging and went to the Americans to report his find. Within seconds all sirens of the camps were shrilling, the search lights went on, soldiers drove up in tanks and trucks and surrounded the camp, rifles directed towards the camp – ready to shoot. Highest alarm. And inside the camp stood thousands and thousands of German men and laughed and laughed. We would never have thought of using these weapons; we were so fed up with war. We had so enough! The Americans were not too pleased when they noticed that we had laughed and had made fun of their fear.

By this time we received decent food, we had shelter and we were treated like human beings. I guess by this time the Americans had come to realize that we were not wild and savage brutes, but ordinary people just like them.

The orders came to empty the camp. I was in one of the first groups that were loaded into trains to be transported into Germany. On the way we had to stop at a station and next to our freight train was another one just like ours, filled with soldiers, prisoners of war, all SS. A lively exchange of greetings and news ensued. In fact, some men changed trains as groups of friends came together, planning to stay together through the next leg of camp life. Lucky me - I did not change my train even though I had recognized some familiar faces in the other train. This train, as I found out later, drove into France and there the prisoners were put into mines to work. And many years later, when in Germany the lower ranks had long been allowed to return to their homes and families, these poor devils were still working in the mines for the French.

It was the end of August when we were unloaded in our new camp in Goeggingen, a town near Augsburg.

CHAPTER 23

GUDRUN'S EARLY YEARS

A unt Erika recalls a night in November 1939:
"That night I will never forget. Irmgard, your mother, was to have her baby at home like all the other SS wives. The official line was that having a baby was no sickness and therefore did not have to happen in a hospital. I had been sent by my father to help. Your father, Gustel, was also there – it was a Sunday and he was not busy being 'the mother of the company', as he liked to call himself. He was with your mother who was in labour in the bedroom in the second story. He was very nervous. The midwife was attending another birth and would be late.

Irmgard screamed and pushed hard. Gustel lost his nerves and yelled at me to 'boil water'. I raced down to the kitchen and did as I was told. On my way up the stairs with a pot of boiling water in my hands I collided with the midwife who had meanwhile arrived and was attending your mother; she had heard me stomping up the stairs and had come to open the door for me. Through the open doors I saw Irmgard's raised legs and an emerging head. I dropped the kettle. Gustel yelled at me to bring more hot water. I found my way to the kitchen and fainted in a dead heap on the floor. Upstairs they needed the water to wash the baby that had meanwhile been born. Finally when no hot water was coming up Gustel raced downstairs to find out what was the delay. He saw me on the floor.

'Oh, die Weiber!' He exploded.

'Women!'

That was your birth. You were a very healthy baby."

And she smiles as she sees it all happening again.

My father was transferred to Berlin, where he was finally able to fulfill his dream: he matriculated from high school with the 'abitur'. He then took special courses in law and criminology at the university, for he had opted for a career as a Kriminalkommissar in the Sicherheitspolizei, the security police.

I remember the air raids and the sirens. Many a night we were plucked from our cots and rushed downstairs into the safe cellars. I can still feel the pull on my arm, wrenched up by an impatient and nervous adult, as I stumble down the long stairs, never fast enough, my sleepy legs not wanting to function, unable to take one step at a time, the siren howling in my ears, scaring me and all. A valise with all the important papers had to be brought along as well as my baby sister, born in November 41, and perhaps some water and food.

The trips down to the cellars were an inconvenience not only to us but also to my father.

"The worst was that instead of studying I had to spend many hours in the air raid shelter underground. Not only did I have to make sure that even the last little woman had made it safely down to the cellar with her survival suitcase but after the 'all clear' sirens had come on I had to make certain that all the women and children made it safely back up to their apartments."

"Why was that your job, Dad?"

"It really wasn't my job but the other man, who was supposed to be the guard for these occasions, had never showed up and I actually was the only man on the block."

Wartime in the big city was an everlasting struggle to feed the family. All food was rationed and food stamps were issued to a person depending on gender, marital status, work performed, and age. There was very little that was edible that was not rationed. Going to restaurants was only possible by trading in food stamps with your bill. My mother and our nanny took turns lining up for hours in long queues of tired and impatient women who inched slowly forward, wondering whatever the grocer would have for sale today for the few precious food stamps they hoarded carefully in their apron pockets, or worse yet, they worried there would be nothing left by the time they would reach the counter.

Meat was scarce and severely rationed, but brains from cows were not rationed, they were 'free' meat, and a desired item for our kitchen – no bones, no waste; they cooked easily into a meal that children could eat. My mother later told me that she was sure that I got 'my brains from their brains'. Sometimes the women came home with another 'free' meat, snails, little gray, small, finger-size creatures. Mama recalls with a wry smile.

"Well, we boiled them, pulled them out of their shells, we sliced them, added some chopped onions, if we had some, put salt, vinegar and oil on them and ate them as a salad. They were not that bad at all – we actually considered them a delicacy."

I cannot remember.

The cache of my memory of Berlin is small, but there is the picture of a table covered with a white table cloth, fancy porcelain cups and silver spoons. There was a cafe where my mother loved to go to with her little girls. Elegantly attired ladies, holding silver cigarette holders in their manicured fingers, sat at tables, drinking from dainty cups, a piano player entertained, gentile laughter and the fragrance of perfume wafted through the room. Our libations were served by a black and white frocked waiter who addressed Mama with 'Gnaedige Frau', who pulled out her chair and who helped us into our chairs. He was very polite to me too and called me 'Fraeulein'. He served me with the same flourish as he did my mother and I copied her polite manners. I revelled in the elegance and decorum of this place and behaved my very best.

I cannot recall my father at all even though he was living with us. But I have a story which belongs to him and this time. It is a favourite of his and it has been told over and over again to his teenage daughters; I have heard it so often I can speak along with him.

"One day in university I had to write a paper in a class on economics. We sat in our desks. The professor entered and marched to his desk. 'Gentlemen, the title of your essay shall be on the topic "Camels as Important Trade Routes". I was somewhat perplexed by the title but commenced to write the title heading on the paper that lay in front of me waiting to be covered with intelligent comments and ideas.'Camels as Important Trade Routes'. Of course the professor had said, 'Canals as Important Trade Routes', but I had misunderstood the word camels for canals. (The German word for camels is 'Kamele' and that for canals is 'Kanaele').

But there I was and I did not question my professor – I accepted the challenge. I knew my geography and my history – and with an ounce of creative thinking – I came up with plenty of good ideas and wrote a long essay, which, I might say, was quite good."

My father looks around expecting our mirth. Watching him chuckling in blissful anticipation, it comes easily. Inge and I oblige him with hearty guffaws.

"Papa, what happened then?"

"I passed hands down."

But for my sister and me the best part of the tale is still to come: A wistful smile curls dad's lips, his eyes twinkle as he looks at our mother and he chuckles. He knows she loathes this story and I think that seasons his tale even more. Mama expresses her sentiments first with tightly pursed lips and raised eye brows and then she invariably erupts.

"I cannot understand that you find this so funny! All you do is make people look at you as if you were an idiot. How could you have been so dense as to get that title wrong? I just cannot fathom why you want to show off with this story which makes you seem a complete fool!"

She hates this story and cannot share our father's joy in divulging his naivete. Perhaps she is envious that he overcame the challenge with flying colours, perhaps she resents the fact that problems don't seem to faze him and that he still finds the event hilarious. What she considers incompetence or source of embarrassment is the core of a darn good tale for him. It shows so much their differences in attitude and character. There is a lightness in him and ease that she completely lacks.

"Oh, Irmgard, don't be so serious. I think it's hilarious how stupid I was!"

And, of course, my sister and I find it amusing to watch both of them in this never changing, repeat performance.

My mother was devoted to raising the best children for the fatherland. She fed us the healthiest food, she read Grimm's stories to us, she sang old ballads to us – she was our life and we were hers. When they came to her door asking her to join a women's service group and to work for the war effort, she informed them that she was raising two girls for the Reich and the Fuehrer and that that was enough for her.

She was proud of her handsome husband who was advancing in career and stature and who carried her along into a circle of ambitious men and modish women. She, who had grown up the oldest daughter of a poor country teacher in Silesia, used to wearing hand-me-downs and never having a penny, found herself suddenly able to wear beautiful clothes and 'be someone', to have money, and to be welcomed into a new social sphere.

For this new society she learned to smoke, to use make-up and to drink. She  loved to show off her children and often took me to cafés because, "Gudrun, you behaved like a perfect little lady and the waiters and the guests admired your impeccable manners and named you 'the little princess'."

But not all outings were good. One late afternoon on our way home, sirens started wailing unexpectedly; they were quickly followed by a hail of bombs. Explosions spewed stones and timber fragments into the air, fires and flames shot across from house to house, people screamed, some were running swathed in burning clothes like flickering torches hurdling themselves down the street. My mother started to run holding fast onto my hand. A fire ball shot up in front of us and she ripped me close to her and in a flash draped her skirt over my head. Holding me tight and her skirt closely over me she walked as fast as I would allow her. But I had already seen more than I should have and the event stayed with me for years. Sirens put me in panic for a long time – and to this day when I hear their wailing howl, goose bumps roll over my body and my heart stops for a second.

There was no letup of daily bombings. Officers' families with children were evacuated away from Berlin. In 1943 we were sent to Lindau, a pretty little town on Lake Constance in the very south of Germany. It was a long train journey in cars that were tightly packed with young soldiers. Good natured bantering, laughing and singing filled the wagon. The travellers were new soldiers and what they knew of war they had seen on the news reel in the cinema - life was still an adventure. They played and horsed around with us and I am sure my mother was glad of that.

My first recollections of my father are of the time in Lindau. He was on leave from Greece and he had brought a live turtle and two flowery house coats for his little girls. We became devoted little maids to the turtle, which we named Marlene, the most glamorous name I knew. We watched in fascination how the clumsy creature crawled over the shiny wooden parquet floor, unhurriedly, her claws making a scratchy sound. We dared a little poke at her and the leathery head with the pearly black eyes retreated under the carapace that was decorated with the most magic design. We fed her bits of lettuce and herbage from the park, or bits of fruit saved from our own ration. My mother did not like the little creature – she had once attempted to climb up her leg and ripped her silk stockings. And besides – the turtle was not cuddly.

Life was so different with dad at home. He tossed my sister and me into the air, he tickled us, and he proudly paraded around with us – he always did things you really weren't supposed to do, such as talk loud, sing full throated through all the verses of a song, burst into belly laughs, make jokes and play tricks on us.

Papa was a wonderful dad and I adored him. He was so full of life.

Here in Lindau we lived in a large building that housed the police offices. Our apartment was spacious and well appointed. The oak furniture was ours. We had leather chairs in our 'Herrenzimmer' the gentlemen's room, we had a library and a piano. More than a dozen wide steps led from the street up to our very spacious hallway – what a wonderful place to play. There even was a backyard with a small garden, a sandbox, and some trees.

The city was small and it was easier to obtain groceries there than in Berlin; there even was a weekly farmers market in the square in front of the church where one could buy vegetables without food stamps. The war was somewhere else. Some of the shops had flower pots in front. I remember because one day when we were in the pharmacy Ingeborg suddenly disappeared and my frantic mother eventually found her asleep in one of the containers, hidden by the flowers, still clutching a cookie that the kindly apothecary had given her.

One morning on our outing to the harbour I found a bloody child's hand on the walled pier. Mama said this was a reminder that it still was war.

It was on a warm and sunny spring day that our lives changed forever. The bell rang and when my mother opened the door, strange men, speaking in a tongue I did not understand, and wearing unfamiliar uniforms, stood there. They had guns. A soldier spoke to my mother. She turned pale and very quiet and went back into the house.

She did not speak much but told me to put on shoes and a coat and help my sister into the same. She got some things from her desk and went out into the garden. When she returned she packed some clothing into a bundle, sat my smaller sister into the pram besides the package, told me to stay with her and then she left the house.

"Mama, you have forgotten to lock the house," I reminded her.

"Gudrun," she replied, "We don't have to. The house is no longer ours. The French soldiers have come and taken it away from us. It is now their house."

"But why?"

"Because we have lost the war."

"What does that mean?"

"That means that soldiers from other countries have invaded our fatherland and they are driving us out."

As I was pondering these strange news, she said to me, "Now listen carefully, Gudrun, from this moment on you must never salute a person with 'Heil Hitler' again."

"But why?"

"There is no more Heil Hitler. Hitler is dead. From now on you must never say 'Heil Hitler' again, only 'Good Day' or 'Good Morning'."

She was quiet for a short while and then a determined look moved over her face and stayed there – she turned to the pram, grabbed its handle and began to walk.

Suddenly life had changed. My mother had changed.

A few days before this event my Aunt Erika had arrived from bombed-out Berlin. She had visited us and told us that she was living in a camp for refugees – confusing terms and conditions for me, a five year old. I sensed that many things were not as they had been. I noticed that the adults talked about different things than a few days before and that they used words that were new to me. I sensed an uncertainty and fear in the air. My mother, having been evicted from our home, made her way to the camp where Erika stayed.

I cannot remember anything about the days in the camp except that when my aunt was about to leave the camp, she looked ugly and unwashed and unkempt. She told my mother to do the same. Mama laughed and protested, "They are French soldiers and they respect women".

Erika informed her "These troops are not regular French soldiers. They are called the de Gaulle troops, and are mainly men from North Africa. These men have no regard for women of any age. They'll rape all – all but pregnant women."

So from then on whenever they left the camp my beautiful blonde mother and dark haired aunt 'went pregnant' with cushions tied to their waists. They coloured their teeth black with soot, dishevelled their hair and they walked bent over and with a limp. Sometimes groups of soldiers approached the women but left them alone with a curse when they saw the two ugly hags.

One day Aunt Erika moved out, washed and cleaned up. She had found a job as a Doctor's aid in the Red Cross Hospital and a place to stay. Immediately she approached the head doctor and asked if she could put up her sister with her two little girls in her room because they were refugees from Berlin.

"Yes," the doctor said, "we could do with some extra help in the kitchen."

Another two army cots were placed in Erika's room – and we had a home.

When Aunt Erika tells the story, she carries on:

"Irmgard and I worked long days because the hospital was filled with soldiers up to the rafters. You two little girls had all the wounded men looking after you. They were the best nannies in the world and you had a wonderful time. We all were safe because the Moroccan troops did not bother a Red Cross Hospital."

Then she pauses and the smile leaves her face.

"But sad events soon took place. One day the head doctor spoke to me.

'Erika, I must tell you that I cannot go on much longer like this. This is the end for my family and me.' He had a beautiful wife and small children. He was high in the Waffen SS – and one day the poor devil shot his wife, his children and then himself."

This was the end of our stay in the hospital. Aunt Erika joined up with eight soldiers who were able to walk. They searched out the highway and planned to head north. Aunt Erika wanted to go to Schwaebisch Hall, the only place in southern Germany where she knew someone: Gustel's parents – my grandparents.

During the day the group walked. Occupation law stated that they had to be off the road by eight at night. So, when evening came the group split up. They went to farmers along the road and asked if they could have a place in the barn. There were so many people walking the highways and roads – and they always got permission to sleep there. Often they were given some food. After two months a ragged and thin Aunt Erika arrived in Schwaebisch Hall.

When Erika headed north my mother headed south. To this day I wonder why she did not go together with her sister to seek out the safe haven of her parents-in-law in Schwaebisch Hall. When Irmgard married the only son of the good burger and cooper master, August Haefner, she felt not exactly welcomed with open arms. In fact she tells the story that when her future mother-in-law who bravely undertook the long train journey to Silesia by herself so she could attend the wedding of her son, greeted them on arrival, she expressed her astonishment to hear that 'they, the family Ernst, spoke German'. I am certain that my grandmother would have never said such an outrageous thing and that it was a tale fabricated by my mother to discredit her mother-in-law.

Young Gustel had chosen a bride 1000 kilometers away from home – nothing like that had ever happened before in this family. In Swabian eyes Silesia was a foreign country, with inhabitants that differed in traditions, customs, names and language, from anything their Swabian and provincial mind was accustomed to. Their Gustel had married a foreigner but his father and mother welcomed her.

Irmgard had always felt herself more of an intellectual, her father's family numbering teachers and professors, men that were university educated and cultured. Her chosen came 'only' from a burger family, his father was a barrel maker – a tradesman, the family petty bourgeois. I am certain that was a step below Irmgard's aspiration, aspirations which had wholeheartedly embraced Gustel's ambitions, promotions and advances in the Third Reich and the SS political and military machinery.

So instead of heading north to family, my mother headed south, walking towards the Austrian Alps that towered on the other side of Lake Constance.

How many days did we walk on in the early summer sun? I don't know. But eventually we came to a place where the farmer would answer my mother's request for work.

"What can you do, young woman?"

"I can milk cows," she answered.

"You've done that before?"

"Oh, yes, I can milk twelve cows a day."

Brazenly she got herself the job. She had never milked a cow before. But this was today and it was a different day.

We were given a room with two large beds buried under red and white, plump feather pillows. A huge wooden closet was filled with old woolen coats and pants which reeked of moth balls. A picture hung on one wall showing a young woman with a naked baby in her arms. She wore a blue cape and she smiled and her feet stood on a half moon. I thought she was very beautiful and I enjoyed looking at her. I liked our room, it was cozy and I felt safe.

My mother helped milking the cows in the morning and then helped to drive them out to pasture. The reverse process occurred at late afternoon. It was hard work – not only had she never milked cows before, she had no experience with herding them. She did not like to use the stick the farmer gave her with instructions to hit the animals hard on the rump in order to get them to move. She never said a word, but observed and learned quickly.

The farm house sat squat in a cleanly swept yard. The wall facing the road was white washed, and above the row of windows which reflected the summery sky from their glass panes wedged between edgings of checkered curtains, was a sight that I found very disturbing. A large, dark, wooden cross was affixed to the wall and an almost naked man was nailed by his hands and feet onto the cross, blood red paint was oozing from his nail wounds and from his right side in his body where a large gash opened his belly. It was so real. I could feel the pain when I looked up into his sad and thin face, tears were rolling down his cheeks and his eyes were rolled up so they showed their whites. On top of his head was a wreath of branches with thorns that cut into his head and there was more blood flowing. I had never seen such a figure before and it bothered me very much. Why would anyone hang such a pitiful statue which showed so much suffering on a wall where everyone could see it? I was only five years old but I knew that one should not advertise such pain and anguish and walk quietly by. I saw that the farmer and his wife stopped and bowed before the statue, they touched their forehead and chest and shoulders, something I had also never seen before.

"Mama, what are they doing?"

"Gudrun, the farmer and his wife are Christians."

"Mama, are we Christians?"

"No Gudrun, we do not believe in their God; we prefer the Gods of the Germanic people."

"Mama, why do they make those strange signs?"

"They are praying to Jesus."

"Who is Jesus?"

"This man on the cross is Jesus Christ, the people say that he is the son of God."

"Mama, why is he nailed on a cross?"

"Well, God, who is his father, wanted that."

"But why?"

"They say that God wanted his son to die for all the sinners in the world?"

"But why?"

"If I remember correctly, that means that he will take all the sins of men on himself so that the people have no sins and can go to heaven."

"Mama, what is a sin?"

"A sin is when you do something wrong in the eyes of God."

I did not understand how God could have his son killed for wrongs committed by other people. Why didn't he punish them?

And I did not think that God loved his son at all if he made him suffer that much for something he had not done. It was all a puzzle to me. But watching the farmer and his quiet wife I was impressed and thought they were good people who had compassion for the creatures of God and for suffering. They also prayed at every meal and called for God's blessing. I liked that. We had never done that at home.

One day the farmer passed under the cross, as he did many times during the day. This time after he had made the sacred signs and movements he looked up to the cross.

"Oh, those damn birds, they are messing up our Christ!"

And he marched into the barn with resolute steps and came back with a long broom and a ladder. Up he climbed, alongside the Jesus, and waving the broom he whacked off the row of swallows' nests that clung tightly to the wall right underneath the overhanging roof. Clumps of gray nests shattered on the ground, little pink and naked fledglings tumbled out. They screamed with their beaks wide open – they were so red inside. Their little eyes were bulging out in panic. Frantic parents swooped over them screeching at the farmer. He climbed down and chased them off with his broom. Then he stomped over the writhing creatures with his dirty boots, back and forth, until nothing moved anymore on the ground. Only the parents still shrieked shrilly and attacked with passionate fury the murderer of their children.

Then I knew what sin was and I knew why the body on the cross cried his bloody tears. Mine were just salty.

I searched for my mother in the barn. I tell. I ask why. She buries her face in the flank of the cow she is milking, her hands keep on the steady press and pull. She has no answer and we both cry.

The couple has a baby. It is sallow and sickly and it smells bad. The farmer's wife carries it with her most of the time and sometimes the baby's feces run through her hands in a yellow, thin and evil smelling stream. I don't think it wears any diapers. And it cries all the time. My mother takes the baby and asks for a basin of water. She washes the limp body and shows the woman how to fold ripped up bed sheets for diapers.

She talks to the young wife who is so pale and who never smiles. She learns that she has no milk to feed the baby. Mama tells her to boil cows milk, to make thin porridge gruels, to boil carrots and greens and how to mash them for her infant. The young mother listens eagerly. Mama teaches her about diapering, of washing and boiling the cloths. The baby receives its first bath from his mother and has its first experience of fresh air and sunshine. Slowly the baby shows life and colour, it gains weight, it smiles and gurgles contentedly and when it now screams – it is for food. The woman looks at my mother with deep gratitude. And when she looks at her baby she now can smile.

I love the barn with the warm smell of the cows mixed with the tang of their urine, and the scent of the hay, the lowing sound the animals make, the metallic jingle of their chains, the sound their grinding teeth make as they chew on their hay, slow and deliberate. I love the way the spider webs glisten in the sunshine that pierces the dark in sparkling and dusty rays. There is an attic where hay is stored. Here I feel right at home. One afternoon as I watch the cows from the attic above, I see a calf being born in a large skin bubble. It plops down, in its slippery balloon, at the hind legs of the cow. The mother cow bellows and strains at her chains which do not allow her to move or turn around to check what has happened to her. I can see the dark and wet body of the baby curled up in its silvery veil. After a while it does not move anymore. It is dead.

Later on I ask the farmer why the baby was born dead. He yells at me.

"You were not supposed to see that. You are a wicked girl. It is a sin what you have done. Good girls do not look at such things. The devil will get you for that, you ungrateful, little spit. Shame on you! Get away from me!"

That man who killed baby swallows right in front of me and right under the Son of God now shouts at me that I am a sinner for having watched a baby cow being born. I cannot understand.

Again, I seek out my mother.

"Mama, why did the calf die?"

"The calf drowned in its sac – if the mother would have been allowed turn around, she would have ripped open the sac and the baby would have been able to breathe."

"But why is the cow tied up?"

"Gudrun, that is just the way it is here."

And she makes me go and play with my sister and the little baby because, "one must always take care of babies and small creatures- they don't hurt anyone and they need us."

The house squats heavy and cold like an oppressing ogre allowing no air or light inside. Does it squeeze happiness and laughter out of its inhabitants?

At noon the family and their hired hands, and now us, gather around a massive table. One round earthenware bowl is placed in the middle of the table. A fragrant steam rises from it. Everyone folds hands, which are not clean, resting arms on the table. Heads are bowed and the farmer intones a prayer which ends with a chorus of 'Amens'. Then hands reach under the table and come up with a spoon which gets dipped into the common bowl filled with some kind of cereal mush covered with a layer of melted butter. Spoons dig a hole into which the golden fat oozes, ready to be scooped up with the next spoonful. And the eaters dig quickly to catch the tasty fat which always flows into the deepest hole. Dig, scoop, lift, swallow, smack. Dig, scoop, lift, swallow, smack.

The farmer's wife is kind. She has provided two small bowls for Ingeborg and me. Our arms are too short, they would never reach to the center of the table. She dishes the mush out to us – with some yellow butter on it. It tastes good.

Not a word is spoken. The only sound is the sucking sound the spoons make as they lift the mush out from the bowl and the swallowing and licking of lips. When the bowl is empty the eaters lick their spoon very clean and then replace it in a leather sling under the table top. Everyone gets up and leaves without a word.

The village was in turmoil. Rumours flew around: The dreaded De Gaulle troops were expected and the village knew that these dark men from North Africa showed no mercy. They took what they wanted and hurt or killed those who tried to prevent them from having their ways. Men and women deserted their villages or hid wherever they thought they would be safe. Inge and I were undressed and put to bed and sternly told not to move out from there. My mother and the farmer's wife climbed up into the hayloft where the farmer hid them under layers of extra hay and old farm implements and tools. The troops arrived. They entered houses and barns. They knew where to look for women. They poked their long bayonets into wood piles and hay stacks. The afternoon held its breath. Men's shouting and women's screaming cut through the silence and scattered its hush. It was a long afternoon. The women in our house were not discovered.

When I saw my mother again her face had changed once more.

Milking a dozen cows twice a day for someone who had never worked with her hands before quickly became too much for my mother. She developed a painful tendonitis in one arm and could milk no more.

"Well, I guess I could use you on the fields weeding beets and helping with the haying," said the farmer, who apparently could be kind too.

And so every morning the three of us left the house and walked to some fields that needed weeding. We carried our midday meal, bread and cheese and a bottle of water, with us. While my mother raked or hoed or pulled weeds, Inge and I played with plants, and rocks, shells of snails, wandering ants, bugs and beetles and whatever drifted towards us with the wind. One day, during our midday meal, Mama made us a doll. It was a stick of wood with a head of a bunch of folded grass. The doll had arms and legs of braided grass, it had a grass skirt, and flowers in its grassy head. This was our first toy in a long time. We made a whole family like that, and a stick and stone house with many rooms, we even made a play garden – and my sister and I were completely happy.

When Mama was not too tired, she told us stories about Heinzelmaennchen, little creatures that lived under rocks and roots of crooked trees, good and helpful creatures that come only out at night.

"Have you ever seen the Heinzelmaennchen?"

"No, but I know people who have seen them and whom they have helped."

I knew I was good and kind and tried to stay up at night to catch the little gnomes – but when I woke up it was always mornings and I never saw one Heinzelmaennchen.

Summer laid over the land. We were healthy and suntanned. One day we were on the road again. My mother wheeled the pram which held besides Inge, a big wheel of cheese and occasionally even me. I remember that we walked a lot, perhaps sometimes we used the train, I don't know. My mother used the cheese to barter for shelter and food and eventually we arrived at the door of Oma and Opa Haefner, my father's parents, in the Gelbingergasse 39, in Schwaebisch Hall.

Chapter 24

GELBINGERGASSE 39

The large house still showed that it had once been a church; its lower medieval half was built of stone, the upper stories built in the seventeenth century showed beautiful timber work. It had a large Roman arched entry from the street into the shop and alongside the house deep stone steps led up to a heavy door and into the living quarters. I was fascinated by the bronze lion head knocker on the door – which we never used as the door was only locked at night. On the other side of the house a bell tower with timber construction on its upper levels rose high in the air.

All of the ground floor was the shop where barrels were made and where wine and schnaps were sold. Oma and Opa lived on the first floor. Uncle Willie and Aunt Berta occupied the second storey.

A narrow staircase led from the second floor up to a large and steep attic which was covered by a huge tiled roof constructed in 1686. There was a spare bedroom and some small closed off storage areas, one of which was used for firewood, one as a chamber for the maid and one for the hired man. From this floor open stairs climbed up to yet another area right under the gable which was used for storing more firewood and one more very small and sparsely furnished chamber. This room was not even properly boarded in and the heat, the cold and the wind had easy access. This was Aunt Erika's bedroom.

Mama, Inge and I were put into the attic bedroom. It had two sloping ceilings and two windows that opened over grandma's pantry, a storey down, which was originally part of the city wall. From the windows one had a view of part of the prison and the outskirts of the town, the valley through which the Kocher River rolled and the adjoining hills dotted with houses, cabins and fruit trees.

Inge and I were very excited about our new place. There was the attic, dark under huge beams, to which one climbed on staircases that got smaller with each storey ascended. There was a door and when it was closed, we were sealed off from the rest of the world. We had never been in such a wonderland of boxes and chests and closets filled with treasures of old toys, and books, and clothes, umbrellas, pictures, photographs.

As if it was not enough to discover a paradise for snooping and playing, soon grandma and her maid arranged large trays made of chicken wire on saw horses which they filled tightly with cut up pears, apples and plums with their stone hearts ripped out. As the pieces dried, they had to be removed to make room for the next batch. Inge and I ate our fill and neatly rearranged the fruit – and we were never found out to be the thieves that we were.

Very exciting was the fall day when firewood was delivered. Early in the morning horse drawn wagons lined up in front of the house, hired men loaded the chunks of wood into big willow baskets which were then lifted up by a hefty block and tackle operated by another man up in the attic. With much hollering of "Clear the street!" and "Watch Out" and "Here she comes!" the heavy baskets were pulled up, swung through an opened window into the attic, emptied and then carefully sent down to the street again. The hired hand or the maid stacked the firewood neatly in its own room.

On that day Oma cooked extra large meals and large pitchers of cider were guzzled down when everyone sat around the table in the living room. Midday rest was longer than usual, probably because everyone was in an almost festive mood and the ongoing chattering was interspersed by bouts of laughter.

Down in the shop, which we entered from inside the house via a spiral metal staircase, was a walled in corner with a wood fired water tank and a bath tub. Every Saturday afternoon was bath day. The maid lit a mighty fire under the water tank and all members of the household, from the master to the littlest apprentice, uncles and aunts, and anyone else who requested one, took turns having a bath. For the many years after when we were living in the barracks, we showed up every Saturday afternoon for our weekly ablutions and, of course, the obligatory coffee and cake afterwards upstairs with Oma and Opa.

The other exciting place was the shop itself. A two part door, large enough to allow a horse to ride in, provided access from the street. The elaborate brass fittings on it were polished daily by the maid, as was the hand bell one could ring for service when the shop was closed. Opa was a cooper by trade. He was sturdily built, a prototype of the 'Alpine Race', as my mother explained, his aquiline nose had a purplish hue and his bald round head was covered with a skull cap. His teeth, proudly referred to as 'still my very own' were black stumps, always clamped tightly around a cigar or pipe.

The master wore a thick leather apron when he was building barrels. First there were raw planks of wood, hauled into the shop from the huge stacks in a neighbour's back garden where they had been drying, they were sawed into correct lengths, which were shaved into staves, wood shavings piling up on the floor, steam was swirling through the air, iron rings were hammered into rounds and wondrously one day there was a new vessel to hold wine – or – as in most cases – cider.

On cider days in fall the farmers drove up with hand pulled or horse drawn wagons filled with sacks of windfall apples and pears. The fruit was placed on a large weighing scale on the ground and the balancing brass and metal weights carefully tallied. The sacks were emptied into a crusher, a large flywheel turned gears and the resulting bits of fruit and juice were dumped into a round wooden press. Two men turned the screw press, first an easy job, then pulling with ever more bulging muscles, groaning and straining. The frothy juice sloshed into buckets which were emptied into huge glass flasks or barrels. The farmer stood and watched, barely permitting grandpa to take a sample drink. So much fruit had to be pressed into that much juice. At home the juice would be sterilized and bottled as apple juice or it would be allowed to ferment in the barrel to become potent cider or 'Most'. The leftover mash was not thrown away either. Either the farmer himself or Opa let it ferment after adding water and then distilled it to fruit schnaps. Nothing was wasted.

When cider season was over, purple Zwetschgen, prune plums, were hauled in. They were allowed to ferment in large oval wooden vats until Opa decided it was time to make schnaps. All other work stopped. The taxman came, removed the seal from the winding and gleaming copper pipes that stuck out from the cement casing that was the distillery. Water hoses were connected, gages, levers, taps and faucets were checked. A fire was built on the floor inside the cement vat – a tricky operation because it had to be fed and kept going at just the right temperature and rate. Then it was finally time for the hired man to bucket the fermented plums into the still. Opa put on his glasses so he could read the different thermometers.

Making schnaps was a fine art and required much knowledge, skill and concentration. Hefty glass bottles caught the clear drops that fell from the copper pipe. August Haefner was a master 'Schnapsbrenner', his schnaps was famous throughout the city and countryside and it was much in demand. It had seen his family comfortably through the war and it still enabled them to have a good life.

The smell of the brew wafted throughout the whole house. When it was distilled it looked just like water. Opa laughed and offered us a sip which we hastily declined. Later in the day some old men from the neighbourhood gathered to test the spirits too, they pronounced their verdict, and it was always "as good as gold."

When all the distilling was done, the taxman came again and sealed the pipes for another year. Taxes were charged according to the hours the still was in use.

In the end there was a line of large flasks filled with different kinds of schnaps: pear, windfall fruit, plum – some were very fine and double distilled for connoisseurs, some just good for mixing drinks or to soothe a tummy ache. Depending on their quality or intended purpose, the spirits were allowed to age and were sold for a different price. One could buy schnaps open, in the amount of a cup or a gallon jug. Schnaps was considered medicine for many ailments and people had a small glass after a heavy meal or to soothe a painful tooth. A sick person was treated to hot tea laced with honey and schnaps – it took the aches away and brought sleep. For those who did not care about schnaps, or for those recovering from an illness, a glass of warm red wine with a raw egg beaten into it, was administered as a strengthening potion. Even children were treated to small doses of these concoctions.

August and Emma were typical provincial burgers with a very set and straight way of life rooted in small town conventionalities and traditions. Their life during the war had not been interrupted significantly. They had not been active Party members but had gone along like so many others. Because of their dealings with cider and schnaps their lives had been spared the deprivations of most city dwellers, they always ate well, they drank well and they basically had everything they needed, even a telephone and a car.

My mother expressed her disdain that they had probably afforded unfair advantage during the years when 'all had to tighten their belts'.

"I would have never taken more than I was given ration cards for. Sacrifices had to be made for the fatherland and for our future – and nobody should be allowed to have more than another."

I know she really believed that. In fact, my grandmother told me that once when my mother had visited and was to catch the train back to Berlin, Oma gave her a parcel indicating that there were two dozen eggs in it, safely packed for transport.

"Your mother refused to take the eggs along, saying that she did not want to have more than other Germans. And she did not take them along."

Not very long after my mother had come to live with Oma and Opa Haefner in the Gelbingergasse in late summer of 1945, she went back to Lindau, where she indicated she had business to finish. She left Inge and me in the care of our grandparents. I was happy where we were. Oma and Aunt Berta loved and included us in their daily lives.

Later on I found out that my mother had gone back to dig up the box she had hidden in the garden. They contained papers of my father and his SS dagger. As she was digging, she was apprehended by French soldiers; they confiscated the box and took her to prison.

"I was actually treated quite well, the food was good and the guards were alright. The worst was when we had to go to the bathroom – a male guard – there were no women guards – had to come with us, and I found that very embarrassing."

And proudly she would always add, "When I was brought before the judge, I defended myself. I told the judge that there was nothing in the box that had any material value whatsoever and I had only wanted to get these items back for my husband, who I did not know whether he was alive or not. I also told the judge, if my husband is still alive, I want the box because it is important for him, if he is dead; I only want these things as a memory of him. And I also let him know that I had two little girls that I had left behind and that I got myself into this predicament only because I love my husband and wanted to do something good for him."

The judge ruled that my mother would not receive the box back but that otherwise she had served her time and he dismissed her. She rode on freight trains back to Schwaebisch Hall and her children.

The house of my grandparents was only one of many old buildings that lined the Gelbingergasse. The almost one kilometer long street had only two side alleys branching off. During past centuries it had meandered inside the city wall leading out into the country side. Horse drawn wagons loaded with barrels of salt had left through this street, farmers had entered here bringing their wares to market. Once there had been a guarded gate at its end.

Later, when we lived at the edge of the city 'on the other side of the tracks', we had to walk almost all of its length to get to Oma and Opa's house. The street was a world in itself: there were four bakers, four butchers, four grocery stores, a haberdashery which used the open street to make ropes for farmers, but stored the flaxen coils inside. There were two shoe makers, a smithy, two milliners, some hairdressers and barbers, four restaurants and some pubs. There was a store that sold only oils that were pressed in the back room. Another store dispensed fresh milk and other dairy products. There was a place where one could buy briquettes of coal by the sack, there was a clothing store, a goldsmith, a plumber, a bookstore that also sold stationery, and a florist. Doctors and dentists informed you about their office hours on enameled signs which were affixed to the wall of the houses. Drugs and medication were dispensed by two apothecaries. There was a store that sold only under garments and corsets. At one end of the street was a large and smelly ancient tannery alongside a creek and at the other end, our end of town, was the laundry with its steamy building and lively drying yard. An American library and youth centre occupied the ancient 'Renaissance House'. There was even a factory in a large five story house, owned by the family Franz, the 'Noodle Franz'. And, of course, there was a cooper and a wine store in number 39. It was a very busy street where a few cars mixed with horse drawn wagons, businessmen, drummers, with housewives in the morning and children in the afternoon when school was out. Most of the houses had three or four stories, the ground floor was the business; the owners lived above and family or renters occupied the upper apartments.

In those days nobody had an icebox or a fridge and housewives had to go shopping every day. It was a morning ritual for Oma and Tante Berta, as it was for most other women, to put on a clean apron before going to buy their daily supplies. Herr Schanzenbach or his good wife, always dressed in a fresh white smock, pumped milk into a proffered metal can, carved cheese from a large round, cut butter from a big yellow block and wrapped it in wax paper before handing it over the counter. Baker Haertle's wife handed over fresh bread or rolls or on special occasions pretzels into a wicker basket. At Wieland's one obtained a bit of wurst or meat for dinner, and at Hagelstein's little shop, where a humpbacked and clubfooted old daughter ran the store for her even older parents, Oma shopped daily for a pint of cooking oil, or a pound of sugar or some tea. At the Konsum, a coop, one purchased radishes, green beans or lettuce, carrots and potatoes. They also sold mustard which was ladled from a barrel into a small jar or sauerkraut which was scooped out from a huge barrel with a large fork into the pot brought along.

The news on the street was fresher than that one read in the daily newspaper and the sidewalks were dotted with groups of men and women standing and chatting, their baskets or shopping bags set on the sidewalk. The street was noisy with ringing bicycle bells and with the clatter of horse drawn wagons.

Inge and I loved the big and busy house. We were friends with all its occupants, the family, the hired hands, the maids and its many visitors and 'Maexle', Opa's beloved mongrel dog. Opa took him along on business or on his morning jaunts to the barber or his morning libation. Maexle was a friendly dog but listened to no one but his master.

December was a very special month. Before Christmas Father Niklaus visited German children. On the night of December fifth, before we went to bed, we put a clean shoe outside our bedroom door; good children found their shoe filled with candy on the next morning, perhaps even an orange or cookies, but bad children found a bundle of rushes in them. I am sorry to say that I always had to share my goodies with my sister Inge.

But we loved the old house most on Christmas. On Christmas Eve Inge and I always showed up in mid afternoon with our parents arriving later. Banned from the living room we huddled together on the dark staircase that lead up to Aunt Bertha and Uncle Willie's apartment in the second storey. We hummed Christmas songs and got very excited when the door to the living room opened allowing a glimpse of the bustle and light inside. We knew the Christmas tree was being set up, and also the table with the gifts.

Eventually the shop closed, all became quiet. Then finally the door was opened and we were allowed in. The shine from the many candles on the tree would blind us. Glittering golden and white ornaments dangled from the tree, silvery lametta hung from the bows, a golden star shone on the top of the tree right under the ceiling. It was beautiful.

On the first Christmas in the Gelbingergasse a figure dressed in a long white robe with long wide sleeves edged with a pretty golden ribbon, a golden halo tied onto a nodding slim rod on the head, entered soon after we had been allowed into the living room. It looked like an angel to me and Oma greeted it as the Christ Child. My sister sank in fear under the table and I recognized the voice of Inge's Kindergarten teacher when the figure inquired whether we had been good children during the year. I thought she knows how we behaved, how can she dress up like that and pretend to come from heaven – this is just like the fairies and goblins, another lie adults dish out to make us behave. But I pretended to accept the celestial greetings and helped my sister crawl out from under the table. We were blessed and then Oma escorted the white clad figure out of the living room.

After renditions of the many Christmas songs Germans love to sing, we were finally allowed to look at the table that had been festively covered with a white cloth and set up alongside the wall where our presents were set out. Individual gifts were not boxed or wrapped but a name card indicated the recipient. Gifts were not brought by the Christ Child or Santa Claus, they always came from parents or relatives.

After the singing and the gifts, we looked forward to the traditional Christmas Eve dinner of cocoa and wieners with crisp white and buttered rolls. This was a feast for us children – we were each allowed one whole sausage – and later when the family did better, we could even eat two! Grandma ate smoked tongue and fine white bread and she always plaintively explained, "I would love to eat a Frankfurter, but 'Ich hab's halt mit der Galle', 'I've got it with the gall'. She also let everyone know that, "the Herr Doctor has implicitly forbidden to eat common sausages or anything with pork in it or, heaven forbid, heavy brown rye bread."

Oma was the only woman I knew who ate white bread during the week; everyone else ate dark rye bread. White bread or white rolls were only for Sunday or for special occasions. Oma also had a standing order for pigeon from farmer Frank for every Sunday when a pork roast was served to the family; she ate roast pigeon. She bought smoked tongue from her favourite butcher for all other special events. When I grew up I thought 'bully for her' and congratulated her in my mind for being such a crafty girl. If it took 'the gall' to make her life a bit special and give her some treats – why not. I reckoned she deserved them.

Christmas Eve was not over yet. We still had to walk home. I still feel the crackle of the cold night, and I still see the black sky sparkling with so many stars. Sometimes snowflakes fell, making that lovely soft and golden grey downwards cone at the street lamps. The town was so quiet – songs were still heard or happy laughter. And we walked home, hand in hand, so content. It was long after our bed time, that by itself was thrilling, and we were so happy with the gifts we carried with us. We were immersed in the magic of the lights and the songs and the spirit of Christmas that fills the heart of a child to overflowing.

At home in our barrack we had our own little tree – it had much fewer decorations on it – a few apples and coloured nuts and only a very few red candles. We received gifts from our parents - no Santa Claus here or Christ Child either – and later went blissfully happy to bed.

Our presents in the first years were all practical and hand made. There were knitted mittens, grey socks and grey stockings. I hated the stockings because they itched and I often took them off on my way to school. Of course, when it was winter, I had to bear them. There were always bloomers knitted in purl stitch. Those I hated even more: at first they fitted but with every wash they stretched and then the crotch hung between my knees. I could pull them up to the armpits but from there they had a nasty habit of sliding down because there was nothing to hinder their gradual descent. The only refuge was to roll the excess knitting into a sausage around my waist and hope it would stay. But the greatest horror was when the elastic broke – which it so often did, and nothing would prevent a sudden drop of underpants to the floor but a quick grab and a careful tip- toeing out of the room.

Later and more prosperous years brought gifts of thick flannel nightgowns and flannel underwear which I was made to wear well into my teens. I loathed the latter thoroughly as shapeless and ugly stuff, made 'for old women'. Worst of all was that this shiny material with the pastel coloured flowers printed on it, never wore out and the only way to get rid of it was to outgrow the garments. Then it was cut into neat pieces which were cut and hemmed and they served for many more years as dish and polishing cloths. It was years before Mama could finally afford real gifts, such as shoes or even books.

Back at Oma's the best Christmas gift yet was the old doll house that she as a child had played with and a grocery store that was put up in the living room every season and stayed until after epiphany. The store was filled with real groceries and candies and play money. Old tins and boxes in miniature with colourful labels were an endless source of enjoyment. The dolls in the completely furnished doll house had moveable limbs and very old fashioned dresses. We were allowed to come every day and play and eat everything edible in the store which miraculously was replaced on every visit. We had a very good Oma.

Chapter 25

JAHNSTRASSE 15

At the end of town between an arm of the Kocher River and an apartment building, was an acre or so of land with three empty and dilapidated shacks standing side by side on it; they were called 'the barracks'. The 'Fremdarbeiter', the conscripted foreign workers who had lived there during the war, had left. To the south of the huts lay a meadow and to the north a largish plot of land that had been subdivided by the municipality into small garden patches which were rented by industrious town folk, eager to fill their bellies with home grown vegetables and their Sunday living rooms with a vase of flowers. The path to the 'barracks' led past these gardens and then veered off behind the white apartment which stood at a gravel road leading out of town.

The small huts, which looked like sheds, were made of wood with the roof sloping towards the river. Inside was a kitchen with a wood stove, a bedroom with two built in bunks and a living room. There was a table and some chairs. An outside pump for water on one side of the three shacks and an outhouse between two of them completed the set up. There was electricity.

One day in the spring of 1946 Irmgard and Erika stood outside the barracks, looking admiringly at them. They looked at the buildings and then to each other.

"We can clean it up."

"We'll plant a garden in front."

"We can even have another one in the back."

"I'll take the one on the left," said Erika.

" I'll take the one in the middle," beamed Irmgard.

"Now we each have our own home!"

The two women smiled at each other and resolutely marched back to town and to some office in the town hall where they signed some papers and paid the next month's rent for two barracks.

We quickly moved into our new and bare home. My mother would have rather bitten off her tongue than asked for help. So despite Gelbingergasse 39 being filled with enough bedding and linens, pots and pans, crockery and utensils, to look after the needs of my grandparents and their maids and hired hands, as well as Uncle Willie and Aunt Berta, Irmgard declared, "No thank you, I need nothing, I'll be doing just fine."

She took us by the hand and wheeled the old pram filled with our few belongings out of town. We slept on the old straw sacks that had been left behind.

We covered ourselves with the old ratty blankets that we had found and heaped another bag of straw on top when we were cold. During the next few days we made forays to the local dump to find some more cooking and eating utensils to augment the few battered metal containers left behind in the hut.

The dump was a busy place. There had been many bombings in town and consequently there was much rubbish accumulated which was eagerly sifted through by the many refugees and homeless women and children. One still saw very few men around. We acquired a pot and a pan, some tin cans which were to serve as cups, a few bits of cutlery and an ancient enameled basin that was decorated with faded roses, which I thought were quite pretty.

"Look children, now we have everything we need."

Inge and I agreed; it was all so exciting for us.

Opa Haefner came by and offered his help. He chopped some firewood but was told by my mother, she had all she wanted and that he need not come again. He only showed up once more when she asked him to help her setting up a vegetable garden. We were to live for six years in the 'barracks' – I cannot recall my grandmother coming once into our house – even though on their weekly weekend pilgrimage to the 'Berg' they had to pass by the apartment that stood between the barracks and the road. I know it was not that she would not have liked to, she was a good and kind woman – it was my mother whose unbendable pride did not allow her to invite the mother and father of her husband into the place she had to live in now.

Food was still rationed. There were stamps for the locals and there were stamps for refugees and ours were never enough. How many soups can you create with just flour and water and some salt? You can use plain white flour stir it with water and then boil it, you can roast the flour to different shades of brown – that makes for a change of taste – an old rind of bread can be added. There are the greens of spring: sorrel, that sour little roadside weed that sends its green succulent leaves up first and which is so eagerly searched out by every urchin and munched happily on the way home. There are lambs quarters and chickweed and stinging nettles and all kinds of weeds and greens that can be collected, washed and chopped and boiled to create a different soup. There is watercress from the creek, field salad from fallow fields, wild onions from the meadows, roots from bull rushes and later in summer and fall there are berries and mushrooms from the forest.

My mother and aunt quickly realized that even with both children out collecting edibles there was never enough food to make our bellies really full. Once Inge and I were tucked into bed at seven o'clock at night they put on coats and bandanas, grabbed a sack and marched resolutely out of town and into the country side. Irmgard and Erika quickly became earnest and skilled thieves of cabbages, carrots, turnips, onions and potatoes. Not every one of their nightly forays was successful, there were many other women and the farmers often waited for them with flashlights, sticks and dogs.

Mama never told us that they stole – we only knew that they went out ('organisieren', that German word implies so many ways), to get vegetables. We were strictly forbidden to take anything from any field or garden.

With an extended index finger waving in front of our faces and with a stern mien she admonished us: "You are the children of an SS officer, and you are not thieves. Don't ever let me catch you either stealing or begging!"

The bread we could buy was soggy and grey and stories went about that bakers added saw dust and ground up acorns to add weight. But we were glad to have it. The rule followed in our house until many years later was that there was to be only one spread on the bread – either hard and bluish looking margarine, or jam, which looked a pretty red and was made from beets and carrots. I was quite into my teens when we were first allowed to have both, margarine and jam, on a slice of bread.

At the end of summer women and children marched off into the woods to collect mushrooms which were then dried at home. We collected blackberries which were boiled down without sugar to make sweet and black jams, we collected sloe berries, which were so sour that they were inedible but when dried were tangy and could be chewed and used like raisins in puddings and baking. Dried raspberry and mint leaves made a pleasant tea, flowers from chamomile and linden and leaves and flowers from sage and thyme made medicinal tisanes. And then of course there was the race for the cherished beechnuts which were found in the forest. The nuts were so tiny, just a small kernel the size of a sunflower seed enclosed in a hard shell. They were hard to find as they were usually covered by layers of fallen leaves – but we still enjoyed rustling through them to find the precious nuts. Back at the oil mill we could exchange them for real oil. Precious oil.

During the summer holidays, when wheat and rye and barley was harvested, women and children trotted to the fields, tin cans in hand, and in hope of great riches, a cloth sack or pillow case in the pocket. Rows of bent over bodies combed the fields, picking up kernels of grain that had fallen out of the ripe cereals. One was lucky to find a whole head with many kernels. The richest harvest was always where the stooks had been erected in wait for the kernels to ripen so they could be threshed - and everyone swarmed to these sites first. Kernel by kernel our little tin cans were filled and emptied into our sack. The flour mill exchanged the grain for flour which was the basis for our daily soup. But if one had flour and oil and perhaps an egg - one could make pancakes – oh – and with blackberry jam- heavenly!

Later in summer we gathered windfall apples and pears, and plums. What could not be eaten or boiled down to make some form of jam, was cut up and dried. I remember the strings of drying apple and pear rings that hung in our living room under the ceiling – spreading such a wonderful fragrance through the room.

Schools were involved in collecting all sorts of edibles too. A huge mountain of raspberry leaves in our school yard grew by the day as students arrived in the morning with a sack full of leaves - amazingly none of the children played on the pile of leaves or fooled around with it – food was just too precious. One day trucks came and hauled the leaves away to be dried and then sold. Classes of children were sent to the fields to gather kernels of grain – we did not get to keep any for ourselves – but I still preferred these days out in the sunshine to sitting in an overcrowded classroom.

Young and eager hands were also used to thin the green rows of early spring beets and turnips. A few weeks later we went to the fields to search for the prettily striped potato beetle that wandered over the green leaves of the potato plants to find a suitable place to lay their stacks of bright orange eggs, eggs that would hatch into voracious larvae devouring the green potato leaves and devastating whole fields. We happily filled our tin cans with these pests. We needed our potatoes.

Everything was collected and for everything there was a person or office or warehouse which exchanged it for something else: cigarette paper foil gave aluminum, newspaper or used paper was exchanged for a few sheets of writing paper. One could not buy paper – it just was not available. In school we used slates on which we wrote with graphite styles – both items were highly breakable.

When we were not out gathering edibles from fields and roadsides, we scoured the woods for cones and for fire wood or the local dumps for treasures that could be used – now or later and which if not useful for Mama would make wonderful things for us to play with. I still remember the time I found a crate filled with test tubes and glass bottles and vials filled with coloured powders. It took me a few trips to haul my find home – but I spent weeks mixing powders, discovering colours and mixing patterns; I learned to pour liquids with a steady hand and I decided I was going to be an apothecary.

Thus we survived.

Shortly after moving into the barracks my mother noticed that my body was covered with red spots. She touched my forehead – no, I didn't have a fever. Next morning we were in the doctor's office.

"Please, Frau Doctor, is it scarlet fever?"

"Oh no, Frau Haefner," smiled Frau Doktor Hermann, "these are bites of bedbugs!"

This was the start of a struggle that was to last many years, almost until we moved out of the barracks. Bedbugs lived in the frames of our bunks and in the grooves of the shiplap that covered the inside of our home. They hid there in the day and they came out at night hungry for blood. My mother, armed with the 'bug spoon' and a night light, performed a daily ritual before she went to sleep: she turned all lights off and then she searched with the flashlight on up and down the grooves on the wall, and the spoon squashed the bugs. The spoon handle became quickly red as did the wall. Her children's blood – but not for long! Night after night for many years she squashed the bugs and she washed the wall – and eventually she won!

Sunday morning ritual was the evacuation of our home and then she went at the walls with a gun spraying deadly DDT. Later on I joked that I would probably be inedible because my liver held so much of the deadly poison.

Opa Haefner come once more to our place and spaded over the grass patch at the front of the house in order to prepare the ground for the planned vegetable garden. Because it was well walked down it was hard work – that was the only other time Mama allowed him to help. From then on it was my chore to turn the garden earth over in fall and in spring. My mother made a nice path to the house, lined with rocks – schlepped there by Inge and me. To one side of the path was the future vegetable garden, to the other a rickety fence and then the future garden of the other barrack. A few weeks later I spaded our plot over again and my mother emptied the contents of our cesspool on it with a bucket. Everybody did that. Then it rained and washed the fertilizer into the soil. I raked the earth – then it rained again. One more raking and we were ready for our garden.

We made beds for vegetables, raising the earth, as the Germans do, into a patch, one meter wide and ten centimeters high; this allowed for good drainage. We planted potatoes and filled the beds with carrots, turnips, onions, radishes, peas and later on cucumbers and tomatoes. I watered and weeded and I loved my garden.

But my mother was not very happy with the results.

"The soil is too poor," she declared, "it needs 'Mist', manure."

She had grown up in the country, the daughter of a passionate gardener. She knew that 'manure was the cure'.

We looked expectantly at her.

She smiled back.

"Here are two pails. Whoever brings one back filled with horse manure gets five pfennig."

Five pfennig was a fortune. Five pfennig could buy fifteen of those sour red and round sweet sugar drops which we loved so dearly.

Ingeborg and Gudrun

Finding horse manure was not difficult. There were not many cars left in Germany and petrol was even scarcer, so all the transporting of goods was done with wagons drawn by horses. Right opposite the house in the Gelbingergase was a restaurant. They sold much beer and cold Sprudel, the sparkling water that all Germans drink; ice was brought on a weekly basis by a large horse drawn wagon.

I used to love hanging out of Oma's window to watch the burly men, sweat rolling over their faces, hefting the dripping ice blocks with great hooks onto their shoulders, where their leather aprons had a special leather pad so they would not get too wet, and carry the large blocks into the restaurant. Naturally the horses had to stand there for some time, occasionally they got a bag with oats hung under their heads – and when they dipped their noses into the bags their other end was busy too and quickly my sister would dash out of grandma's house, bucket in one hand, shovel in the other. And because the horses were hefty Belgians their leftovers were hefty too!

Inge made much more money than I did – I was too embarrassed to collect much. Inge laughed about Miss Piminy Niminy and went forth waiting for the horses to fart and to poop. She had no compunction to picking up the steaming 'apples', and if she had no shovel she used her hands. I believe she made a small fortune that summer.

It was a long time before our garden gave up its first harvest – before that, some hungry times had to be lived through.

Mama bought three chickens; they had names – an indication how precious they were: Trienchen, Bienchen and Sabinchen. I loved to hear their enthusiastic cackling when I poured my handfuls of freshly picked dandelions or stinging nettles to them. I gathered worms and June bugs for them, caterpillars and moths – but never ladybugs. I said thank you to the hens when I collected their eggs and they followed my movements with quiet clucking.

When we sat down to our meals, we prayed. This was new. But we did not pray to the God of the Christians and the name 'Jesus' was never mentioned.

My mother taught us to say, "Liebe Sonne, Liebe Erde, Deiner nie verges-sen werde...", "Dear Sun, dear earth, we will never forget about you ..."

We gave thanks for our meal and then we prayed fervently for the safe return of Papa and of Uncle Manfred. Nobody knew if he even was still alive. We prayed for years for them to come home. One day my father arrived and from then on, we prayed only for Uncle Manfred.

One day a much handled and smudged letter arrived; most of the writing was censored with a thick black line, but there was a pencil drawing of a gaunt face. Manfred was alive – somewhere in Siberia. Dreaded words. Some

Uncle Manfred

time later, and who knows how long after, childhood does not measure time with a clock or calendars – our prayer was answered, he came home too and we prayed no more.

My mother never complained. During our first months in the barracks, she went every day to the employment office and every day she went to stand in line for her ration of bread and potatoes or cabbage or carrots or whatever there was. She weighed less than ninety pounds. Often she told us at supper that she would eat after we were in bed. Only much later did I realize that she did not eat at all.

My hands and face were covered with sores. I coughed a lot and often in the morning when I woke up I could not open my eyelids because they were caked together. It took minutes to carefully scrape away the yellow crusted pus before I could open my eyes. Sometimes my mother had a cloth with warm water to soften the sticky mess. I was not well in the day and instead of sleeping I was plagued by nightmares about fires and screaming children, and the sounds of bombs and sirens tortured me.

Naturally we had head lice and fought those with an evil smelling concoction from the apothecary that had to be rubbed onto one's scalp. That and everyday grooming with the louse comb eventually rid us of the pests. But lice and bedbugs were nothing compared to the worm infestations we suffered. Tiny little pin worms were just very itchy and did not matter much to me, but one day I had two foot long round worms bore their way out of my eye during school. Shaking with disgust and horror and fear I pulled the two wriggling creatures out of my eye. I stuffed the white worms into my pocket to show my mother when I came home. She took them and me to see Dr. Hermann.

"Oh dear, this child has everything – now its roundworms."

She prescribed huge purple pills that had to be swallowed whole.

My much admired Dr. Hermann got me on a list of malnourished children entitled to two liters of fresh milk a week. Happily I walked twice a week the three kilometers along the Kocher River to 'my' farm, where, after having braved the outraged gander, whom I greatly feared because he was always chasing me with flapping wings, his horny beak open making threatening noises, I received the warm milk carefully measured into my pail. At home I boiled the milk slowly then stashed it in a bottle into our cooler underneath our living room floor– where the rats could look at it but not get at the precious drink.

We shared our home with rats, they lived underneath our floor. Their intelligent black eyes seemed to look at you with a challenge. I knew they were smart and greedy and very clever. Their whiskers were mobile and alive antennae and their tails were thick and naked ropes. Our cold storage was a little shelf accessible only after lifting up the trap door in the living room floor. One had to be lying on one's stomach and then reach down into the black. Everything had to be in a metal pail or in glass or the rats would get it. Sometimes I saw their black, pearly eyes when I reached down and I could hear their ghostlike movements. Mama always screamed at them to make them go away. I did not like the rats – somehow they scared me. I always felt that if they could they would come out at night and start gnawing on my fingers on my blanket. I kept them safely tucked under.

One summer I had to abandon my singing role as the witch in 'Hansel and Gretel' because I almost choked to death from tonsillitis the night before the performance. I was heartbroken because with all my eight years I was stage struck and had no greater wish than to perform. Instead of an audience of many admiring my singing I soon had an audience of nurses struggling to hold me down on a special operating chair and a surgeon barking out orders. The hospital had no anesthetics and used nurses to keep a patient from moving.

The surgeon sat in front of me and with scalpel poised ordered me to open my mouth. The nurses had my upper body and my arms pinned down, but not my legs and so I kicked the physician who in a flash slapped my face, then he clamped his knees around my legs like a vice. Thus immobilized I had to endure and watch him as he lifted out the bloody lump of swollen tissue from my mouth. After waving it in front of my nose he dropped the first one in a kidney shaped basin – flump – and then threatened me that he would keep on cutting if I would not sit still. I sat still.

There was no painkiller and there was no ice cream for me in the hospital. I was eight years old and I wet my bed that night. When the nurse discovered that she scolded me and then put a huge thick red rubber sheet under me. There was no cloth sheet on top of it. All the other children watched carefully, some snickered. No one said a word. I was filled with shame.

I did not sleep much that night, but sat on my rubber sheet with my hands on my screaming ears, rocking to and fro with pain.

During the following winter I caught some bug and developed such a fever that my mother thought I would surely die. In desperation she ran to Dr. Hermann in the middle of the night and brought her to our house. By that time I was delirious but I can still remember – with a shiver – that the two women took off my nightgown, which was sewn from USA donated sugar sacks with printed yellow flowers on it, lifted my naked, burning body and gently laid me on top of a dripping wet sheet they had placed on the table, and then wrapped me up in it like a mummy. Soon I was shivering with cold. I was unwrapped and another ice cold and wet sheet was draped over the table and the procedure was repeated. One woman stayed with me the other ran to the river for another bucket of icy water into which the now warm sheet was dunked.

The two women worked all night to break the fever – so my mother explained to me next morning when I woke up. The fever was gone. Mama was late for work and I was very hungry.

On one of their nightly forays Aunt Erika and Mama discovered a field of sugar beets. A few nights outing and the two women had a pile of the tubers deposited behind the barrack.

Inge and I stood wondering what Mama and Tante Eka would do with this huge amount of ugly, purplish white turnips which did not look at all edible or inviting.

They smiled. "You just wait and see."

We soon found out. On Friday night the tubers were washed at the pump house, cut into chunks, placed into a large pot, carried into the kitchen, put on the wood eating kitchen stove and covered with water. We kept the fire going under the pot until the flesh was cooked to a mush.

The next morning, after the sugar beets had cooled off and could be handled, the mush was ladled into a pillow case. The case was then hung up with a string from the ceiling, a bucket placed underneath and yellowish thick juice started to run out and then dripped all day long and during the night. We were careful not to upset the bucket underneath which was filling up with sticky, sugary juice. The next day Mama and Aunt Erika took the much deflated pillow case down, rearranged the mush into the center. Then both started to twist the pillow case each from her side in a different direction and they squeezed the last ounces of juice out of the mush into the pot.

Inge and I watched in fascination and in anticipation – of course we had stuck our fingers into the juice and tasted it – it was sweet and rich like a late summers evening. The women poured the juice back into the large pot set it on the stove and slowly boiled it down. The syrup became darker and sweeter and thicker. When it was deemed 'done' it was ladled into tin cans which we had found on the city dump and washed and scoured with sand until they were shiny. Most were closed with bits of paper tied down with string. Lucky forays to the dump yielded jars from the Americans – they had lids. They were cherished!

Mama and Aunt Erika spend many evenings chopping and boiling – and when winter came we had a large stash of cans filled with thick syrup. Porridge with black treacle! Sweet tea. Pancakes with treacle. We were happy!

I do not remember how many liters the two women made – but I do recall with somewhat of a shudder how long it took our family to finally get rid of the last of the syrup: six years later in 1952, when my father had long come home, when we had finally enough to eat and had already moved to Stuttgart, we celebrated the last spoonful which was equally divided up between the four of us and swallowed with exaggerated grimaces.

From the barracks it was a long walk every morning to school. I recall that for my first three years we were sent home every day after lunch. There were so many children now with the added refugees and there were not enough qualified teachers, because former Party members were excluded from the class room. Classes were staggered through the day in the one main Elementary School. At home I did household chores, after that I was free to do whatever I wanted. Mostly I wandered out of town, crossed the Kocher River on the old wooden roofed bridge that had been damaged in the war and required very careful attention in order not to fall through into the water, and headed to the 'Berg'.

The 'Berg' was a hillside rising from a meadow that followed the meandering Kocher River. At one time the steep hillside had grown grape vines on its laboriously and carefully constructed terraces. At about the turn of the century the farmers pulled them out because the grapes produced wine that was too sour. Most of the former vineyards had been sold to burgers from town who used the plots as weekend retreats. They built rustic cabins, which one could only reach on foot; they planted apple and pear and plum trees. Many raised raspberries and currants and had small garden patches on their deeply sloped lots.

Oma and Opa also owned one of these lots and they had built a cabin there. Opa came out every Saturday afternoon with Maexle, his beloved dog. The apprentice or the maid brought his provisions and many bottles of cider and wine in a hand pulled cart. Everything had to be carried up to the cabin on the narrow zig zag path. Many of Opa's friends met there later on for cards and libations.

It was a lovely valley overlooked by ancient ruins from which in the Middle Ages robber knights had extracted their toll from the burgers that travelled with their salt wagons from the city. When I went there only farmers driving their oxen carts moved on the road that wound alongside the river. I could watch herons and hawks, swallows and chickadees. The meadows were yellow with primulas and cow slips in spring and autumn brought purple crocuses. A cornucopia of fruit and berries, ripened hazelnuts and the famously sour sloeberries grew on the hills. During the week the cabins were deserted and I felt I owned the whole valley. I loved the 'Berg'.

My class mates envied my freedom. Their mothers were at home and waited for their children to come from school. And here I was – no mother at home – and had so much freedom. I had proven to Mama that I was responsible and trustworthy enough to be left alone at home, I had promised not to play in the old quarry where a grenade had torn off the leg of a child; I had promised not to pick up things that were made of metal, not to taste mushrooms or berries I did not recognize and not to go away with strangers.

I was considered very grown up for my age and Mama was certainly responsible for one aspect of that; I never threw temper tantrums. There was the matter of the large tin into which Mama had placed hundreds – or so it seemed to me – of bits of knotted string people at the office had cut off from parcels, and which she had collected. Whenever I had a fit of temper she told me to undo the knots, the number of which depended on the size of my outburst, and to make neat little packets of string that could be used again. I got very, very good at persistently and uncomplainingly – or she would have added another handful to it! - undoing countless knots. I certainly learned patience and eventually I learned to control my temper!

I do not know when my mother found out that my father was still alive and a prisoner of war in the American Sector. Did she cry? Did she dance for joy?

I don't know.

Later on Mama never talked about those days and she kept her thoughts and emotions to herself. One's own feelings were never up for discussion. A German and especially a Prussian always kept their "Haltung", their composure, an attitude much like the British 'stiff upper lip'. The display of excessive passion or grief or excitement was not becoming – only the plebs demonstrated such an improper exhibit. I sometimes wonder if she had ever allowed herself to feel desperate when she recognized that her whole world had changed. Everything she had held dear and known to be her truth had been destroyed, derided and taken away from her. She must have been devastated at having been cheated of her dreams and she must have been angry when she realized that she had been lied to – but it is also possible she still thought and felt as before and she looked at the Allies as an enemy who had unjustly invaded her fatherland and who had cruelly taken away everything she had cherished. I do not know.

I only know that she fought to stay alive and for her children to stay alive. She looked after us, she begged for us, she stole for us and she slept with a butcher's knife next to her bed until Papa came home again. I am quite sure she would have used it if she had had to.

If she had doubts or worries or fears, we never knew. She dealt with adversity head on, grimly determined to conquer devils, evils and weakness.

"Gelobt sei was hart macht." Praised be what makes you tough – that was her mantra. That is what she hammered into us every day.

When one spring an overflowing Kocher River threatened our little home she was not in a panic. She collected the chickens from outside and brought them in the living room and deposited them, with water and food, on top of the closet. Inge and I were sent to the grandparents in the Gelbingergasse with the message that she was fine and intended to stay in her house and that they should not bother her but leave her alone. This happened on a Friday afternoon. Inge and I skipped happily in to town. We loved going there. Back in the Jahnstrasse the water rose, the Kocher River poured over its bank and flooded the valley. Neighbours came and told her to leave her house. Mama sat on the table and told them to go away. She was going to stay.

Naturally my mother never told the story afterwards – she does not speak about defeat or losing. The neighbours watched the proceedings from their flats high and safely up in the apartment and passed on the happenings. Late in the afternoon a fire truck drove up on the road. Three firemen in uniform waded through the now quite deep water. They entered the house and probably informed her that they had come to evacuate her even against her will. Did my mother know that it was policy to save a person even against their choice if public safety was in question? Eventually they picked her up, carried her out of her house and loaded her into the fire truck. I remember that she spent the night with us at my grandparents. I also remember that she did not speak much and that she had that special look on her face that made no one want to talk to her. Inge and I were quite afraid of her when she had on her 'iron mask', her outward announcement of deep disapproval. It was best to leave her alone.

Overnight the water fell and on Sunday afternoon we marched resolutely down to Jahnstrasse and into our house. The three chickens were fine. We lifted them down and took them back into the backyard into their now very muddy and soggy home. Their clucking convinced us that they were very happy to be home again. As were we. It took some time and many buckets of water, lugged by Inge and me from the outside pump, to clean the rooms from the mud and dirt.

That night I resumed the daily ritual again of combing and brushing Mama's hair. This was our together time – I chatted away and she sat quietly, eyes closed – at home and in peace.

In those first two years in our barrack life revolved around food and warmth. My mother bought a wagonload of scrap wood which was unloaded behind the barrack. The wood was thin and burned up in a flash in our kitchen stove. Forever out to increase our stash of fuel Inge and I picked up pieces of wood wherever we saw some. Often we would wander into the woods and collect dried branches and sacks full of pine and spruce cones for kindling. Later on Mama bought coal briquettes to burn in the little potbelly in the living room. They were shaped like loaves and left one's fingers black and greasy. They also needed much kindling wood to get going but they kept the room warm for a long time.

I loved school but I did not like my class mates. There were only a handful of refugees in my class – but we were marked. Some of these children spoke a dialect that was difficult to understand and did not sound German at all. They were a source of humour for the locals.

Some of the children were Roman Catholics – papists in a city that prided itself to have been one of the first cities to have become protestant Lutheran. Melanchthon, Luther's disciple, had taught here in Schwaebisch Hall and the citizenry was predominantly Lutheran and there was still a dislike and mistrust of Catholics and the newcomers from the east felt that animosity. The children became an easy target, they were taunted by their class mates for being 'rosary yokels'.

Some of 'us' wore different clothing, some even wore their traditional costumes. Most of us were barefoot and in winter our shoes were 'funny', like too big, or men's shoes or boots. Our socks were mended and mended again and some, like mine so often, were mended with yarn of a different colour – and I was mortified and tried to hide the patched up heels or toes. Most of us had only one dress, protected by an apron. Our clothes were stitched together from old women's dresses, dark and drab. Some of our attire was sewn from dyed material of Third Reich flags; all households had a few and none were needed anymore. Those dresses were dowdy and indestructible, perhaps beaded with a pretty crochet or white piping – but nothing could hide their origin – and the children pointed their fingers and snickered. Sometimes our flag dresses were prettied up with a little red apron – one just like Little Red Riding Hood wore

– but its flag origin was quickly recognized too and they let us know they knew. The local children would not play with us; they laughed at us and told us to get back to where we came from.

Mama told me to let them laugh and to ignore them.

"Get even with them," she advised, "be quiet but rise above them."

She mused, "They don't know any better. They hate what is strange and different. They are the plebs. But you are not. Your father is an SS officer."

Chapter 26

ERIKA AND CHARLES

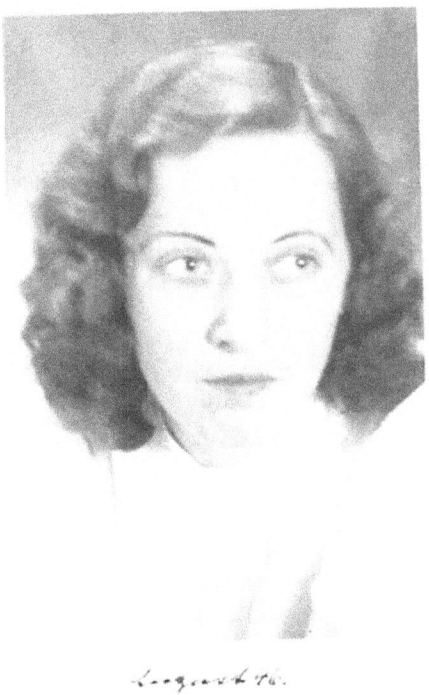

Lagerteld 46.

In Schwaebisch Hall I was happy to accept the upper attic room that August and Emma Haefner had offered me. I didn't mind the raw tiles above my head and the wind whistling through the wall, I was safe and I had food to eat. I much enjoyed my king's view of the lovely Kocher Valley through the tiny window under the gable of the massive roof.

Every day I went to the employment office in Schwaebisch Hall to ask for work, any kind of work, only to be told that I had come in vain. I could sense that they did not like me, I was a refugee, and I was taking jobs away from the locals. Sometimes they even asked me why I didn't go back to where I had come from. But I kept my tongue and kept on showing up every day. I needed a job and I was going to get something eventually. One morning the clerk offered me a position with the Americans. She sort of sneered at me that that was all they had to offer me. Imagine her surprise when I replied that I would love to take a job with the Americans, I spoke English and had office experience.

The Americans, the occupying forces in Wuerttemberg, had taken over a large factory in town that manufactured appliances and machine parts. They needed personnel for the office. I went for the interview and was hired to be in charge of payroll.

All went well and a few months later a new boss took over. His name was Charles Vanek. Because I spoke English, I had to accompany him on his trips to buy steel for the manufacture of nuts, bolts and appliances. One day just outside a small town he got awfully sick. I ran into town and to the nearest pharmacy. The apothecary came with me bringing quinine tablets. Charlie had been able to tell me that he had a malaria attack, a disease he had picked up in the war in New Guinea. It took about three hours before he was able to drive again.

Charlie lived in the factory which was just a block away from the Haefner house in the Gelbingergasse. A fat and slatternly woman was employed as the cook for him and the other Americans. Since I did the books, I knew that she spent much too much on supplies and food and I told Charlie so. He replied that he needed a cook and what was he supposed to do. I told him that I had a sister who was an excellent cook who was also very clean, not like the slut who was looking after him now. I also informed him that my sister was honest and would not steal him blind like the present cook.

Charlie agreed to hire Irmgard. But it turned out there was a problem; the problem was not Charlie, the problem was my sister, your mother. When I broached the subject of cooking for the Americans to her, Irmgard was outraged.

"How could you possibly imagine that I would cook for the enemy?"

That was your mother – so typical. But after she thought over it for a while it did not take too much persuasion. Your mother had no money, no food and two little girls and she decided to take the job.

Your mother took her job very seriously. She spent the first week cleaning and scrubbing the kitchen from top to bottom; she had to sift all the flour to get rid of the masses of weevils squirming in it. She was bowled over by the amount of food supplies that were there. She sorted and rearranged the pantry. Part of her duty was to fill out a new requisition form every week.

One day Charles visited her in the now spanking clean kitchen. He was hugely surprised by the visible change and he mentioned that he was equally surprised at how little food Frau Haefner was ordering – compared to the long lists her predecessor had handed in.

And your mother hurled back at him in righteous indignation, "Do you think that I steal food from YOU?"

Charlie just smiled. He had been forewarned by me that Irmgard still had a huge 'chip on her shoulder'. Charles and the Americans were still the enemy and Irmgard was still very proud and unbending.

One day Charlie spoke to her, "I understand that you have two little girls. Why don't you bring them here every day so they can have their lunch in the kitchen? And please, do me a favour: I hate left-overs, please take all the leftovers home."

From then on you kids came every noon from school, which was just across the road, and had lunch in the kitchen. Both you and Inge started to grow and fill out, what with all the good left-overs!

Charles was so very kind. After I had worked for him for three months, he asked me where my husband was. I told him that I was a war widow. When I asked him if he was married, he answered that he had lost his wife in a car accident in California.

And so we fell in love.

Charlie was such a gentleman. He was courteous and very dignified and I appreciated it so very much that he did not rush me in any way.

One day Charlie said to me, wouldn't it be nice if you had a little place of your own. And he bought the two barracks we were living in. Yes, Charlie bought them – one for me and one for your mother and you two little girls. And then we found your father and he got furniture for you and me and life started to become very good indeed.

It was Charlie who helped bring my father over to the west. Charlie arranged to have him denazified and to get his teaching papers back so he could start teaching as soon as he got here. Not long after he brought his wife Trudel and daughter Sigrid over to the west – they were smuggled over.

When we got married in 1948 and left to go back to the States, we gave my father the house. Charles had paid 1000 Marks for each barrack.

Charlie was such a good man."

***When my mother became the cook for the Americans, we had to leave our house very early every morning. I brought my little sister Inge who was not yet of school age to grandma or another lady who looked after her and then returned to the kitchen until it was time for school.

At noon I crossed the street from the school to the factory. The kitchen was in a sort of tower on top of the factory. There was a flat roof and it was like a terrace adjacent to the place where Mama worked. Every noon in nice weather I sat there at a little table anticipating the wonderful noonday meal, the fragrances of which spilled out of the door. Those meals, with meat and vegetables and gravy were followed by tasty desserts. Uncle Charlie had a sweet tooth; he was especially fond of pancakes made with canned fruit. I remember those especially because I quickly learned how to make them myself.

I helped my mother in the kitchen with dishes and peeling potatoes and other things like that, because school still was only half a day every day. Aunt Erika put me on payroll – or so she said. Every Friday I lined up with the workers and passed by the window where she handed out the envelopes. I felt so grown up and important. Only years later did she tell me the truth – I had actually not been on payroll, my wages had come out of hers!

Now, when I lined up in the school yard with all the other children, the old army dish in hand, to receive my daily ration of 'Schulspeisung', the food given to all the children in the American occupied zone, the Hoover meals, the stews and thick soups that were daily ladled out of huge steaming metal milk cans, I did not need to eat it but could carry that food to Tante Berta who received it gratefully.

For many families this meal was the only decent meal they had during the day. I had liked all the meals except the one on Saturdays, where it was hot cocoa with noodles in it. It was sweet and good – I am sure – but I had hated it. For many children this was their favourite meal of the week and they looked forward to it with great anticipation.

My mother cooked for about a year. She quickly refreshed her knowledge of English and soon advanced to be Charles' secretary and interpreter. By this time, she had also found Papa and was able to follow his sojourns through different prisoner of war camps.

My father had been able to secure a job in the kitchen – the most coveted job in a POW camp and consequently he was well again. As his health increased so did his enterprising spirit. He had finagled to gain access to wood and tools and men with skills and talents and had built furniture for us in his camp. How he was able to transport those pieces with GI guards right to our barracks and install them there with their help will forever be a monument to him, human ingenuity, and the kindness of the Americans.

Our living room had a home made couch that opened into a bed. There was a new table, chairs, stools, a cupboard and a closet. The pieces were of pine and well made, and their painted lines and decorations looked very pretty indeed.

He had also carved two large plaques. One was nailed to Aunt Erika's barracks next to the entrance door, the other one found a place next to ours. Aunt Erika's house was "Villa Tigerkralle" or 'Tiger's Claw' – and it showed a fierce beast with extended claws. Ours was much more peaceful:

it showed a relief of a lusty sparrow dropping a piece of poop onto a carved earth with the outlines of Europe painted on it. "Villa Sperlingslust", 'Villa Sparrow's Delight'. I believe it nicely expressed my father's philosophy at that stage of his life. To hell with the world.

When I left Germany for Canada in 1964, I asked for the plaque and my parents gave it to me. Naturally it has occupied a place of honour ever since. To me it expresses defiance, courage, fortitude, care and appreciation of the beauty of life – traits I admired in my parents.***

Chapter 27

GUSTEL AS PRISONER OF WAR

B eing closer to home we hoped to finally get more information as to the state and the fate of the had-been German Reich. Other than that the war was lost and that Germany was occupied by the Allied forces, we knew nothing. Later on, in the weeks and the months in the new camp, we had a fantastic network of people who brought us the news about what was happening in the world. We were strongly isolated from the population around us. But the lucky ones among us who had family and who knew where their families resided, received eventually permission to have visits from them here in the camp.

Life in this camp was very different because here we were allowed to work. Our barracks had taken over the kitchen for the American officers, with the result that they had good food and we got back to our normal healthy condition, like what we had been before our first camp experience.

Originally the Americans had former conscripted workers do the kitchen work but they were not as clean as we were and their meals did not taste quite as good as the ones cooked by us; and they stole even more than we did. One day some of the lower ranks started to treat us in an uncommonly mean way and even as prisoner of war we could not take such treatment without a protest and so we fought back the only we knew: we went on strike. En masse we left the kitchen – we marched out in formation singing the SS Treue Lied: " Wenn alle untreu werden, so bleiben wir doch treu…".

The Americans were not all pleased with our singing demonstration and they, of course, also missed their customary and well prepared meals. A following discussion between them and us led to the agreement that we would go back into our kitchen and cook for the officers if they would ensure that their men would treat us decently. We also had to agree that we would not steal one single item, not even the smallest pinch, for two whole days.

This way the Americans were again happy with the clean kitchen and the tasty food served on time – everything was again tip top. Of course, nothing else was to be expected from a bunch of men like us.

In Goeggingen the American officers resided in a house where also the offices of the CIC were located. One day they came and asked for a contingent of men to move a piano from the ground floor up to the third floor. Naturally I volunteered. The Americans had many women personnel and they flocked into the stair well as we were carrying the piano up to the third floor. Three men had the front end lifted and dragged it upstairs and I was at the rear, all by myself, carrying the heavy piano. The ladies looked with round eyes, chattering and admiring my strength. They were all over me with their ohs, and ahs, they even touched my arms. My goodness, they were a crazy bunch of girls.

That was my Papa! He loved it when he was the center of attention especially when his audience included the 'fairer sex'- as he loved to call the ladies. He was a natural charmer and he had to flirt with all the girls – no matter what their age. Sister Inge and I used to love watching when Papa used his wily ways to get a shy store girl to blush and stammer with embarrassment. In restaurants the waitresses were usually made of tougher stuff and their banter drew the attention of the rest of the diners enticing Papa to even wittier remarks. My mother tried to hide her discomfiture by pretending to be only interested in her cigarette while under the table she tried desperately to kick sense into her wayward husband. But Papa only wanted the challenge to get the girls to pay attention to him. There was never any other intention. He was a proper gentleman, gallant to the ladies and true and faithful to his wife.

When kitchen duty was done, we drove the scraps out to a hill outside the camp. It did not take our men long to notice that old men and women were frequent visitors scrounging through the garbage for edibles. The Americans had the habit of discarding any can that had a dent. Strange how clumsy we suddenly became when unpacking boxes and pallets, suddenly there were so many dented cans that we had to throw away. For two to three weeks the scavengers enjoyed a good harvest at their garbage hill. I suspect they had not been able to keep their good fortune to themselves and must have blabbed, because more and younger people began to show up at the site. They started fighting with the older people for cans and started to chase them off. When we noticed that, we no longer took dented cans to the landfill because we did not want them to have to fight for the food. And we most certainly did not want the younger ones to confront the older people.

The first artists became noticeable in our camp. We had painters and we had many wood carvers. We had made our own carving knives and now a lucrative trade ensued with the Americans. I still recall a beautiful chess set one prisoner had carved: Indians against Negroes. It was absolutely fabulous. He got so many cigarettes for that one; he could keep the whole camp in smokes for a long time.

*** One Christmas I found a carved farm set complete with buildings and fences, barns and a bevy of many animals on the gift table. Papa told us in a letter how many prisoners had helped carve this wonderful toy. I still recall how I loved that set. My mother received wooden ladles, salad forks, trays and candle holders – all well crafted and beautifully designed.***

A station of dentists had also sprung up. We had first class dentists with us. Some were professors at universities. The Americans, even though they had their own dentists, seemed to prefer to have their teeth fixed right here in our camp and they often paid with gold. But a dentist is not much good if he does not have a proper chair. Someone had scouted out that the seats of searchlights had swivels and were adjustable to different heights and angles and therefore were ideal for a dentist chair. Soon the Americans discovered that we had five or six dentists working at the same time. Our good doctors relieved the Americans of so many materials that there was enough left to treat us men too.

According to international contracts and regulations we as officers did not have to work. But I could not sit around all day without something to do. We were trucked in the morning to a former warehouse of the Wehrmacht from where we took what we needed for our enterprises and work. It is amazing how much stuff could be tucked away in a truck when the Americans did not watch too carefully. Wood, rope, metal, especially aluminum came from the warehouse. We fabricated whatever we needed in the camp.

Here in Canada I still have an aluminum slotted spoon and aluminum measuring cup, a wooden candle holder and tray, beautifully hand crafted in that camp.

It happened that when someone needed clothing at home, a man ordered a certain size from the team and they brought it from the warehouse. Almost all the American camps were run by our men. One day the American military police came with siren blaring and blue light signaling to pick up one of our men. And why? There were German sergeants who ran the administration of a warehouse for the Americans. The Americans drove them to the warehouse and made them open the doors so they could get out what they wanted or needed. The Americans used their own supplies for trading purposes with the local Germans. Of course, there was always something in it for our men too.

I had started a carpentry shop where we made furniture from the wood we brought from the Wehrmacht warehouse. After we had made the tools needed for our wood work, I made a table and chairs, a chesterfield, beds and a closet for my family and then worked with other men to make furniture for their families. Sometimes the families came and took the furniture away from the camp. But mostly we arranged somehow that the Americans drove it to the homes. I cannot recall how I managed to do it but one day an American truck drove me and my furniture all the way to Schwaebisch Hall some 250 kilometers away and the driver helped me move the furniture into our house.

From the fall of 1945 throughout the year 1946 I was in Goeggingen together with approximately one thousand men. We were considered prisoners of war but nobody bothered us in any way. We were waiting for the end; meanwhile we kept ourselves busy and useful to whoever needed our work and help. The American trucks drove our men to wherever they were needed during the day. Someone had the great idea to equip the truck with a false floor under which contraband could easily be transported without getting us in danger of being discovered. Our families were all suffering terribly from lack of food and clothing. Whatever we could get to them, we did. They could use it themselves or use it on the black market as a trading item. We filled boxes with foodstuffs and clothing and whatever else we could organize. Prisoners were allowed to send mail and so we drove to the post office with our hidden parcels. Our guards leant their rifles against the walls of the post office and helped carry in our many parcels. They were an awfully decent bunch of men.

We had men who were absent from camp for days on end. Either they stayed at home or they stayed with a girl friend of old or more likely of new. It was so organized that a car stopped at certain points in Augsburg and someone climbed in and someone climbed out. Some of the bodies were female – but the Americans did not catch on to that for quite some time. It was a long time before they noticed that there were women in the camp. One of our Polish guards though must have noticed something because on day he said to me with a smirk, "How come your comrade has big bust like woman?"

One day a huge mustering was ordered. There were four women in the camp but they were quickly dressed as men, their hair hidden under some old caps. We knew that about twenty men were not present. We went to speak to our American sergeant, a Jew by the way, about their absence. He wrinkled his brow and shook his head, then sent the jeep of with blue light and siren, military police to bring back the lost sheep. He was very aware that he had to have all his men present otherwise he would be in serious trouble, no less than the absent men. The jeep collected a few of the stray sheep but some were not to be found. When we realized that some men were still missing, we knew we had to come up with a plan because we would not have wanted our sergeant to get into trouble on our behalf.

We decided that the counted men were to amble down to the gravel pit but then turn around and return on a back path, stand in line and be counted once more. To create a diversion, we called on the owners of all pets, by that time we had a small zoo in the camp, to make themselves be seen where the American guards were standing, counting and writing numbers down. We all knew what animal lovers the Americans were. Shortly our animal owners congregated in an animated bunch around the guards who tried to count. There was a lot of petting and laughter and quite a commotion. Some of us other guys got involved in some other silly activity and that was sufficient time for the men to get back from the gravel pit and to get in line gain. The numbers expected coincided with the numbers counted. When I think back – the things we did.

Your mother visited me one day. As she was walking along the fence she noticed a prisoner walking by; he had a pail in his hand. The pail was an old, commercial size American tin can which had been fitted with a wire handle. She did not say a word but I saw the look in her eyes. When it was time for her to enter the room where we allowed to speak to each other, I was able to hand her her very own pail. We tried so hard to help our families on the outside. I knew of one man who supplied his family for three weeks with food cans from the camp.

Besides the furniture that I could make for our home, I was also able to get clothing. We had set up a dye shop because we could hardly walk around in the German field grey.

At one time one of our men had once left for home and another man took his place. After some time, the stand-in man had to leave the camp and so we were short one man. The Americans had not noticed that until one day a man arrived at the camp gate, identified himself and asked to be let in again. His family could no longer feed him because he had, of course, no food stamps. And, naturally, because he had no papers, he was unable to apply for some. And so he returned back to the camp.

One day men from the kitchen detail noticed that beer barrels were unloaded from trucks. The label indicated good Bavarian beer. I ambled through the storage area where the barrels were kept and in old cooper fashion, kicked the lower barrels with my boot and rapped the upper ones with my fist, and lo and behold, I discovered a barrel that was full. Excitement lifted us a foot off the ground. First, we hid the barrel so it could not be taken away from now until home time. Then we smuggled it into the truck, nobody noticed us. The gate at the camp was more difficult. There was a Polish guard and we were not too sure about him. But we figured he would never guess the truth and so three of our men shouldered the barrel, and as if they were on official business, marched past him into the camp. What a party we had that evening in our barracks!

I was as lucky after the war as I was during the war. If I would have fallen into the hands of the Russians, I don't think I would have survived. They would have found out in short time who I was and what I had been doing in Ukraine and that would have been the end of me. There were so many places in the Ukraine where I had been for some time and where things had happened. Someone would have recognized me for sure. With the Russians I would not have had a chance.

But with the Americans it was a different story. Our life was good. We worked, we ate well and we could even help our families. We could do so many things.

Once I needed a motor. We searched and found a good one in a warehouse. Not long after the Americans wanted to use the elevator in that warehouse – but the elevator would not work. They inspected and discovered that the motor was missing.

Of course, the Americans were often with us. When we ran out of aluminum, which we needed to fabricate kitchen utensils, they told us where we could find remnants of downed airplanes. They drove a few of us to the place and helped us bring the parts into the camp. We carried on with our fabrications. Many of these were made for the Americans who used them themselves or sent them home to their families.

One day when we had to march through Augsburg to see a film. Didn't we march through the city, singing our old SS songs: 'In Reih und Glied' and all the other old and familiar songs! The guards let us. Imagine! What guys!

At one time the old commander was to be replaced with a new one. There were many applicants for the job. The Americans told us they preferred to work in camps that held former SS men. They did not like to supervise a camp full of Wehrmacht because there was nothing but fights and trouble. They laughed, "The SS men in the camps are bandits; they steal and they are full of oats sometimes. But on the other hand there was an overall discipline and there were no problems with the inmates."

The Americans had no problems with us; this is true. And of course, we were not beyond admitting that we enjoyed that they were vying to be commanders of the SS – the feared SS!

One day we were transported to Bad Aibling where the Americans dismissed us into the hands of the Germans who put us into special camps, the 'Internierungslager', internment camps. There we were sorted into two groups: the lower ranks which could be sent home and the others who were wanted by the German administration, men who had been involved with the Party or the SS. This how I landed in the "Hohenasperg", an old fortification which had for a long time during German history housed many prisoners within its old and thick walls.

Many famous Germans had been locked up in there, most, like the poet Schubart, for political reasons. I, who was only a First Lieutenant, was in illustrious company. There were other high risk offenders like me in here. For example, there was the High Minister of Labour Service, Reich Labour leader, Konstantin Hierl.

One day he came into the library where I had been assigned to sort out the many books the population had donated to us inmates.

He asked, "Do you have Karl May?"

I assured him that we, indeed, had many volumes.

He laughed. "Thank heavens. For years I have wanted to read them all and now I will finally have the time to do so."

Other dangerous criminals who shared the high risk prison with me were, for example, an old man in his seventies. He was a farmer from this area who had joined the Home Guard two days before the end of the war. He had worked in the SS barracks in Ellwangen and his task had been to collect horse manure around the place. They were short on cars but they used plenty of horses at that time. And for that service to the Reich, they had brought the old man to the fort. All attempts to set him free and send him home were fruitless.

It was not long before I became the official driver for the many big wigs that came here. I was known to be from the area and to know the region like my back pocket. One day I had to drive some bureaucrats who did not know the route, I made a detour over Schwaebisch Hall where I dropped in on my family and said, 'hello'.

The truck I had been assigned was also used to ferry people around. One day one of my passengers told me that I should consider that I was not driving a BMW motorcycle and that I should not lean into the curves as much as I was toppling the riders from their seats. I guess I had been a pretty rough driver – but I listened to him and tried to make my passenger's lives much easier. Mostly though, I had to haul coal. There I could show what stuff I was made off. The trucks were consistently highly overloaded and the road up to the fort was one of the steepest. It had, of course, not been designed for motorized traffic. I always made it.

The French were once looking for a former Kriminalbeamte, a criminal civil servant, but the Americans informed them that no such man was in Hohenasperg. There must have been tension between the two administrations and they did not want to hand the man over, who was in fact here.

We were maybe three hundred men in the ancient fortified prison. I knew that I would soon be involved in a process because the following had happened: all the memos, reports and papers which the Einsatzkommandos in Russia had sent to their superiors or even the RSHA, the Reich Security Headquarters, in Berlin, had according to good German custom and tradition been kept securely hidden in an abandoned mine, were discovered after a German friend had pointed the authorities in that direction. Therefore, when the trials of the Nuremberg Process started they had already the original papers, and in the reports from detachment

4a Blobel, the name Haefner is mentioned. I got to see that myself when I spent some time in Nuremberg as a witness and I knew that there would be a time when they would come for me.

When I left Greece, every paper, every report, every scrap was burned as we were ordered. I made sure that nothing was left. Of course, we had also sent our regular reports daily to the Reich Security Headquarters as required.

When I had my own day in court, I was classified as a main guilty party, I was after all, an old Party member, I was a Kriminalkommissar and I had the EKII. I was sentenced to spend more time in prison and I also had to forfeit all my possessions, which were to be confiscated. But that was easy since I literally had nothing.

They sent a man to check on our conditions in Schwaebisch Hall. The man was an old craftsman from Schwaebisch Hall, a former Social Democrat. He was so embarrassed when he entered our home, the old barrack, where formerly conscripted workers had been housed. We showed him the straw sacks my wife and my two girls used in their beds and the tin cans from which they ate. I did not mind watching him sweat with embarrassment. He quickly signed the papers stating we were paupers and left in a hurry.

The process against the Einsatzkommandos had started in Nuremberg in April of 1947and I received the order to be transferred to Nuremberg to the Palace of Justice where the IMT, the International Military Tribunal was taking place. All the commanders of the Einsatzkommandos were there. Ohlendorf was; Rasch was no longer available to speak; he was very ill with Alzheimers disease.

The leaders of the Einsatzkommandos were there, Blobel, Schulz, Blume and Braune. The guards in Nuremberg were former Estonian SS men, that is former Waffen SS, who had received a general pardon and who had succeeded in not to being handed over to the Russians but instead been accepted by the Americans. I got to know one of them quite well.

I was there as a witness for Blobel. I was free to wander in the wing where I was quartered until eight at night when the doors of the cells were locked. I had a chance to talk to Blobel and his defense lawyers. I also got to have a look at the court papers and learned that the Americans had word protocol, that is every word that is said, no matter by whom, was recorded. Later, in my own trial I tried to get the court to adopt this method also, but was unsuccessful.

Of course, we went along with the daily proceedings. My cell had another inmate, a German-American, who had been the leader of the Hitler followers in New York. He told me a lot about the American justice system. They could not get him with any of their laws until one clever attorney dug up an old law which forbade bringing a woman from one side of New York to the other side because that was considered kidnapping. One day he was actually driving his secretary through New York and that is when they nabbed him. They brought him to Nuremberg so he might speak out against the Germans. I never knew what happened to him because my time in Nuremberg was quite short.

So much was twisted in the reports and in the questioning. Many people did not speak the truth and that upset me very much. The judges also played their games. One day I told a defense lawyer that I would like to stand up and tell the truth. He told me that they had built up a case that had to prove that the SS was guilty for everything.

"If you get up and involve the Wehrmacht, then you'll live not another twenty four hours."

I respected this man very much. He was to be my own defense lawyer later on. I consulted a few other lawyers and then let things be and was quiet, unfortunately, perhaps. Maybe some things would have been different.

I was carrying meals in the wing and that was a terrific opportunity to get to know people and to talk to them. I learned a lot and gladly parted with any information I was able to gather. There were two or three trials going on at the same time and everyone was interested who, for example, was lined up as witness, and also for whom. Alfred Krupp was there too and I passed messages for him as I carried out my waiter duties.

I also worked in the American clothing warehouse and helped myself to a wonderful pair of trousers and a pair of boots. Up to that time I had still been walking around in the remnants of my old German uniform. There was only the minor problem of how to get these articles past the guards until I remembered the old saying 'give a dog a piece of bone and he'll not see the carcass in the bush'. I laid a woolen blanket on top of my bag and when the guards saw that they took it away from me with a hurrah. They never noticed the pants or the boots underneath.

I once had a chance to speak to Ohlendorf.

"Sir, you said that the security police had the absolute order to shoot all Jews. That was perhaps an unwise statement because that means that all of us who took part in the training course, all the hundreds with me and all the hundreds who came after, will have to face the court."

"That is correct. It is too late now and I cannot take it back,"

I asked him what had really happened.

He answered, "Dear comrade Haefner. If I would open my mouth and speak all the generals who were active in the south would have to face the tribunal."

He did involve two generals who were active in that region and they were sentenced too. They did not get the death penalty. The famous General von

Manstein received twenty years which he never served. All the really big generals served only a fraction of their punishments. They quickly were released – they were all Wehrmacht, of course.

When I once spoke to an American captain, a man who was originally from Hamburg, he said, "Herr Haefner, don't tell of the Wehrmacht and their involvement. No one will listen. It was agreed upon to have the SS take all the blame because we cannot, simply cannot, punish the whole German nation or incarcerate the whole German population. You will have to get used to it – all the blame will be laid at the feet of the SS." And that is how it happened.

Our translator from the Ukraine was here too, a captain Waldemar von Radetzky, a Baltic German, he was sentenced to twenty years but was released after seven or eight. All the men in Landsberg were let go after seven or eight years and were all allowed to go home. Blobel, Braune, and Ohlendorf were hanged on June 7th, 1951 in Landsberg Prison. I knew all three personally. Rasch had died of natural causes in November 1948.

Another reason that none of us had ever spoken was that there was an unwritten law not to involve more men than were already involved. Enough lives had been lost. We did not want to implicate more and cause more deaths. There had been rumours that the Americans were going to kill all SS. We did not know the future. We knew we had lost the war and our motto now was: let us get out of it with as few repercussions as possible.

That too is what I tried to do in my trial of 1965. I knew nothing would happen to the Wehrmacht, they were immune. Nothing ever did happen to them. I know because things with which I implicated them in my trial were not recorded in the official documents. There were orders not to document certain happenings, not to document anything that went against official policy.

I sat in Hohenasperg until summer 1948 and then I was let go. I knew that this was not the end of my involvement with the justice system. I knew they would come again for me one day.

Chapter 28

Opa Ernst In Schwaebisch Hall

O ne day in the spring of 1947 an old man moved into the Tiger Claw barrack, Aunt Erika's house, next to us. He was tall and gaunt with a shock of white hair on his head and an eternal pipe in his mouth; that was my grandfather from Silesia, Opa Ernst.

In December of 1945 the borders across Germany had opened for mail. Herbert had written to the Haefner family in Schwaebisch Hall, where Irmgard and Erika had found refuge. Both wrote to their father in January, "causing the greatest joy!"

My grandfather's memoirs read: "I have never in my life written and read so many letters as in the following months. The girls supported us in the kindest way with extra food. They sent us flour and oats, semolina, milk powder, egg powder, cocoa, sugar, coffee, fat, dried fruit. They also sent us pliers, solder material, saws, nails, paper, envelopes, pencils, glue and so much more. And last but not least, Erika sent me cigarettes and tobacco. During the span of thirteen months, we received a total of 194 parcels, practically one every second day one. I know some got lost – so the number sent was even higher."

All this made possible by Erika and later my mother by working for the Americans.

Erika asked him to relocate to Schwaebisch Hall and after some hesitation he agreed. Since so many refugees in the east wanted to move away from the communist Russians and live in the American sector this was not an easy enterprise but with Charlie's help he succeeded.

I do not know what Opa Ernst thought when Charles came for his frequent courting visits to the barracks. I remember Uncle Charles so very well – he had a voice very much like Paul Robson and often Charles' voice would ring out over the Kocher River and we listened spellbound to his rendition of 'Oh Shenandoh' and 'Old Man River'. Once Papa came home the two men, who got along splendidly, frequently sang together.

I often wondered what my grandfather had thought about accepting help from the former 'enemy'. He must have been aware that without Charles' help he might have never succeeded in relocating in the west. Much later Aunt Erika shared with us her own great sorrow about being aware of her father's great disappointment when she married an American and immigrated to the US. Her father discouraged the relationship between his daughter's new family and himself in the ensuing years. He could not get used to the fact that her husband Charles and her daughter Helga, born meanwhile in El Paso, had become more important in Erika's life, than he, her father. He must have resented also that she wrote in glowing terms about her new country, its freedoms and its riches she was able to enjoy.

When in the early sixties Erika and Charles returned to the States after their two years stay in Pattonville, the American base near Ludwigsburg in Wuerttemberg, where Charles had been working, the two families no longer spoke to each other. There had been visits but they became less frequent and in the end the father never even said good bye to his daughter. Erika found the break and her father's selfishness and intolerance very hard to bear.

Sharing the 'Villa Tiger Claw' with Erika was probably not desirable for Opa Ernst and he quickly built an addition which became his room. Inside the house he 'ruled' from his self-made wooden 'Easy Chair' which was flanked by a shelf that held his pipe and smoking paraphernalia and an ever increasing stack of books. The chair had an inbuilt and swiveling lectern with a ledge for the book, a lamp and a page holder. There was a place for his coffee cup, a radio, then a turn table and records. I watched in fascination how one man commandeered people and matters to make his life as comfortable as he could have it.

Opa Ernst was a good gardener. His lettuces grew straight into the sky, his peas were verdantly green and lush, I had never seen bigger and more colourful cucumbers, tomatoes and squashes. He was a master compost maker – compost that was as black as the ersatz coffee we drank and sweet smelling and heaven for his pumpkins. And he grew those strange looking, exotically beautiful plants – tobacco. They were his favourites. He babied them, cut the leaves when they were just ready for him. He hung them using a needle and thread, on a string underneath his roof until they were dry, to be later on rolled, cut and then stuffed into his black brown pipe. They actually smelled quite good when he set them alight. Some leaves he cut very finely and rolled them into white paper and smoked them as cigarettes. He also rolled his very own cigars.

Opa Ernst was never without smoke rising from his face – and like the deity of Mount Vesuvius, his head was crowned with a cloud of white hair; he had a rumbling voice, he was distant and awesome and to be feared because one could not predict what he was going to do next.

As I have mentioned already, we had three precious egg laying hens. One day Mama announced that it was very fine that I supplemented their feed with gathered greens and the occasional bug or worm, but that she was sure the egg output would vastly increase if the chickens were given free access to all the goodies that our garden provided freely for them. She said not only would that benefit the chickens but that I, the slave of the garden, would have less work weeding or picking damaging insects from the garden because the hens would do it for me. Well, good. I had to agree – besides one did not argue with Mama.

I saw that the chickens were equally agreeable to the plan when I let them out. Only there was a problem – Mama had omitted to tell the chickens that they were not supposed to get greens and worms from Opa Ernst's garden. So, after the first day and some rather scary violent verbal eruptions from Mount Vesuvius next to us, I was told I had to herd the chickens. Naturally as hard as I ran and scolded and then ran some more – the chickens scattered and destroyed much in his beautiful garden. The herding plan did not work. Vesuvius erupted some more, which did not bother the chickens very much, but had me sobbing and crying. Finally Mama consented to locking up the chickens again and I returned to being in charge of supplying Trienchen, Bienchen and Sabinchen with my garnered dietary supplements.

A little story blimp on paper, but in reality it took many days before my stubborn mother gave in and released me from the impossible task of being a chicken shepherdess.

Opa Ernst had much patience with his garden, tinkering with wood, designing machines and making them work, but he had little patience with my sister or me. Inge actually stayed clear of him. In fact Inge was rarely at home. She much preferred life in the Gelbingergasse. Before and after kindergarten and later on school, Inge spent all her spare time there visiting and being everybody's favourite little girl, even Opa Haefner's with whom she spent many hours, watching him silently when he was making barrels.

One day Aunt Trudel and their daughter Sigrid, arrived from the East and then Opa Ernst was even less interested in me or my sister.

Chapter 29

Papa Comes Home

It was on a summery day in 1948 when I happened to look out from our front door and my eyes caught the sight of a head bopping up and down alongside the fence that separated the garden plots from the Jahnstrasse that passed alongside the white apartment building and out of town. A man came striding fast and with a purpose towards the end of the fence. The head moved around the corner and the figure of a man approached our barracks. I recognized him as the man who had brought the furniture some time back. My father.

"Papa!" I yelled and ran towards him. He swept me up and whirled around with me in his arms. Papa had come home and he had come home to stay.

When I think back, I realize that I actually did not know my father. He was there when I was a baby and a toddler in Pretzsch and Berlin. In later years I saw him when he was home on furlough from Austria and Greece. I saw him once again after the war when my mother visited him in a POW camp not too far away from Schwaebisch Hall. We took a bus to visit him.

I remember so vividly the huge bare ground which was surrounded by a high chain link fence and extra strands of coiled barbed wire. Watchtowers reached up and I saw they were manned by soldiers. Within the fence was a huge bare field on which many men either sat or stood or walked about. Mama told me that they were prisoners of war and that Papa was somewhere in that crowd. I did not recognize my father – all faces looked alike, dark and gaunt and unshaven. But then one man smiled, waved his hand and started coming towards us. I ran towards the fence wanting to touch his hands.

"No!" A scream out of dozens of throats cut through the air.

"No, don't touch the wire. It will kill you! Get back!"

I stopped and stepped back. My mother wondered why the men had screamed.

"The fence is electric and would have killed her in an instant".

Papa got busy with our little house. By the time winter came he had built an extra bedroom that ran the whole length of the house and into which one had to step down two steps from the living room. The room was subdivided by a large closet, made by him in prison camp. On the left side was a bed where Mama slept. Between the foot of the bed and the wall was an army cot and that was where Papa slept. Inge and I had two small beds on the other side of the closet. By removing a wall from the old bedroom Papa enlarged the little kitchen, he built a counter with a sink and installed POW handmade cupboards. He dug a deep ditch from the water pump to the kitchen, laid a pipe, and soon we had the luxury of running water. He incorporated the outhouse into an anteroom annexed to our house and we had indoor plumbing, our 'Plumps Kloset' – still gravity operated but so much more convenient than before.

In the back of the yard Papa built a large slatted shed that held firewood, a work place with a workbench and the much enlarged chicken coop with an enclosed outdoor run on one side. And best of all, he reserved on the other side one back corner of the shed for me. Nestled under the overhanging roof he built a sort of half open verandah enclosure with a book shelf, a bench – and I had 'my house'. I was ecstatic.

We had acquired a grey tabby cat, Pusso, and he loved to sit on my lap purring away when I read for hours on end in 'my house'. The river with ducks, fish and brilliantly colored kingfishers was only a few feet behind me, overhung by the wispy branches of an old willow tree. I could hear the water, the twittering and singing of so many birds, the odd slap of a jumping fish and I quickly got to know the different sounds the ducks made when they reared out of water, where they treaded water to start flying or when they put on 'the brakes' when sliding into landing. It was a child's paradise.

Papa painted the outside of the house a dark green and the window frames white. Inge and I collected more football size stones with which we re-edged the path to our front door. A few sandstones make perfect steps. We amassed more stones and surrounded the front of our house at a two foot distance and planted flowers and bushes. Soon our poor old barracks looked like a neat and friendly jewel. We were all very proud of our Villa Sperlingslust.

All of the improvements were done mostly after work and on the weekends. Papa spent the day as a labourer's helper – the only work he had been allowed to do. He worked for his father sawing wood. Every morning after he arrived at the Gelbingergasse, he walked down the back alley to the garden that spread from someone else's house down to the road. Steep steps had to be climbed up to the plot of land that the Haefner family had rented for many years. A Greengage plum and a quince tree, vegetables and some flowers grew there; in one corner stood a wooden chicken house with a large run safely under wire that housed a noisy flock.

Years ago, apprentices had neatly stacked raw planks of oak so the wood could dry and weather before it was made into barrels. Now Papa carried the heavy boards down the steep steps, loaded them into the four wheeled hand pulled cart that was specially designed to pull barrels, and hauled the wood up to the street in front of Opa's house. There an electric saw was set up. I guess he sawed the planks up for barrel staves and also a lot of firewood. Every evening the wood had to be put away or stored somewhere, mountains of sawdust had to be discarded, the saw had to be cleaned up and the street had to be swept before he was able to limp home with his cane. An old injury sustained when he plunged down a river in the Ukraine was acting up and gave him much pain. He never complained.

Papa often helped me and Inge with the supper dishes, then we sang and he taught us to whistle and we had so much fun. He knew so many songs and he knew all the verses. When we were in bed – and summer or winter it was unfailingly at seven o'clock – he sweetened our unhappiness by sitting on the steps from the living room into the bedroom and he played on the violin that Mama had bought for me the year before. Oh – he could fiddle! Inge and I sang and he often did too. Papa had a good voice and he enjoyed our 'even song' as much as we did. He always signalled the end of the evening's concert with Schubert's 'Wiegenlied' and unquestioningly we said our 'good nights' and contentedly fell asleep.

I loved to watch Papa's toes wiggle on a Sunday morning when we all slept in a bit late. He always was an early riser – but he waited patiently until Mama stirred. There he was, his arms folded under his head, eyes bright, his lips humming a song and his toes, poking out from under the too short blanket, wiggling the rhythm to the song he was humming. When he saw that I was watching him, he grinned and winked at me.

Papa loved physical work and he sweated and grunted as he lifted and heaved loads. If it wasn't too hard and he still had energy to spare he whistled or yodelled or sang. When he was done with the work he loved to dip his whole head into a bucket with cold water and emerge, shaking off the water in a flood of drops like some Newfoundland dog, and laughing out loud in sheer joy of having gained back his strength and being a free man again. He so obviously loved life. That is how I saw him.

But he had his dark side too. He could drop into gloomy brooding and the next minute explode in fiery tantrums. During these episodes I tried to stay far away from him. In one of these dangerous moods he stumbled over my toy box – a small cardboard box that held my treasures – a few coloured glass bottles retrieved from the dump, the hand-made farm, its barns and animals lovingly carved by himself and inmates in the POW camp, and my only doll. Waltraud – I still remember her name. I don't know where I got her from, most likely from the dump. She had barely any hair left, missed one leg and one eye; she had a dress on that I had stitched myself from pieces of cloth that I found in grandma's mending kit. Papa turned and with a face black in rage stamped on the box until everything in it was smashed to bits. He screamed that I was not entitled to toys.

"Why should you have all that when others have nothing? Who in hell do you think you are?"

I went crying to Mama. She just hugged me and said, "Gudrun, this is what the war has done to him. War changes men."

And I wondered about the war. It seemed to me that it was a horrid monster. I had seen that it destroyed and maimed and killed. I knew that it separated men from their wives and parents from their children, people from their land and their homes. I was learning that it also divided time. There was the time 'before the war', there was the time 'during the war' and there was the time 'after the war' and the three were totally different worlds.

The time 'before the war' was a good time. The older people remembered it as a time of butter and meat, pretty dresses and shoes, there was singing and dancing, there was peace and it was a good life. The time 'during the war', had none of that. Men went away and left the women and children alone, margarine was blue, there was no meat and one had to line up for potatoes and milk. Dresses were turned and shoes were patched and studded with nails so they would never wear out. It was a time of blackouts and sirens and falling bombs, and danger and death. And 'after the war' was the time of defeat and occupation, when the fatherland was taken away, when nobody had anything, when children died because they had stumbled on hidden mines or had played with grenades and where everything changed, from the daily greeting and salutation, to the newspaper, the radio and the neighbours.

Floods of people had come from the east and they were called refugees. On their way to the west children lost their parents, mothers lost their children and many perished. Everybody listened every morning to the Radio when the Red Cross Service was on. Lists of thousands of names of children, men and women were read out; names of displaced persons who were looking for members of their families. I can still remember when after many years the last of these programs was broadcast and we celebrated that everyone had found who they had been looking for.

The 'after the war' era was the time of many deprivations but it was also the time of the magic 'black market' – a term a child could hear many times during a day. I am quite certain that it existed in the 'time before and the time during' but I am also certain that my mother would have never made use of it as she did now. The American connection had probably something to do with it. I always asked Mama to take me there – I knew one could get shoes there, butter, cigarettes and anything one wanted – but she always waved me off. In my mind it was a market straight out of 'Thousand and One Night' – with stalls lined with treasures and beautiful things – much richer and much more fantastic than the Saturday morning farmers' market on the stone cobbled place in front of St. Michaels Church. I loved that one too – the vegetables and eggs and cheeses and flowers were very pretty and good to look at. But Mama never took me to the one of my dreams. "That is not for children," she said and I had to content myself with that. It was many years before I found out what the 'black market' really was. What a let down!

Chapter 30

Manfred As Prisoner Of War

We rode our horses and headed west – always towards the west. In the east were the Russians. We had one truck with supplies with us besides our horses. One night we made camp in an abandoned farm. For some reason I had decided to sleep outside, but beside the fence. In the early morning when I went to the truck, I saw the driver hanging out of the cab. He was dead; someone had cut his throat right through.

We rode on and came to a canal which we intended to cross. Two women partisans stood on the bridge and one of them shouted in broken German at us, "If you are smart you'll give us your weapons!" I just swore at her, took a grenade and tossed it in front of her, gave my horse the spurs and was not twenty meters gone when the grenade exploded and she was dead. After about ten kilometers we heard noise behind us and saw some Czechs driving after us in a stolen military vehicle. I saw a machine rifle on the cab and about thirty men behind in the truck. They were bound to catch us. I yelled to my men.

"Left to the forest and get in line!"

We drove the horses away from us into the trees and took position. We shot them all. Naturally we took their truck and drove on.

It must sound all so callous and senseless, but it was either them or us. We were scared silly but we were also desperate. We knew what they would do with us should they catch us. So we got them first. That's war and I do not dwell on it. A good thing we still had automatic rifles. It saved our hides more than once. They had come out in 44 and they were very good for us.

And then we fell into a trap. A high ranking Czech officer, Anders, had collected around himself about 2500 men into a freedom fighter corps. We fell among them and that is when they took us all prisoner. That happened on May, 12th,, 1945 in the afternoon at twelve thirty. That is another number I will never forget.

They put us into a camp and locked us into barracks. Everywhere we looked were automatic rifles pointed at us. We heard a lot of women screaming – they were raped everywhere – it was awful. They were German Red Cross nurses and radio operators that had been captured. When some of our men tried to come to the aid of the women, they were shot.

They took us to Czechoslovakian barracks west of Prague. They lined up the soldiers who had any rank along a wall and killed them all with a flame thrower, 8000 men. Many of them were boys who had joined just weeks before. My turn came too. One day they hauled me outside. I was a NCO, a corporal at the time. I was put alongside that wall which was splattered with blood and the brains of thousands of men they had slaughtered already. Behind me was a ditch dug by the prisoners, about three meters deep and two meters wide, half filled with bodies. As soon as the salvo started, I let myself fall into the ditch and in falling they shot off my finger.

Here, look, the top is missing.

He showed me his decapitated finger and continued his story.

I lay in the ditch and was quickly covered by dying comrades, blood and urine oozing over me. Later on the Czechs were all dead drunk and no one checked the ditch. In the night I crawled out from under the dead bodies. I carefully checked if anyone was in sight then I quickly dove under a hedge and through it and ran away from the camp. Just at that time a column of prisoners was marching by, I joined them and marched with them until Bruenn some 250 kilometers away. We did not get even a drop of water and, of course, nothing to eat. Some of us ripped off a few blades of grass and chewed these. Just before the city we met the first Volksdeutsche. They had been made to wear a yellow ribbon around their arms and they were made to sweep and clean the streets.

A Panzertruppe of the Waffen SS came along on their way to Bavaria. They had stayed in their tanks and they had stayed together. The Russians did not want to make room for them on the road, so the tanks just drove close to the trucks and shoved the Russian trucks into the ditch. The tanks kept on driving and the Russians finally gave way. And these guys – despite the capitulation, they did not give up. They drove all the way to Bavaria.

I once heard a Russian officer admit that they had been at their end also. He indicated that if the war would had another two weeks they would have had to give up. He said, "We were bled dry. We had nothing anymore to give."

The Russians rounded up all the farm animals of the Czech farmers, about three to four hundred head, and drove them through the standing wheat. Every bit of the beautiful crop was trampled down in a swath forty meters wide and Russian riders drove them. I can tell you that after that there were not too many Czech farmers yelling, "Heil Moscow!"

Dysentery broke out after we were quartered in Bruenn and many prisoners died. I was lucky again and survived. I still had a pistol with me and bullets hidden in my belt and the heels of my boots. The Russians hauled us down to Romania where we were finally loaded onto an ancient freighter with the Crimea as our destiny.

Six men were allowed on deck and I was one of them. We were not quite two kilometers out of the harbour when the ship hit a mine. There was a hole in the ship the size of a large stove. The ship started quickly to sink. I bolted to the hatch and yelled down what was happening. But many of my comrades were too weak already because nobody ever fed us, and they barely moved. I took a dive into the water and swam back to the harbour. By the time I made it to the beach I just collapsed with weakness. But I made it while many of my comrades had not. I am sure most of them drowned.

Russian soldiers gathered us up and threw us into cattle wagons. They took us to Moscow where we were made part of a propaganda and victory parade through Moscow.

My next stay was a camp about two hundred kilometers east of Moscow where the prisoners had to cut peat. We did that by standing up to our belly in ice cold water cutting specific size slabs with a special spade. The pieces were dried and later on used to heat stoves. We did this for ten hours a day. In summer it got quite warm and we were surrounded by clouds of flies and mosquitoes. That is where I got malaria. Of the 800 men who were first with me 727 died. We were housed in an American army tent, forty meters long and six meters wide to the left and the right of a sort of pathway. We slept on small wooden benches without blankets close together like sardines. The guards, who were Mongols, demanded that when we marched to work we were to sing at the same time. And well – we sang our old marching songs from times gone by.

'Alte Kameraden' and 'Wenn wir schreiten Seit an Seit' and many, many more. The Russians were marching ahead of us, proudly victorious and we were marching behind, buoyed up by the songs we knew so well, with one eye crying, with the other laughing because of the silliness of it all. They had conquered us and they could tell us what to do but they did not know what we were singing and how it made our spirits soar. Our old songs instilled courage in us and we had to laugh at the irony of it all. And it was fun – something we had not had in a long, long time.

Every morning the Russian army physician entered our tent and demanded to know who and how many had died during the night. If the tent eldest couldn't come up with at least three dead bodies he got nothing to eat."I'll make you pay for that!" She would shout and then stomp out.

One day I with eight other men had to cut wood for the sauna because the day after we were to be deloused. Of course we all had lice because we barely managed to wash. There were two guards and a farmer with a sled drawn by three horses. A huge dog was also there. Suddenly the Russian soldier took his rifle.

"What are you doing?" I asked.

"Take your time, you'll soon see," he replied.

Slowly he shouldered his rifle, took aim and shot the dog who fell in an instant. I guess he was just trigger happy.

The farmer was hopping and yelling.

"If you don't shut up I'll kill you too," the guard said coolly.

Then he took the dead dog and threw it towards a tree.

A prisoner buddy, Erwin Dien from Bludenz in Austria, was a butcher. When we returned that evening from work to our tent, we got a spoonful of water soup served in a bowl made from a tin can. On the bottom of the can were embossed letters and we could read: Oscar Meyer, Chicago, 1944. The Russians had eaten the meat and we got the tins and water soup with some cabbage or carrots in it.

The Kommandant, a German, came at night and choose a few of us to go down to the sauna and prepare the place for tomorrow's delousing. The sauna was located outside the camp and no guard was there this night. Erwin was there too. I said to him,

"Listen, Erwin, this afternoon a guard shot a mighty big dog and I am sure it is still where he tossed it."

Erwin showed great excitement.

Outside it was minus thirty degrees cold. We told the men in charge of heating the sauna to really heat up the oven. Then Erwin got the dog which by this time, of course, had frozen solidly. Naturally we could not skin the animal because the skin had frozen to the meat. So we hung the dog close to the oven to thaw it out.

After a while Erwin started to skin it and cut it up. Slowly, in front of the hellishly hot oven the dog thawed as he was working on it. We had a bag of rock salt which we smashed with a stone and so we had seasoning for our meat. I cannot recall how it came about that we had a pot – but we did – and it was a big one. Ah, the tantalizing smell of the boiling meat. We did not even wait for the meat to be boiled fully but fell to it. With a few sprinkles of salt, it was a feast. The other half of the dog we covered with some salt and hung it in the pot high in the chimney for a future feast.

The next morning the Kommandant came. We had been so busy with the dog that we had forgotten to go back to barracks for what euphemistically was called breakfast. Wondering why we had not shown up for our watery morning soup he declared that something was afoul because he had never in all his years seen that prisoners who were able to walk had not shown up for breakfast. Prisoners who were not hungry as wolves must have been up to something.

He asked us if we had butchered a goat of which there were many but we could honestly deny that.

He went with us to the sauna. Suspicious as he was he kept on searching and it did not take him very long to discover the pot hanging high up under the roof. He took it down and discovered remnants of our meat in it. He marched straight back to camp and went to Karl, a German doctor from Berlin. He shoved the pot under his nose and demanded to know what was in it. The doctor inspected it and said dryly,

"That, Herr Kommandant, is the meat of the village cur."

Following that the Kommnant made all the men line up in U-shape. He set the pot in the middle and announ-ced pointing at Erwin and me,

"These miserable examples of humanity have eaten half a dog last night.

They planned to eat the other half by themselves today."

The other prisoners looked enviously towards us as we stood in front of the pot with the wonderful food which was now so far out of reach to us.

We never got to taste the other half.

Well – that's what you do when you are hungry.

From our site there was a small spur line about five kilometers long. There were about fifteen wagons transporting the peat to the main line. For the last kilometers the spur ran parallel to the main line. The train had an old tractor mounted on an iron frame above the wheels that used a chain to get the train moving. The driver had to start the engine manually. One day he got hit by the crank, the winch handle, and he fell dead on to the tracks. None of the other guards wanted to drive this devilish contraption after that anymore. I believe they were not only very ignorant and backwards but also very superstitious. I, on the other hand, was used to diesel motors and driving tanks and I knew what to do and so I volunteered my services. I started the motor after I reset some gadgets and drove the peat train for about three months. A guard with a rifle always sat on the last wagon. I sat on the front box and when we went around a corner he could not see me. I knew that. I was going to make full use of that.

The name of the train station was Kommissarovka. The main line was about twenty five meters away from our spur line and there were many bushes between the two tracks. I heard the main train chugging through the train station; I did not stop our train but put it on slow and jumped off my box. I ran through the bushes and jumped up on the brake house of the big train.

My good old peat train kept on going but then it hit a buffer stock. The impact dislodged six wagons that jumped the tracks and the guard fell down. He shouted and he swore, waving his rifle about but shortly he found himself alone and in charge of the peat train. He ran back to the camp to report the events. Then the poor sods from the camp had to come and empty the turned over wagons.

They had to set them back on the tracks, load them up again because they still had to bring the peat to the station so it could be loaded onto the large train. These poor buggers, they got nothing to eat for the two days they had to work for what I had done. I felt sorry for them but I had to do what I thought was best for me. I had enough of Russia. I wanted to go home.

Three months later they dissolved the camp because too many prisoners died. Every day around six or eight men – they died mostly of starvation. They were just dug in and the Russians planted cabbages on them afterwards. This I learned from previous prisoners later on.

I arrived in Vladimir with my large train. For the people around I could easily pass for a Russian. I was wearing the typical local attire; a dirty quilted jacket and pants, boots and a fur cap with flaps. I also spoke passable Russian and I had a plan. I went to the conductor of the train and told him that I was ordered to go with him to Smolensk and that my official job was to grease the axels.

He said to me, "Good, get to work."

So I went and got myself an oil can, a key, a wrench and a hammer and I became one of the crew. The train's engineer was Ukrainian and he knew that I was not a prisoner and not a Russian but he never said a thing. The train conductor was Russian but he was okay too. In fact, whenever the train stopped I went in front to the engine and got myself hot water for drinking, he gave me tea. They gave me bread too because they were issued food for these long trips. It was not much but it kept them going and so I did quite well.

When we arrived in Smolensk, I noticed that masses of police were standing around the train station. I was just on my way to the locomotive to get some more hot water, when one of those approached me and ordered me to show him my pass.

"I don't have it on me."

"Why not?"

"Do you think I carry my documents with me so that you can stick your stupid eyes in them. I am sure you can see that I am working here. Go to the front and ask the engineer."

And he did just that. The engineer told him that I was part of the crew and that I was working on the train.

"Okay, you can go."

*** Uncle Manfred gave us all Russian conversations in Russian! I had him translate the Russian phrases later into English for me. ***

And just as I was climbing into the locomotive to be safe, there came a Mongol around the corner and pulled me down at my belt.

"You come with me to the Kommandant!"

The engineer said, "He is crew, he works here."

But the Mongol just muttered something and took me along. He brought me to the Kommandant and he interrogated me.

"Where do you come from?"

"From Perosnaya."

"Where is that?"

"About twenty six kilometers away from Kharkov."

He consulted a map and nodded.

"How large is the village?"

"About two and a half kilometers wide."

"How many inhabitants?"

"About twelve hundred."

That was also correct.

I knew all that because I was there during the great Tank battle at Gerdorot which had lasted for about four weeks.

Despite that they took me along and put me in prison.

There I found out I had a tapeworm. Not only was I starving because they gave us not enough to eat, but I was also feeding a voracious guest in my gut. I was sent to the hospital to get rid of the worm. The doctor there had a clock, the only one in camp. In the evening I had to go to bed and at midnight they served me a kilogram of peeled onions and after I had eaten those, they served me two large salted fish. They gave me nothing to drink and my guard was standing next to my cot. I almost died I was so thirsty. Next morning at eight o'clock the doctor came with six large pills. He put the clock on the table and said to the guard, "No matter what happens, make sure he eats one of those pills every two minutes."

After the fourth pill I couldn't hold it any more. I jumped off the bed, heading towards the latrine with the guard after me – perhaps he thought I was running away - but I just had to go! I did not get very far. In the corner was a low basin prepared for me and that is where I sat down, curled over in twists of gut wrenching pain. It was not pleasant what was happening to me. I thought I would lose my bowels! And then there was a ball of white worms in the bowl.

When I had emptied myself, I collapsed in utter exhaustion.

They carried me to my bed and washed me a bit. The guard brought another fellow who came with a spool and they proceeded to unwind the tapeworm in order to measure it. The beast had two heads with suckers on it. I am sure after a few more days with him in me I would have been dead. The physician came by, looked me over and asked, "How on earth can you get a tapeworm? Prisoners are never fed meat – so how did you get that one?"

"I don't know." I said.

But I knew where I had got it from.

They kept me there for another ten days. They fed me a floury soup and even some bread and that put me back on my feet again.

Once I was able to work, they brought me back to the camp.

My next camp was at Pankilova. We had Rumanian guards and they were really awful. On August 22nd in 1944 the Rumanians, who had originally been on our side, changed sides and went over to the Russians. The Russians did not really trust the Rumanians in the camp. They had rifles and they were made to watch the prisoners, but I always felt they were not much more than prisoners either.

I was there only a short time when our camp, which held about 2500 men, was attacked by partisans, troops and fighters that were against communism. They slaughtered all of the twenty two guards. Then they told us that if we were to throw our lot in with theirs, they would take us back to Germany. At least sixty of us joined them and I was one of them. The others were left without trouble in the camp. A short time later the people of the village informed the authorities that the camp had been attacked by the partisans and killed all the guards. When the new troops and guards arrived to take charge of the 'orphaned' camp and its prisoners, we had vanished.

We made a sort of headquarter camp in a large forested area not far away from our former camp and there, in 1946, I was issued another rifle once again. I had become part of the partisans and did guard duty. Some time later though, I realized that my time of freedom had come to an end. Two or three divisions of Russian army troops had encircled us and I reckoned that if I was going to be captured together with these partisans things were not going to be easy for me – so I bolted. But of course, I was captured again and put back into a camp.

In Vladimir I worked in a factory making tractors; I was in the hall where they were hardening crank shafts with oil stoves to be used for tractors. There were iron floors. I was wearing wooden shoes which were covered with canvas and extra soles of hardened ice and earth. One day when I was in there warming up someone came along carrying a huge crowbar in his hand. I lost my footing on the warm iron floor because the ice soles were melting and I fell down. Unfortunately, I hit the leg of the worker who was just passing by. He got mad, took the crowbar and brought it down on my head. That broke my skull in a clean split!

In hospital they lifted part of the cracked skull, cleaned it out, covered my brain up again, used staples to hold the bone together and sewed the skin back over it. I suffered for more than a year from problems with balance.

Here, touch my head, you can still feel the bump where the bone had split all across my skull. And I am sure if I would not have been wearing my Russian cap, made of felt and fur, he would have killed me. And the man was only eighteen years old. They sent him to Siberia for twenty five years.

A day later a Russian skewered a man with an iron rod that had a very long and pointy end as he was coming out of the toilet – and nailed him to the wall. There he hung and there he died, bleeding to death. Many, many things like that happened to us prisoners.

At another time they had me working in a coal mine in Siberia. I was there for more than half a year. We had to get coal out with pick axes and then push the wagons filled with the shiny chunks above ground. It was very dangerous and very hard work. We worked a few hundred meters underground and it was very hot, over thirty degrees warm. That was good but we sweated so much and that made us even weaker. When we came up it was minus forty degrees cold. Many of the prisoners got sick and died. It was winter outside and they put us into earthen dugouts with a roof over us. That is where we slept. The floor was pounded earth and the walls were earth too. Only the roof was made of timber, there were whole trees with rushes to cover them. Inside it rained dirt and bark and insects.

There I bolted once more. My plans were to travel through Siberia with the train and then to get through the Black Sea to Turkey. But they caught me again and stuck me in another camp.

At another time I escaped with a plane to Leningrad but they caught me and I landed in prison again from where they deported me to a work camp. At minus thirty we had to dig ditches for cables. The ground was so solidly frozen that no pick could loosen the earth. So one of us held a punch and the other whacked it with the hammer. Every half hour we were allowed to get into the shop to warm up a bit. Here we stole a truck and made passports. Our plan had been to head west and go over Brestlitovsk to East Berlin to officially pick up goods apprehended from the Germans, owed as reparation items to Russia. We were the men to get them and drive them back to Russia. That was our plan.

The Russian border guards found our papers to be in good order and they let us through – but I am sure that was so only because they could not read. I had made a stamp of the Soviet Star with a cut up potato and had fabricated a wonderfully authentic looking document. I was really proud of it. My comrades in this escapade had equally impressive papers.

This was in 1948. One of us was Viennese and about five hundred meters from the border he jumped off the truck and disappeared. We kept on going but the Polish border guards stopped us and sent us back. I guess they could read. We turned back discussing the idea to pretend to be going back and then try to cross the border at a different location. Unfortunately, we did not get very far with this plan. Some guards came after us and without much ado they arrested us. And that is when I was sent to the infamous Lubyanka in Moscow.

It was not the Ritz, let me tell you. I got a liter of water and 200 grams of bread per day. My cell was five meters long and one and a half meter wide. There was a lamp on the ceiling in a tin screen with an inside made from shiny tin, which glared down at me day and night. There was no window and I quickly lost track of all time. The only thing that marked the flow of time was that every few hours someone came to get me for interrogation.

I was in the Lubyanka for four and a half months. One day they got me out of my cell at night. In 1944 a comrade of mine had been taken prisoner by the Russians. He had a photo of me in his jacket which they, of course, had found. By now it was the year of 1949. The interrogator told me that I had to go into the next room where he had a collection of German military uniforms. He instructed me to put on the very same uniform I had been wearing in 1944 and put all my medals on.

I put on the uniform I had been wearing during that time. He took the photo and looked at me and studied us for a short time. Then he pushed a button and two Mongol guards with rifles and bayonets entered with an officer behind them. He said to them, "Go and take the jeep and take him with you."

That was all he said – nothing else.

I thought for sure they were going to shoot me.

They sat me in the jeep with one guard on either side, the officer next to the driver and off we went.

Two and a half hours later we arrived at a station and we got into a train. I think we travelled almost five days on the train. We went through Kharkov and then from there to Perosnaya, where I had been once during that famous battle in 1942.

The whole village was assembled outside their houses and I, wearing a Stahlhelm and a German uniform with the Iron Cross II and the Silver wound badge, the equivalent of the American Purple Heart, pinned on, walked, flanked by two Mongols, down the street slowly so that all the villagers could inspect me. Then we came to the place where we had had our field kitchen set up. And old woman of about sixty years approached me. She said, "Good day."

I greeted her too.

The officer asked her, "Do you know this man?"

She answered, "Well, yes, of course. He was a good man."

She had daily come to the kitchen to peel potatoes and do other jobs and I had always given her a loaf of bread to take home. Often I gave her also a pail of soup. Those poor people had nothing to eat.

I remember I also gave her once a 'Voelkischer Beobachter', our German newspaper, which her husband craved because it made wonderful cigarette paper.

I breathed a sigh of immense relief and thanked the old woman from the bottom of my heart.

When I think back today – if only one of them would have said that I had done something bad, they would have shot me on the spot. But nothing of the sort happened. And that was amazing because they all had good reasons to hate the Germans and this was their chance to get rid of one more of them.

I had perhaps another week in the Lubyanka after that and then they let me out.

Something else happened when I was in my solitary cell. In March of 1949 a Russian Jew, lieutenant colonel Epstein, came to me one day and told me I would be his driver. He was in charge of all the prisoners of war in Moscow. I was aware that his previous driver had died. I also knew that he knew I could drive cars and that I spoke Russian.

I looked at him quietly and said, "I want to go home. I don't want to be a driver."

He looked at me for a long time and then he said, "I promise that you will get to go home this year."

I replied, "When a Russian opens his mouth once he tells ten lies."

I knew that he could just take his pistol out and shoot me like a dog. But I had had so enough. I just couldn't stand it anymore. I wanted to go home with every fiber of my heart and my body. Going home was all that filled my thoughts and dreams.

He told me that he would give me his hand and that I would get home. We both shook hands and looked each other in the eye. That is how I became a driver for a while. It was a very welcome change from hanging around a small cell. I wore Russian clothes, the brown belted jacket, but I had to wear a band around my sleeve which spelled out 'prisoner of war'. I got decent food to eat. I did not mind driving him around. I had it actually quite good.

I had to drive him to the Kremlin a few times. There the German generals Seidlitz and Paulus, the ones of Stalingrad fame, were teaching Russian officers military tactics. Epstein was taking part in these exercises and I had to drive him there. It was there that I saw Stalin a few times, sometimes he was not six meters away from me.

When I think of those two generals I think of Stalingrad. It was Hitler's fault that they lost 93 000 soldiers as prisoners of which only seven thousand survived. All the soldiers knew that the generals had almost begged Hitler to put an end to the senseless fighting there and that he had forbidden it. How easy it was for him to order all the men to fight to the last while he sat comfortably in his Wolfschanze. It makes me so mad to think of all those poor men.

And here I just remember something odd. In one of our camps, I noticed children playing in a specially fenced off area. To my astonishment I heard them sing and play in German. I asked them how they came to be in this camp and they told me that their fathers were engineers who had been working on the V2 up at Sweenemuende. The Russians had taken the scientists and their families to Russia, where they were working in research.

Shortly before Christmas 1949 it was announced that another transport of German prisoners was to leave for Germany – and my name was on the list. On December 28th, about 2000 prisoners got on this train. And we truly were the lucky ones because this was to be the very last train of German prisoners of war to leave for Germany. This was the famous last train. I know there were at least another ten thousand Germans left, mostly officers that had been sentenced. I had been sentenced too – to twenty five years of hard labour because I had participated in 1943 to dynamite a bridge in Kiev, of course I had been ordered to do so by my superior. I got the twenty five years because I had damaged Russian public property. The punishment was to have been served in Siberia. But this was rescinded because I was able to prove that I had worked under orders and that I had had to obey or else run the risk being shot by the Germans.

I am sure that lieutenant colonel Epstein had something to do with my newly won freedom. Without him I would have never made it home.

The train left the station on December 28th. We were locked in the train till Brestlitovsk and were not allowed out. We had potatoes with us so we had to eat. I believe at least five men died on this transport. Many of us were sick and of course, we were all severely undernourished. And when we were through Brestlitovsk we rolled into Poland and there the Polish border guards took all the Russian guards and locked them into the trains.

The Poles and the Russians were not friends, in fact they actually hated one another. That was probably caused by Stalin who had seized so much of eastern Poland. Our guards were locked up but we were allowed to get out and walk around. The Russians scowled at us through the tightly shut windows. Some Poles gave us something to eat and we quite enjoyed the fact that the Russians got nothing.

On the way back home a former Lagerkommandant, a German who was the commander of one camp, was murdered. Our men on the train did that, of course. He had been a terrible man and he had never taken the side of a prisoner in any camp. One man knifed him to death and when we crossed a river they simply threw him out. No one missed him.

We passed through Frankfurt at the Oder and then through East Germany, the part that had been taken away from the Germans by the Russians, and was now part of the communist bloc. It had been founded in 1949 as the German Democratic Republic. There we saw our first East German Volkspolizist, the East German police, he was just a young kid – like they all were. And here we were in January of 1950. We still had potatoes left and so we handed them out to the population because we could see they did not have much to eat. Once the news got around, people arrived with bags and sacks to get some potatoes from us. Naturally the potatoes were frozen but once you thaw them slowly in ice water they become edible again – it always depends on how hungry you are!

Two young police appeared drawing their pistols, trying to intimidate us. Those young whippersnappers were barely nineteen years old. I went towards one and took his pistol away.

"You little bastard you."

I took his pistol and threw it in a wide arc away.

"You think that we former soldiers who have been in the war would be scared of your shitty little piece?

And they both slunk away.

I heard someone saying that by giving potatoes to the people here we were actually putting shame on the DDR, who it seemed, could not feed its own people enough, that they were so hungry they did not mind accepting food from former prisoners of war. That, of course, was true.

At Moschenburg we crossed the border. I was walking on and was not ten meters across when I heard a young policeman hollering after me.

"Come back! Come back!"

I knew what that was all about. I turned around.

"Oh, stuff yourself!" I shouted and kept on going to get on the train heading west. I knew if they would get a hold of me they would arrest me again.

I was finally allowed to leave the train in Ulm. Two American military police came towards me. They called my name and took me between them. They told me that I was to come with them to the Kienlesberg Kaserne where they were stationed and that they would want to interrogate me. I grabbed my earthly possessions, a towel, a piece of soap in a bag and came along. What else could I do?

They knew that I had been working in Vladimir in the tractor factory. How they came to this knowledge is still a mystery to me, but they knew it. That was the place I got hit over my head – they knew that too. They also were informed that I had been laying cables for a factory that made aluminum for airplanes in Moscow. I had used a piece of that aluminum to make a little box for my tobacco. They knew that too – I just wonder how.

During the interrogation they showed me aerial photographs of the plants I had been working in and they quizzed me about anything I remembered about the places. I quickly realized what the interrogation was all about. What they were really after was my tobacco box. I told them that I could not just hand it over as it held too much of a sentimental value for me. I earnestly explained to them that it represented five years of my life spent in prison in Russia. When I saw how badly they wanted the box, I told them that it would be much cheaper to pay me a good price for it than sending a spy out there to get another scrap of the coveted metal.

"I would be quite happy if you'd buy it for 800 Deutsch Mark."

And that is what they paid me for it. They gave me two cartons of cigarettes every day. I was rich now. I got a suit made from rayon – that is paper in other words. You washed it two times and it fell to pieces. Then they gave me official release papers into the Bundesrepublik Germany. I had another one like that from the Russians. I bought a ticket for the train to Schwaebisch Hall.

It had been in 1944 when I had been stationed in Nuremburg that I had visited the Haefner family in Hall. That was the only time I had met them. When I arrived at the train station in Schwaebisch Hall in January of 1950, I found it still totally bombed out. Business was done in a barrack shack. I headed straight downhill for the center of town. It was market day and there were plenty of people around.

"Please, where is the Gelbingergasse?"

When I got there I bid my astonished relatives a good day and then Liese, Gustel's sister, walked me down to the Jahnstrasse where my father lived with Trudel and little Sigrid. He lived right next to Irmgard and her two girls. Funny – we had all been moving around and the Haefner family had been here all the time, already for a few hundred years and they seemed to be permanent.

Chapter 31

MY FAMILY

When my father came home in 1948, he worked as a labourer for his father. After a few years he became a salesman for a large wine company in Stuttgart and we moved away from Schwaebisch Hall. In 1954 August senior passed the business on to my parents and we moved back and into Gelbingergasse 39 into the apartment Uncle Willie and Aunt Bertha had been living in. They had found a place elsewhere. Oma and Opa still lived above the shop. The time for cider and barrels was gone and my parents started a retail and wholesale business for wine and spirits. The business was in my mother's name and Papa was just an employee.

The early years were hard. My parents worked from early morning till late at night and my sister helped them every day after school. I don't think she ever forgave me for my 'easy' time in boarding school away from home which I had entered in the fall of 1954.

Papa bought wine by the tank load and filled recycled bottles which meant that he had to clean and wash them before use. I remember so many days, when I was at home during school holidays, sore and stiff crouching on the floor, operating the small and unpractical motor driven filling machine. I suggested to my father,

"Papa, why don't we put the machine on a table and I can sit comfortably and fill thousands of bottles without breaking my back?"

"No, Gudrun, that is not possible. We have always done it this way and that is how it is going to stay."

"But Papa," I wailed.

"No, it's going to stay the way it is. Period. End of discussion."

Papa never allowed me to put the machine on a table and do the work in relative comfort. And no matter how much I pleaded and promised an increased output and less spillage or waste, he would not change. He could be very thick headed and much opposed to changing what was a tradition.

Papa corked and I glued the labels on using wallpaper paste. Inge packed the bottles into crates and Papa lugged them down into the cellar. Mama ran the store and did the books.

Business was slow at first – but I remember the excitement of one business day before Christmas when we took in so much paper money that the till jammed. A giggling Mama had to extricate whole wads of money which she then just stuffed into a bag – no time to run upstairs to put the marks away. That night, before we celebrated Christmas, we celebrated the pile of money, now in neat heaps, on the kitchen table. We counted more than 1000 DM – we were on our way.

Twenty years later when the store was sold it had become a thriving business. My father even delivered the wine to the castle in Langenburg when Queen Elizabeth visited her husband's, Prince Philip's, relations, the Battenbergs. I was amazed when Mama related that to me – had she become what she had scorned all her life: a 'Spiesser', that arch German mix of conventionality, provinciality, and commonality. Was she proud to be supplying goods to Her Majesty the Queen? Had she become her parents-in-law?

My mother told tales about Odin and Freya and from the Germanic Edda but never spoke of a Christian God or the bible. She said to always speak the truth, to be tough to oneself and not indulge in ones weaknesses but to be kind and charitable and tolerant to others. She would never allow me to steal or to beg. She valued education and the arts. From very early on she bought books or enabled my sister and I to go to libraries. She bought me a violin and worked extra hours to pay for my lessons. She frowned when we showed her the tickets Opa Haefner had given us so we could go to the circus. Very reluctantly she gave permission. She would never allow us to go to a variety show even though we could have gone with Opa when the annual fair was in town.

"Variety shows are only for the plebs."

And when I asked who and what the plebs was and if it included Opa and Oma and Aunt Berta – who loved to go to these shows - she would agree that those three did not classify as plebs. And when I insisted that she explain to me what 'the plebs' was, she smiled wryly.

"Gudrun, they are every easy to identify: you will always be able to hear them."

She imposed few rules on me and when the chores at home were done to her satisfaction, I enjoyed unfettered freedom. When I left in 1954 to go to boarding school, she said to me, "There will come times when you will have to make decisions. When you don't know what to do, stop and ask yourself, what would Mama do in this case."

She could have given no better advice.

Oma Haefner was altogether different. She looked like a grandma out of a picture book with her white bun that gradually over the years got smaller. She had 'weak feet and ankles', and therefore wore only handmade boots of very fine leather that reached up to her mid calves. She only wore dark dresses with long sleeves rolled up to her elbows. Her large apron had two very deep pockets that held a spotlessly clean handkerchief in one and usually a few coins in the other.

Oma loved to sing and smile and be nice to people. She loved to have company for the sacrosanct daily afternoon coffee, the 'Kaffeklatsch', where members of the household came together for good coffee, jam sandwiches or even cake if an elevated social standing of the day's guest warranted that. For important guests a tablecloth and the better cups were brought out.

She never spoke about being tough and strong, I don't recall her ever using the term 'weakness' or 'discipline'. She never talked about 'the plebs'. She did not condemn or chastise if we did something wrong. She consoled us with: 'you are just a child and you'll learn', or 'better not do that again' or 'it doesn't matter'. She enjoyed spoiling a child with small indulgences like a small coin from her pocket, a spoon of honey or an apple or a pickle – I always preferred 'sours'. Grandma did not care much about higher schooling and academics. The basics of the three R's were quite enough. She much rather talked about relatives, neighbours, the news in the Gelbingergasse and the daily newspaper.

She was especially interested in reading in the daily paper about people that had died. Since my grandparents had lived in Schwaebisch Hall all of their lives and because of their wide business connections, they knew everybody in town and outlying villages and therefore went to everyone's funeral.

Oma relished dressing up in her very best black; she wore a hat and black gloves and she had an especially fine and white 'funeral handkerchief' embroidered with delicate lace. Opa wore a suit, the chain of his heavy gold watch glittering on his immaculately black vest; and a Homburg hat that made him look very impressive. Both walked to the cemetery with their walking canes, joining the ever increasing stream of people and their subdued conversations towards the old grave yard. A funeral was always a most satisfying social event.

Oma loved to tell stories about the time when she was young.

"We were so many girls in our family that we always had a good time. When we got ourselves ready for an outing, we would wet our hair, braid it into many long plaits, place them on the ironing board and one of us would iron them. When the hair was dry, we would open the braids and carefully comb the curls so they spread like a wave around us. We looked so beautiful. We put flowers and colored pins into our hair or combs. Our frilly dresses had high collars and underneath we wore seven white and embroidered petticoats, in winter they were woolen and dark as were our stockings. Most evenings all of us girls would lean out of the upper storey windows and sing. The neighbours in the street would open their windows and listen and clap or sometimes they would join in. It was wonderful."

And grandma would stop and dab her eyes in happy memory. Invariably this story would be followed by the story of the raisins.

"My father was a master pastry maker. He owned a 'Konditorei' where we sold cakes and tortes, and pastry, sweets, chocolates and other fine confectionery. Because our father was in a wheel chair, we girls had to do all the baking and selling in the store. Of course, we got all of our supplies in sacks. Sacks of raisins and almonds and currants and candied fruit and peel and we had to sort them into different bins in the bakery and in the store. Our father used to sit in his wheel chair and supervise. When we had to fill the cans in the shop with these goodies we always had to whistle."

Quizzically she looks at me, a twinkle in her eyes.

"Why that, Oma?"

"So we couldn't eat!"

"It was custom that all girls when they were of a certain age would leave the house and go to another household to learn cooking and keeping house. I went into service at a boarding house in Heidelberg for two years. The work was hard. We had to make up rooms and meals for a dozen men. We took care of their laundry too. We worked from six in the morning until eight at night and on Sunday we were allowed three hours of free time to go for a walk in the park. I was not even allowed to go to church on Sundays because that is when the master and mistress went. Once a week we were allowed evening service. I learned a lot and also fine French cooking. Though I must admit, I was happy to come home again because I had been quite lonely there."

"Our father did not allow any of us girls to marry because we had to do the baking and run the shop. So, when he died, we were already in our thirties and then we all quickly married. I married August who was four years younger, and my younger sister Berta married his brother Willi. Both lived in the Gelbingergasse in the very house I am still living today – this was their parents' house."

Oma was a good hausfrau and an excellent cook. She had her suppliers come to the house with their little horse or hand pulled wagons on their way to the market. Grandma canned and pickled many different vegetables and fruit. The jars were stored in long rows in the underground cellar together with bins of potatoes and apples, wheels of cheese and barrels of raw eggs. In fall she dried apples and pears and plums on large trays in the attic. Grandma made her own vinegar and different berry liqueurs. She also made her own Spaetzle, Swabian pasta, but she did not use a machine to press the dough through small openings like I do, hers were scraped quickly and masterfully from a wooden board into the boiling water. I loved watching her; it was like a dance.

Every Saturday she baked cakes and 'Kuchen' for Sunday afternoon coffee in the 'Berg'. The round cake tins which were much larger than the ones used in North America, were carried to a near- by baker. I loved watching the master placing the cake tins on a long ladle and then shoving them into the hot oven; when they were done, he pulled them out and placed them with the many others on a shelf. Every tin had a small paper inserted with the name of the household on it – now baked to a golden brown. I paid a few pennies and then carried the fragrant fruit pies or the yeasty, raisin studded Gugelhopf back to Oma.

Oma was almost 86 years old when she died and it was not her gall that finished her life, but rather hopelessness and depression. Her husband had died in 1958 and my mother had wanted Oma's apartment for business space. Oma accommodated them for a while by giving them half of her rooms. But my mother still did nothing to make her life more agreeable and Oma was not happy. The lonely old woman then moved in with her daughter Liese whose husband Karl was bothered by the continuous presence of Oma and so they put her in an old age home. Not long after her son Gustel was put into prison and I guess she had no more reason to live. She died soon after.

My sister Inge said to me, "Oma's life just faded away like a burnt out candle."

I am glad she never knew that her son Gustel was not allowed out from prison to attend her funeral.

My sister Inge spent much time with Opa Haefner watching him make barrels for wine and cider. Inge loved the tools, especially the wooden planes of all sizes and widths and she tried them all out. Different hammers were used for different tasks, there were some to be used for nails and then there were some for the use for wood. There was a huge anvil and a turning stone to sharpen axes. Grandpa wore a thick leather apron and a skull cap when he worked. There was always a cigar clamped between his teeth preventing too much talk. Inge quickly learned for which tool he was turning around or which he needed. She handed it to him without a word. He liked that and Inge became his favourite apprentice.

"Too bad you're not a boy." He once said. Inge was very proud.

Opa Haefner was not a man of words with children. I sometimes enjoyed sitting with him at his table when he had his morning break at ten o'clock. I watched him spoon up the bowl of soured milk and bite into a thick slice of brown rye bread. We did not talk. Sometimes Oma served a slab of Swiss cheese which he cut into squares, skewered each with his pointy knife and then ate with the bread. Occasionally he pierced a chunk of cheese and held it towards me. That was a treat.

When he was done with his breakfast, he put Maexle on a leash and went a few blocks down the street to a pub where the masters of the local trades met for their morning drink. In Opa's eyes life was straight forward: a man learned a trade, got a practical education from the military, looked for a well paying job after his service, then married a good girl with whom he could raise a decent family and thus have a prosperous life. It was easy to be a good citizen. One did one's business as best one could, read the daily newspaper, kept one's nose clean, paid one's taxes and let the politicians make the big decisions because there was nothing one could do anyway; the police kept order and bad people went to prison. Girls were alright if they learned how to sew and cook and keep a tidy house. A man was the master of his house and church was alright for spinsters and old women. He lived the Swabian motto: S' Lebe isch nix anders wie schaffe, schaffe, Haeusle baue, Steure zahle, schterbe, which translates to: life is but work and more work, you build a house, you pay your taxes, and then you die.

Aunt Liese was the ten year younger sister of my father. Her second husband was Karl Voegeli, a tool maker, who worked in the factory Uncle Charles had run during the American occupation. They bought a house in the country and had three children.

And then there was Aunt Erika. By the time she married Charles in 1948 she was wearing lipstick, high heeled shoes, very stylish dresses and even hats! She smoked and she could drink. She preferred Bourbon. She loved life with a hungry passion. She was a working girl, she was smart and she was worldly. She was no little wife walking behind her husband.

When I was older, I got to know and appreciate my maternal grandfather, Opa Ernst. He encouraged reading and 'intellectual loafing', questioning and wondering; he thought discussions and differences of opinion were very acceptable if not desirable. He considered art and music to be a very important part of a person's education. He did not think it was wrong to be at odds with the opinions of the family; he did not think to be a loner was to be snickered at, and he did not think that everybody would want to march in a parade and he gave little value to the opinion of the crowd.

The best indication how different the two families were, is my memory of presents: in the Haefner house gifts were for practical use for now or later. In the Ernst house the gifts were always books, mostly from the classics.

But it was not all work for the Haefner and Ernst families; they loved to come together and they especially loved to celebrate birthdays. What was not to celebrate? They were now all living in the same city, everyone was healthy, everyone was doing fine, those wanting a job had one, their children were thriving, there was free time, and there was money – the past was the past and everyone had a future.

On these occasions the women made huge platters of garnished, open faced sandwiches of smoked salmon, smoked meats, herrings pickled and jellied, and different cheeses. My mother would make a gallon of her famous herring salad, Trudel made a special confectionary and Oma would make her renouned Rheinischer Bund dessert. When the party was somewhere other than our house my father had bottles of wine and champagne and sparkling water brought to the house during the afternoon by his hired man, was the party at home Papa would bring up from the cellar his best wine and champagne.

After the feasting and toasting local and world politics were contemplated and discussed and later the men and women would tell amusing events from their youth and then, of course, the war – I remember one of my father's: Gustel and his troop went skinny dipping on a hot summer's day, a colonel came driving by, and Gustel and his men clambered out of the lake, stood buck naked at attention and saluted their superior. The walls shook with laughter as the family members outdid each other with hilarious stories. One of the best story tellers was Opa Ernst and we all listened spellbound. And then, of course, the family sang – and how we could sing. The number of songs was limitless and so was the endurance of the singers.

It was often almost daylight when the party finally dissolved and everyone went home.

Chapter 32

MANFRED IN SCHWAEBISCH HALL

I was just skin and bones when I arrived at Schwaebisch Hall in January of 1950 and the doctor sent me to the hospital. There they gave me thin soup to eat because they were so scared that if I ate too much I would get very sick. I know of a case where a friend of mine, who also came home with me, went to his father's farm. There, of course, they celebrated his homecoming with good farmers fare, ham and rich and creamy sauces and cake. He was dead after two days. So that is why the hospital put me on a starvation diet. Cabbage soup – to which I was well used to – and dry bread was all I got at the beginning; slowly they increased the quantity and the quality of my food and slowly I came back. But I was always hungry and often in the evening I secretly left the hospital and walked down to the Villa Tigerkralle. It was not very far. There was always a pot with freshly boiled potatoes waiting for me. My father and Trudel did not have much to share either, but because I had come back from Russia, I had privileges for extra food.

I had come back with malaria and I had to eat quinine tablets and it was late February when I was finally released from Hospital. I moved into Villa Tigerkralle with my father and Trudel.

Right away I looked for work. My first job was in a saw mill. I got there every morning on a bicycle that had a tire on the front wheel and on the back only an inner tube fastened with wire. Every time I clattered over the cobble stones the tire went schlupp, schlupp, schlupp – for five long kilometers, at every turn of the wheel when the wire hid the stones.

I knew how to work, I knew about wood and timber but at this job the workers were exploited – there is no other word for it. When the machine had just a few seconds rest, the boss came running, screaming, "Why aren't you working?"

I ran all the time and it was heavy, heavy work and at the end of the week I came home with fifty nine marks - that was take home pay after all taxes, insurance, healthcare and what not had been taken care of. I gave forty five marks to Trudel and so I had fourteen marks left for me.

Sometimes I bought some tobacco and sometimes a bar of chocolate. Chocolate, something I had not had for so many years, was a dream for me.

Of course, we were very resourceful. My father tended a big garden and he also had thirty rabbits. We pulled a small handcart to the 'Berg' and cut grass for them. I remember how amazed I was at the amount of greens thirty rabbits can eat.

After one year living with my father, he said to me one day, "Manfred, its time for you to move out. Go and get a room for yourself."

By that time I had decided to become a surveyor. With the high school education I had, I would have to take less time than the required three years of apprenticeship. The State also allowed me 180 DM a month because I was over twenty five years old instead of the forty marks for young people. It was my time to get lucky.

When I attended courses, I had to be really careful because I needed money to keep the tank of my motorbike full. I had just bought one and Opa Haefner had lent me three hundred marks to buy it. I signed a cheque and I did not know what that was. I also signed that I had to pay one hundred DM a month to pay off my debt. I got 180 DM a month from work, 100 to pay off the bike, 60 went for my rent and so I was left with 20DM. I ate only dry bread, drank milk and occasionally I had an apple.

I lived out of town in the only place I could afford, some old barracks that had once housed conscripted workers. There was a common room where I sometimes spent the evening. One evening an old man asked me if I would play chess with him. I agreed and so we played chess. When I got to know him better I found out that he was the former Minister of Labour in the Third Reich, Reichsarbeitsminister Hierl. I guess he had no more money than I had.

*** The very same person Gustel had encountered in the POW camp in Hohenasperg; he must have been free by then too.***

I started working in the surveyors' office in 1950. In 1952 I passed my first exam as one of the two out of twenty who sat for them. I took more courses and slowly worked my way up and in 1955 I finally became a surveyor.

I was very poor – because to take the courses it always cost extra money. I remember that when I went dancing, I ordered a bottle of coca cola and asked the waitress to bring two glasses.

Not only did I not have too many girlfriends – what was almost more important for me was that my tank was forever empty. Being more resourceful than rich I came up with an idea: It happened frequently that someone would ask me to give him a ride. And I would answer, 'Yes, sure – but my tank is empty'.

So who ever really wanted to have a ride with me had to contribute to fill my tank. I always drove them. I used to empty my tank into an old jerry can but leave about two liters in the tank and so accumulated enough gasoline for me when I wanted to go somewhere – alone.

"By the way – your mother drove for weeks behind me to work.

***Perhaps that was the reason that she never would allow me to catch another ride on Uncle Manfred's bike after the one he had offered which I consequently had accepted! I had decided that riding on a motorbike was not on my wish list anymore. ***

In 1955 my father, who had found a job as a teacher again, retired and moved out to the country into a small house. This was the place where his mother visited him from East Germany in 1957. I remember how small she had become, but she was still curious about everything. Unfortunately, she fell sick and after a few months she died. She was buried in that little village. She was ninety two years old. Not long after he and Trudel moved back to Schwaebisch Hall into a nice and modern apartment.

On Easter 1959 he spit up blood. An old army doctor diagnosed lung cancer. He had been a heavy smoker all his life. He went for radiation treatment to Heidelberg but it was no use. He died on February 4, 1961, all alone in the hospital. He was buried on the seventh, the day before my 37th birthday. It was very hard for me. I never celebrated my birthday that year, I only wanted to be alone.

I got married to Annemie and we lived at the beginning in her parents' house. I still always needed money and so I came up with the following idea: commercial chicken breeders kill little cockerels because they want only laying hens. I found that I could buy them for a dime a piece. One day I bought thirty cockerels. I had built them a small shed where they could spend the day. In the evening after I came home from work, I would let them out so they could wander into the nearby park and nibble on greens and bugs. When it got dark, I locked them up again. It was a good plan and it worked for a while. Then, one night I forgot to lock the door and in the morning the little cockerels, who had by then grown into much bigger ones, had flown over the fence and wreaked havoc in neighbours garden. I woke up when I heard him screaming and hollering chasing my birds away.

That put an end to my chicken enterprise. I slaughtered all thirty, gave him two, all the chicken heads for which he had asked, some money and then he was satisfied.

Soon after that Annemie and I left for our belated honeymoon on my motorbike. We took two roasted cockerels with us. It was a late honeymoon because we had already a little baby girl. Grandma at home looked after her. On our second day as we sat in the ditch munching on our cold roast chicken, that is cold roasted cockerel, Annemie started to cry.

"I want to go home to my baby."

She did not stop crying for her baby.

I told her to stop crying and went on driving. I wanted to drive up to Salzgitter to visit Auntie Tilchen, my mother's sister, who had moved there after the war. Uncle Erich and she were to celebrate their fiftieth anniversary. But listen, what happened: The day before the anniversary he went into the cellar to get a bottle of wine. He tripped and fell down the cellar stairs and he broke his neck. So the people who came to celebrate his anniversary stayed to mourn his death. He did have a big funeral.

Annemie, wanted me to be with her for all her birthings. It was terrible, but I watched all of them and I became sick after everyone. I had five children, four girls and one boy! I will never forget Wolfgang's birth. It took seven hours. The midwife had a moustache and we had to call the doctor and I fainted when I saw him taking out his instruments. A few days later I came down with sciatica – from all the stress. My father-in-law had to carry me up to our room.

In 1956 I joined the Bundeswehr. They had called for veterans to train and instruct the new recruits. I will never forget, when I was out in the yard and heard for the first time in many years: "Rechts um, Marsch!" I thought, 'oh my God, what have I done!' I was thirty two years old – too old to be ordered around. But I stayed; they needed old soldiers because we were the only ones who knew something about the military business. I became a drill sergeant with a salary of 850 DM – that was a lot of money. When we got American tanks, I was the only one who knew how to drive and handle them. I moved about seventy tanks to the barracks. I took some courses and eventually I became sergeant major.

Here I must tell about something that happened during this time: Some students from the Goettingen University protested against the build up of the military by sitting in the gate of the barracks. I wanted to march out with my company and another one wanted to get in. They blocked the way and did not move. I ordered them to get up but they refused. Well, I had to do something. So without much ado I opened the water hydrant, got a large hose and watered the ground in front and around them. It was freezing cold but they did not move.

Manfred in the Bundeswehr

I phoned my superior and asked him for a caterpillar. He balked and did at first not want to release one for me. I ordered all cars on the road to stop and then I phoned the police to come with their paddy wagons. When they arrived the protesting students still did not move. By this time the caterpillar had started to move slowly and carefully towards the students to shove them off the ground. The students were loaded into the paddy wagon – some had ripped pants – they had frozen to the ground. My picture and story came in the newspaper and I was the hero of the day.

Come to think of it – I had actually just followed regulations where it stated that because we were only thirty kilometers away from the border, the entrance to the barracks must be kept open at all times.

When I reported to my commander he said, "Ernst, you did a good job. Outstanding."

I set my sights higher and wanted to become an officer. But to my great chagrin, I was one year too old, and so I went back to being a surveyor. I became a leader in the reserves and spent much time with the men and also the American army on weekends and longer periods in summer. I enjoyed that.

Chapter 33

AN AUSTRIAN CONNECTION

I n conversations with my parents who I relentlessly bored for more stories from their past, I had heard the name Ernst Hallerwedel. I was told that he once had been a friend of Erika's and I knew that whenever Erika visited in Germany Ernst invariably showed up too. I had never met him. Mama never elaborated on their relationship. In 2001 Mama pressed a small book into my hand and told me to read it carefully, that it would explain much about the past. It had been written by Ernst Hallerwedel in 1998; the German title read "Die Verratene Generation", "The Betrayed Generation".

One chapter in the book told the story of Ernst and Erika. It was titled: "Erika – The Story of a Confused Love".

In 1937 Ernst placed an ad in the magazine of the German Faith Movement. "Viennese Man looking for German girl to correspond with." Ernst received twelve letters. Two of the girls that answered had the last name 'Ernst'. One, of the same age as Ernst wrote from Heinersdorf, the other, three years younger answered from Halle. Only later did he find out that they were sisters, Irmgard and Erika Ernst. Looking at enclosed photos he chose the younger girl, Erika. They got involved in serious correspondence. In June 1938, after the annexation of Austria, Ernst travelled by train to a Party meeting and arranged to meet Erika in the railway station of Leipzig.

He remembered that we both were 'very shy and did not speak much but were lost in each others' eyes'.

Shortly after, Ernst accepted a job in the air force ministry in Berlin. Erika met him in Berlin and later in Halle. Erika invited Ernst to visit her parents in Heinersdorf. With a friend who owned a motorcycle he went to Heinersdorf. There her father, a teacher and 'Ortsgruppenleiter', the local leader of the Party, mustered him sternly. Ernst remembered his wife Trudel as a 'rather colorless looking Hausfrau' and he also saw the Hitler Youth, Manfred.

Slowly the relationship progressed. When in 1938 Erika contracted pneumonia, Ernst visited her in his black SS uniform in hospital, an event, he pointed out, which resulted in improved treatment of the patient.

In April 1939 Erika visited his parents in Vienna and both took a few days hiking in the mountains, 'sleeping in communal dormitories' as it was pointed out.

Then Ernst was drafted into the Wehrmacht and they rarely saw each other. 'The first shadow fell on the developing love, when Erika and her family expected that they become engaged'. Ernst did not feel that he was mature and professionally safe enough for such a step. He was still a student and he did not want to burden Erika with the possibility of having to stay with a wounded veteran for the rest of her life. He wrote to Erika ending their relationship 'irrevocably'. Secretly though he hoped that 'their love would be tough enough to overcome this obstacle'.

Erika who had joined the Labour Service wrote poems and vignettes and stories about her experiences at work. Many of them were published in local papers. She dedicated one small volume of stories to him.

Ernst wrote, "There was a living record of the time and the youth we belonged to. It was a dream of national greatness and social community of all people, a faith in Fuehrer and the Reich... Germany was the faith of Erika as it was also mine, and our hope as it was with millions of people in all German lands....I know that today, half a century afterwards, nobody can understand or believe what we believed in."

In 1942 Ernst happened to be travelling through Gruenberg and he contacted Erika. Erika's father advised her not to meet him, but she did. They met in the railway station: 'She was pale, silently she handed me a piece of paper, her marriage license, then she turned and walked out of the room. Frozen and unable to think I remained behind'.

In 1945 Ernst joined the millions of displaced persons looking for relatives through the International Red Cross searching for Erika. A year later he received a letter from Erika's father: 'Erika is alive. She lives in Schwaebisch Hall.'

The first letters he wrote got lost but eventually he succeeded in contacting Erika.

The first letter from Erika is dated February 1948. In it she told Ernst that she had lost her first husband, with whom she had been very happy, and that she was engaged since the previous year to her boss, an American.

Ernst wrote in his book: "I was shaken: Erika, my German girl from then, wanted to marry an 'Ami', like tens of thousands of other German women...With last minute desperation I wanted to fight for her. I called her but she refused to accept my call. She had someone tell me, 'Tell Ernst, I am committed'."

Later on, Erika and Ernst resumed a voluminous correspondence. In a letter from 1966, Erika wrote: 'when I saw you after such a long time in the waiting room, I knew that I would always belong to you. Only you. But I also felt that I betrayed the man whose name I carried...'

'In another letter from 1966 she wrote:...My first marriage was not a marriage like I understand marriage today, but I know that I made my husband very happy...Then I thought it was love. Today I know it was spite. I had to show you that I could live without you...'

In another letter we read: 'It was a blessing that we lost the war. Winning would have resulted in greater chaos.'

Erika wrote that she admired the way the Americans helped the Germans after the war; she pointed out that they treated her kinder than the locals of Schwaebisch Hall did who told her, the refugee from the east, they wished she 'would go back where she had come from'.

Ernst figured that 'she had already succumbed to the re-education and propaganda of the 'American way of life'. He realized that he had lost Erika and one year after Erika married Charles, Ernst married Ingrid.

Ernst quoted a letter from Erika, written in 1956 in Pattonville, an American military base in southern Germany where Charles was stationed upon their request. She wrote,

'What I miss here is the wide space, the freedom, the camaraderie and the openness which I have met in America. The Germans are stiff and petty, provincial and narrow minded. In the USA you can practically do what you want as long as you don't break the law. Whereas here everyone is staring at you like you were a circus clown. And I have never witnessed in the States the hatred that I witness here. The German is much more of a herd animal than the American will ever be. Perhaps there is not enough space here.

I realize that I must have changed without being aware of it…the homeland that I once left is no longer the same for me…perhaps the countryside and the culture, but otherwise…?'

Ernst wrote at the end of the chapter: 'And then our correspondence petered out to occasional greetings across the pond.'

After Charles died 1979 in San Antonio, Texas, Erika visited Irmgard and Gustel a few times in their little retirement house in Eckartshausen and that is where she again took up her relationship with Ernst Hallerwedel who had since lost his wife. For a while it looked as if the old flame was to rise up again. Ernst had become passionate in his pursuit of health and fitness and he abhorred smoking. At one time he invited Erika, who was a chain smoker, to come and stay with him in his house. Erika agreed. But nothing came of it. Erika explained that he wanted her to quit smoking and that 'was more than I was willing to sacrifice.' They quarreled, Ernst drove her back to Eckartshausen and that was finally the end of their romance.

Who was Ernst Hallerwedel who but for a few twists of fate could have become my uncle? Ernst was born in 1914 as Ernst Wedel, in Austria who after the annexation became a German. He worked in Germany as an aircraft engineer.

During the war he served with the German Army. Ernst's memoirs told of his childhood in Vienna where in the winter of 1920/21 so little food was available that the poor started to die of starvation. International charity organizations intervened and soon trainloads full of children were sent to Switzerland, Sweden, and Holland. Ernst spent one and a half years in Holland and when he came back to Vienna he was well fed and loaded down with gifts, but very dirty. In all the time he had spent with his caregivers, two spinster ladies and their two bachelor brothers, fanatic Lutherans, he did much Bible reading and praying, but he never had a bath. Taking a bath was considered a sign of vanity that played straight into the hand of the devil.

Ernst grew up during the 'dictatorship of Dollfuss', where a Catholic and clerical state was set up in Austria under the guidance of the Pope in Rome and where a person voicing disagreement with the church could land a prison term. Depression, unemployment, and misery of the urban population made life in Austria very hard. Ernst became a National Socialist in 1930, joined the SA and became politically very active. A civil war threw Austria into chaos in 1934. In 1936 the successor to Dollfuss, Schuschnigg, signed a non-aggression pact with Hitler. Political unrest and uprisings followed. In 1938 Schuschnigg was made to resign by Hitler and Austria was annexed by Germany.

Ernst, a passionate National Socialist, was there when Hitler undertook his 'Blumenfeldzug', his triumphant entry in March 1938 through an enthusiastically welcoming Austria. His entrance into Vienna is described by the author: "I received permission to wear the black Austrian SS uniform. Around three in the afternoon Hitler drove past us with leaders of the German Wehrmacht and the SS amid indescribable cheers from the population. Our troop was in a car wearing our black SS uniforms. A few German police asked us who we were. I replied. They left but soon returned and then they spliced us into Hitler's parade, about four cars behind him. With excitement came tears – and I must confess I was not ashamed.

Later on we listened to the passionate words of the Fuehrer who exulted that after seventy two years we were back in the German Reich. For me, as a convinced National Socialist this hour was the high point, the pinnacle, of my political life!

You cannot imagine what followed: For the next three days and nights millions of men women and children thronged through the large plazas in Vienna, screaming, singing, jubilating, waving homemade swastika flags. It was crazy.'

On March 18 the bishops presented a letter to the Gauleiter expressing their joy at the union of all German speaking people, pledging their support to the new Regime. They urged all citizens to vote in the upcoming plebiscite and do their duty as Germans and to stand for a German Reich and 'we expect from all Christians that they know what they owe their people.'

Hallerwedel notes that 'simple people, labourers and farmers told me that when our cardinal welcomes the Fuehrer as liberator of Austria, then this really proves that Hitler was sent by God to lead us out of our misery and troubles'.

The protestant churches also pledged their loyalty to Hitler.

The plebiscite on April 10th resulted in a 99.73% support for the unification of Austria with the German Reich. Diplomats and consuls from all countries as well as Cardinal Eugenio Pacelli, later Pope Pius XII, rushed to express their sincere congratulations.

The first doubts about the new regime rose in Ernst when he slowly realized that of all the leaders and prominent figures that had lived and worked underground for so many years and furthered the cause of national socialism in Austria, only a very few were rewarded by the Party by being called for office or promoted into higher positions. Ernst himself never rose higher than to the rank of a first lieutenant.

His disillusionment increased when he became aware of the strict and brutal practice of the racial laws that forbade marriage with Jews, Jews to hold office or Jews to have businesses. Many Jews left the city; he mentions the lineup of people at the Polish consulate wanting to immigrate to their country – naturally without any goods or money. Jews that immigrated were not allowed to take anything along with them, their possessions were confiscated by the state.

Ernst obtained a position as an engineer with the Aviation ministry in Berlin. Sometime later he had to report for military training. He loathed the brutal sergeants, mindless Prussian militarism, stupid rules and regulations and the endless marching and parades he had to endure and he wondered how soldiers, trained in that puppet fashion, would ever perform when confronted with modern weaponry and real conditions in the field.

He was first sent to France and the following was one of his experiences there: Somewhere between Caen and Bayeux he reported to a commander, a 'bull of a man one did not want to cross' who inquired whether Ernst spoke French. Upon admission that he was somewhat conversant, he was ordered to accompany the mayor of the town where Ernst negotiated quarters for the men. Rudely awakened very early next morning he was ordered immediately to the lieutenant in charge.

A young French boy, handcuffed and shaking with fear, flanked by two soldiers with helmets and rifles stood in front of the lieutenant who screamed at him in German. Slowly Ernst found out what was going on. The thick cable, their communication to headquarters, had been damaged during the night. The soldiers had apprehended the young man on the meadow where the cable ran through. The lieutenant threatened loudly to hang the saboteur within the morning.

'I went with the lieutenant to the mayor and then to the family of the young man. Naturally there was a great commotion and much crying and yelling. I tried to tell the mayor that the lieutenant could not just hang the young man and that he should stop worrying. Meanwhile the cable had been fixed and I was ready to leave the scene. Suddenly the mayor appeared together with the father who was dragging an obstinate cow on a rope. We all went to the lieutenant. Very excitedly they pointed out to him how badly the mouth of the cow was burned and blistered. Both men outdid each other in explaining that probably the cow had bitten through the cable during the night. The mayor promised that from now on someone would watch the cable during the night so that such things could not happen again.'

Very much relieved Ernst translated all. Well, the lieutenant, probably tired of the whole commotion, sent the young man home together with the two guards and Ernst.

The parents were overjoyed – the father pointed to his young daughter, who was rather pretty, as Ernst recalled – and indicated that it would be alright if Ernst went into the house alone with the girl. The young girl reddened embarrassedly as did Ernst who turned around and left with the two soldiers.

Ernst's laconic remarks at the end of the story were: "The radio cable was only of low voltage but the poor cow had been treated with high voltage. I wonder if the lieutenant had noticed that too?"

Ernst saw military action also in Norway and northern Germany. On May 6th, 1945, his company received the order to lay down their weapons, because the Canadian Division was going to overrun them later during the morning. The men obeyed 'with moist eyes and swallowing hard'…

He continued in his book: "An almost six-year-long superhuman and hard struggle by all the German people, on the front and at home, had come to a terrible end. My generation lived their best years of their lives during this time. These years of the maturing youth are now lost, truly we are a 'betrayed generation'.

For me this was the most conspicuous change of my young life which I had put totally in the service of the National socialist idea. My deepest conviction was that this 'idée' could only be supplanted by a better one but never through the material superiority of an enemy and his weapons. That was a bitter end! The last entry in my diary, which I was able to carry with me through my time as a prisoner of war, reads: Long live the Great Germany! May 6th, 1945.'

After some months as a prisoner of war of Canadians he returned to Vienna only to find a totally different political situation. He found himself persecuted and as a former Nazi on a list of war criminals. Apprehended he spent time in prison and then on the run, hiding from being caught again. In order to disappear from the radar, he changed his name to Haller in 1946. He eventually crossed the border and escaped to Germany. Without papers he did not find work in industry but had to make do with jobs mostly for the US on their bases.

In 1949 he married Ingrid Pape as Ernst Haller. During this time he started to build up his career; he gained respect and recognition with scientific papers and lectures. In 1955 because of a general amnesty in Germany, he was able change his name back to his old name Wedel.

In 1955 Austria gained its neutrality and the occupation forces left the country. The Austrian government tried to eradicate its Nazi past and a general amnesty finally erased his name from the list of war criminals.

This led to a new problem: the Germans took his German passport away from him and his wife – because now they were supposed to be Austrians again. This posed a huge problem for him because he had since found a position with Siemens in Bavaria and his children were in German schools. So both he and his wife refused to apply for Austrian passports. They were issued a provisional pass in Germany and not allowed to leave the country for two years. Finally, in 1956 he was able to get a German Passport and now finally 'could the former war criminal live in Bavaria as a free German citizen'.

P.S. A German court ordered him in 1955 to take up the name Wedel again. He petitioned the authorities to allow him to call himself Haller-Wedel. Today in his passport Ernst's name is Wedel, in public his name is Hallerwedel. In 1965 he received an official document instructing him that he and his wife would now have the name of Hallerwedel. The hyphenated name Haller-Wedel was allowed only when used in the capacity of an author. His three children were to be named Wedel.

Long live German bureaucracy!!

Ernst Hallerwedel became quite famous as a founder and leader of the local 'Volkshochschule', a well respected and nation wide institution for continuing education in Germany. Always an avid athlete Ernst became a 100 km runner in his sixties and a marathon runner in his seventies. In his eighties he took up parachuting. His accumulation of medals was impressive. He died in 2009.

Chapter 34

GUSTEL'S TRIAL

In summer 1965 the Queen of England came to Germany for a visit. Of course, she went to the nearby Castle of Langenburg to visit the relatives of Prince Philip. She also came through Schwaebisch Hall- and the reason I remember this event is that on the very next day the police stood at my house.

"We have orders to arrest you."

I had known that one day they would come for me and so this was no surprise.

They wanted to handcuff me but I asked them if they were crazy. I pointed out to them that I absolutely no intentions of escaping. So they loaded me in the car without the handcuffs. My charges were that I deprived one hundred Jewish children of food and water and then ordered the survivors to be shot.

Our lawyer, Dr.Pfeiffer, was in the area but after getting into contact with him I realized that he had not the slightest idea of what lay before me and so I got myself another lawyer. But before he washed his hands of August Haefner, he charged us 3000DM, the bandit, the rotten scoundrel. He was a former SS captain of the general SS from the Sudetengau.

Right from the start I informed the presiding judge that I had no money for a defense lawyer and so I the state provided me with one, a Dr. Aschenauer. Then I found out that others had been arrested. We were brought into prison into an isolation cell. The cutlery was taken away after my meals and when I went for my customary walk, no other person was allowed to be there. There was to be no contact among us. My first trial was about the Jewish children of Belaya Cerkov and of course there was the one about Babi Yar.

You ask how did it happen that I was charged in 1965? An old letter had been forwarded to the authorities. In it the liaison officer of Reichenau had written to his family about the story with the one hundred children in Belaya Cerkov and he had mentioned my name. One day later, when I had returned from Kiev and he was at the meeting, he found out that it was not me who had arranged that but the Wehrmacht's field commander, the Austrian colonel. But he obviously had other more pressing things to do than sit down and write another letter to his family telling them that it was not really me who was guilty of the children's murder but rather it was the Austrian colonel. I will not blame the writer for it – he died later in Russian prisons after he was captured in Stalingrad.

Because of Belaya Cerkov the events of Babi Yar became public and other men who had been in the same detachment with me were arrested and charged.

They all had been at the gorge; well, one man had to count the people, one had to take care of the clothing, one had to check on the guards there. They all got sentenced from twelve to fifteen years. I know they, lower rank officers like me, had just followed orders. My colleagues knew nothing about the children

What happened to my colleagues from then, I do not know. I did not try to re-connect. Understandably they were not happy with me either.

I had known for many years that I would have to face justice for what had occurred in Ukraine but what made me very bitter was the fact that nothing ever happened to the people from the Wehrmacht who were involved in the killings of the Jews. Eberhard, the commandant of Kiev said to me, 'The Jews have to be shot. This is your task. Period.' That is what he told me. I testified to that in court and there was no other evidence against my words.

When I inquired at my trial why he had not been called, the judge told me that 'the man was 78 years and too old to stand trial.' I could cite case after case where the Wehrmacht gathered the Jews and then handed them over to the SS for shooting. One of these incidents was told to me by a journalist who covered my case. I wrote this in a letter to your mother and it went through without being blackened out – my letters were always censored. Were the attorneys not negligent in their duty in the light of such evidence?

Last year (1995) when the trade unions in Germany wanted to stage an exhibition that would have shown how the Wehrmacht had been involved in the extermination of Jews, the CDU government in Bonn prevented the event citing as a lame excuse that it would damage the reputation of Germany in the world. 'No need to dig it all up again!', but SS Captain Priebke in Rome accused of shooting of Italian hostages – that is different. That poor devil was freed by the Italian courts, however the German courts wanted to try and sentence him again, this time at home.

I also know that when the pioneers built a bridge over the Dniepr River in Kiev, they had commandeered Jews to do much of the work and when they were done they threw the Jews into the river and shot them. I did not witness this personally but I have been told about these events by soldiers who did witness them. The commander of the regiment was present in court at my process and he had loudly decried the shooting of Jews. When he heard my testimony, he turned white and started stuttering. The judge managed to find a sergeant major and a lieutenant from his regiment who corroborated my story, they also declared that their commander had done nothing to stop the shootings.

Don't you think that when a commander of the regiment does nothing to stop these actions, he is guilty? Do you think that anything happened to him after these testimonials? Nothing happened to him! He was in the Wehrmacht.

Once I had the district attorney in our house in Schwaebisch Hall and I told him that I thought we, in Germany, had a system where the little fish get caught, and the big ones get the Verdienstkreuz, the Order of Germany. He replied, 'You have to prove this.'

I told him that that was not a problem for me and I told him about the 42 000 Jews in Simferopol that General von Manstein had had shot.

'How do you know about this?'

'Very simple. I was for some months in Nuremberg and knew some of the commanders personally through my work in Pretzsch, and we talked about these affairs. Major Braune reported how the shooting came about – the order had come from Manstein."

The district attorney was quiet and then said, 'You are correct, we are quite aware of that.'

General Field Marshall von Manstein had ordered on Christmas in 1941 that 42,200 Jews were to be shot in Simferopol. He was also responsible for the 40,000 Jews that died in their freight trains sitting at the Hungarian border. The German administration and the German government knew about these events.

At a British Military Tribunal held in 1949 in Hamburg von Manstein had been sentenced to eighteen years. Churchill, Montgomery and many others intervened and the sentence was reduced to twelve years. He was let out in May of 1953.

Eventually Herr von Manstein received the highest order of the German Republic for his role as senior defense advisor to Konrad Adenauer and the rebuilding of the German Army, the new Bundeswehr.

St.Petersburg, or Leningrad as it was then known as, was under German siege for three years. How many hundreds of thousands starved to death. Are the Wehrmacht units not guilty of those deaths? I am sure there were Jews among them too. A certain lieutenant von Weizsacker was there too and helped for three and a half years to starve out the population. Did he not aid in killing civilians?

I spent less than three months in the Ukraine in 1941 where I was made to do things I did not want to do. I did what I was ordered to do and what I could not avoid doing. That cost me eight years of my life.

In 1945 this same von Weizsacker was the leader of a battalion and when the call came to advance: Vorwaerts, Kamerad! he turned, he deserted his battalion and escaped to Sweden. Officer? Honour? Another one thousand officers stayed with their men to the bitter end.

This is the former Bundespraesident Herr von Weizsacker. Is that justice? And I, a lower rank SS officer, am sentenced for many years because I was made to watch the shooting of Jews? Is that justice?

What about the men in high positions? The men who ordered all this madness? A very few paid for what they had done. What about those who quietly complied and who did not raise a voice of protest? How about the Gauleiters? The Kreisleiters? The generals? The ministers? Who got punished in the end? We, the lower ranks who took orders from them, we got blamed and we received sentences and we lost our pensions. And how about the high command of the Waffen SS from whom we lower ranks took orders? It was the captains, the lieutenants, the men who had to obey orders, they were the ones who had to pay.

"If you don't do it you will be shot!"

Nobody speaks about that today.

When I spoke about this during my trial the district attorney did not protest. Interestingly enough, these comments are nowhere to be found in the court records.

I especially asked for word protocol, which means that every word spoken in court was to be recorded. It never happened. So much of what I said and what I could prove without a doubt, was not recorded. The chairman of the court to whom I complained about that answered me that he received the records only eight days after the day in court, because of a lack of office and writing personnel, and he added, 'You cannot expect me to recall facts and words from eight days before.'

The woman who stenographed the proceedings admitted to me one day that many things that were said in court were not recorded or purged from the written record of the trial.

I was told by a judge that things said in my favour were not recorded and that the court had instructions from above that all guilt was to be laid on the Gestapo and the SS and that the Wehrmacht had to be kept out of it.

I often wondered where these judges were during the war and what they had been doing but I refrained from asking because I did not want them to be even more against me. How could I have dared to expose 'das deutsche Arschkriechertum', the German brownnose system – my father always told me, "You may complain about the devil but never to his grandmother."

Some of the judges were annoyed with my insistence on pointing fingers at the Wehrmacht. But why should I not. Not only did I give testimony about their part in the shooting of thousands of Jews, I also knew how they had implicated us during the IMT, the International Military Trials in Nuremberg, where they had sat silently and let SS officers like Blobel, Braune and Ohlendorf shoulder all the blame. These three officers said nothing to implicate the Wehrmacht – and they could have.

A priest of the Wehrmacht who was there in Belaya Cerkov, who is a Bishop today, was subpoenaed to Darmstadt as a witness. But he never showed up citing health reasons. But Dr. Aschenauer, my defense lawyer, found a newspaper clipping that put the good Bishop to be in Lyons in France, consecrating new priests on the very day he was supposed to appear in court, the day he had excused himself for medical reasons. Aschenauer advised not to make waves because we did not want the Catholic Church and the Catholic intelligence against us.

I had discussed with Dr. Aschenauer the possibility of finding someone in Israel to testify on my behalf. Weihman was probably dead but there had been children on the train to Mauthausen. This event had occurred in the beginning of April and since there never had been mass shootings in Mauthausen there was a chance that we could find survivors.

Aschenauer said to me, "You must know, even if Weihman is still alive, you still don't know if he would testify for you. Maybe he would denounce you too. I do know of Jews who had testified for members of the SS and who had consequently got into great trouble."

And Aschenauer told me the names of two Jews who had spoken in favour of SS members and who had surprisingly suddenly met a violent death.

Later when I was in prison for the second part of my sentence, I spoke to a Lieutenant Colonel who had been commandeered from the Waffen SS to a camp with Jews in Poland and he told me, "A Jewish woman had told during the trial that the conditions in that particular camp had been relatively good and decent and that guards did not overstep the bounds of decency and law. And on the next day she counteracted her testimony in court. Someone had pressured her."

On one hand I cannot blame the Jews for that but it is regrettable that they have all agreed to find the guilty in only one segment and that the others all were given a halo. I guess our present government has chosen a course of least resistance.

The investigating judge was a decent man; I could talk to him. I was accused of having shot many Jews in a small village between Belaya Cerkov and Kiev but I denied it vigorously. The next day the judge apologized indicating that records had shown that a battalion from the Wehrmacht had done that.

I was accused to have shot 36 000 Jews in the south at a place the name of which I have forgotten. I admitted to have been there to see the Higher SS and Police Leader but I had nothing to do with the shootings. The judge in the next session apologized again and admitted that I had been correct – the Jews had been shot by the SS Police Regiment South Russia, as I had told him. Following this disclosure, I informed him that the same regiment had shot 42 000 Jews at another place and 10 000 south of Belaya Cerkov. Again, the judge had to admit that I had been correct.

We counted – Roskorov – 42 000 Jews, 36 000 in the place the name of which I had forgotten, 10 000 Jews in the village south of Belaya Cerkov and on. Everything had been reported and recorded. The investigating judge could see that until the end of September, the time when we were recalled to the Reich, about 242 000 Jews had been shot by the police regiments. Of course, those men had to obey orders just like the others, were they Wehrmacht or Gestapo.

33 771 Jews were shot in Kiev. We had one troop to do the shooting, the police had two battalions there and ten troops for shooting; they agreed to that number later. That meant that we had shot one eleventh, that is 3 070 Jews of the 33 771 Jews that were shot; the others were shot by the regiments of the police.

The police regiments were composed of police and reservists who had nothing to do with the Wehrmacht. They were under the direct command of the Higher SS and Police Leader and the Wehrmacht did not dare something against him. We in the Gestapo could not order these men at all.

In my trial a case came up where I was sentenced because this time I had been ordered to watch some events. In the reasoning for his sentencing the judge elaborated that 'I, with my mere presence had practically forced the men to obey orders'. That is probably true – but I also was forced to obey orders.

The following had happened: Blobel ordered me to attend an autopsy saying that as a criminal commissary I should have an idea what that entailed. I agreed. When I got there a Dr. Panning from the Wehrmacht was there, I knew him because I had once described him the route to a command post. There were also a few colleagues present and other men as well as five or six Russian soldiers.

We were surprised to see Russian soldiers because generally there never were Russian prisoners of war – they were all always shot – the Wehrmacht only kept communist functionaries whom they handed over to us for shooting. We found out that Dr. Panning had brought the prisoners himself.

When we had gathered there the doctor looked at us and said, "Well, can we start?"

We four officers looked at each other and finally one nodded his head.

None of us knew what this was all about. We saw that the doctor had a large box with him – we were to find out that it contained rifles of British, French and German origin. Now the following happened: the Russian soldier had to lay down and then a German soldier was given a rifle and he had to shoot the Russian at certain places, the arm, the thigh or the shoulder – and so the poor devil was shot three or four times and finally he received his last shot that killed him. The corpses were then taken into a cellar under a chapel and laid on tables where autopsies were performed to find out what happened to the body when it was shot by different kinds of rifles or ammunition. Some of the Russians had even received shots into their stomachs.

Just my presence at the event brought me three years in prison even though I had done nothing and had had no clue whatsoever of what was to occur. We had understood that it was to be an autopsy of already dead persons.

In the decision in this case the judge summarized: Haefner does not dispute the fact that he participated in the execution as a commanding officer. He had realized that he was not only present as an observer but in his capacity to give orders he psychologically encouraged the men in their terrible deeds and prevented resistance. And that is what he wanted to do. On the other hand he is believable in his expression of distaste of the affair, that he only was present on Blobel's orders to assist Dr. Panning during the experiments that had been ordered by Blobel. This shows that he merely did his duty. It is not to be taken into consideration that the accused believed that because of the oath he had sworn he had to participate in this criminal execution …that was an error in judgment and is no excuse.

The events with the children brought me three years of prison – I followed the orders of the Fieldmarshall and attended the shooting of the last of the children - I was made to attend.

The judge added another three years due to the events in Kiev and when the judge read out the ruling he added in his own words, 'because he did nothing to prevent the shooting of the Jews in Kiev.'

I would have loved to see those generals who would listen to a lieutenant's ideas as to what they should or shouldn't do! It couldn't happen then and it cannot happen today because that would result in utter chaos. Little lieutenants do not counter act generals' direct orders.

*** The judge's final sentencing read as follows:
"… in general ,the accused was totally aware of the illegality of the happenings. The easily avoided error of a misguided sense of compliance to official orders cannot be used as an extenuating circumstance because he was aware of the injustice of the proceedings. On the other hand he has shown beyond a doubt that he seriously attempted to withhold himself from the murderous happenings.

The accused could prove that he was mostly involved with partisan counter activities… in later years he could show that he spoke for persons accused under the homeland security provisions, as he had helped French conscripted workers…. it is also to take into consideration that he was interned from 1946 to 1948 and partially paid for his Nationalistic past….but this cannot be counted in the present ruling… It must also be taken into consideration that the accused was honestly interested in helping to clarify the events that had happened by the use of his very good memory and he has shown that this open attitude stemmed from an openly visible change of attitude and regret.

At the shooting of at least twenty six children of Belaya Cerkov, Haefner participated only marginally and without real influence, even though the suggestion to have the Ukrainians shoot the children, came from him. This happened only because he did not want his men from the Waffen SS to have these deeds on their conscience and so he tried to keep them away from this task. On the other hand, Haefner supervised the shooting of the children which was executed by Ukrainian volunteers. Even though Haefner is to be believed when he insists that he was extremely upset by the order to supervise, which speaks for him, it must be taken into account, that the victims of this base and cruel execution were of the age of two to seven year old children, whose only 'crime' was to belong to the Jewish race and to have Jewish parents. With consideration of all circumstances a sentencing of four years in prison seems appropriate.'

At the executions in Kiev Haefner did participate for two days, lead by base motivation, in the cruel and inhumane killing of 33 771 Jewish men, women and children by supervising at the bottom of the ravine and by administering two so called Fangschuesse, shots in the neck.

Even so his participation was very intensive and the number of victims is very high, he did here also try to withdraw himself from the proceedings. He acted under order and especially the immediate order of Dr. Rasch, when he climbed down into the ditch to administer the shots in the neck. In consideration of all circumstances a sentence of six years in prison seems necessary but also sufficient."

Considering another case (executions of Jews and mental patients in Wassilkov, events which are not mentioned in these notes), the judge summarized "that Haefner was in charge of some aspects of the operation but that he stayed mostly in the background and did not more than was absolutely necessary in his position. He was not present at the place of execution and even asked Blobel again if the persons had to be shot, even though in his position as leader of the detachment he could have given the order himself. Taking into consideration the gravity of his contributions, the number of victims and the personality of Haefner, a sentencing of five years in prison seems appropriate."

In the end the judge ruled that "a total sentence of nine years was appropriate to his guilt, was necessary and sufficient. Time served as well as the five months he spent as a witness in Nuremberg in 1947 were to be taken into consideration. With reference to the magnitude of the injustice and the acts as well as the personality of the accused, his civil rights were to be suspended for five years.' ***

I served part of my sentence from 1965 to 1969 when I was released for health reasons. They came again for me in 1973 and then in the spring of 1976 I was released. Herman, your sister's husband and a member of the Wuerttemberg diet, had spoken to the Minister of Justice of his state and Minister of Justice of the state of Hesse, they intervened and my sentence was reduced to eight years. I was allowed to leave, before the assigned time – in the spring of 76.

Now it is finished – forever.

They did send me a bill for one million German Marks.

I must say that during all those years the family supported me whole heartedly. During the trial your sister Ingeborg drove every day to be present at the proceedings. Her husband was often there too. Your mother did not attend any of the trials; she was running the store and I believe these proceedings would have been too difficult for her to attend. She came often when I was in prison and then your sister or my sister Liese ran the shop.

When I came home in 76 I was sixty four and your mother was sixty two years old; this time we sold the business. After everything about me had been dragged out in the newspapers I did not want to face customers anymore. Many people were neutral and never spoke to me or about me, many customers spoke to your mother in a kind and encouraging way, many thought, that 'bygones should be bygones' and did not see why I should go to prison because these things had happened during war and I had just followed orders, but we had also hate mail and lost some customers.

Irmgard had for years been buying retirement savings stamps with every spare Pfennig she got her hands on. Even though I had been a civil servant in my position as a Kriminal Kommissar and entitled to a pension, because I had been a member of the SS my pension was disallowed. This was not the case with the bureaucrats and the Wehrmacht; they all got their pension. If it would not have been for your mother we would not have had much to retire on.

We bought a small house in the country, moved our furniture into it, packed our bags and left for a five months long visit to Canada.

***My sister Ingeborg remembers that generally the customers were neutral and did not hassle her or my mother during the process and when he was in prison. She told me that she herself actually never discussed with Mama the events for which Papa was on trial because she knew this to be too painful and devastating for her. Inge also realized that Mama needed all her courage and iron will power to get through this trying time.

This was not an act of denial. Inge says, "Mama was shattered. She had not known any details of Papa's time in Ukraine and it took all her strength to get over the shock of what Gustel was accused of. It was a very difficult time for her not only because of what Papa was facing but she also had worries about their future."

My mother had to face the public every day, and as proud a woman as she was, that must have cost her a superhuman effort. It was during this time that she began to suffer from asthma and heart problems which would render her almost an invalid and which eventually caused her death.

I had found out about my father's involvement in Babi Yar by reading Time Magazine and before my mother had written to me about Papa's imprisonment. My gut reaction was utter numbness and disbelief and then the overwhelming feeling that I could not bear this but that suicide would in some way pay for his actions. To this day I remember how I walked away from the University Library and then across the High Level Bridge in Edmonton looking down into the murky Saskatchewan River determined to atone for what he had done. Then I remembered a lesson Papa had taught me: my little sister was always in trouble and in good old tradition Papa punished her with strikes over her behind. One day Inge had again done something wrong and expecting the painful punishment cried in fear. I ran to Papa and begged him not to hit my sister but me instead. And to my great surprise he did. It hurt badly and I never asked to be punished for my sister again. Despite the anguish the memory made me smile. I remembered the lesson; and also the other one I had been taught that only Jesus could take the sins of man on his shoulders. But I was not a believer. After some time the thoughts of atonement for others vanished and slowly I turned and walked back again.

Later in that fall of 1965 my mother had written a letter to my husband and I asking if we would leave Canada and come to Schwaebisch Hall to help with the business. I thought long and hard and wrote her that I would remain in Canada - this was the most difficult decision I ever had to make. Mama respected my decision without any comment and never mentioned it again.

When I was a teenager there had been violent clashes between myself and my father when we discussed the Third Reich. In my youthful ignorance I had made brash accusations after which my father threw me out of the house. My mother engineered peace and I resolved never to talk politics with my parents again. The only other time I ever asked my father to speak about the Third Reich was almost forty years later in 1996. By then I was much wiser and quieter and only asked questions.***

Chapter 35

THE SUM OF MY FATHER

Gustel, my father, was raised in the tradition of obedience to authority in the family, in business, and in the community in the tradition of the Lutheran church. This ingrained custom of order was completely at odds with the chaos of the times of his youth in the later twenties and early thirties.

It was a time of weak government, extreme inflation, no social programs, no labour laws, no pensions for war veterans, rampant petty crime resulting from the poverty of millions of out of work citizens and the glaring disparity of the multitude of the poor and the riches of a small minority of landowners, real estate tycoons and big business barons with a 'Cabaret' mentality without regard for the majority.

This conflict between my father's orderly upbringing and the chaotic world of his youth made him a perfect candidate for a Hitler whose speeches offered work for all, social programs for workers, free education for skills and professions, law and order in the streets, in business, in government and most of all a national pride in a unified Germany. Hitler enabled the masses a way out of their dead end lives by instilling hope in progress and hope in their future.

Gustel and millions of others joined the National Socialist movement with the purest of motifs and unwittingly they became slowly caught up in the moronic ideology of a mad man. My father, like millions of others, had to pay the price.

My father was an intelligent person but not an intellectual. He believed in the movement and he was drawn into a no-way-out system. His crimes against humanity took place in a three months period in 1941 when he was drawn into Hitler's maniacal cauldron of murder. He was twenty nine years old.

Genghis Khan, Ivan the Terrible, Hitler and Stalin ordered mass slaughter of populations and millions perished, Roosevelt ordered the dropping of a multitude of incendiary bombs on Dresden and other German cities killing hundreds of thousands of civilians, Truman withheld peace talks with Japan in order to gain time to be able to drop Atomic bombs on Hiroshima and Nagasaki which annihilated 250 000 people in mere seconds. Johnson ordered the spraying of Agent Orange and carpet bombings of north-south routes in Vietnam.

Hermann Goering said at the Nuremberg War Trials:

"Naturally the common people don't want war: neither in Russia, nor in England, nor for that matter in Germany. That is understood. But, after all, it is the leaders of the country who determine the policy and it is always a simple matter to drag the people along, whether it is a democracy, or a fascist dictatorship, or a parliament, or a communist dictatorship. Voice, or no voice, the people can always be brought to the bidding of the leaders. That is easy. All you have to do is tell them they are being attacked, and denounce the peacemakers for lack of patriotism and exposing the country to danger. It works the same in any country."

George W. Bush was of that same mindset when he riled up his congress, the senate and the population and hurled his country into his supposed 'War on Terror' in Iraq. Today we know that the reasons he gave such as Saddam's procurement and training of Al Queda terrorists and Iraq's amassed biological and nuclear weapons of mass destruction were unfounded. No such weapons were ever found in Iraq and it turned out that Afghanistan was the motherland of Al Queda.

Men like these choose to make war, citing colonial, territorial or ideological reasons, for religious supremacy or corporate gain and often these reasons intertwine. They choose not to make war against poverty, ignorance, social injustice and health problems like malaria or Aids. These are equally crimes against humanity.

Worldwide the thirties were a time where young men without work and with nowhere to go joined the military, even went abroad to fight in international brigades like the ones in Spain. Perhaps they were tired of the stultifying humdrum of the poverty at home, perhaps they were idealistic, and perhaps they did want to make the world a better place. The lower ranks have always been filled by the poor, the disenfranchised, men from the periphery of their society who saw the military as a chance for advancement and a better life. My father was one of them.

My father was a cog in that giant wheel of power that a handful of leaders turn without regard for humanity and as it is more and more evident without regard for our whole planet.

My father chose obedience and compliance in duties he knew to be absolutely wrong and criminal. He knew what was right and what was wrong but he honestly believed that there was no way of avoiding participation in the crimes he committed. He chose personal survival rather than what he believed to be certain death if he did not do as he was ordered. If he regretted that choice it was his conscience he had to wrestle with.

Our memories are the true reminder of things we have done. I feel deep empathy with the man who was made to commit unspeakable terror and then had to remember the horrors which were on his conscience for the rest of his life. I will never understand why he did the things he did – but I cannot judge. I did not walk in his shoes.

My father was not given to brooding but we knew his conscience weighed heavily on him. For years he was chronically sick with stomach ulcers and other ailments until his final trial was over, then he became healthy and well again, even though he was always plagued by nightmares.

He served his sentence as a penance that relieved some of the mental torment that he had suffered for years. At the same time, he felt once more let down by the system that allowed a group of men who had ordered and committed the same crimes as he was accused of, to go free.

In prison he worked on ancestry research for the City of Schwaebisch Hall and our family's genealogy. I am certain he was sadly aware that he was the last to carry the name Haefner. His German grandsons are 'Kraft' men and they do not resemble him, only his Canadian grandson does. Jamie looks like the elder August and my father rolled in one, solid with a square bald head, alert eyes and an easy laugh. He even has some of the characteristics of his grandfather like the open and easy way he converses with everyone, the habit of making longwinded speeches, a delight in innocent practical jokes and a penchant to work with his hands.

My father was able to exercise in prison; he even made the Seniors Gold medal of which he was very proud. His ulcers healed and he began to look forward to a peaceful life in old age and retirement. He spent it mainly working on other people's family trees and helping his children's families on their farms in Germany and Canada as long as he was able.

My father was a decent man who liked to help people out. In 2002 when my mother and I visited Lindau and the house that had held the police offices, Mama remembered that often women would call on her – she who had nothing to do with the police – and ask for Herr Haefner. When my mother wondered why, the women, and it was mostly women who came, explained that officer Haefner had told them to go to that office as the place where they might find help in obtaining papers to cross the border into Switzerland.

My father was an honest, kind, hard working and jolly family man. He was generous to a fault, even giving my boyfriend, that strange man from Canada, free use of his car when he visited for the first time. Jim was most impressed by this gesture of trust and generosity and he never forgot it. Papa was a man without guile, never ever holding a person's education, race or religion as a reason to like or dislike, to associate or distance himself. He got on well with family, friends, community and strangers.

I don't want to excuse my father or whitewash what he had done. I can only look at the man that was my father and say: My father was 'ein guter Mensch', my father was a good man.

Chapter 36

THE LAST CHAPTER

I saw my father for the last time in the spring of 1999. He was 87 years old and suffered from Parkinson's Disease. It was difficult to see him eat with a bib. We drove around with him to visit old places and people he had not seen for a while. It was time to say good bye. He knew it and we knew it – my heart was heavy. When we left, I knew I would never see him again. He died in June.

I did not go to his funeral. Jim drove with me through the Okanagan countryside, we dug out bushes and trees, which I then planted here and there around our place – memorials for my father. I saluted the man who had bravely and courageously fought his last battle.

In October we flew to Germany and took my mother away from her memories and her sorrow on a holiday in Austria. She had never been there because Papa had been afraid to enter the country because of his activities during the war.

Mama told us how Papa in hospital had valiantly resisted to be kept alive against his will by repeatedly pulling out the tubes and wires they had stuck into him. She herself had opposed the doctors who had wanted to implant more tubes and had insisted that he be allowed to die. She spoke of the difficulties she had had in finding a minister willing to give Papa a Christian funeral. She does not remember much of that day – but she treasures the little basket with cards of condolences. There were many.

"Look, Gudrun, so and so had written."

It was important.

Austria was autumnal and soft and richly healing. We had rented a small guesthouse and by the time we left the Wolfgang See, Mama was able and willing to wear a brightly coloured head scarf. Before that she had only worn black and had shuddered at the suggestion of something other than the traditionally somber mourning colour.

When I phoned her later from Canada again, she told me that she felt much better now and that she finally did everything she had always wanted to do, such as have soup for breakfast, sleep in till nine, or go to bed at different times each night, all the things Papa had never acceded to because everything had to have order. The defiance was healing and good for her; after a short time, she settled back into her old, habitual routine, got up on time, ate a 'proper' breakfast and went to bed at ten thirty – as she had done for many years. She had had her time of rebellion and freedom and now she could manage.

For the next three years Jim and I visited Mama and took her on a few weeks' holidays: once more to beloved Austria, a May time vacation and family reunion at Lake Constance where even Erika from Texas joined us for a few weeks, and our last, an early spring time in the Kaiserstuhl, that lovely wine growing area straddling the Rhine River.

That was the year she finally let herself be checked for colon cancer. She survived an operation but disliked the rehab centre where too many people told her what to do. She decided, as she told me over the telephone, that she 'now had enough and wanted to be with Papa.' She quit taking her heart pills – she had for years suffered from emphysema and heart insufficiency – and after two days she simply slept away. That was in 2002; she was just a few weeks short of her eighty eighth birthday.

After Aunt Erika finally quit working in her mid-seventies, she enjoyed her retirement in her house in San Antonio, Texas. She was socially active, she travelled, she took up running; she enjoyed gardening and her dogs. She was a beautiful lady who turned many older heads; she had quite a few proposals for marriage but turned them all down, 'even the one from a millionaire who loved to polka'. She said she did not want to lose her freedom.

Erika, healthy in mind and body, and still smoking like a chimney, lived by herself until it became no longer safe for her to continue. Her daughters found her a place in a veterans' hospital. Half a year later she died of a stroke in August of 2007. She was 90 years old.

Uncle Manfred and Annemie divorced in the seventies. Upon retirement he set up his holiday trailer in a camp ground at Lake Constance and enjoyed working as its manager for twenty busy and interesting years. He made a garden and proudly displayed his flowers and veggies. He had a sailboat and with Jockel, his Dachshund, cherished the time on the water. In his mid eighties he quit working but still spent most of the year in the camp ground but now as a paying guest. Manfred was a generous and sociable fellow and over time he had a succession of lady friends. With some he lived for years, with others he entertained just a visiting and holidaying relationship. When he was 83 years old, he sent me a card showing him and his companion parasailing over the Mediterranean Sea close to Crete. He once more visited us in Canada but his girlfriend did not want to fly over the Atlantic and so he came alone. Manfred rode his motorbike until he was 88 years old, but he never trained his dachshund not to throw up when they went driving in his car. He was fit and able to stay in his home until just a few months before he died in September 2013.

My sister Ingeborg married Herman Kraft, a farmer and aspiring politician. They had five children. She divorced him in her early forties. After living in Italy for a few years – Jim and I met gondoliere in Venice who enthusiastically recalled her, the statuesque blonde woman whom they named Julia, and they remembered her beautiful voice – she moved to the most northern parts of Germany. Inge has a real talent for languages and writing and today she is involved in helping to document the rich history and language of the people of this area.

I have finished the tale that I have promised to tell; now the ghosts of the past are released and the spirits of the dead are free. This is peace.

Everyone has a story to tell. It behooves us to honour memory, to record it and to pass it on in hope that coming generations will be vigilant and not repeat the human catastrophes of the past. I know no better way to end than with words written by Martin Niemoeller. Initially an ardent supporter of National Socialism, he soon became disillusioned and eventually led Protestant clergymen in opposition to Hitler. Hitler had him arrested and Pastor Niemoeller spent eight years in concentration camps. The Allied Forces freed him in 1945. These are his words:

IN GERMANY I DID NOT SPEAK OUT

First they came
For the communists
And I did not speak out
Because I was not a Communist.

Then they came
For the Trade Unionists
And I did not speak out
Because I was not a Trade Unionist.

Then they came
For the Jews
And I did not speak out
Because I was not a Jew.

Then they came for me
And there was no one left
To speak for me.

Martin Niemoeller

Let Us Not Forget
Oliver, 2010 and 2021

BIBLIOGRAPHY

Hallerwedel, Ernst. "Die Verratene Generation", Ernst Hallerwedel, 1998

Hoehne, Heinz, "The Order of the Death's Head", Verlag der Spiegel, Hamburg, 1966. Penguin Books, UK.

Rhodes, Richard. "Masters of Death", Vintage Books, New York, 2003

Shirer, William L. "The Rise and Fall of the Third Reich", Crest Books, New York, 1959

ABOUT THE AUTHOR

Gudrun was born in war-time Germany. She immigrated to Canada in her twenties, became a teacher and later also a farmer in the Peace River Country in Northern Alberta. Retired to the Okanagan Valley, she and husband Jim travel the world, when not busy running a B&B and a small farm.

Books published:
Borobudur By Chance,
An account of a family backpacking tour for one year with two pre-teen children.

A Duty of Remembrance, The Story of My German Family

Together with husband James, their memoirs:
The Past Behind: Book I, Parallel Lives
                 Book II, That's Life

www.gudrunmoore.com